fushigi yûgi™

The Mysterious Play
VOL. 6: SUMMONER

Story & Art By
YUU WATASE

FUSHIGI YÛGI
THE MYSTERIOUS PLAY
VOL.6: SUMMONER
SHÔJO EDITION

This volume contains the FUSHIGI YÛGI installments from Animerica Extra Vol. 4, No. 6 through No. 11, in their entirety.

STORY AND ART BY YUU WATASE

English Adaptation/Yuji Oniki
Translation Assist/Kaori Kawakubo Inoue
Touch-up Art & Lettering/Andy Ristaino
Design/Hidemi Sahara
Editor (1st Edition)/William Flanagan
Editor (Shôjo Edition)/Yuki Takagaki

Managing Editor/Megan Bates
Editorial Director/Elizabeth Kawasaki
Editor in Chief/Alvin Lu
Sr. Director of Acquisitions/Rika Inouye
Sr. VP of Marketing/Liza Coppola
Exec. VP of Sales & Marketing/John Easum
Publisher/Hyoe Narita

Printed in the U.S.A.

Published by VIZ Media, LLC
P.O. Box 77010
San Francisco, CA 94107

First edition published 2002

Shôjo Edition
10 9 8 7 6 5 4 3 2
First printing, March 2005
Second printing, October 2006

www.viz.com
store.viz.com

PARENTAL ADVISORY
FUSHIGI YÛGI is rated T+ for Older Teen.
Contains sexual situations and realistic violence.
Recommended for ages 16 and up.

CONTENTS

STORY THUS FAR

Fifteen-year-old Miaka and her best friend Yui are physically drawn into the world of a strange book—*THE UNIVERSE OF THE FOUR GODS*. Miaka is offered the role of the lead character, the Priestess of the god Suzaku, and is charged with a mission to save the nation of Hong-Nan, one that will ultimately grant her any wish she wants. Yui, however, suffers rape and manipulation, which drive her to attempt suicide. Now, Yui has become the Priestess of the god Seiryu, the bitter enemy of Suzaku and Miaka.

The only way for Miaka to gain back the trust of her former best friend is to gather all seven Celestial Warriors of Suzaku together, summon the god, and wish to be reconciled with Yui. Now that Miaka seems to have found all seven, she only needs to retrieve her love, the Suzaku Celestial Warrior Tamahome. But he has been drugged by love-struck Yui and her general Nakago in Seiryu's kingdom of Qu-Dong, and when Miaka, Chichiri, and Tasuki go there to rescue Tamahome, they find that the drug's hold on Tamahome's mind is too powerful. They are forced to escape, leaving the traitorous Tamahome behind.

THE UNIVERSE OF THE FOUR GODS is based on ancient Chinese legend, but Japanese pronunciation of Chinese names differs slightly from their Chinese equivalents. Here is a short glossary of the Japanese pronunciation of the Chinese names in this graphic novel:

CHINESE	JAPANESE	PERSON OR PLACE	MEANING
Hong-Nan	Kônan	Southern Kingdom	Crimson South
Qu-Dong	Kutô	Eastern Kingdom	Gathered East
Diedu	Kodoku	A Potion	Seduction Potion
He-Yan	Waen	A Palace Room	Eternal Peace
Bei-Jia	Hokkan	Northern Kingdom	Armored North
Wong Tao-Hui	Ôdokun	A Chinese Name	King Bright Path
K'o-Ju	Kakyo	Bureaucracy Exam	Department Trial
Hsing-Shin	Shôshi	A Second Exam	Ministry Test
Tai Yi-Jun	Tai Itsukun	An Oracle	Preeminent Person
Shentso-Pao	Shinzahô	A Treasure	God's Seat Jewel

No da: An emphatic. A verbal exclamation point placed at the end of a sentence or phrase.

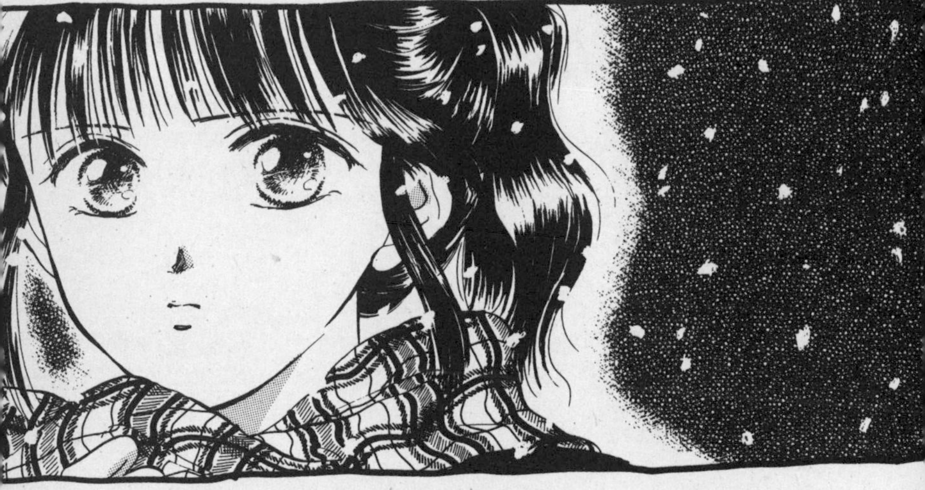

CHAPTER THIRTY-ONE

THE WAY TO GOODBYE

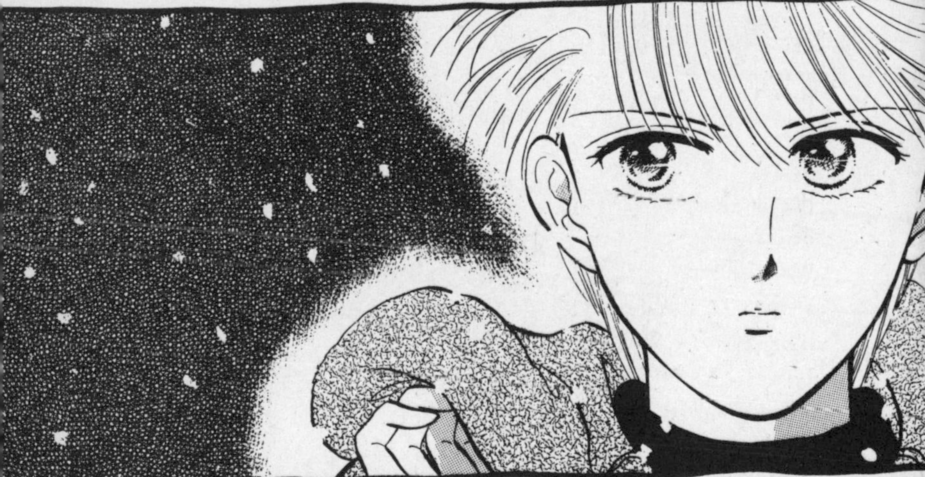

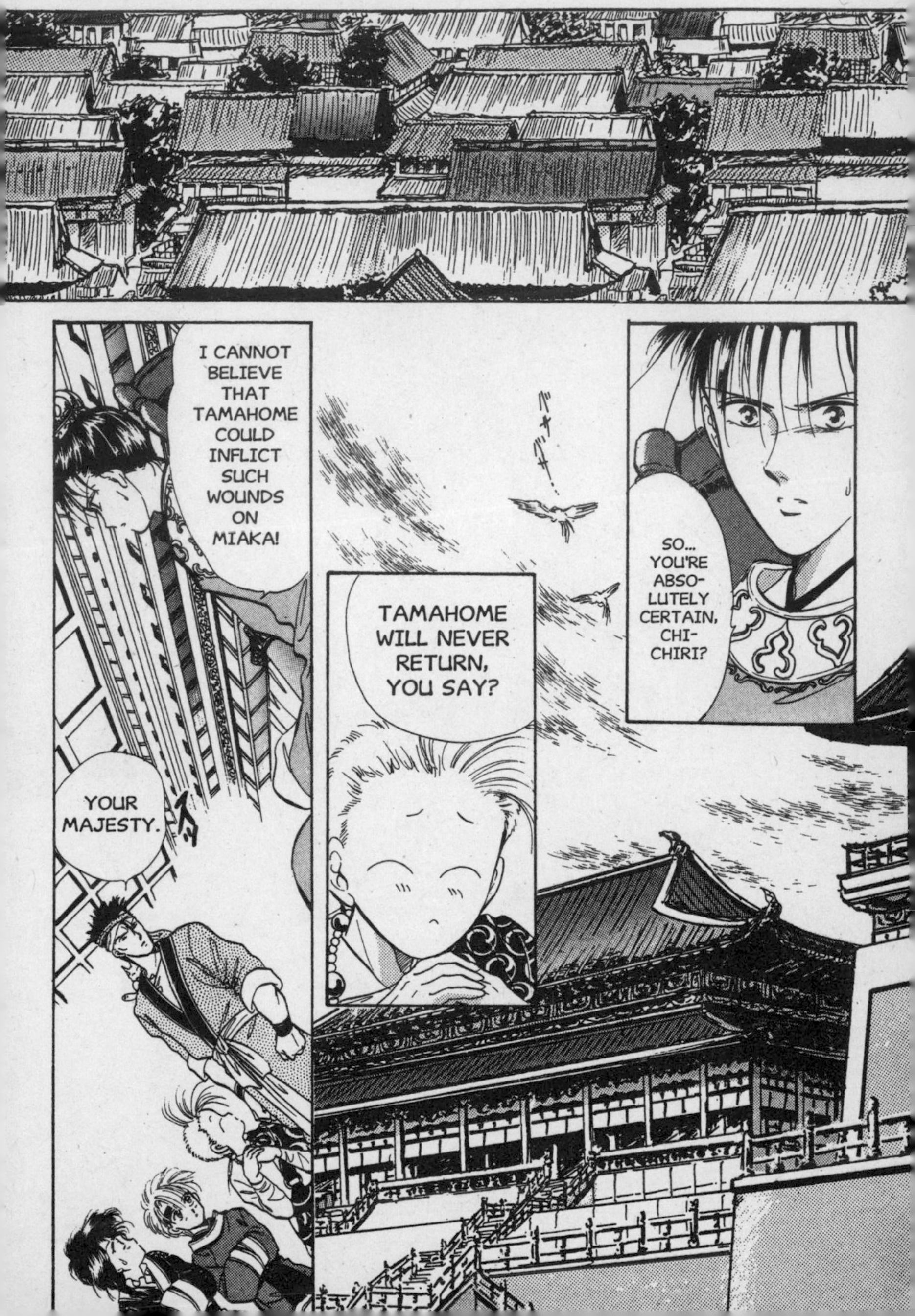
SO... YOU'RE ABSO-LUTELY CERTAIN, CHI-CHIRI?
TAMAHOME WILL NEVER RETURN, YOU SAY?
I CANNOT BELIEVE THAT TAMAHOME COULD INFLICT SUCH WOUNDS ON MIAKA!
YOUR MAJESTY.

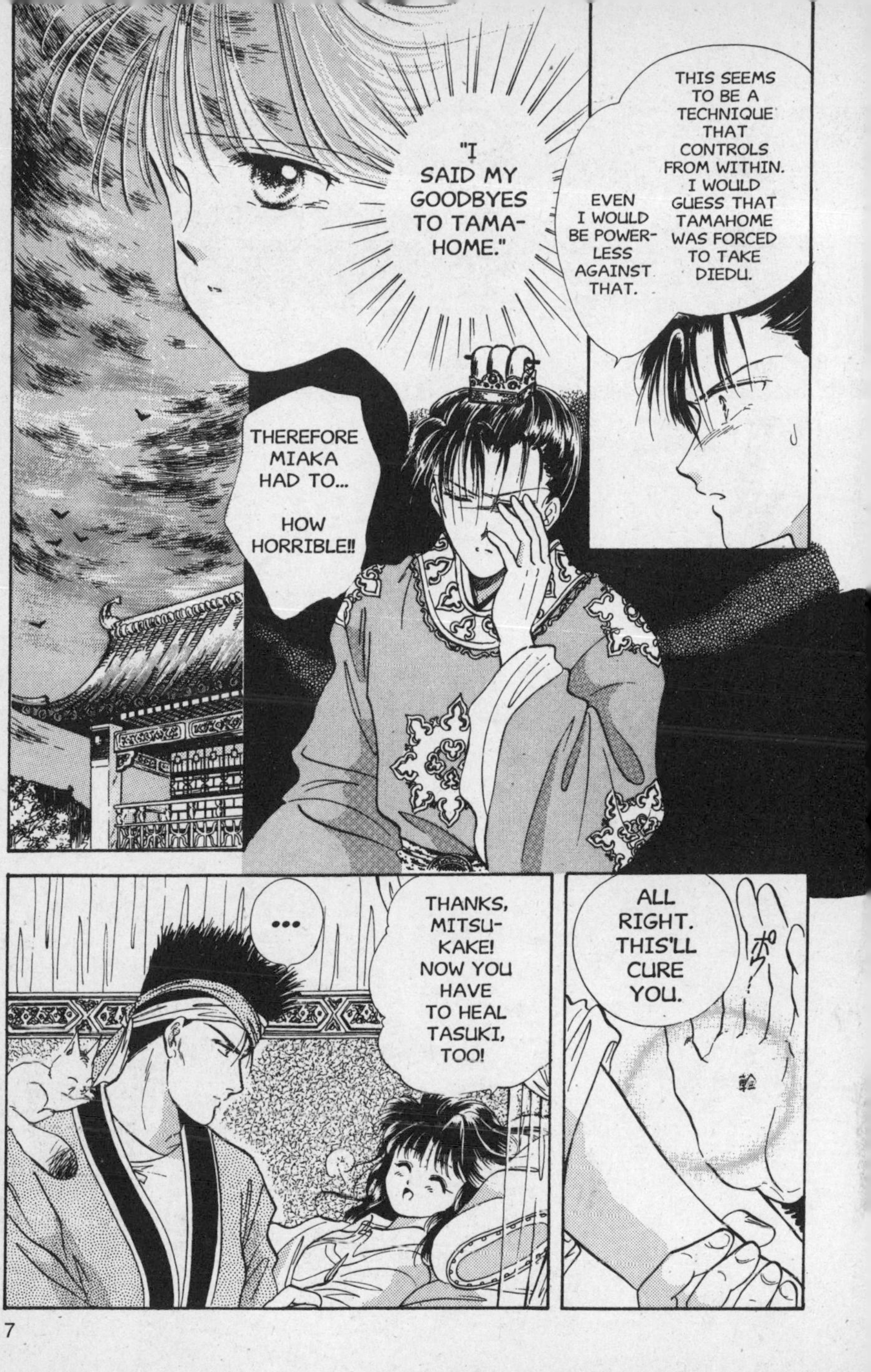
THIS SEEMS TO BE A TECHNIQUE THAT CONTROLS FROM WITHIN. I WOULD GUESS THAT TAMAHOME WAS FORCED TO TAKE DIEDU.
EVEN I WOULD BE POWERLESS AGAINST THAT.
"I SAID MY GOODBYES TO TAMA-HOME."
THEREFORE MIAKA HAD TO... HOW HORRIBLE!!
ALL RIGHT. THIS'LL CURE YOU.
THANKS, MITSU-KAKE! NOW YOU HAVE TO HEAL TASUKI, TOO!
...

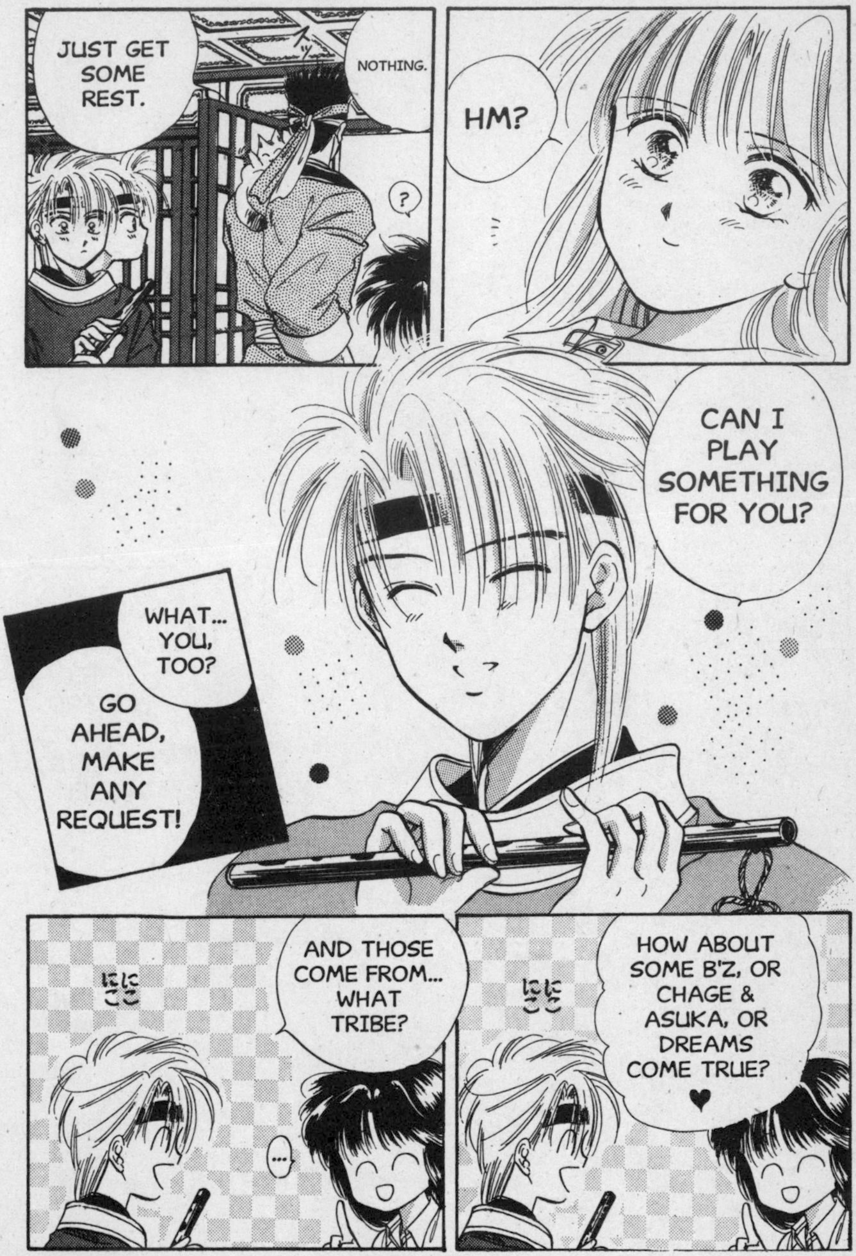
HM?
NOTHING.
JUST GET SOME REST.
?
CAN I PLAY SOMETHING FOR YOU?
WHAT... YOU, TOO?
GO AHEAD, MAKE ANY REQUEST!
HOW ABOUT SOME B'Z, OR CHAGE & ASUKA, OR DREAMS COME TRUE? ♥
AND THOSE COME FROM... WHAT TRIBE?
...

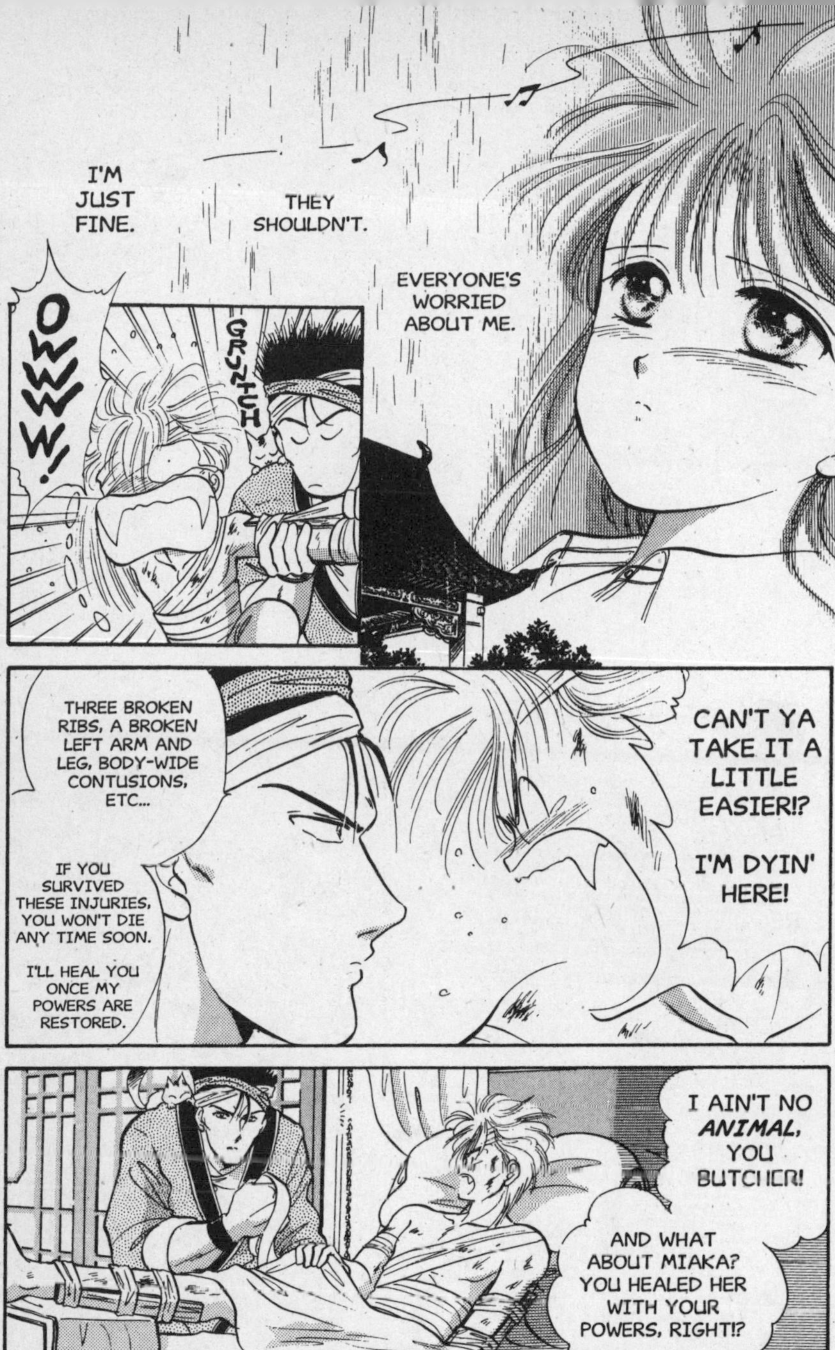
EVERYONE'S WORRIED ABOUT ME.
THEY SHOULDN'T.
I'M JUST FINE.
GRUNTCH
OWWWW!
CAN'T YA TAKE IT A LITTLE EASIER!?
I'M DYIN' HERE!
THREE BROKEN RIBS, A BROKEN LEFT ARM AND LEG, BODY-WIDE CONTUSIONS, ETC...
IF YOU SURVIVED THESE INJURIES, YOU WON'T DIE ANY TIME SOON.
I'LL HEAL YOU ONCE MY POWERS ARE RESTORED.
I AIN'T NO *ANIMAL*, YOU BUTCHER!
AND WHAT ABOUT MIAKA? YOU HEALED HER WITH YOUR POWERS, RIGHT!?

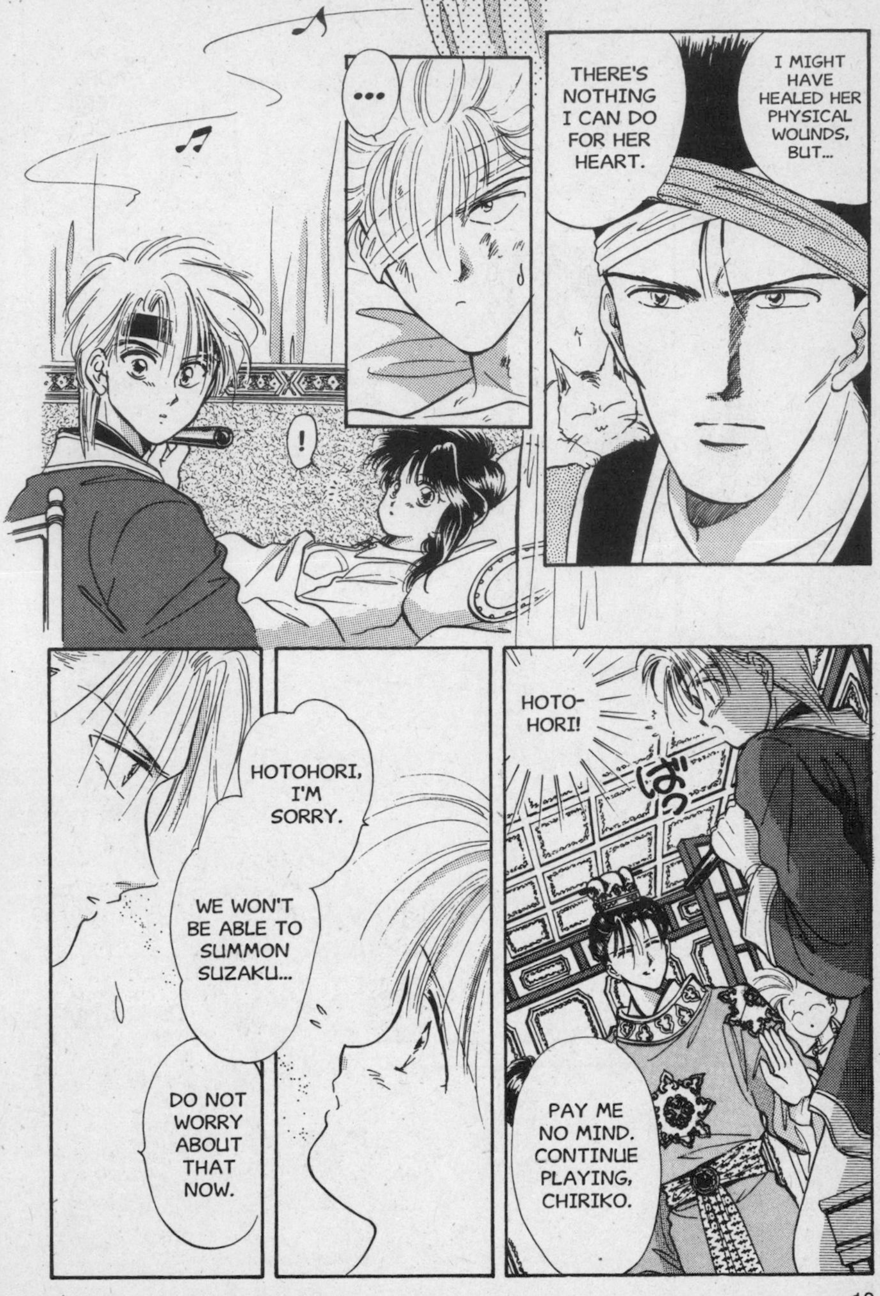
I MIGHT HAVE HEALED HER PHYSICAL WOUNDS, BUT...
THERE'S NOTHING I CAN DO FOR HER HEART.
...
!
HOTO-HORI!
ばっ
PAY ME NO MIND. CONTINUE PLAYING, CHIRIKO.
HOTOHORI, I'M SORRY.
WE WON'T BE ABLE TO SUMMON SUZAKU...
DO NOT WORRY ABOUT THAT NOW.

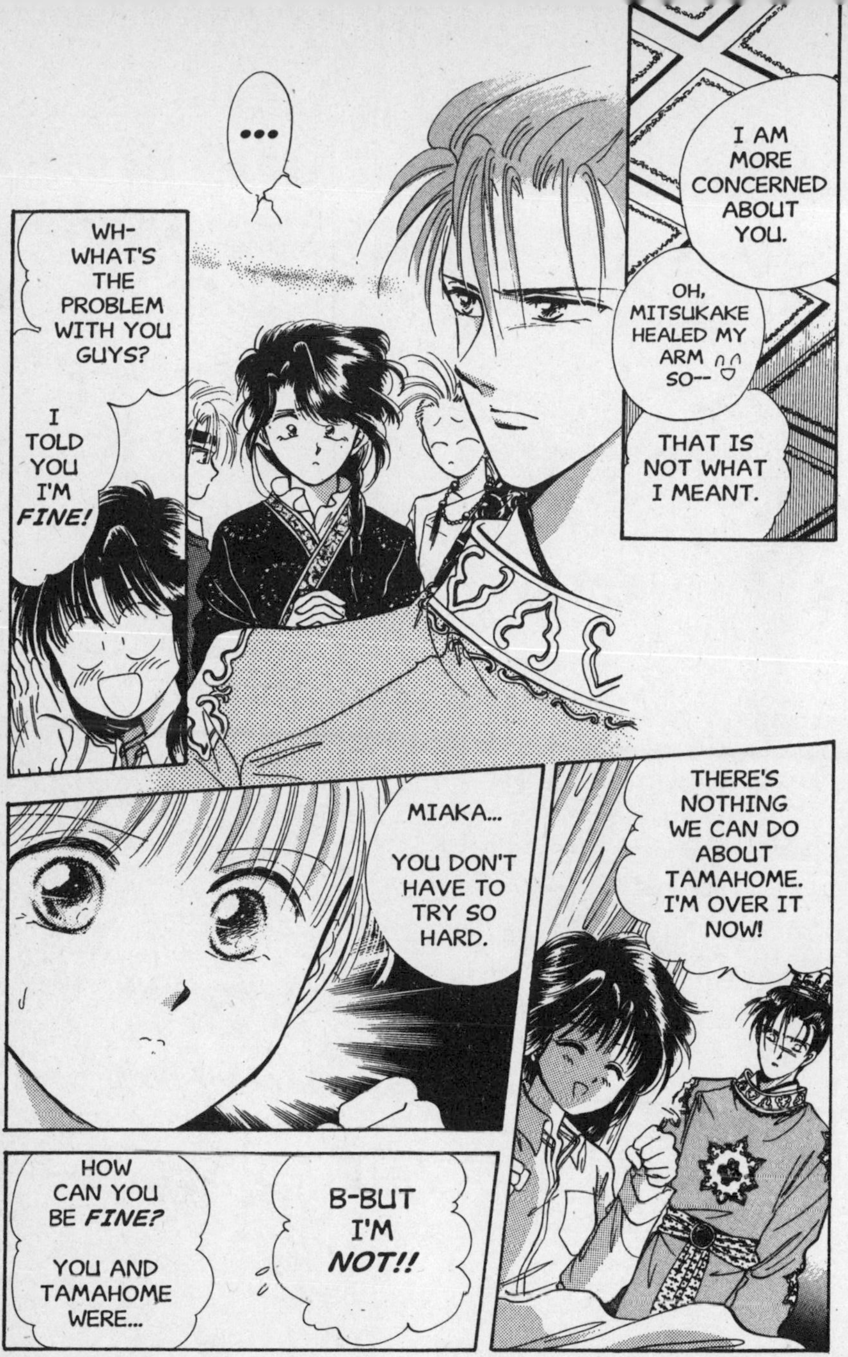
I AM MORE CONCERNED ABOUT YOU.
OH, MITSUKAKE HEALED MY ARM SO--
THAT IS NOT WHAT I MEANT.
...
WH-WHAT'S THE PROBLEM WITH YOU GUYS?
I TOLD YOU I'M *FINE!*
THERE'S NOTHING WE CAN DO ABOUT TAMAHOME. I'M OVER IT NOW!
MIAKA...
YOU DON'T HAVE TO TRY SO HARD.
B-BUT I'M *NOT!!*
HOW CAN YOU BE *FINE?*
YOU AND TAMAHOME WERE...

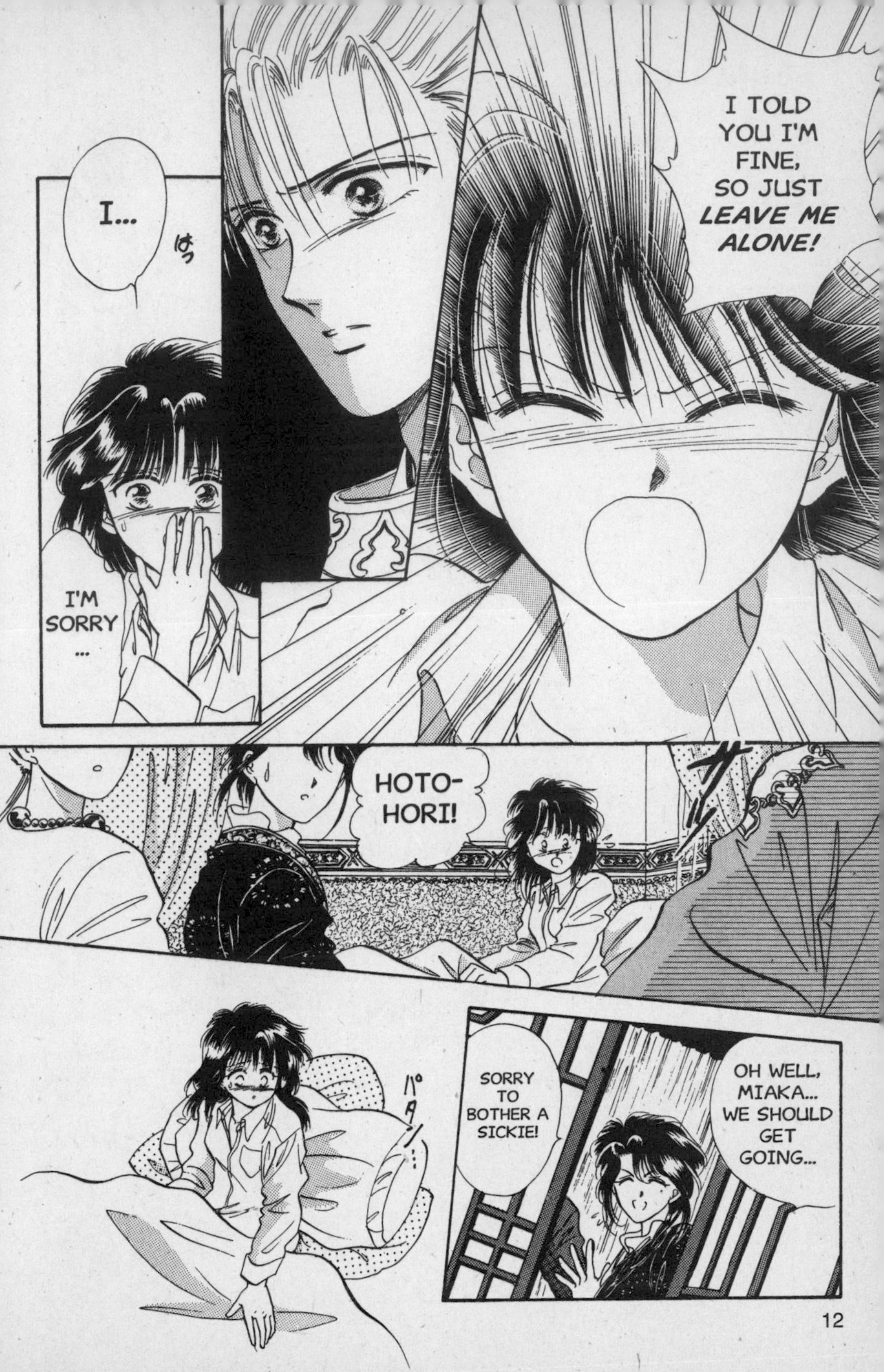
I TOLD YOU I'M FINE, SO JUST *LEAVE ME ALONE!*
I...
はっ
I'M SORRY ...
HOTO-HORI!
OH WELL, MIAKA... WE SHOULD GET GOING...
SORRY TO BOTHER A SICKIE!
パタン…

Hello. Thanks to you, we've reached volume 6! As a matter of fact, I currently feel pretty normal, which is unusual for me while I'm writing these free-talk sections. So what state of mind was I in previously?

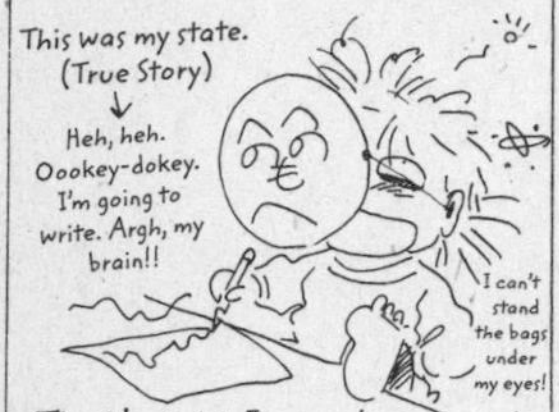
This was my state. (True Story)
Heh, heh. Oookey-dokey. I'm going to write. Argh, my brain!!
I can't stand the bags under my eyes!

That's right. I was sleepy and tired, stressed, overworked and completely fed up! A person has to have some free time once in a while! Not that I have free time now, though. So starting now I'm going to throw away that ugly, overworked-looking mask, and put on a different, bright-eyed, cheery Watase mask.

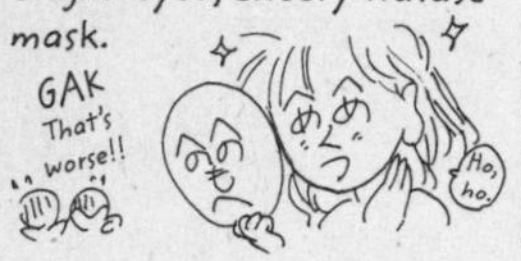
GAK That's worse!!
Ho, ho.

All right, enough with the boring banter. Well, it's summer, so I'm thinking of sharing a real-life horror story I actually experienced. Those of you who don't like horror can skip these sections and just read the manga. I won't be put out. Promise! Those of you who do like horror, keep in mind that it's not a great story, but you should check it out. Actually, it was worse on my assistants than it ever was on me. All I know is that I'm grateful we finally moved.

To be continued...

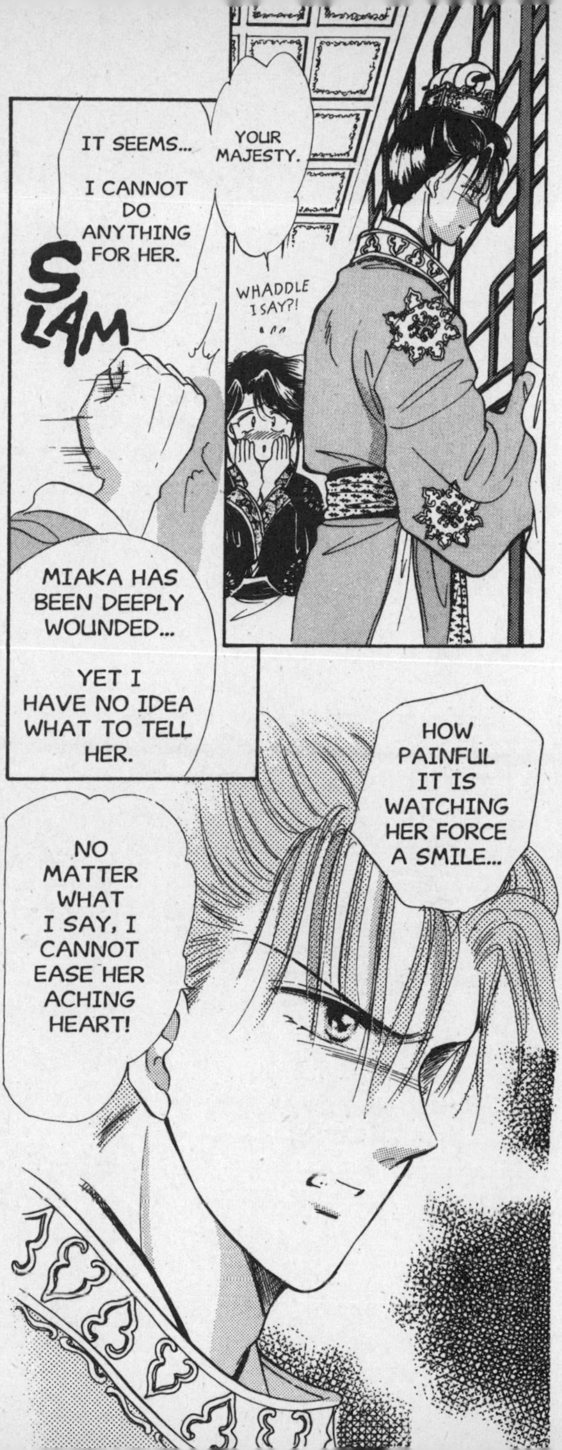
YOUR MAJESTY.
WHADDLE I SAY?!
IT SEEMS...
I CANNOT DO ANYTHING FOR HER.
SLAM
MIAKA HAS BEEN DEEPLY WOUNDED...
YET I HAVE NO IDEA WHAT TO TELL HER.
HOW PAINFUL IT IS WATCHING HER FORCE A SMILE...
NO MATTER WHAT I SAY, I CANNOT EASE HER ACHING HEART!

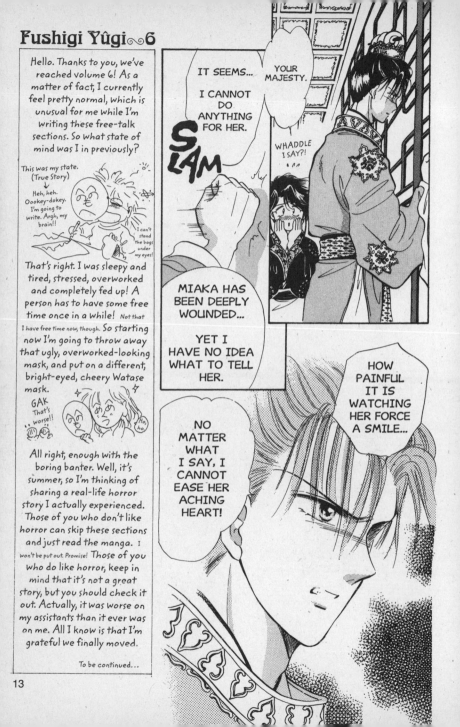

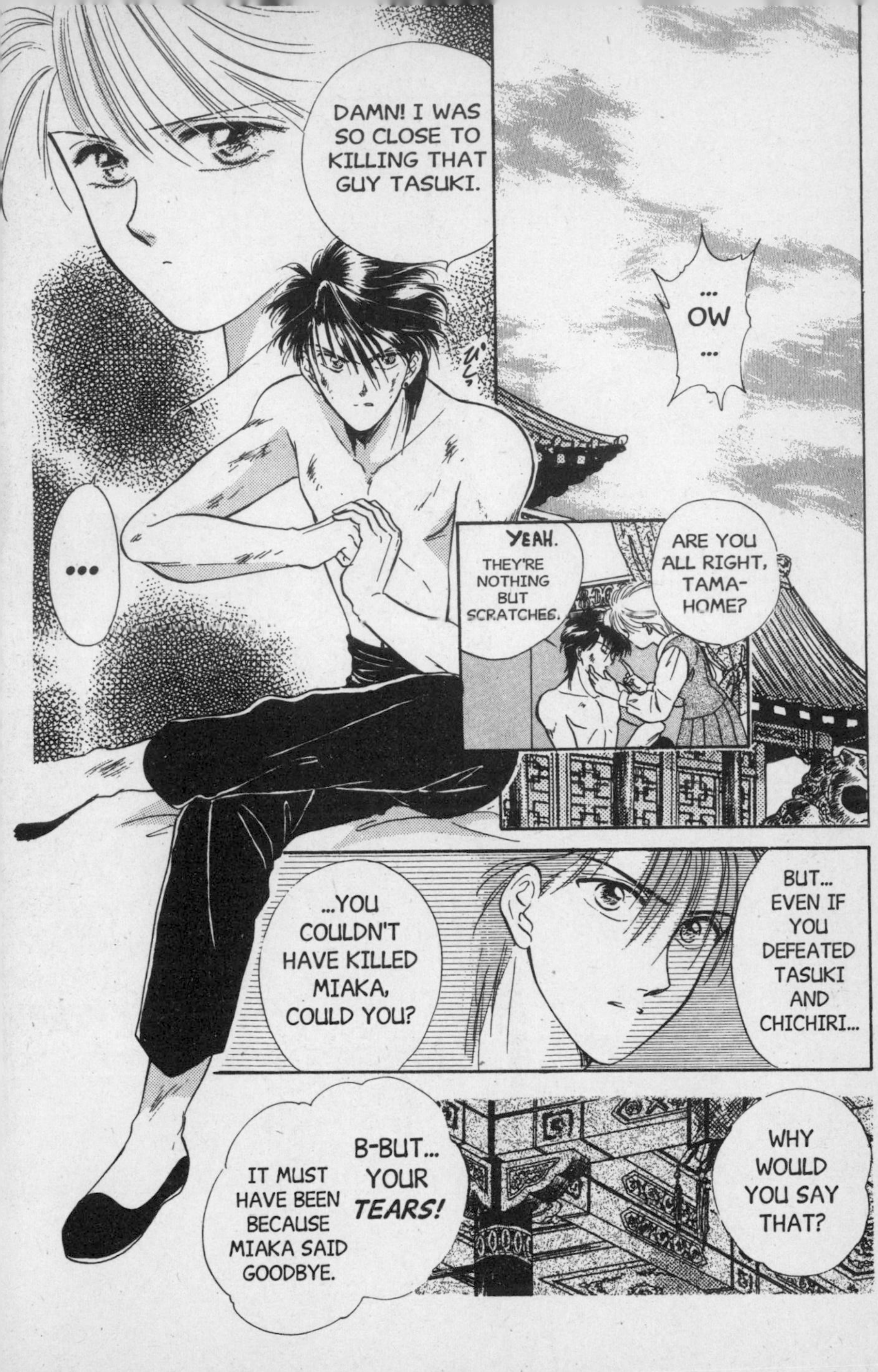
... OW ...
ARE YOU ALL RIGHT, TAMA-HOME?
YEAH. THEY'RE NOTHING BUT SCRATCHES.
DAMN! I WAS SO CLOSE TO KILLING THAT GUY TASUKI.
...
BUT... EVEN IF YOU DEFEATED TASUKI AND CHICHIRI...
...YOU COULDN'T HAVE KILLED MIAKA, COULD YOU?
WHY WOULD YOU SAY THAT?
B-BUT... YOUR TEARS!
IT MUST HAVE BEEN BECAUSE MIAKA SAID GOODBYE.

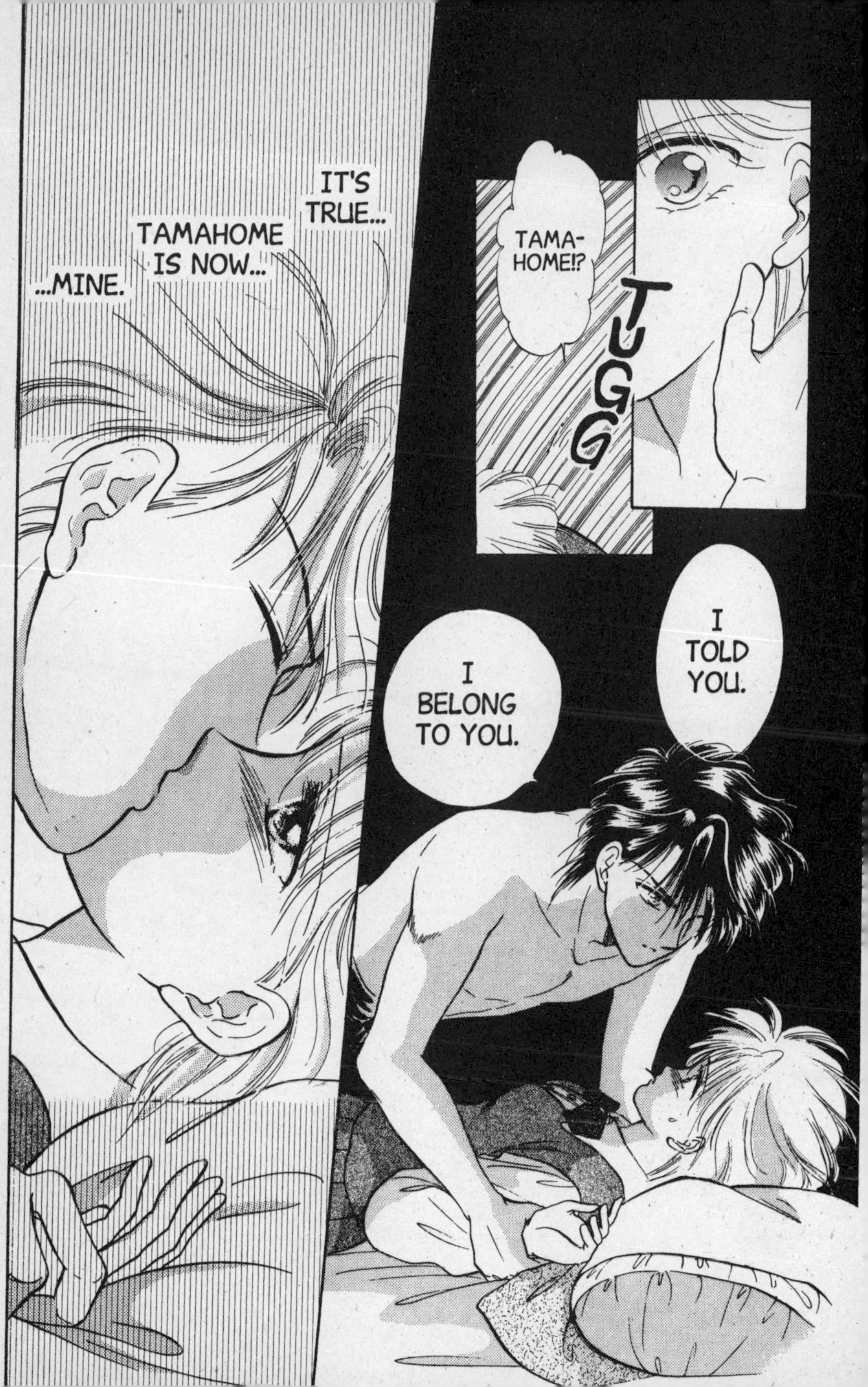
TAMA-HOME!?
TUGG
I TOLD YOU.
I BELONG TO YOU.
IT'S TRUE...
TAMAHOME IS NOW...
...MINE.

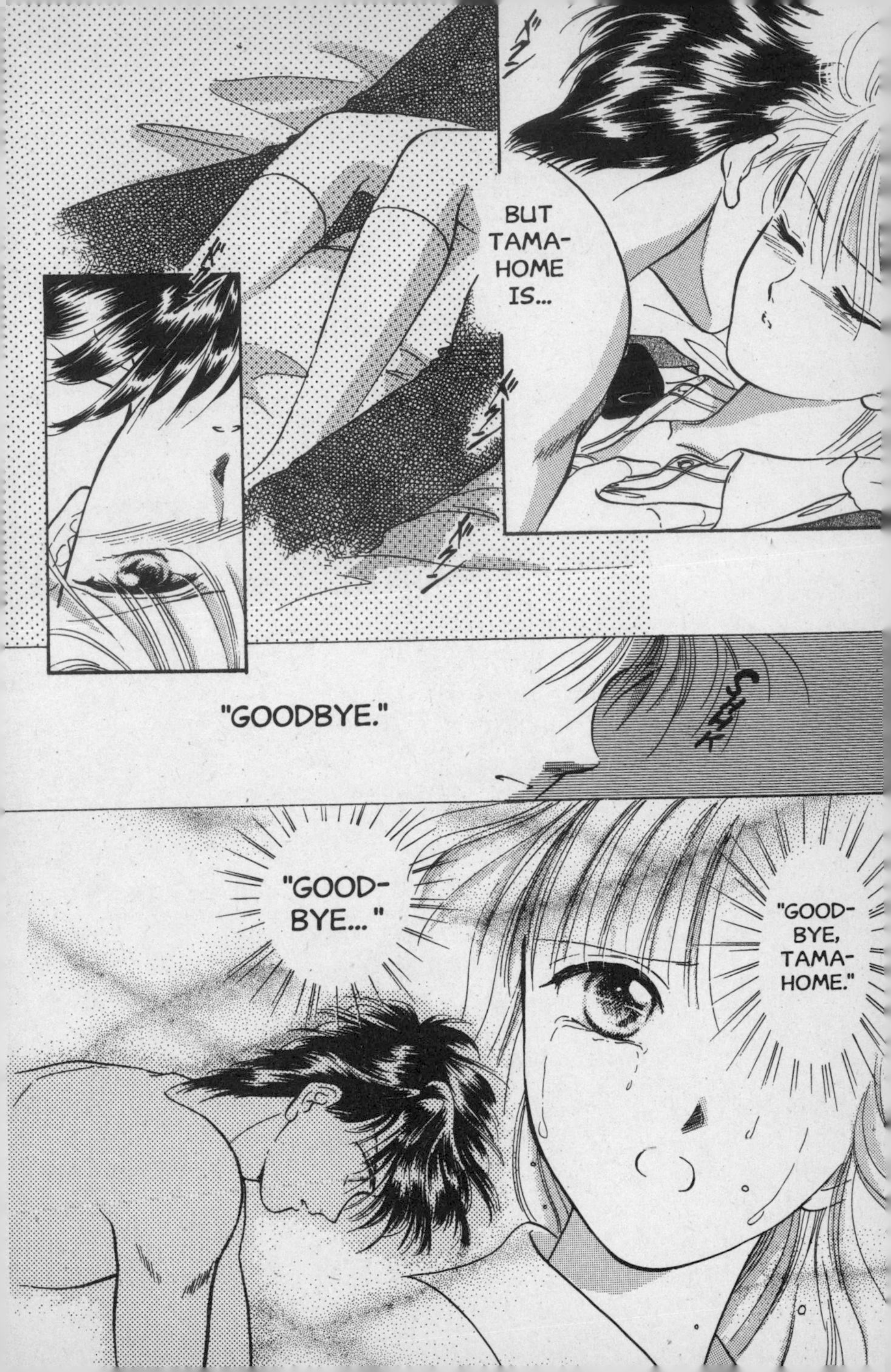
BUT TAMA-HOME IS...
"GOODBYE."
SHK
"GOOD-BYE, TAMA-HOME."
"GOOD-BYE..."

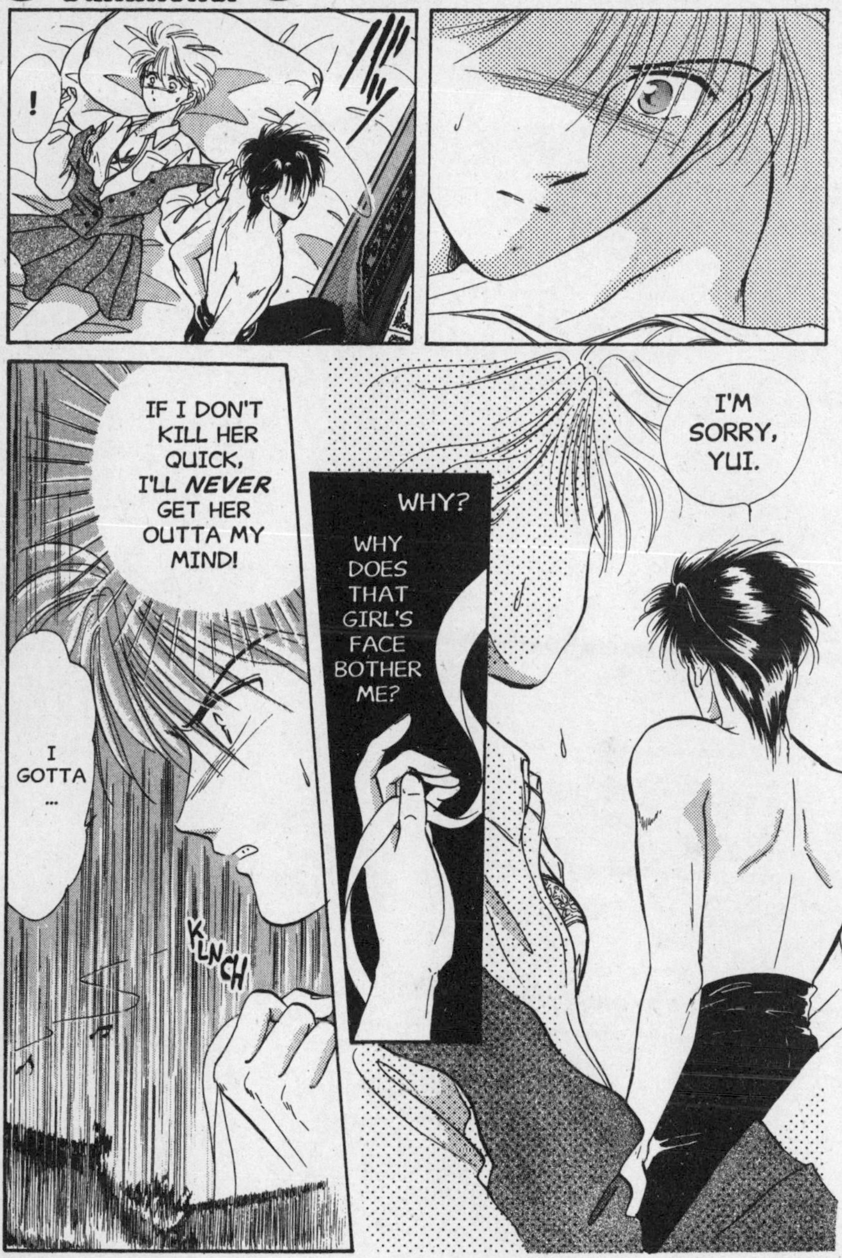
!
I'M SORRY, YUI.
WHY?
WHY DOES THAT GIRL'S FACE BOTHER ME?
IF I DON'T KILL HER QUICK, I'LL *NEVER* GET HER OUTTA MY MIND!
I GOTTA ...
KLNCH

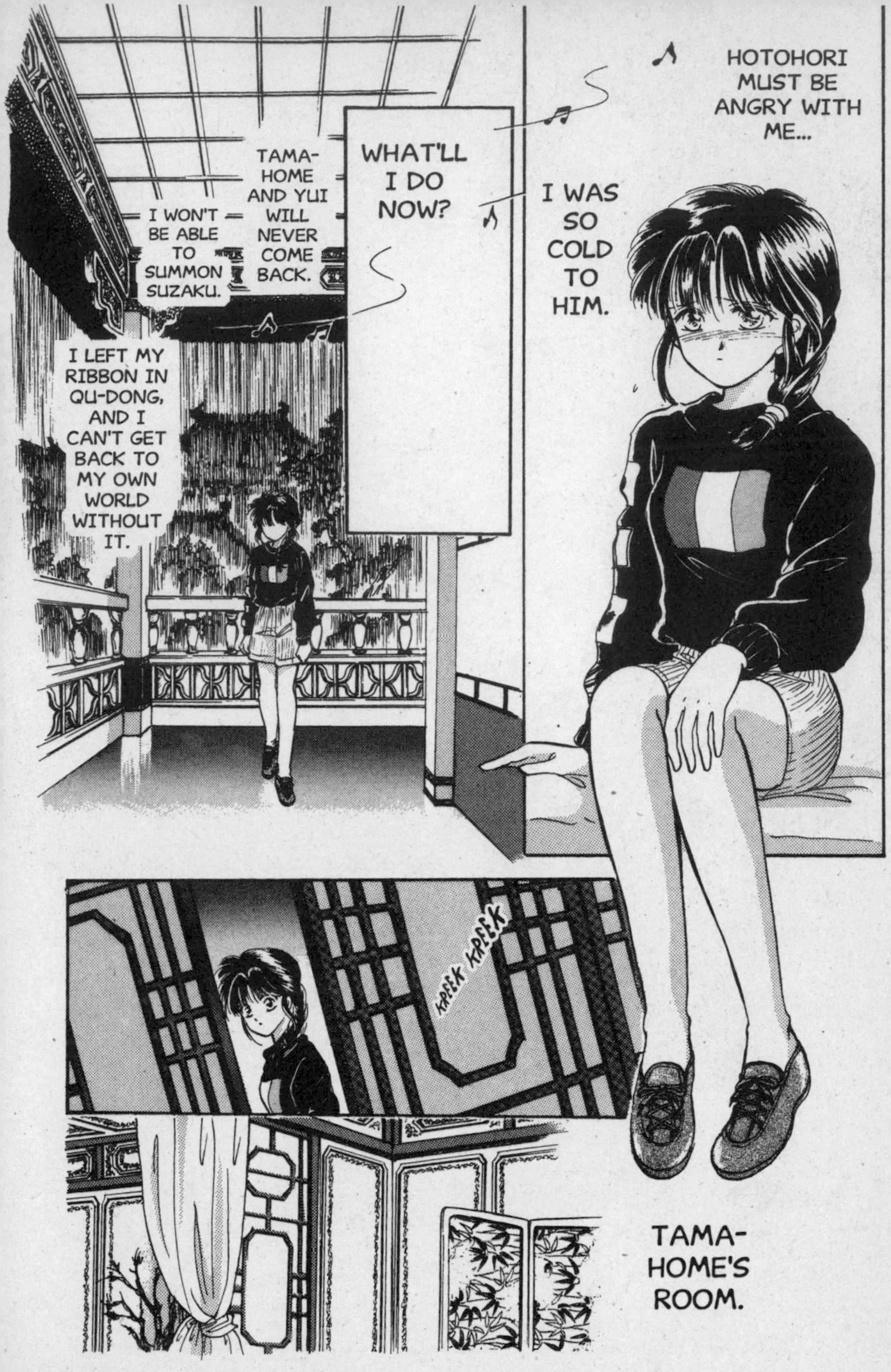
HOTOHORI MUST BE ANGRY WITH ME...
I WAS SO COLD TO HIM.
WHAT'LL I DO NOW?
TAMA-HOME AND YUI WILL NEVER COME BACK.
I WON'T BE ABLE TO SUMMON SUZAKU.
I LEFT MY RIBBON IN QU-DONG, AND I CAN'T GET BACK TO MY OWN WORLD WITHOUT IT.
KREEK KREEK
TAMA-HOME'S ROOM.

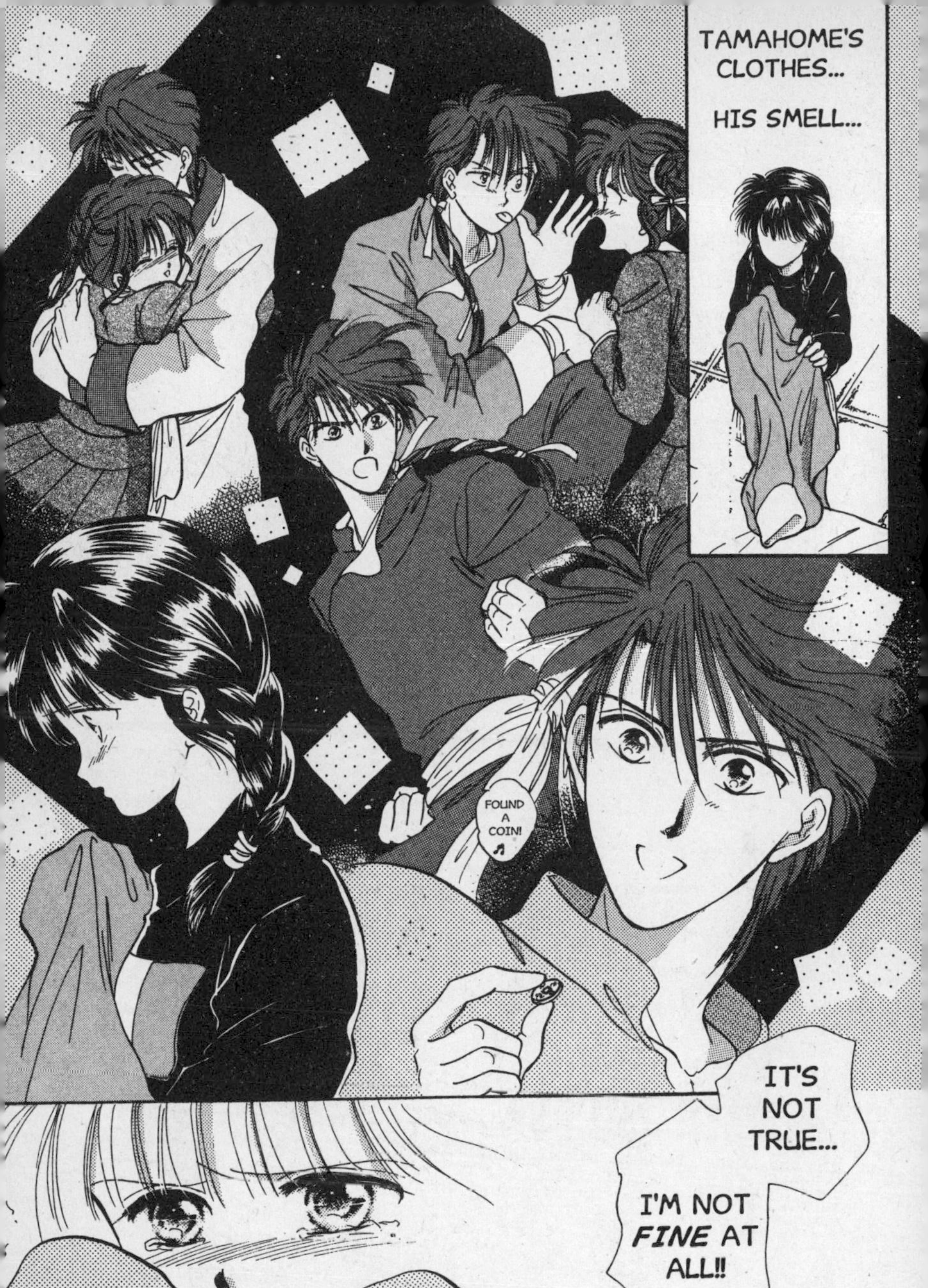
TAMAHOME'S CLOTHES...
HIS SMELL...
FOUND A COIN! ♪
IT'S NOT TRUE...
I'M NOT *FINE* AT ALL!!

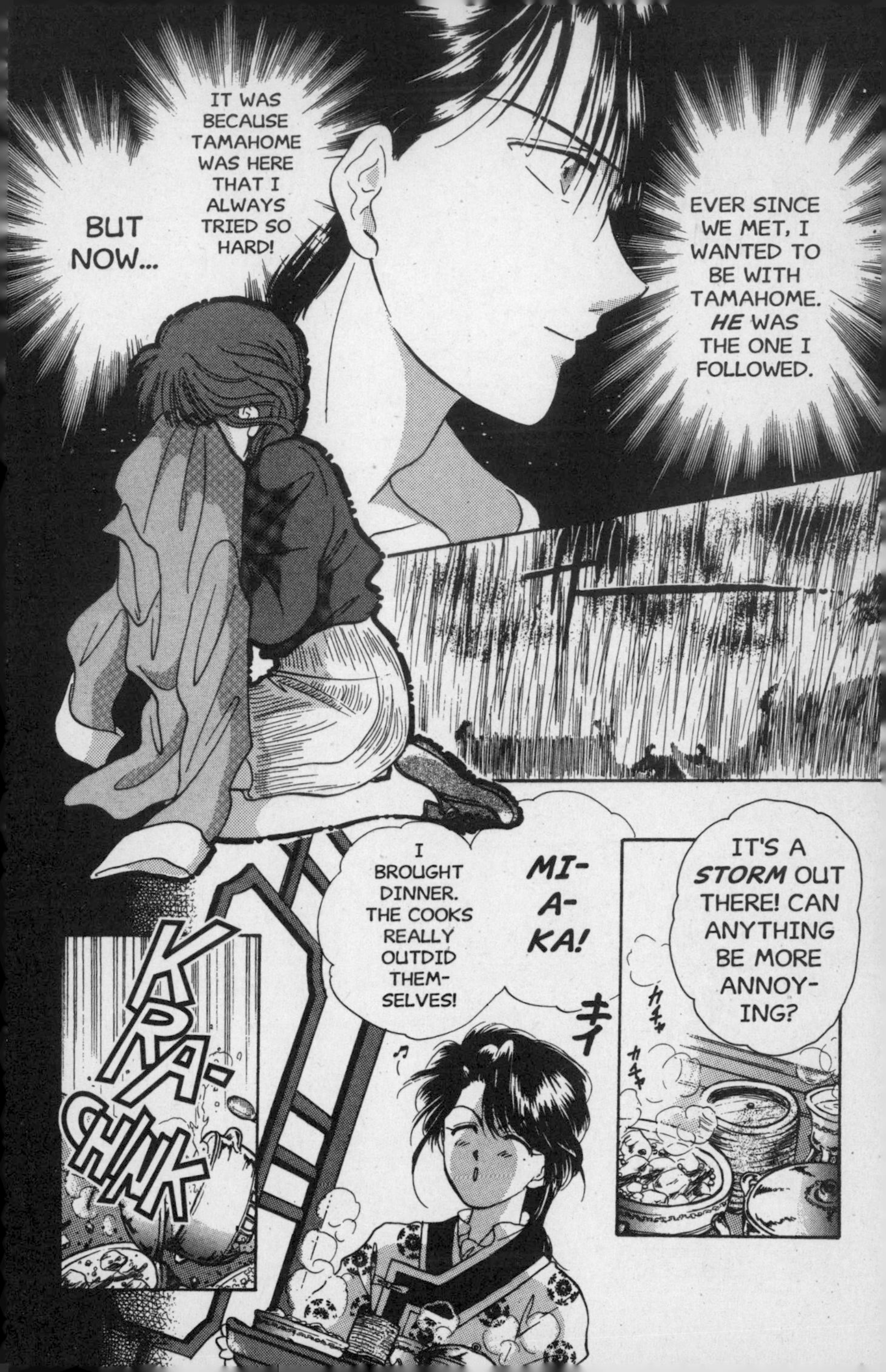
EVER SINCE WE MET, I WANTED TO BE WITH TAMAHOME. *HE* WAS THE ONE I FOLLOWED.
IT WAS BECAUSE TAMAHOME WAS HERE THAT I ALWAYS TRIED SO HARD!
BUT NOW...
IT'S A *STORM* OUT THERE! CAN ANYTHING BE MORE ANNOYING?
カチャ
カチャ
キイ
MI-A-KA!
I BROUGHT DINNER. THE COOKS REALLY OUTDID THEM-SELVES!
KRA-CHINK

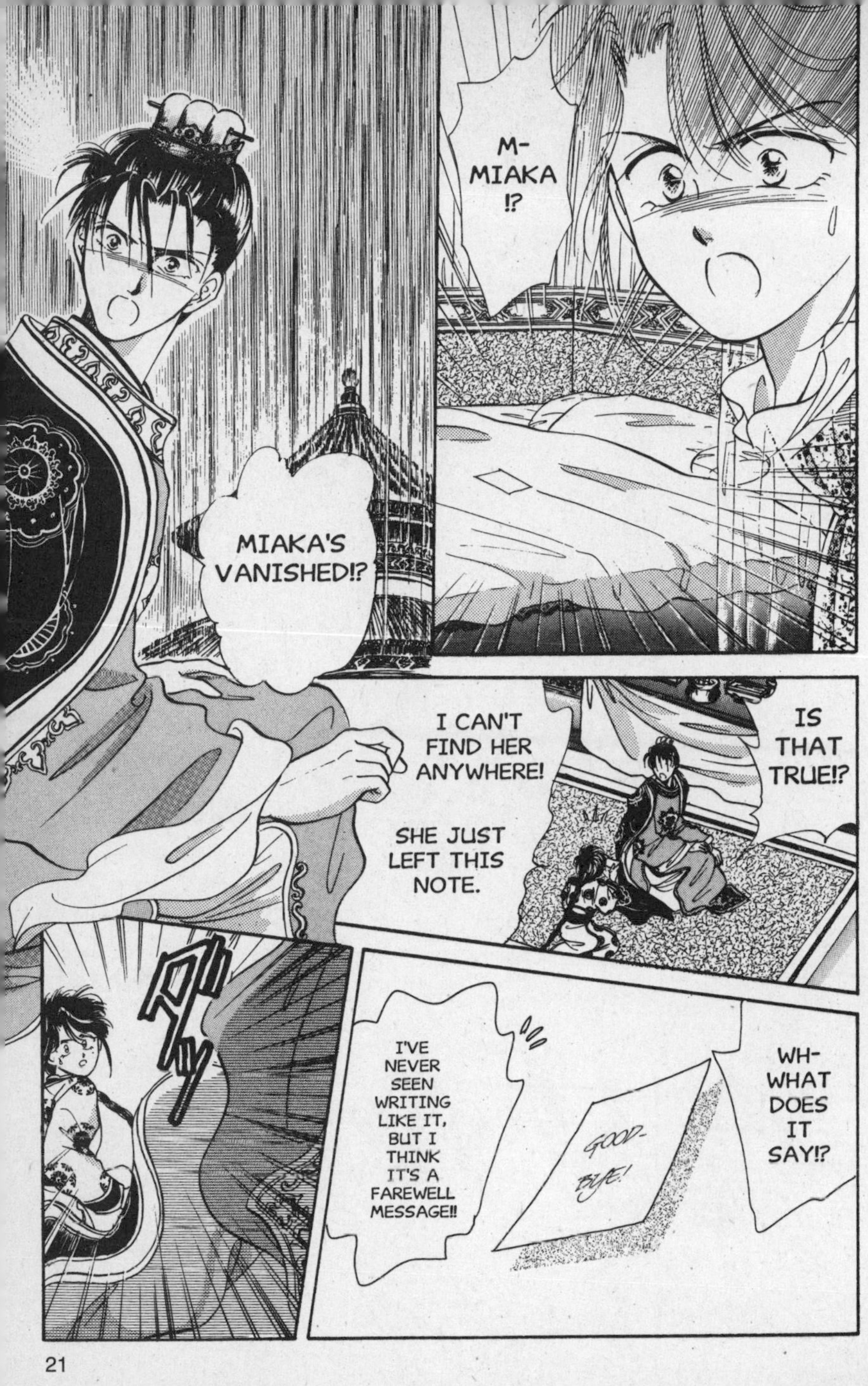
M-MIAKA!?
MIAKA'S VANISHED!?
IS THAT TRUE!?
I CAN'T FIND HER ANYWHERE!
SHE JUST LEFT THIS NOTE.
WH-WHAT DOES IT SAY!?
I'VE NEVER SEEN WRITING LIKE IT, BUT I THINK IT'S A FAREWELL MESSAGE!!
GOOD-BYE!

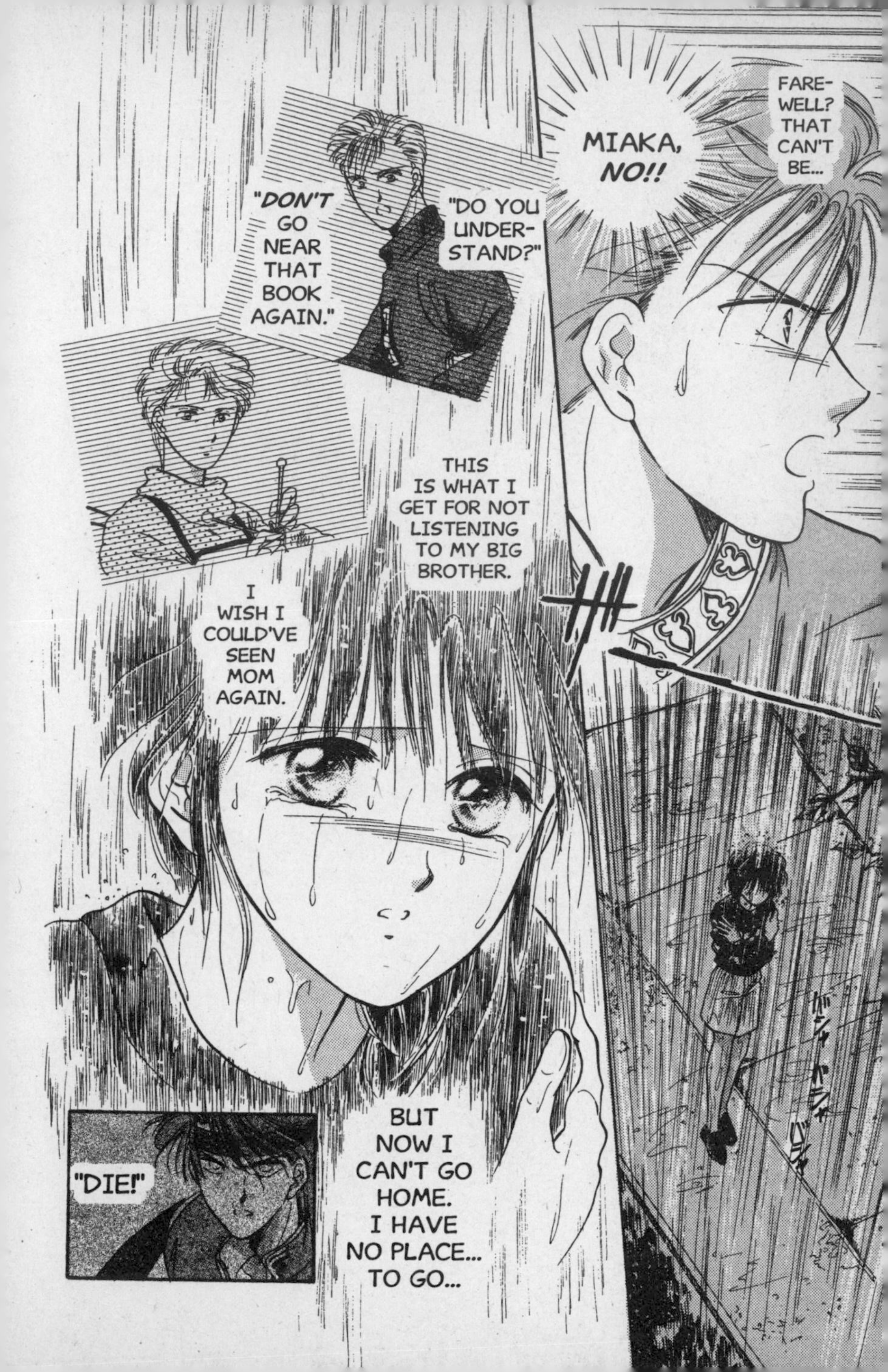
FARE-WELL? THAT CAN'T BE...
MIAKA, *NO!!*
"DO YOU UNDER-STAND?"
"*DON'T* GO NEAR THAT BOOK AGAIN."
THIS IS WHAT I GET FOR NOT LISTENING TO MY BIG BROTHER.
I WISH I COULD'VE SEEN MOM AGAIN.
BUT NOW I CAN'T GO HOME. I HAVE NO PLACE... TO GO...
"DIE!"

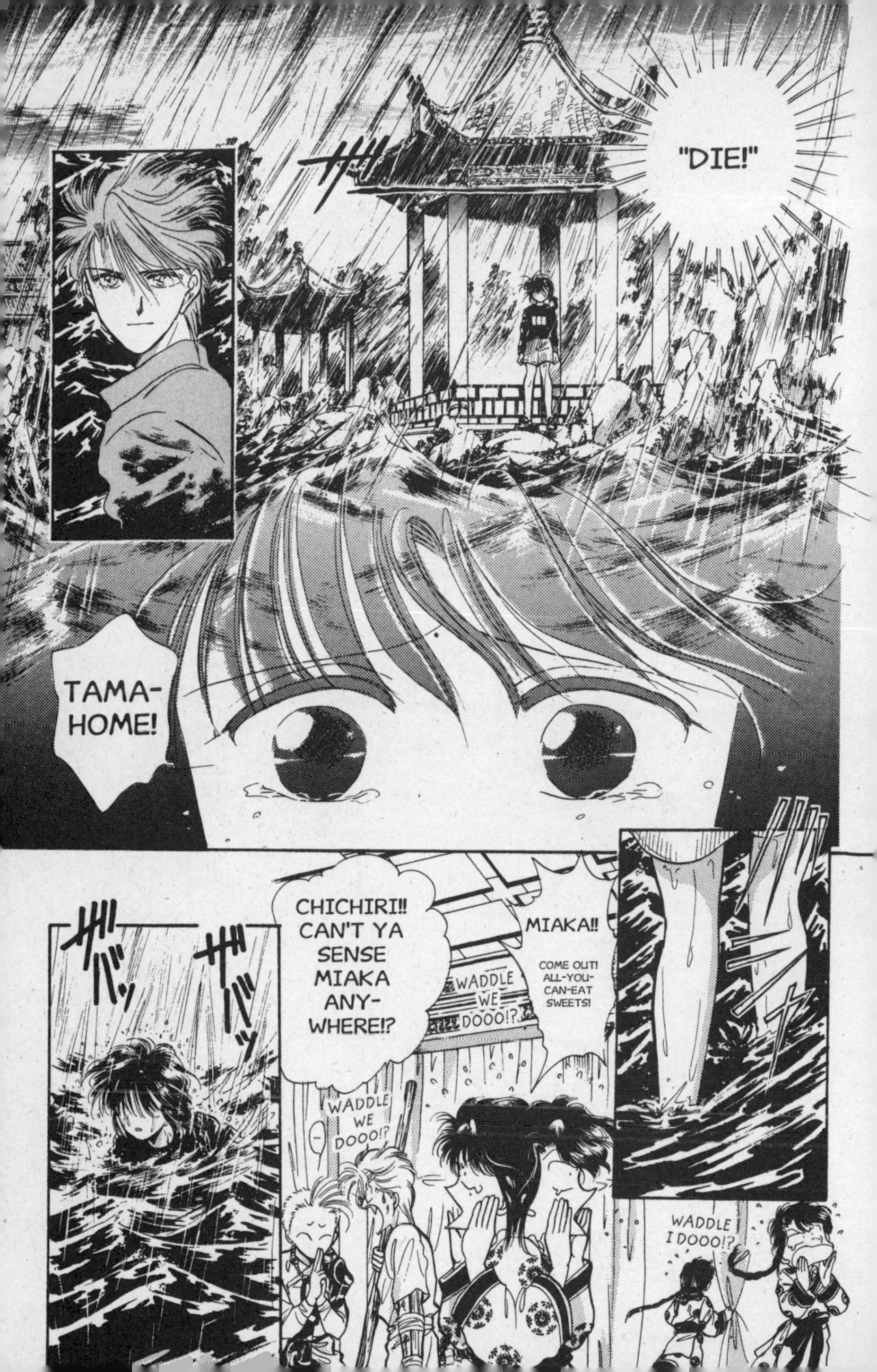
"DIE!"
TAMA-HOME!
MIAKA!!
COME OUT! ALL-YOU-CAN-EAT SWEETS!
CHICHIRI!! CAN'T YA SENSE MIAKA ANY-WHERE!?
WADDLE WE DOOO!?
WADDLE WE DOOO!?
WADDLE I DOOO!?

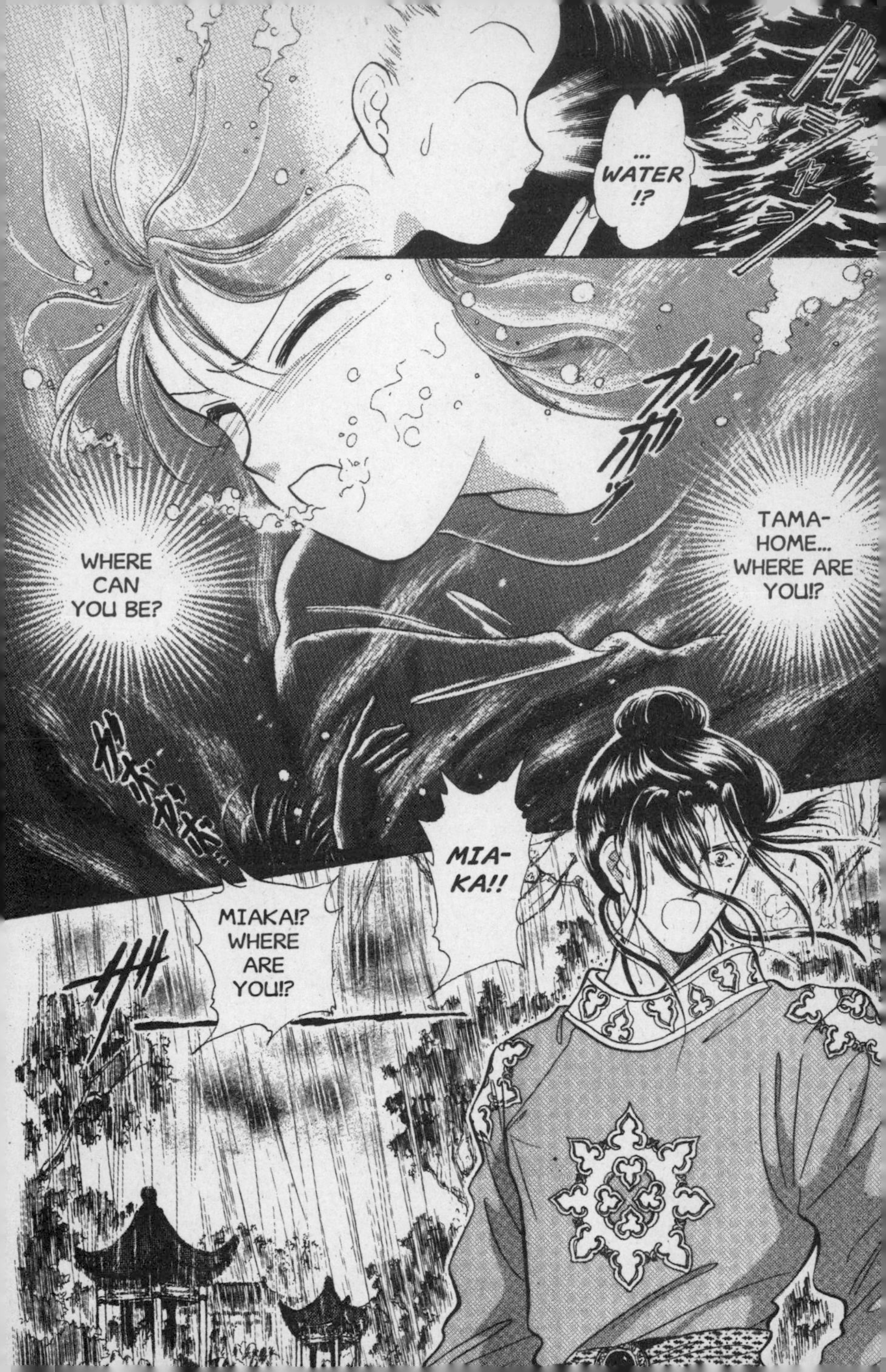
...WATER!?
TAMA-HOME... WHERE ARE YOU!?
WHERE CAN YOU BE?
MIA-KA!!
MIAKA!? WHERE ARE YOU!?

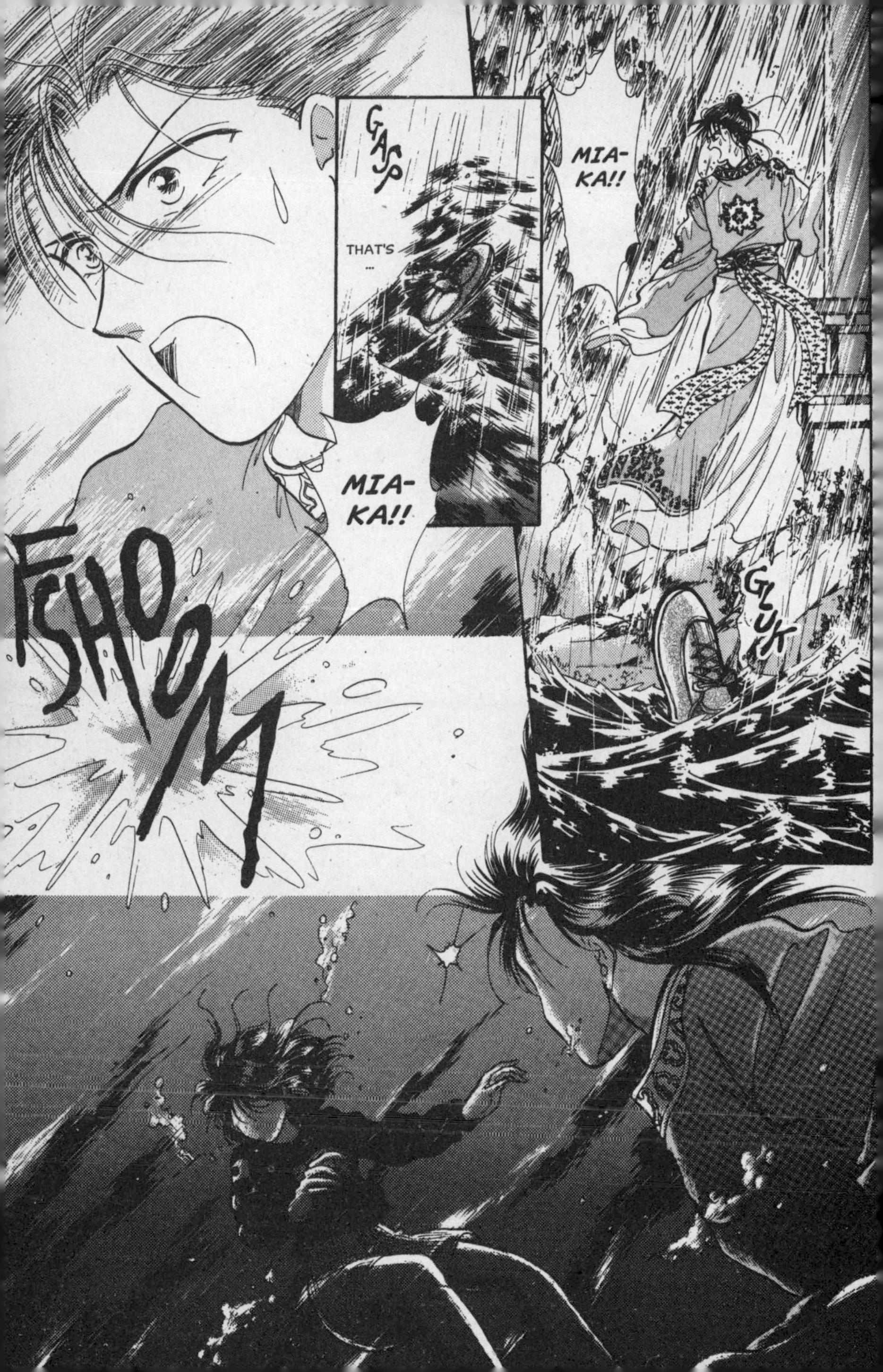
MIA-KA!!
GASP
THAT'S ...
MIA-KA!!
GLUK
FSHOOM

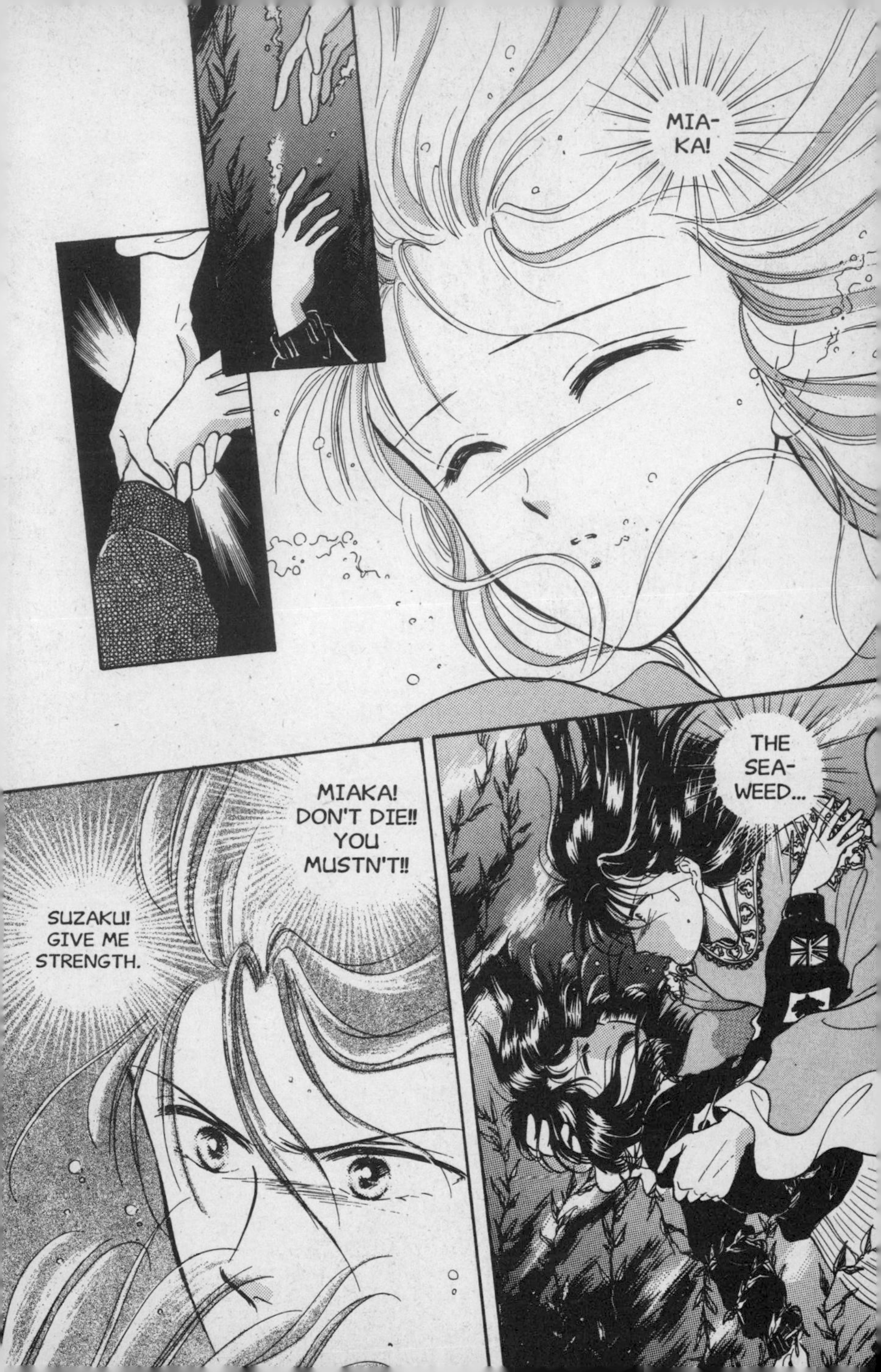
MIA-KA!
THE SEA-WEED...
MIAKA! DON'T DIE!! YOU MUSTN'T!!
SUZAKU! GIVE ME STRENGTH.

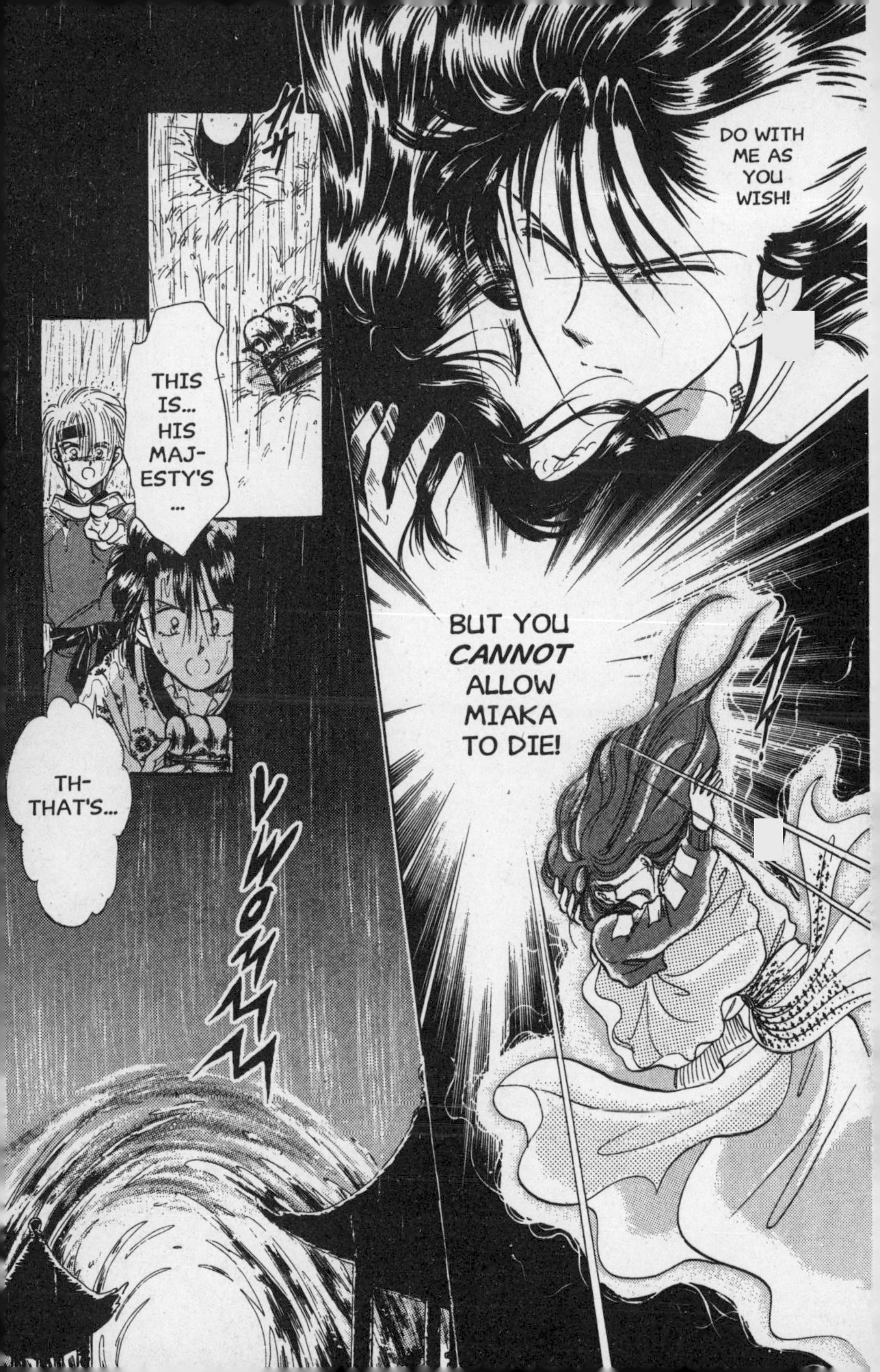
DO WITH ME AS YOU WISH!
BUT YOU CANNOT ALLOW MIAKA TO DIE!
THIS IS... HIS MAJ- ESTY'S ...
TH- THAT'S...
VWOMMMM

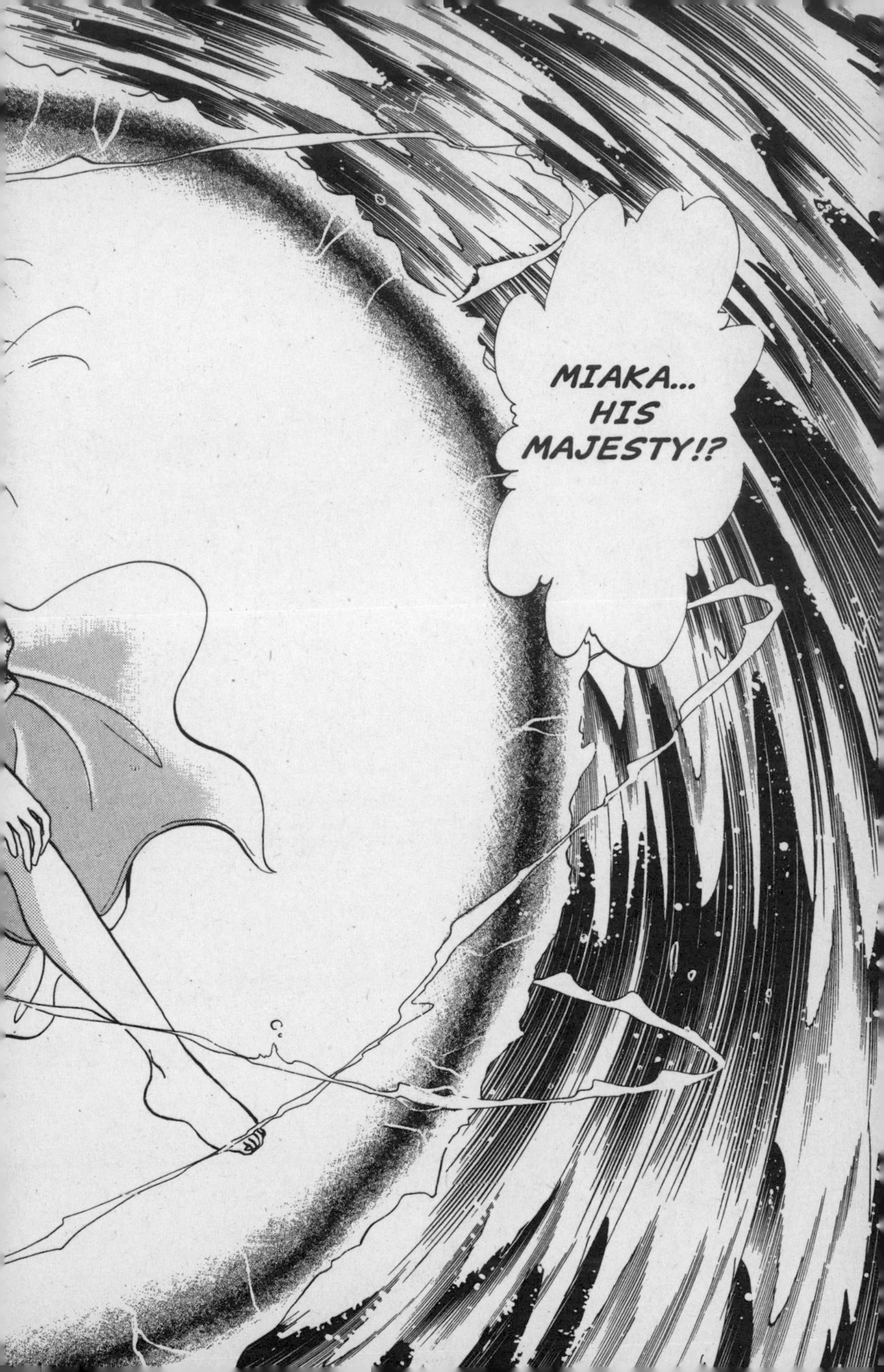
MIAKA... HIS MAJESTY!?

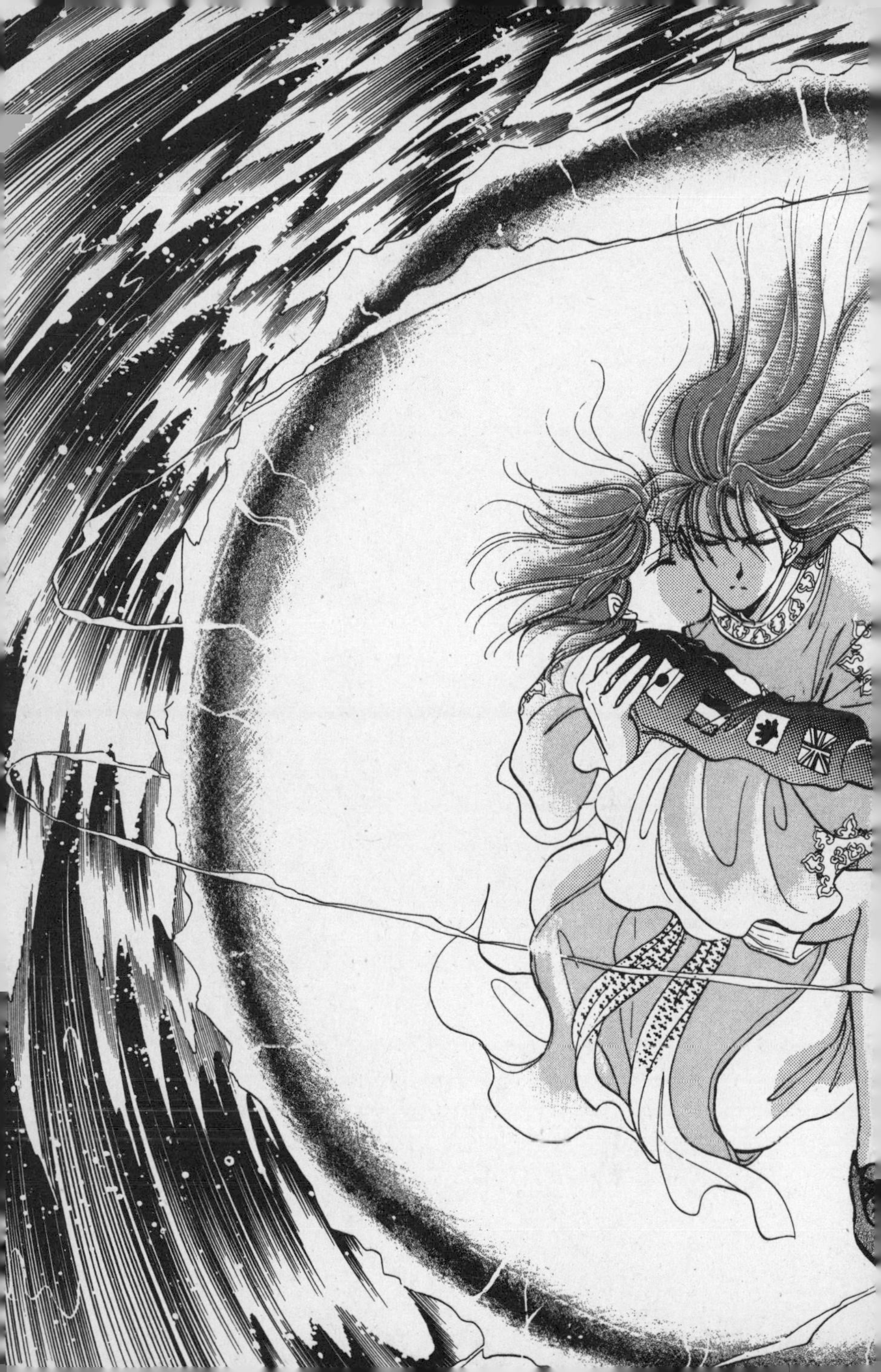

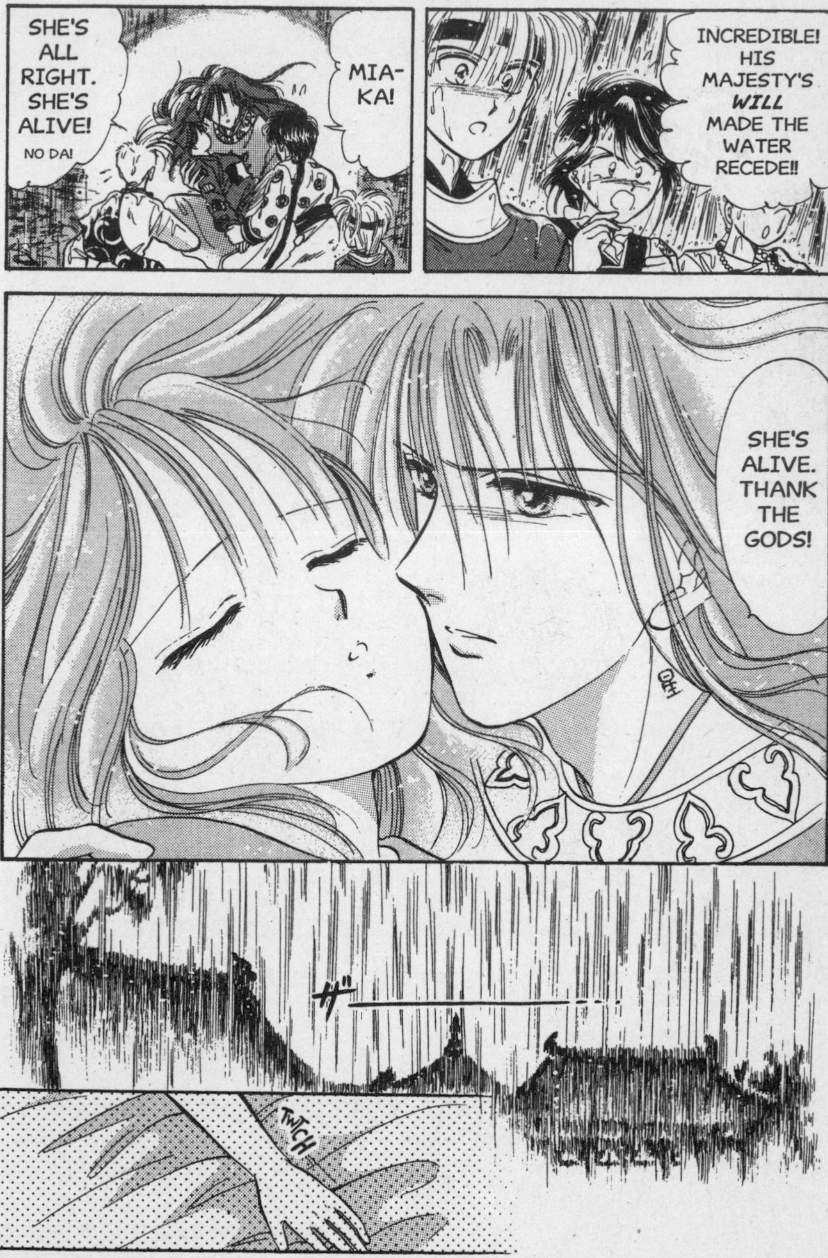
INCREDIBLE! HIS MAJESTY'S *WILL* MADE THE WATER RECEDE!!
MIA-KA!
SHE'S ALL RIGHT. SHE'S ALIVE!
NO DA!
SHE'S ALIVE. THANK THE GODS!
ザ————
TWITCH

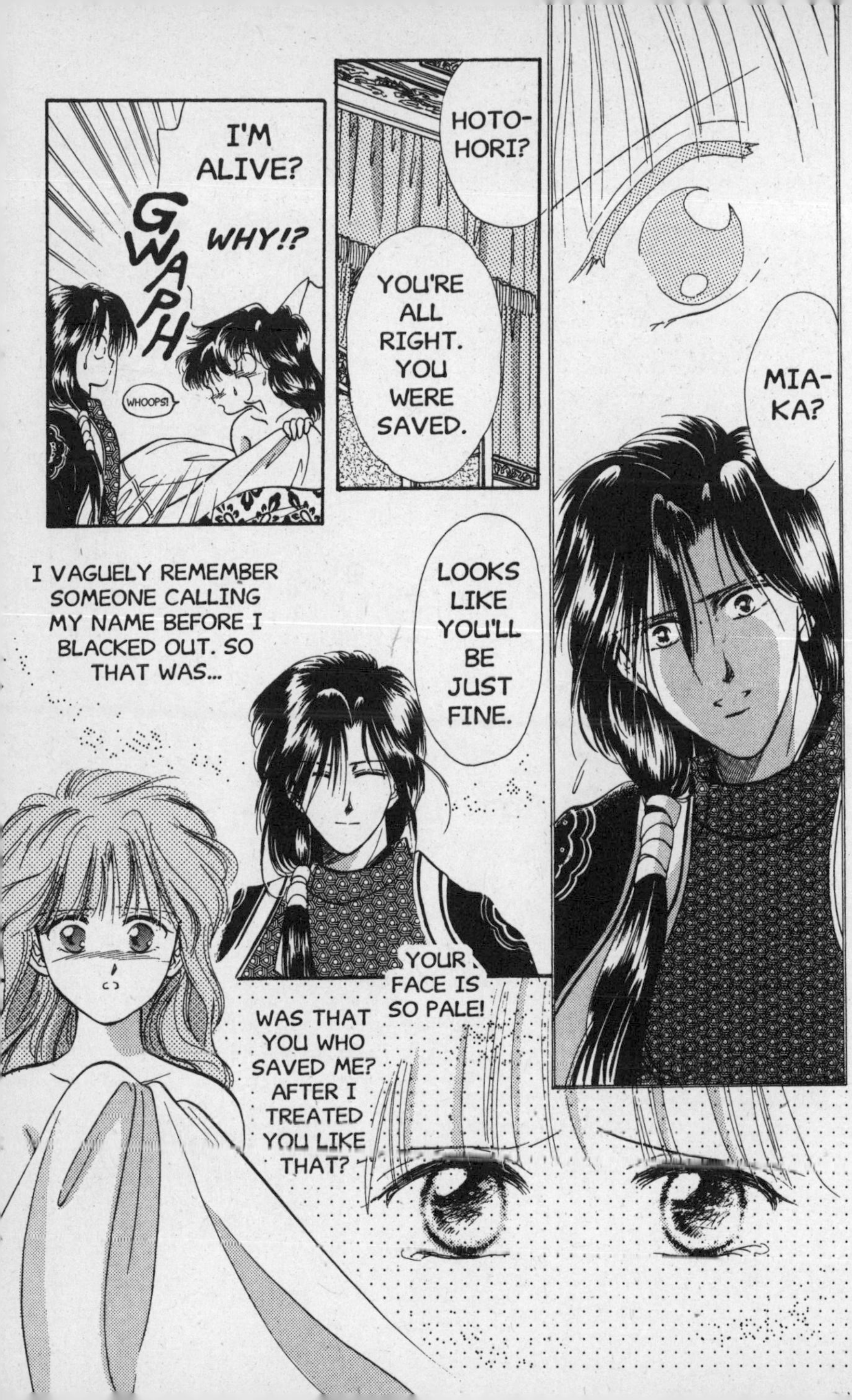
MIA-KA?
HOTO-HORI?
YOU'RE ALL RIGHT. YOU WERE SAVED.
I'M ALIVE?
GWAPH
WHY!?
WHOOPS!
LOOKS LIKE YOU'LL BE JUST FINE.
I VAGUELY REMEMBER SOMEONE CALLING MY NAME BEFORE I BLACKED OUT. SO THAT WAS...
YOUR FACE IS SO PALE!
WAS THAT YOU WHO SAVED ME? AFTER I TREATED YOU LIKE THAT?

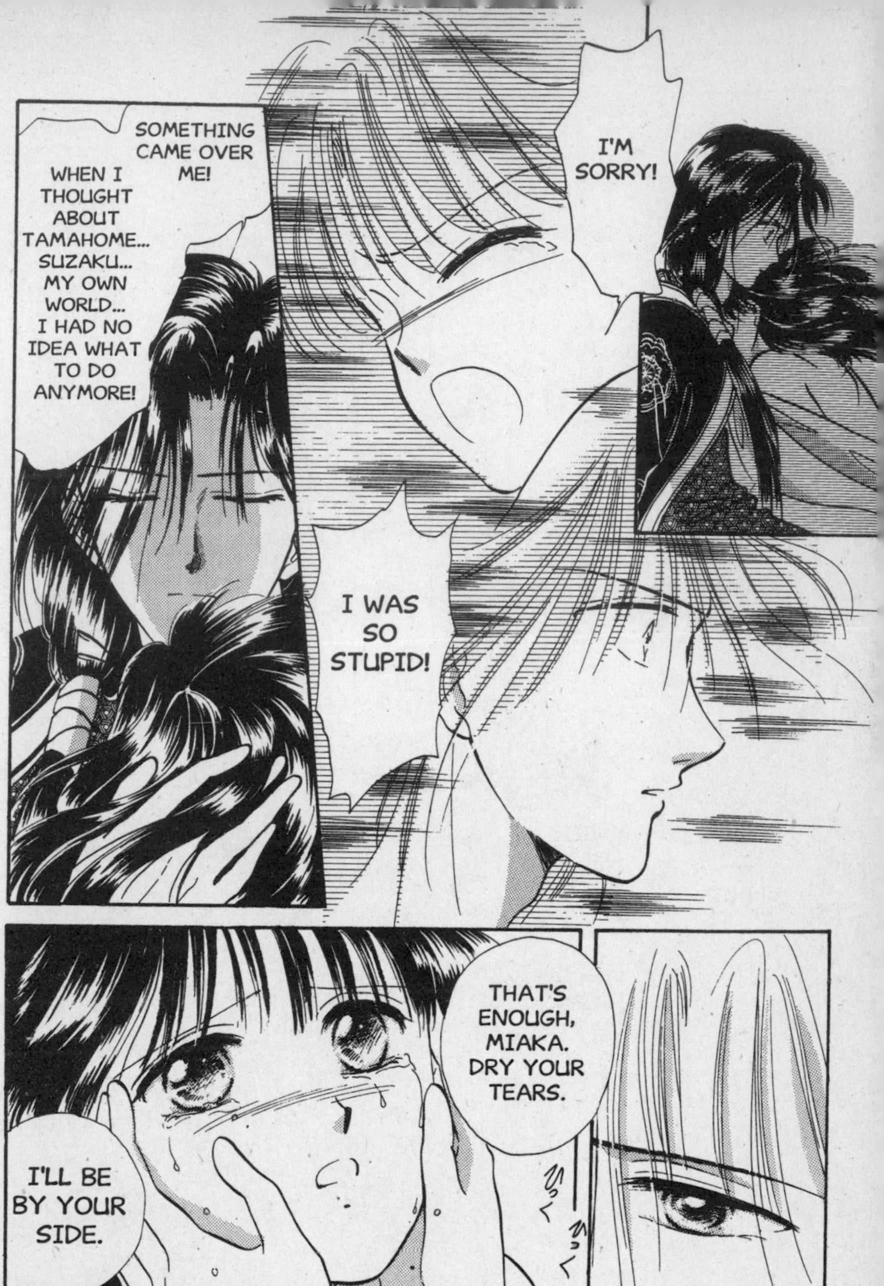
I'M SORRY!
SOMETHING CAME OVER ME!
WHEN I THOUGHT ABOUT TAMAHOME... SUZAKU... MY OWN WORLD... I HAD NO IDEA WHAT TO DO ANYMORE!
I WAS SO STUPID!
THAT'S ENOUGH, MIAKA. DRY YOUR TEARS.
I'LL BE BY YOUR SIDE.

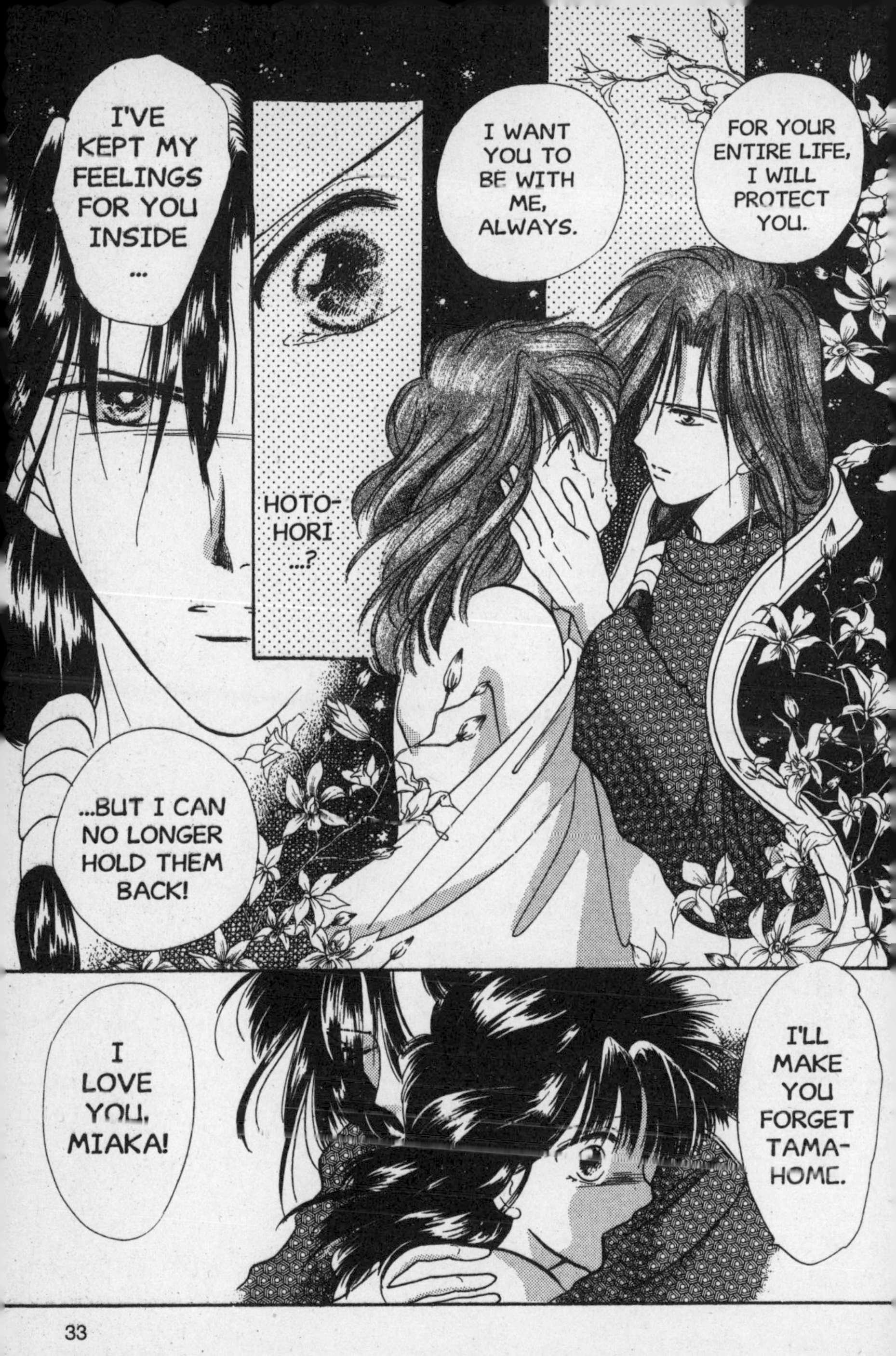
FOR YOUR ENTIRE LIFE, I WILL PROTECT YOU.
I WANT YOU TO BE WITH ME, ALWAYS.
HOTO-HORI ...?
I'VE KEPT MY FEELINGS FOR YOU INSIDE ...
...BUT I CAN NO LONGER HOLD THEM BACK!
I'LL MAKE YOU FORGET TAMA-HOME.
I LOVE YOU, MIAKA!

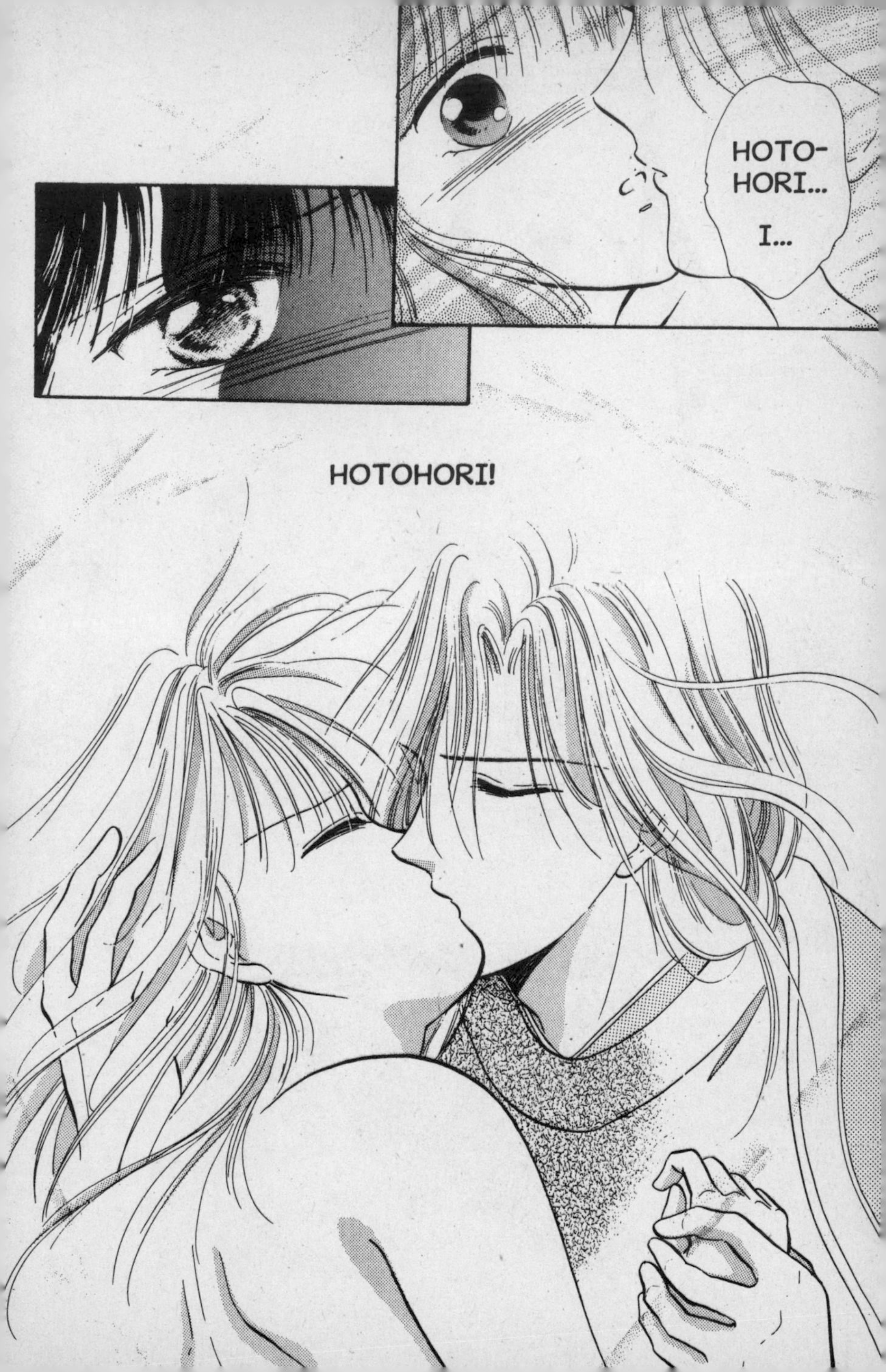
HOTO-
HORI...
I...
HOTOHORI!

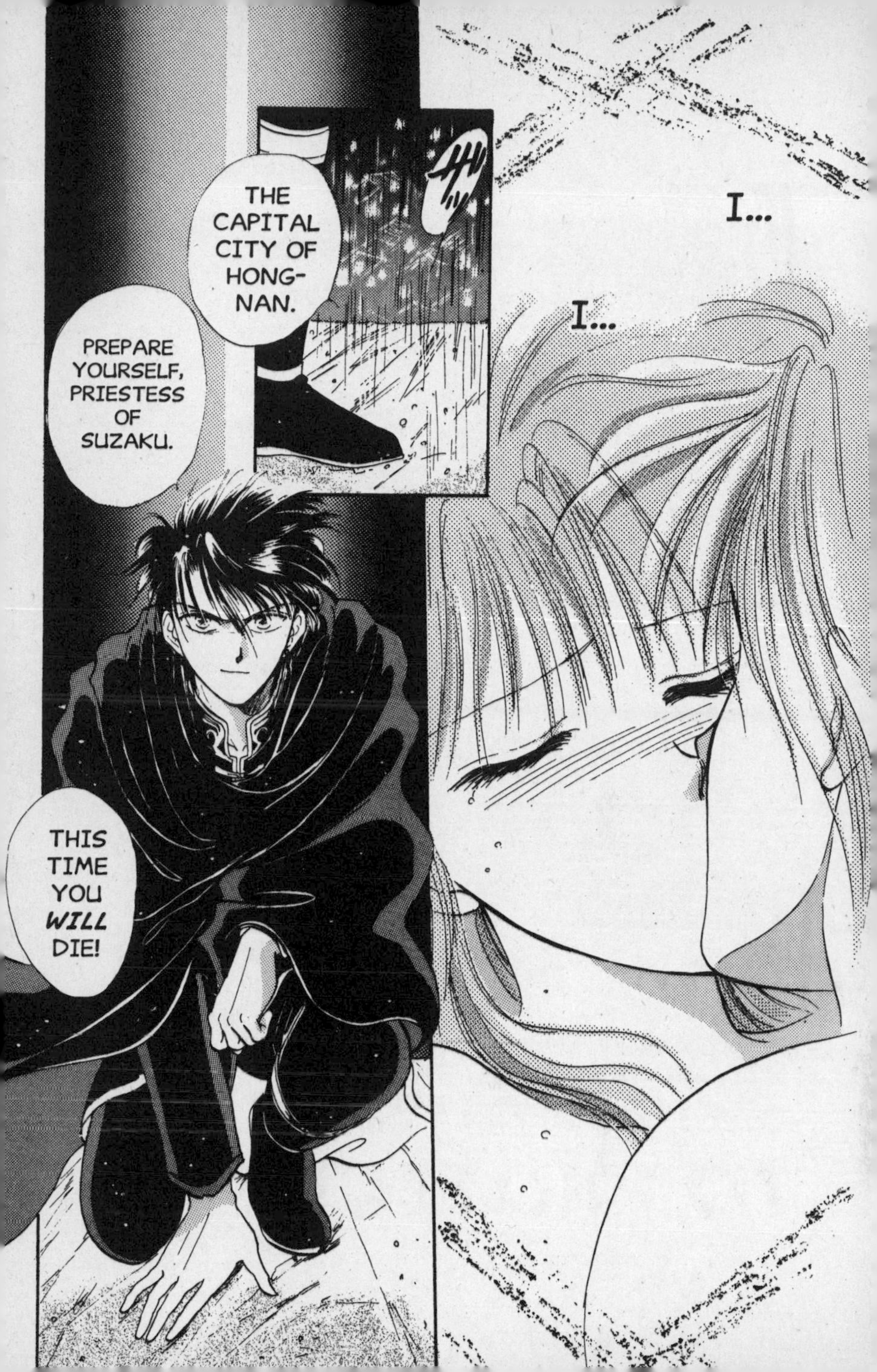
I...
I...
THE CAPITAL CITY OF HONG-NAN.
PREPARE YOURSELF, PRIESTESS OF SUZAKU.
THIS TIME YOU *WILL* DIE!

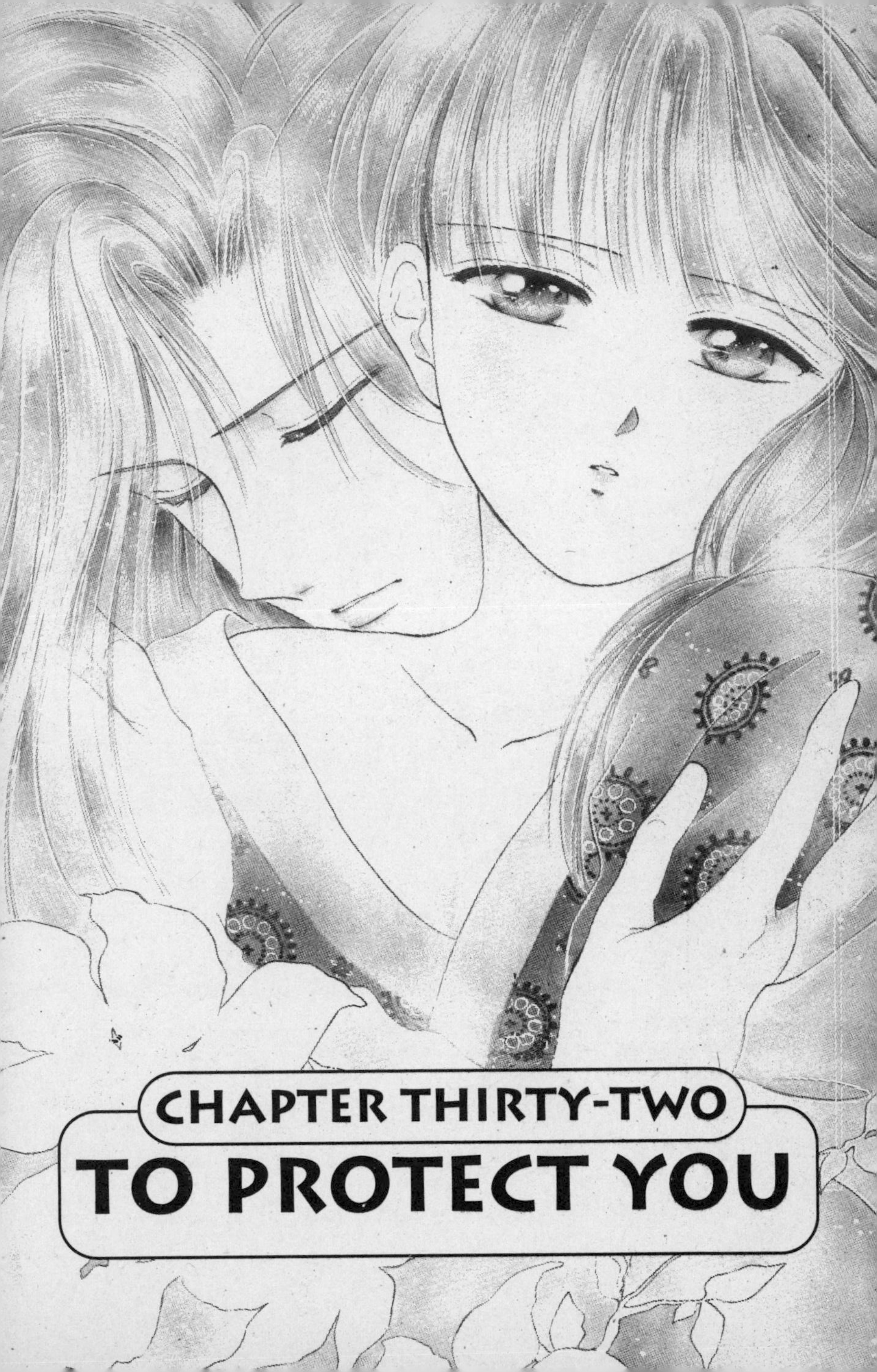

CHAPTER THIRTY-TWO
TO PROTECT YOU

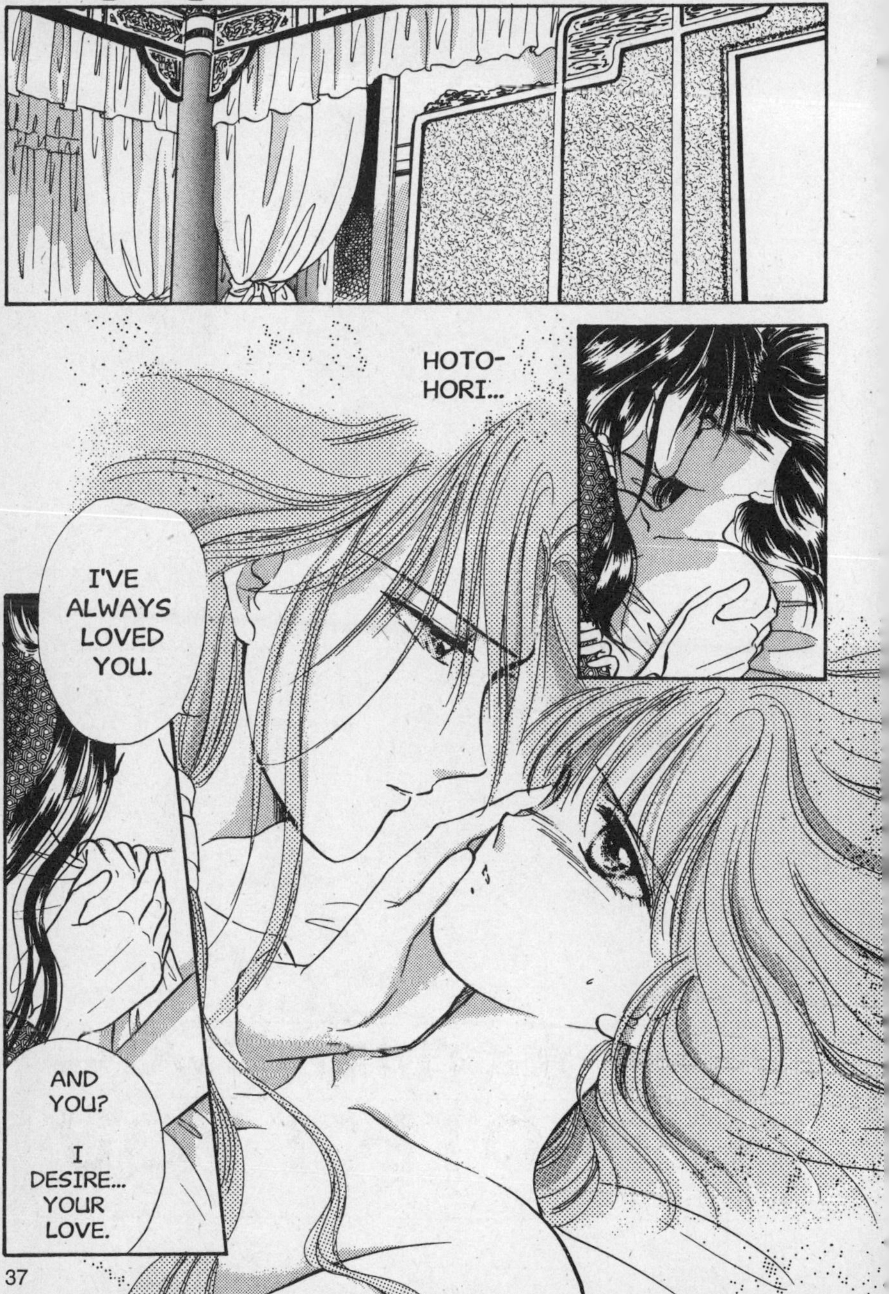
HOTO-HORI...
I'VE ALWAYS LOVED YOU.
AND YOU?
I DESIRE... YOUR LOVE.

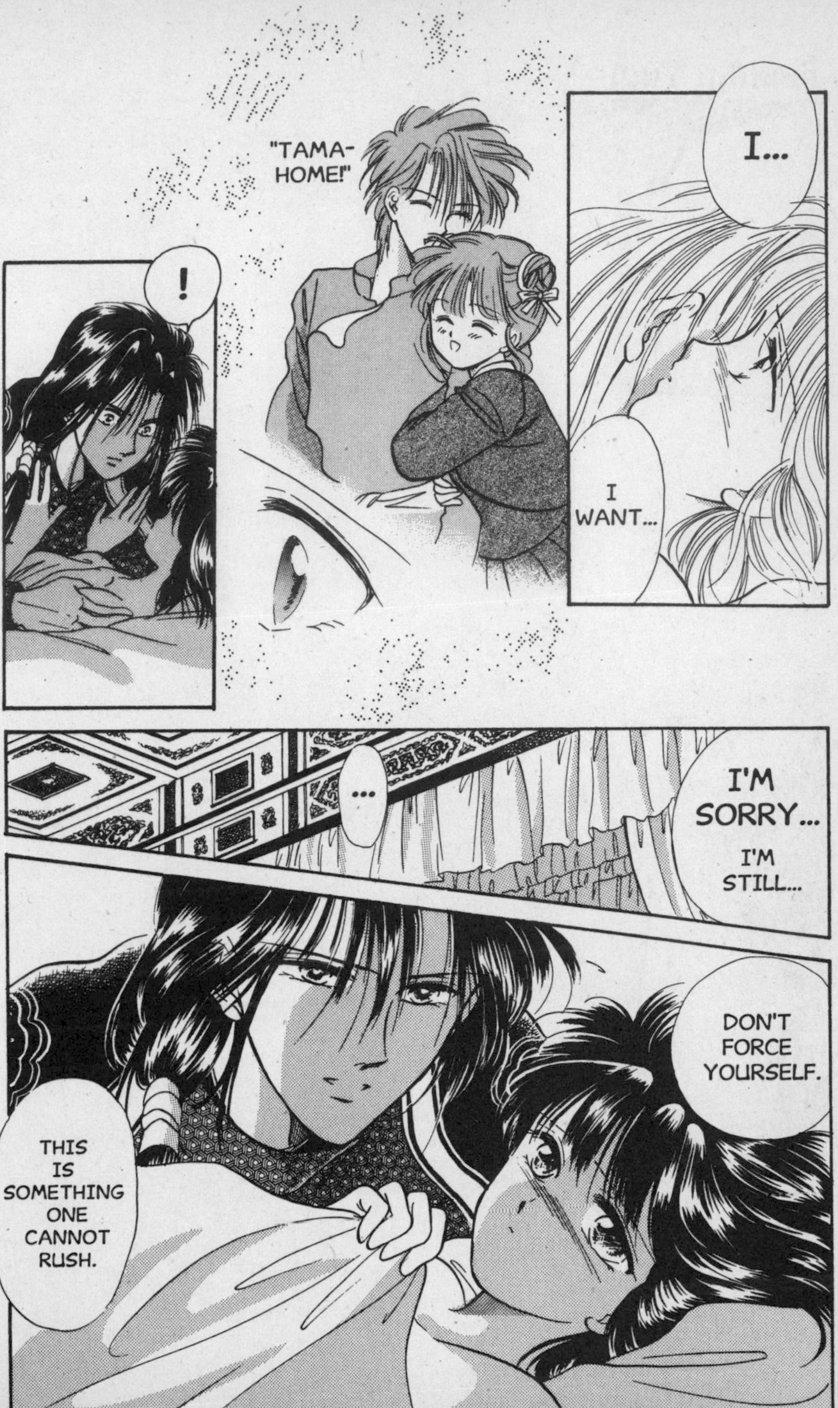
I...
I WANT...
"TAMA-HOME!"
!
I'M SORRY...
I'M STILL...
...
DON'T FORCE YOURSELF.
THIS IS SOMETHING ONE CANNOT RUSH.

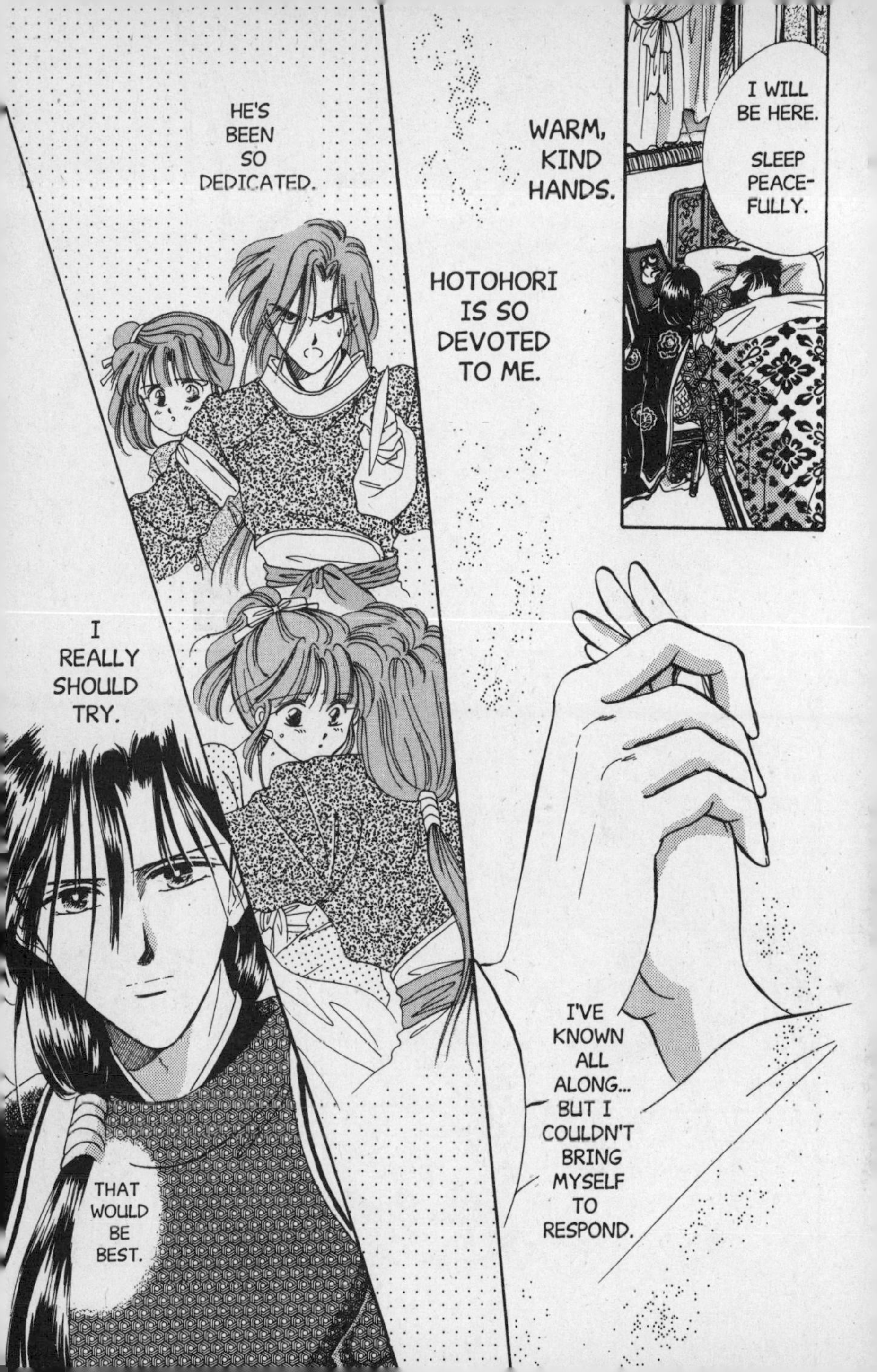
I WILL BE HERE.
SLEEP PEACE-FULLY.
WARM, KIND HANDS.
HOTOHORI IS SO DEVOTED TO ME.
I'VE KNOWN ALL ALONG... BUT I COULDN'T BRING MYSELF TO RESPOND.
HE'S BEEN SO DEDICATED.
I REALLY SHOULD TRY.
THAT WOULD BE BEST.

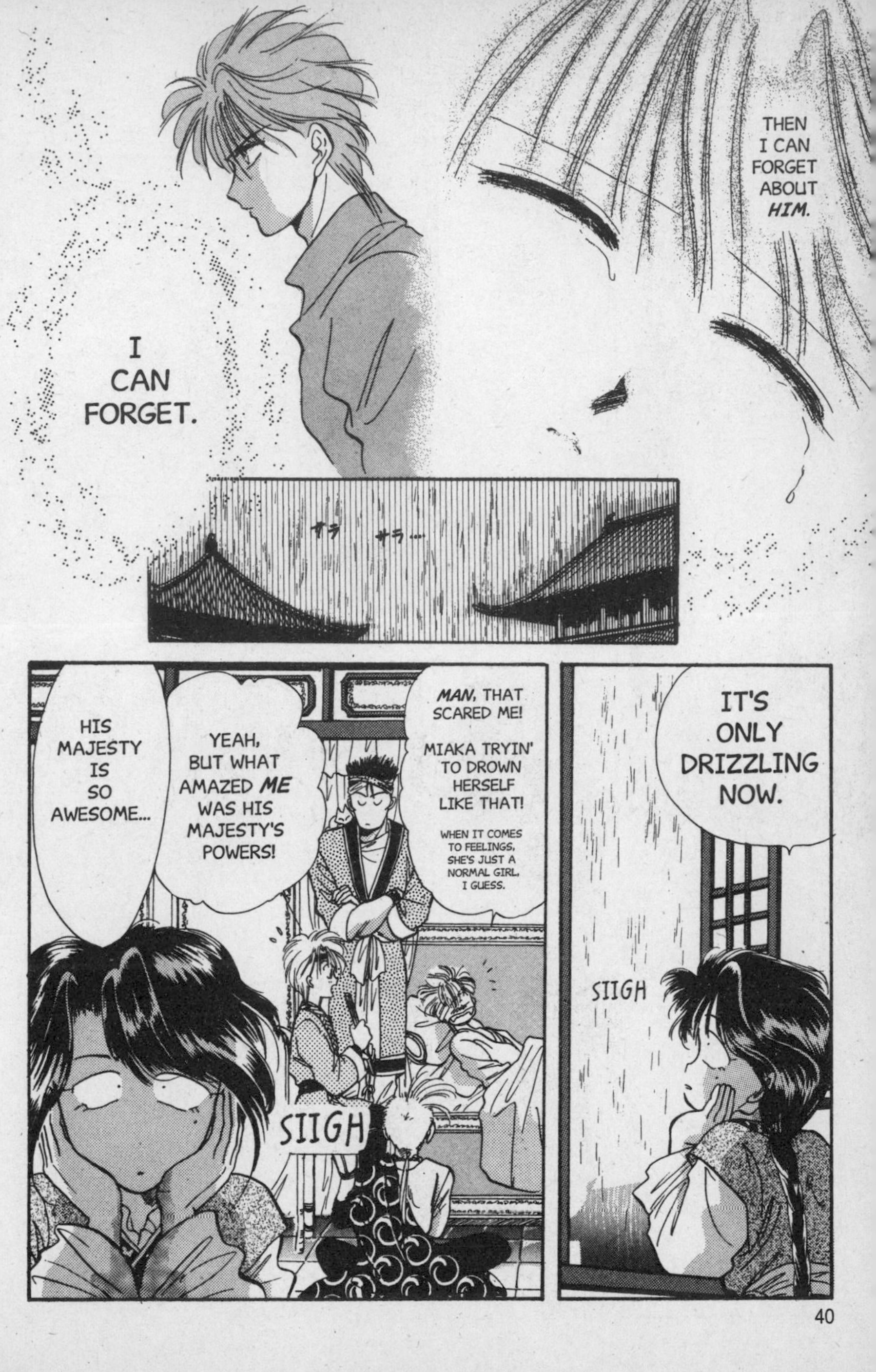
THEN I CAN FORGET ABOUT *HIM*.
I CAN FORGET.
サラ サラ…
IT'S ONLY DRIZZLING NOW.
SIIGH
MAN, THAT SCARED ME!
MIAKA TRYIN' TO DROWN HERSELF LIKE THAT!
WHEN IT COMES TO FEELINGS, SHE'S JUST A NORMAL GIRL, I GUESS.
YEAH, BUT WHAT AMAZED *ME* WAS HIS MAJESTY'S POWERS!
HIS MAJESTY IS SO AWESOME...
SIIGH

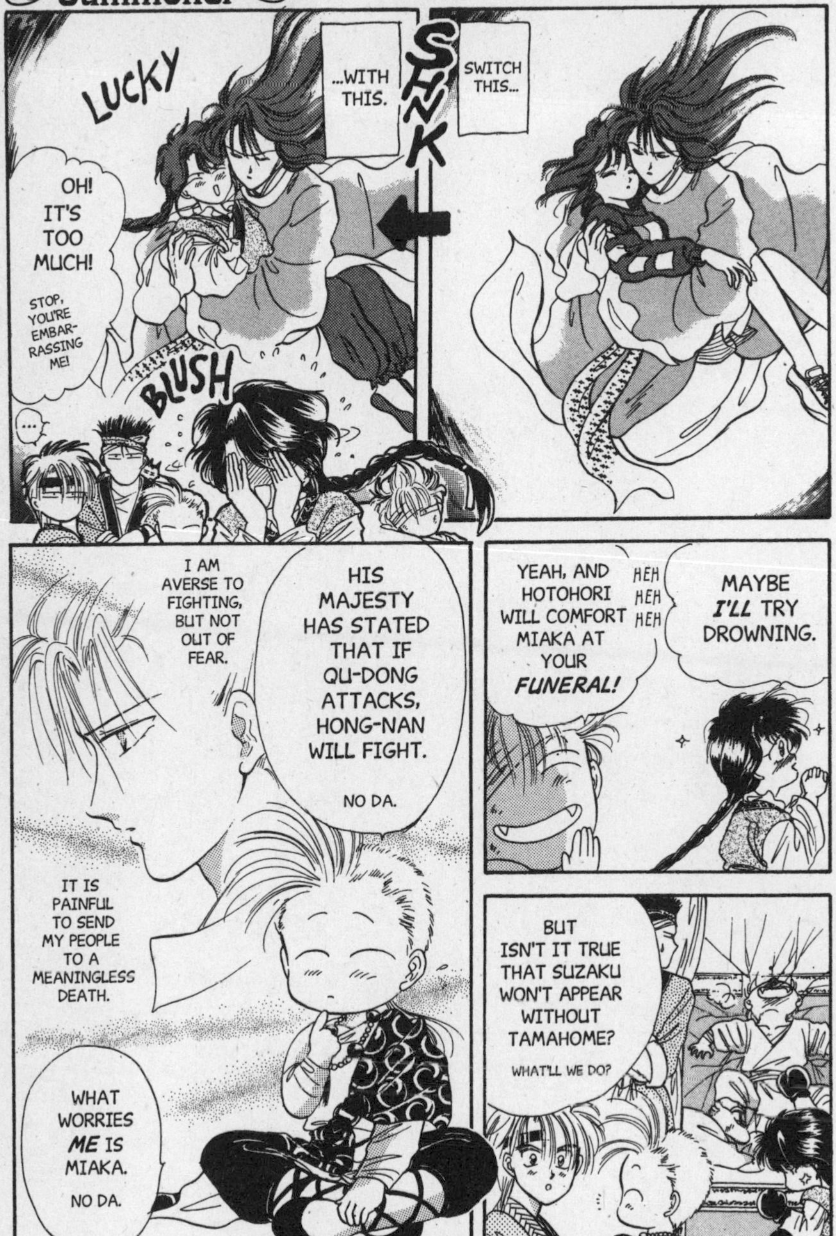
SWITCH THIS...
SHNK
...WITH THIS.
LUCKY
OH! IT'S TOO MUCH!
STOP, YOU'RE EMBARRASSING ME!
BLUSH
...
MAYBE I'LL TRY DROWNING.
HEH HEH HEH
YEAH, AND HOTOHORI WILL COMFORT MIAKA AT YOUR FUNERAL!
BUT ISN'T IT TRUE THAT SUZAKU WON'T APPEAR WITHOUT TAMAHOME?
WHAT'LL WE DO?
HIS MAJESTY HAS STATED THAT IF QU-DONG ATTACKS, HONG-NAN WILL FIGHT.
NO DA.
I AM AVERSE TO FIGHTING, BUT NOT OUT OF FEAR.
IT IS PAINFUL TO SEND MY PEOPLE TO A MEANINGLESS DEATH.
WHAT WORRIES ME IS MIAKA.
NO DA.

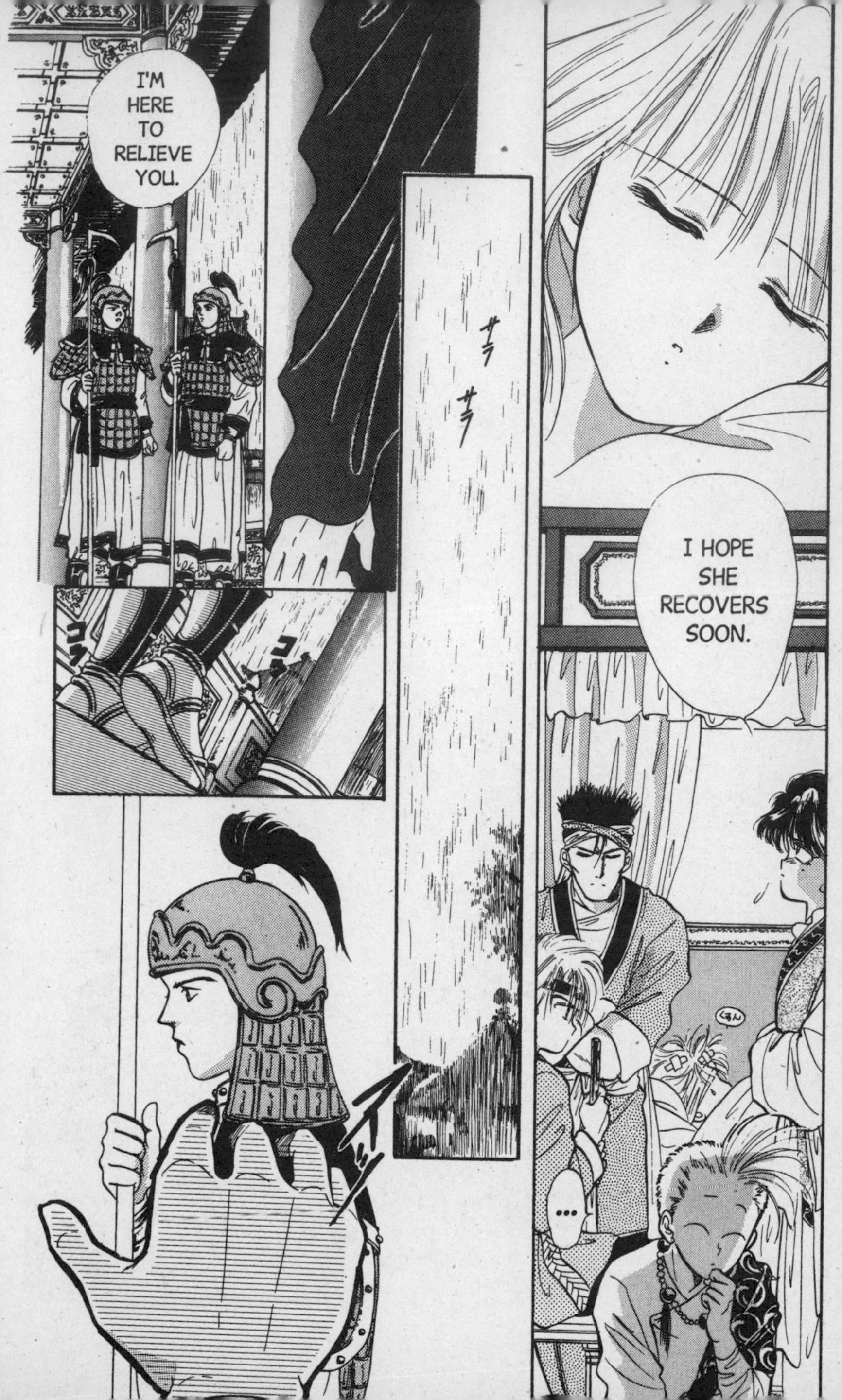
I HOPE SHE RECOVERS SOON.
...
I'M HERE TO RELIEVE YOU.

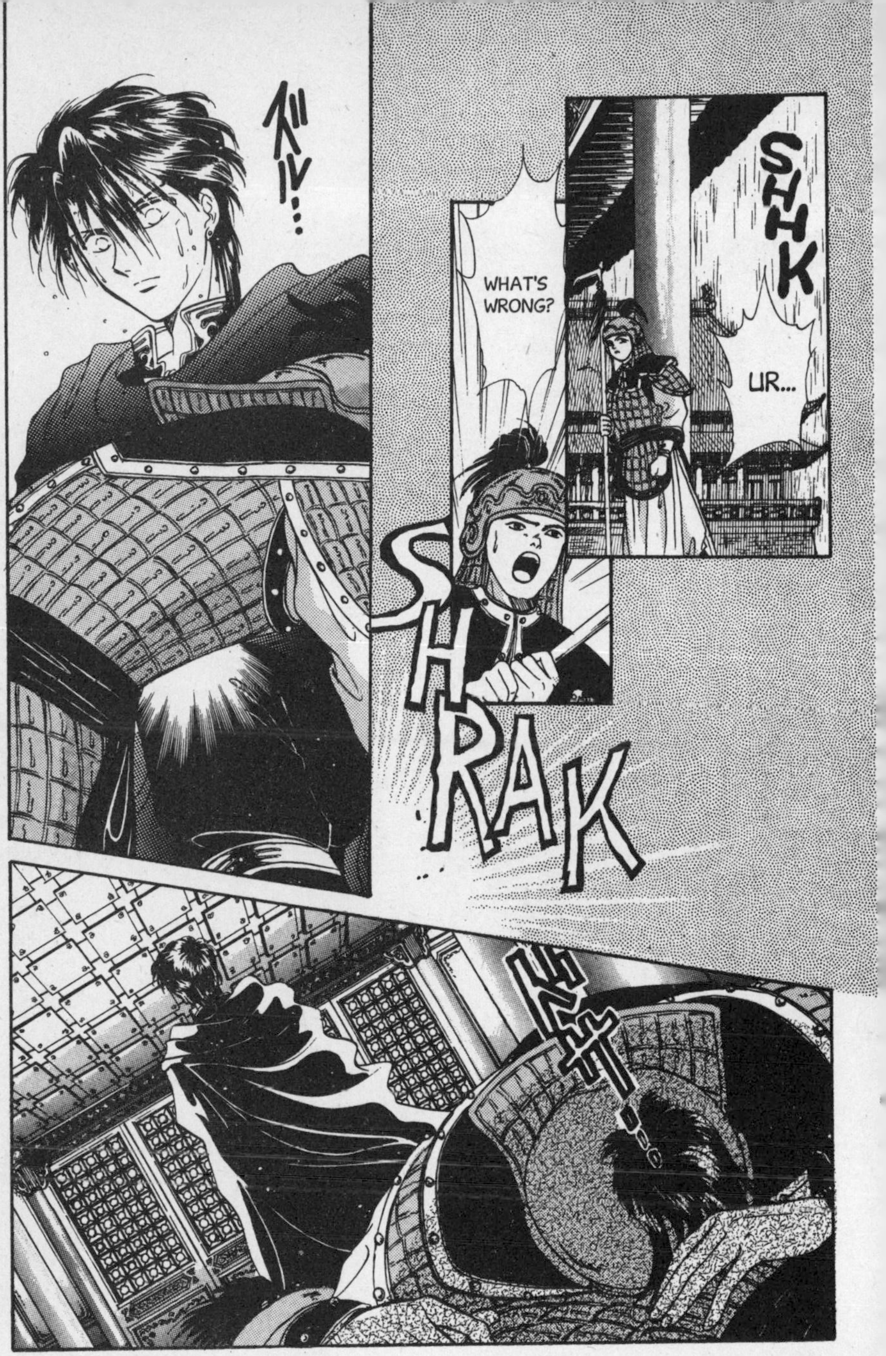
SHHK
UR...
WHAT'S WRONG?
SHRAK
ズル…

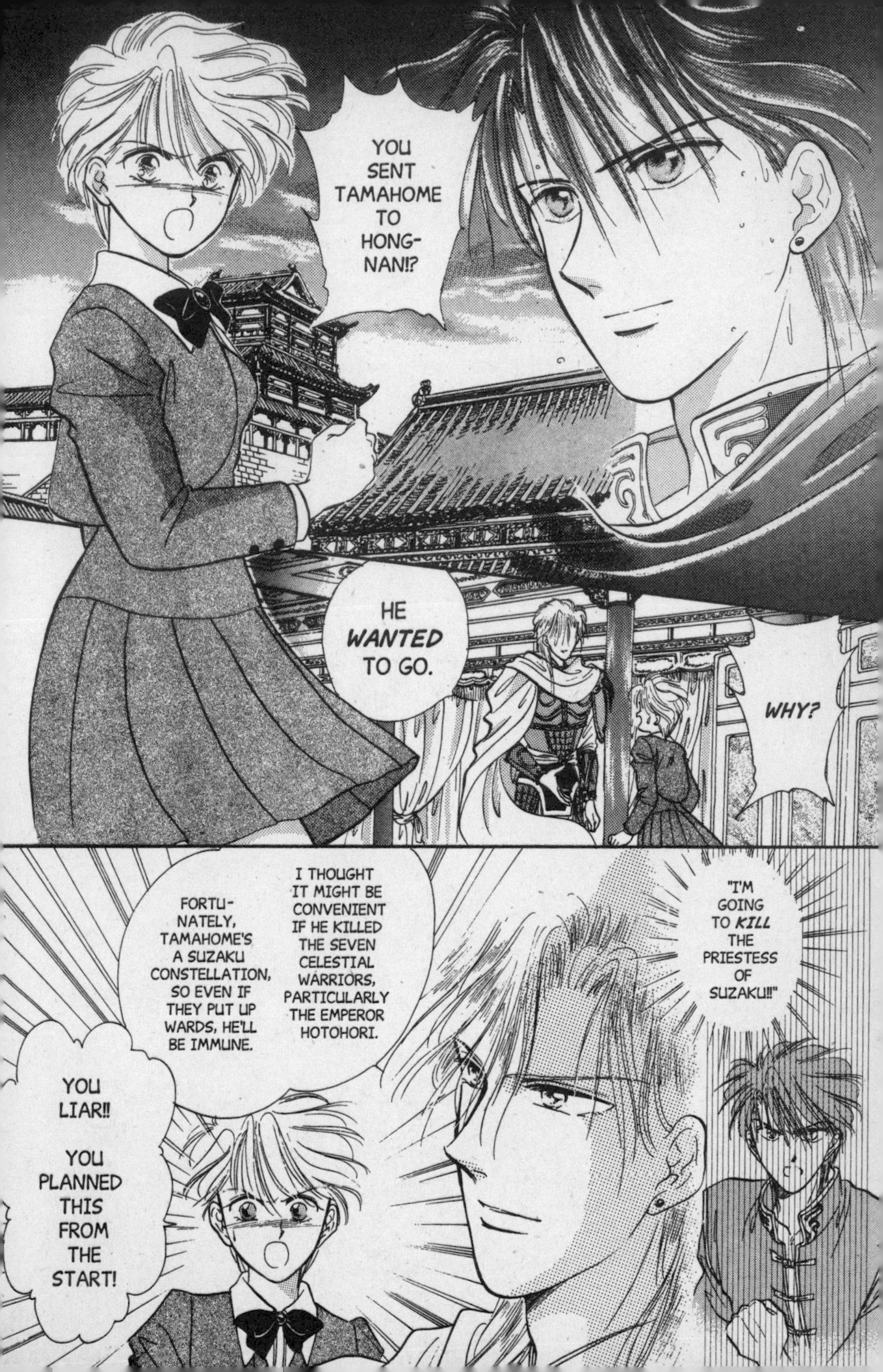
YOU SENT TAMAHOME TO HONG-NAN!?
HE WANTED TO GO.
WHY?
"I'M GOING TO KILL THE PRIESTESS OF SUZAKU!!"
I THOUGHT IT MIGHT BE CONVENIENT IF HE KILLED THE SEVEN CELESTIAL WARRIORS, PARTICULARLY THE EMPEROR HOTOHORI.
FORTU-NATELY, TAMAHOME'S A SUZAKU CONSTELLATION, SO EVEN IF THEY PUT UP WARDS, HE'LL BE IMMUNE.
YOU LIAR!!
YOU PLANNED THIS FROM THE START!

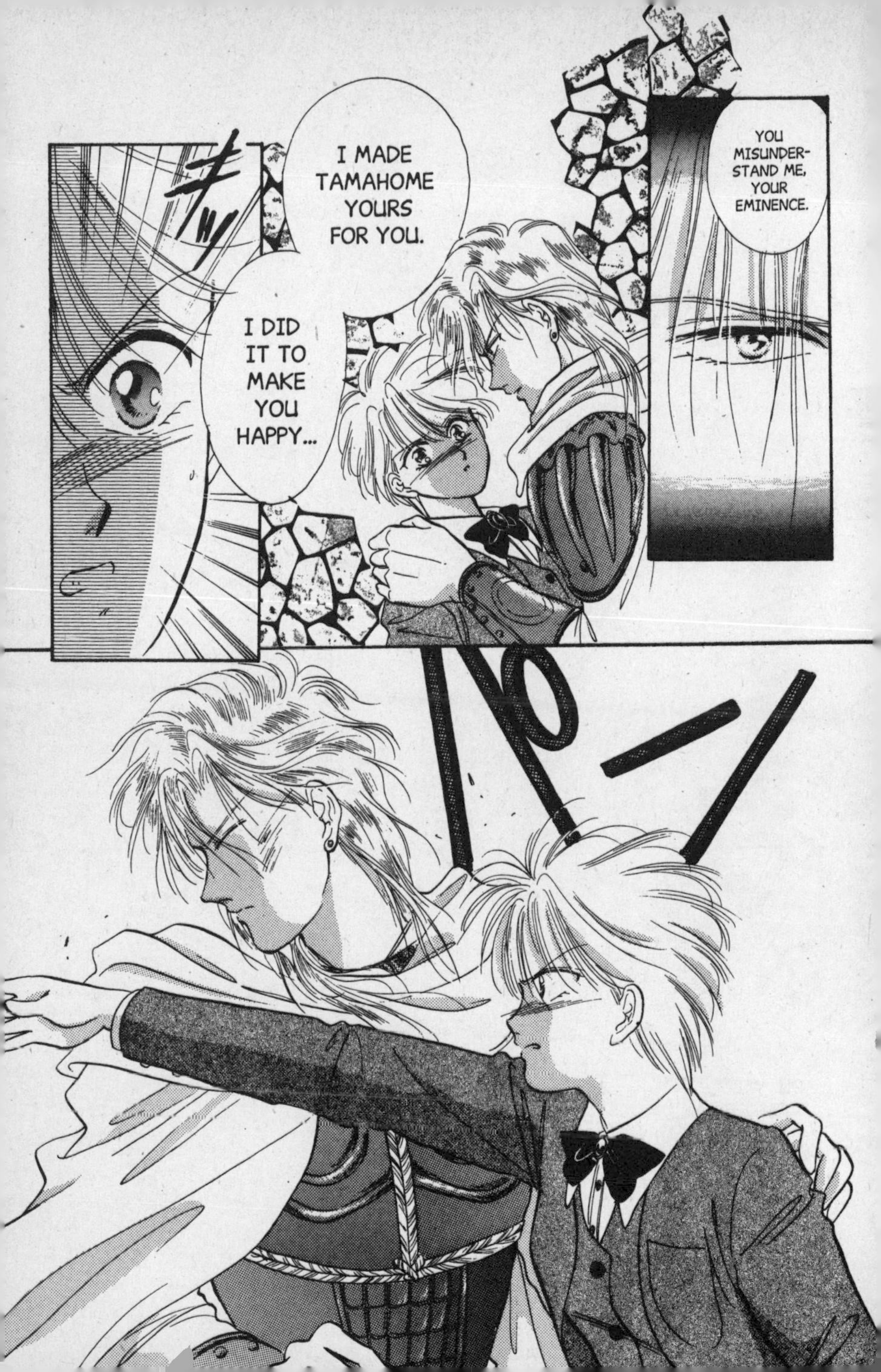
YOU MISUNDER-STAND ME, YOUR EMINENCE.
I MADE TAMAHOME YOURS FOR YOU.
I DID IT TO MAKE YOU HAPPY...

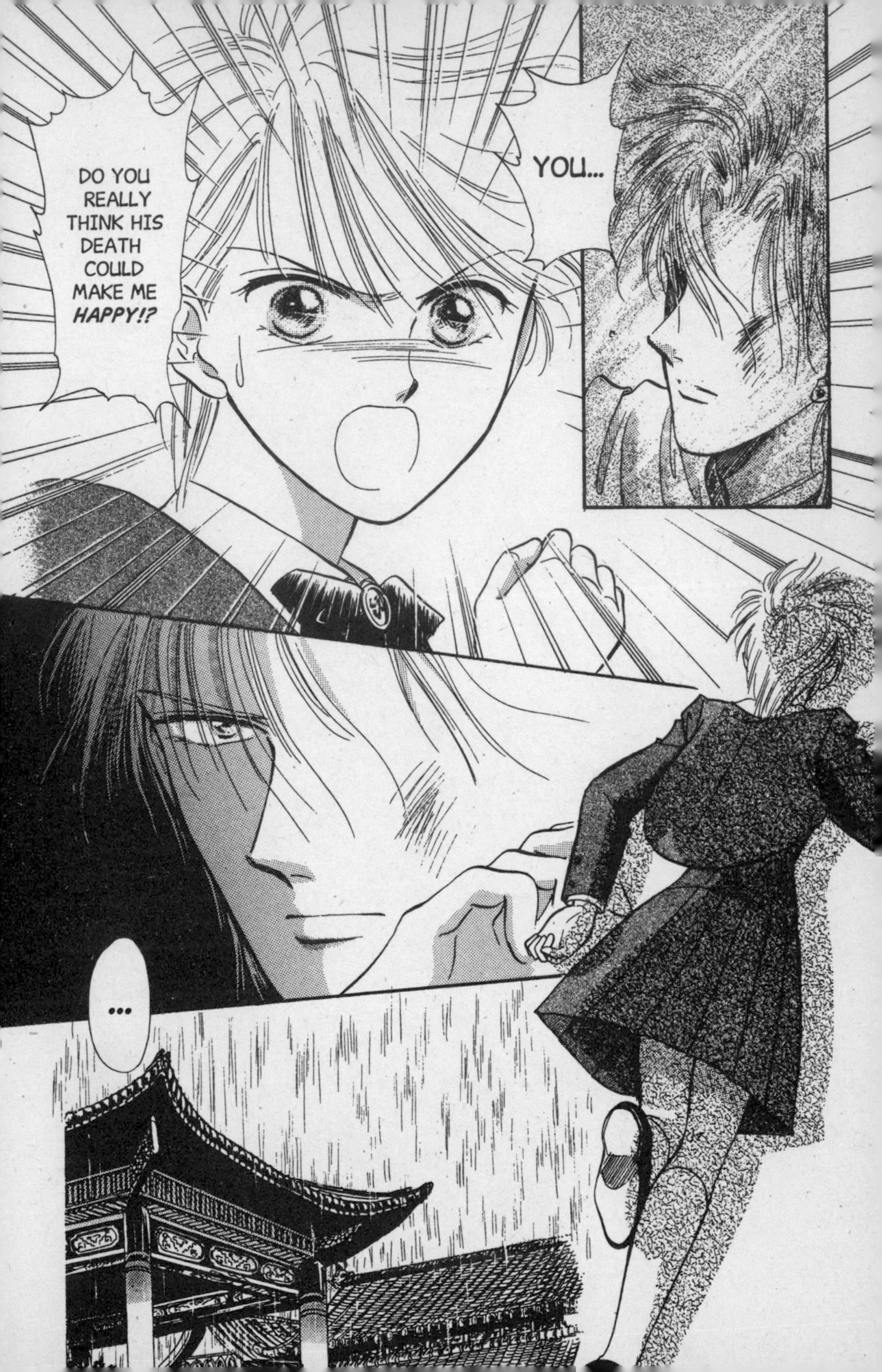
YOU...
DO YOU REALLY THINK HIS DEATH COULD MAKE ME *HAPPY!?*
...

Fushigi Yûgi 6

On with the story. Three years ago, I moved from Osaka into a house in Tokyo. That's when this strange, and I suppose, retrospectively interesting, incident occurred. It started when my assistant (at the time) K. awoke from a deep sleep to find she couldn't move! Of course, our schedule was such that we would work all night and wake up in the afternoon. That could have been playing tricks on our health.

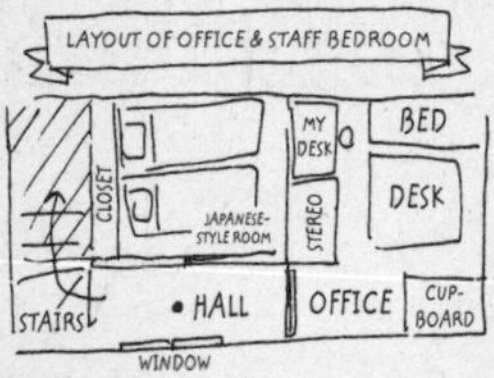
LAYOUT OF OFFICE & STAFF BEDROOM
MY DESK
BED
DESK
CLOSET
JAPANESE-STYLE ROOM
STEREO
STAIRS
HALL
OFFICE
CUP-BOARD
WINDOW

The assistants were sleeping in their bedroom, and I was downstairs taking a break with my mom. I went up to wake them around noon, but before I came upstairs, according to all the assistants, a woman looked into the bedroom. (Was she trying to wake them up?) Then she went downstairs. Apparently, this had been going on for the last six months, and everyone assumed it was my mother. But neither my mother nor my brother ever went upstairs. So the question became, "Who could it possibly be!?" Some saw a light shining on her face, others saw her feet, or even heard breathing (it was a dark room) or the rhythmic sound of footsteps ascending or descending the stairs.

(To be continued...)

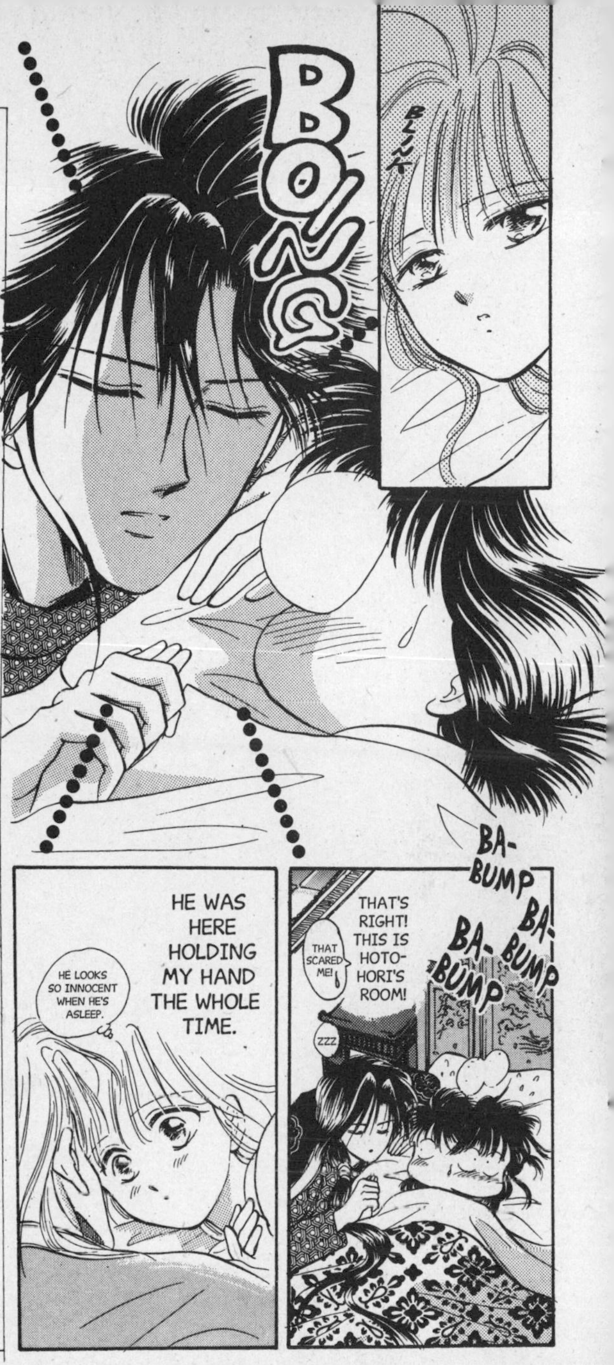
BLINK
BONG
BA-BUMP
THAT'S RIGHT! THIS IS HOTO-HORI'S ROOM!
THAT SCARED ME!
ZZZ
BA-BUMP
BA-BUMP
HE WAS HERE HOLDING MY HAND THE WHOLE TIME.
HE LOOKS SO INNOCENT WHEN HE'S ASLEEP.

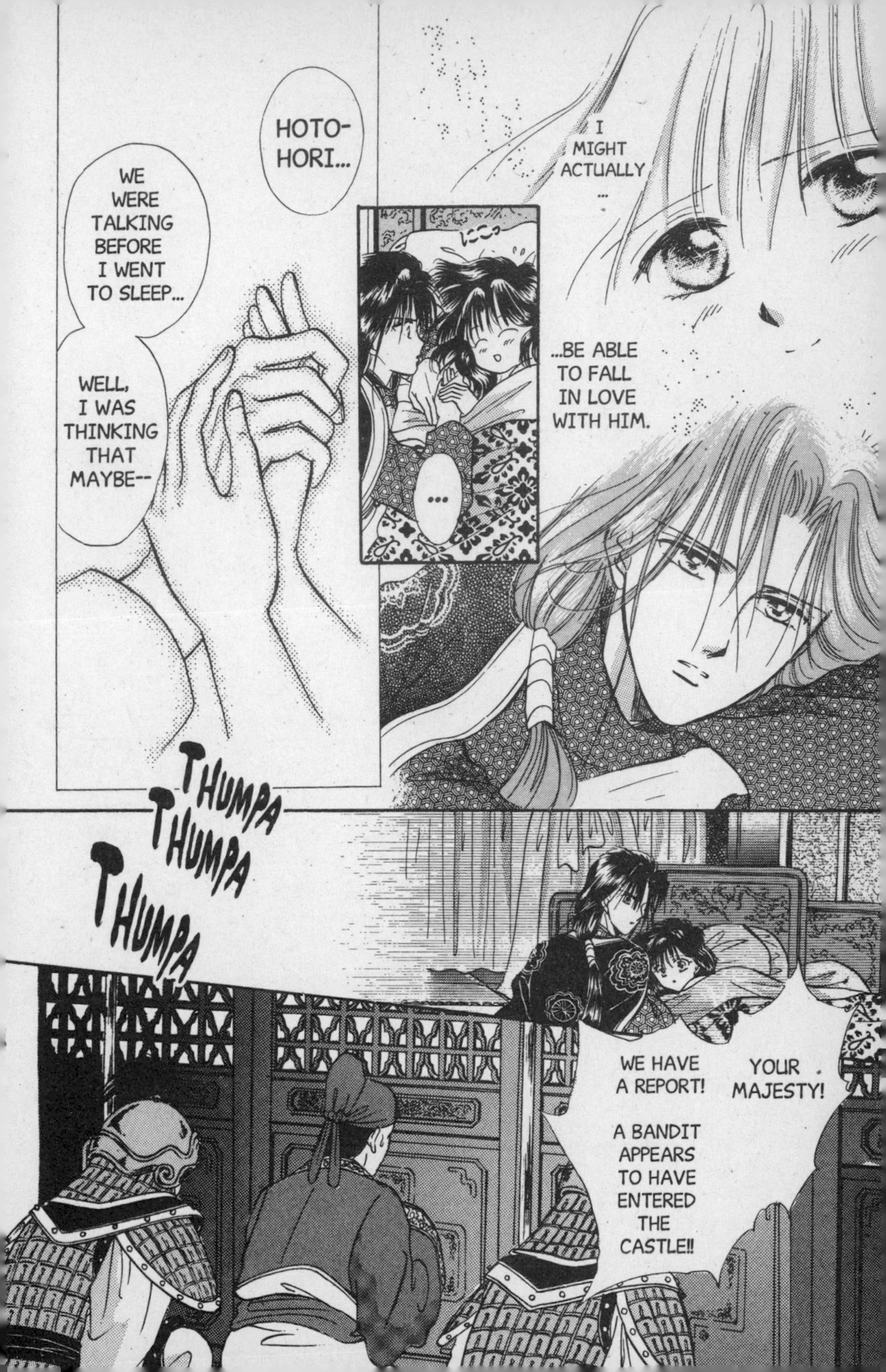
I MIGHT ACTUALLY ...
...BE ABLE TO FALL IN LOVE WITH HIM.
にこっ
...
HOTO-HORI...
WE WERE TALKING BEFORE I WENT TO SLEEP...
WELL, I WAS THINKING THAT MAYBE--
THUMPA THUMPA THUMPA
YOUR MAJESTY!
WE HAVE A REPORT!
A BANDIT APPEARS TO HAVE ENTERED THE CASTLE!!

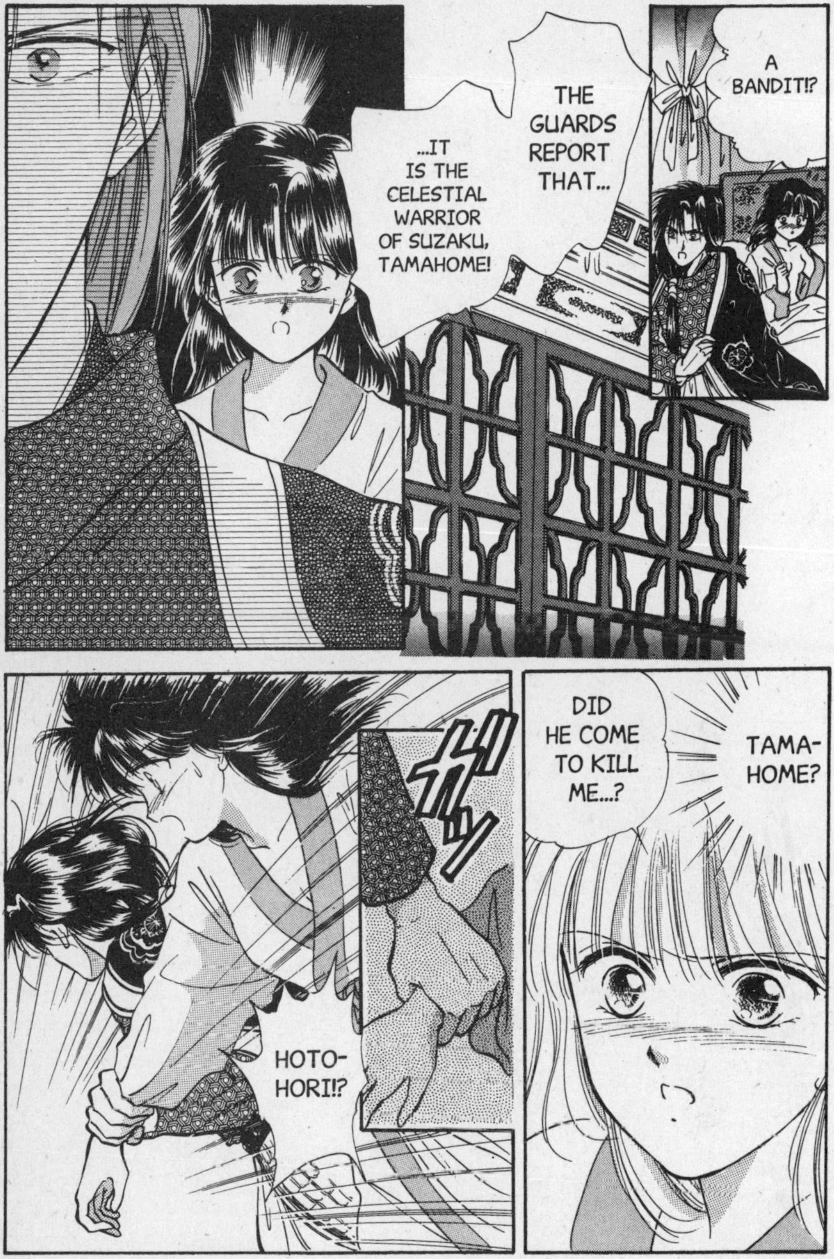
A BANDIT!?
THE GUARDS REPORT THAT...
...IT IS THE CELESTIAL WARRIOR OF SUZAKU, TAMAHOME!
TAMA-HOME?
DID HE COME TO KILL ME...?
HOTO-HORI!?

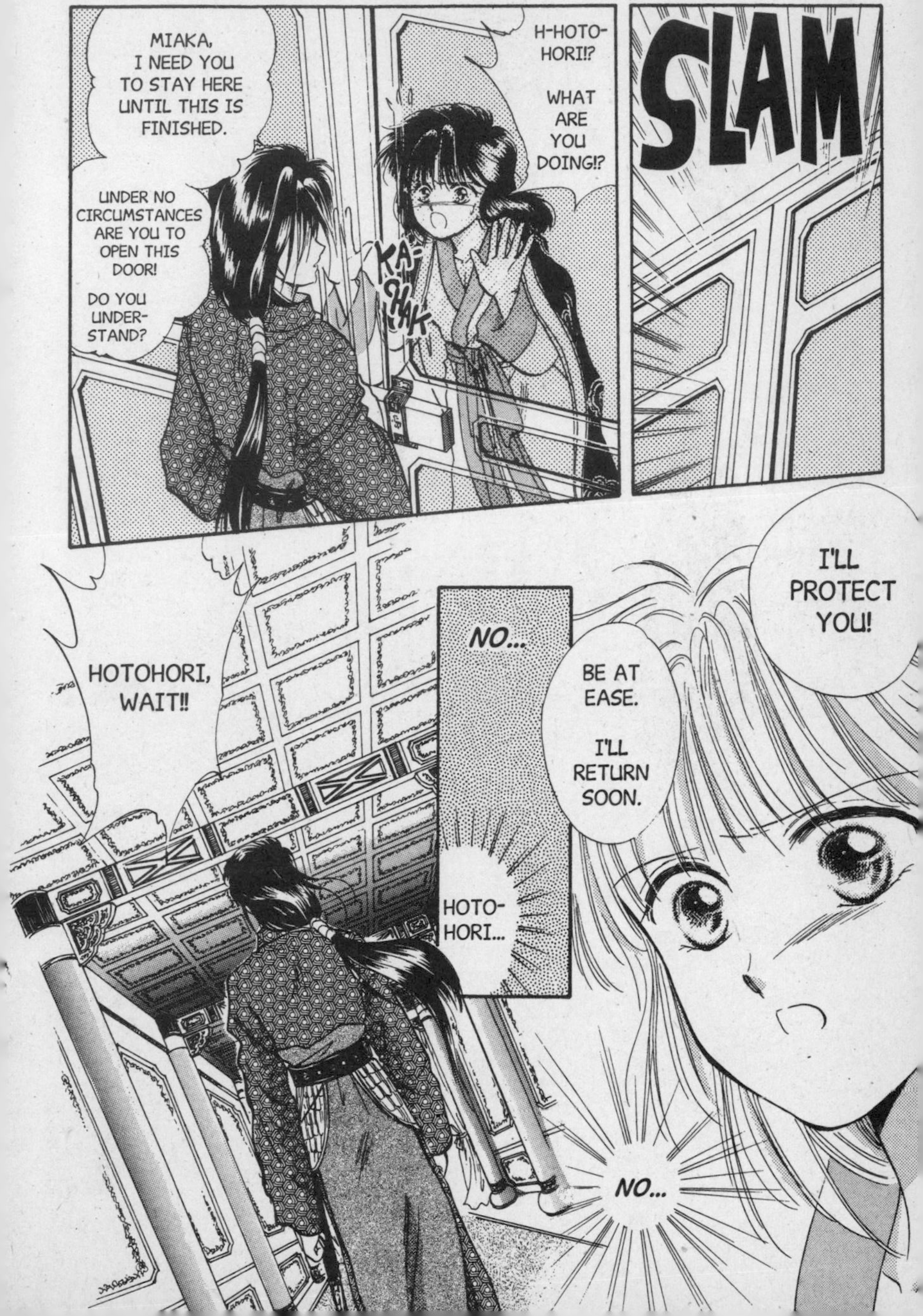
MIAKA, I NEED YOU TO STAY HERE UNTIL THIS IS FINISHED.
UNDER NO CIRCUMSTANCES ARE YOU TO OPEN THIS DOOR!
DO YOU UNDER-STAND?
KA-CHAK
H-HOTO-HORI!?
WHAT ARE YOU DOING!?
SLAM
HOTOHORI, WAIT!!
NO...
BE AT EASE.
I'LL RETURN SOON.
I'LL PROTECT YOU!
HOTO-HORI...
NO...

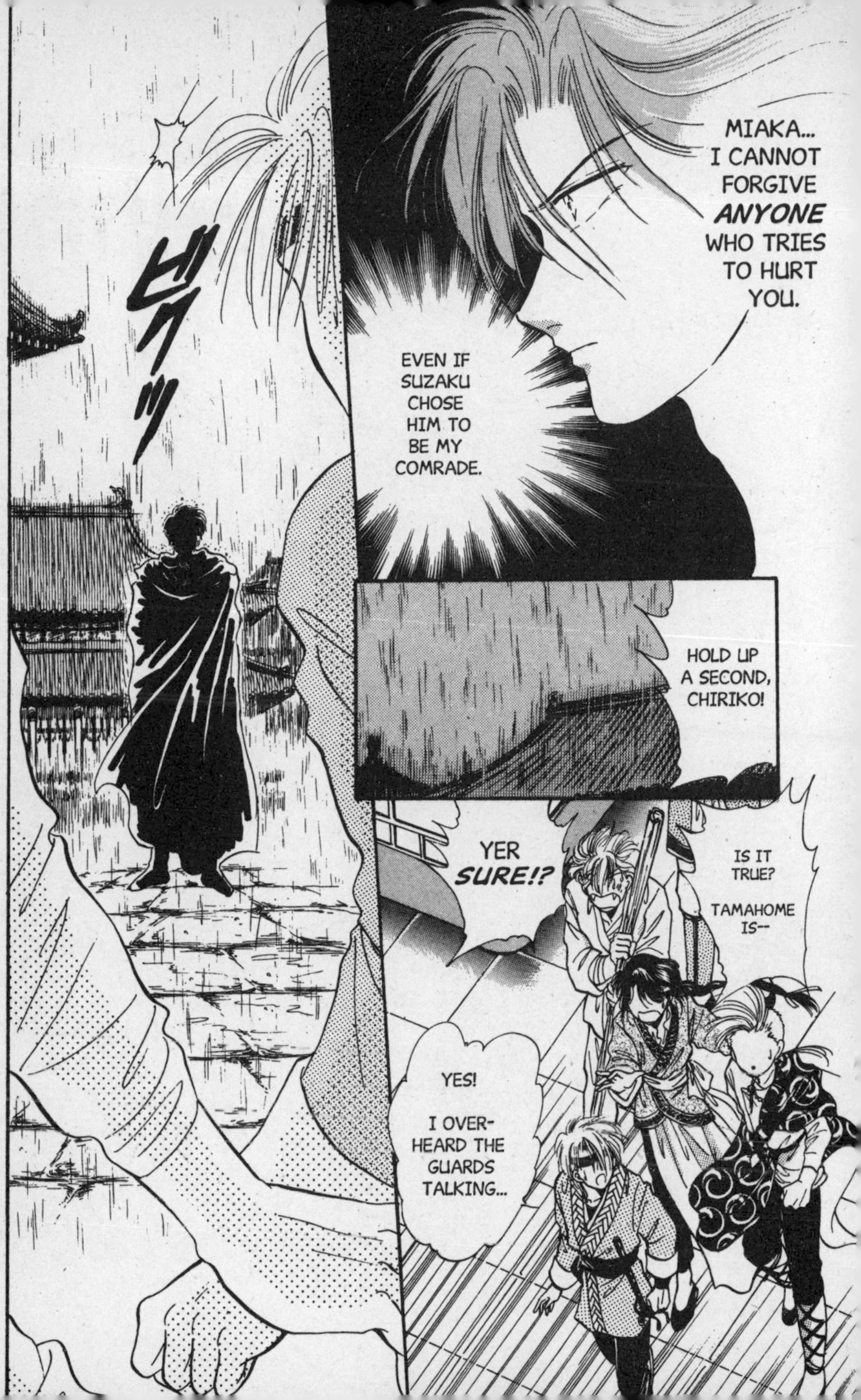
MIAKA... I CANNOT FORGIVE ANYONE WHO TRIES TO HURT YOU.
EVEN IF SUZAKU CHOSE HIM TO BE MY COMRADE.
HOLD UP A SECOND, CHIRIKO!
IS IT TRUE? TAMAHOME IS--
YER SURE!?
YES! I OVERHEARD THE GUARDS TALKING...
ビクッ

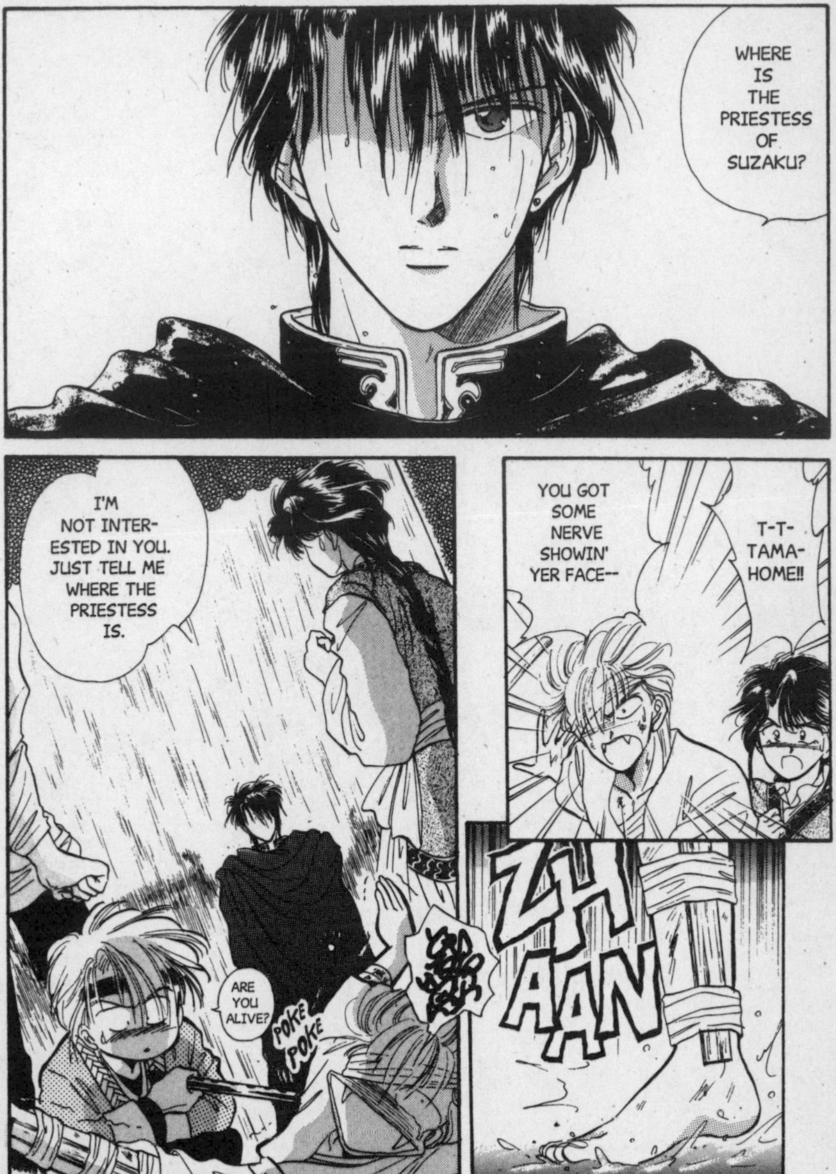
WHERE IS THE PRIESTESS OF SUZAKU?
T-T-TAMA-HOME!!
YOU GOT SOME NERVE SHOWIN' YER FACE--
ZHAAAN
I'M NOT INTER-ESTED IN YOU. JUST TELL ME WHERE THE PRIESTESS IS.
ARE YOU ALIVE?
POKE POKE

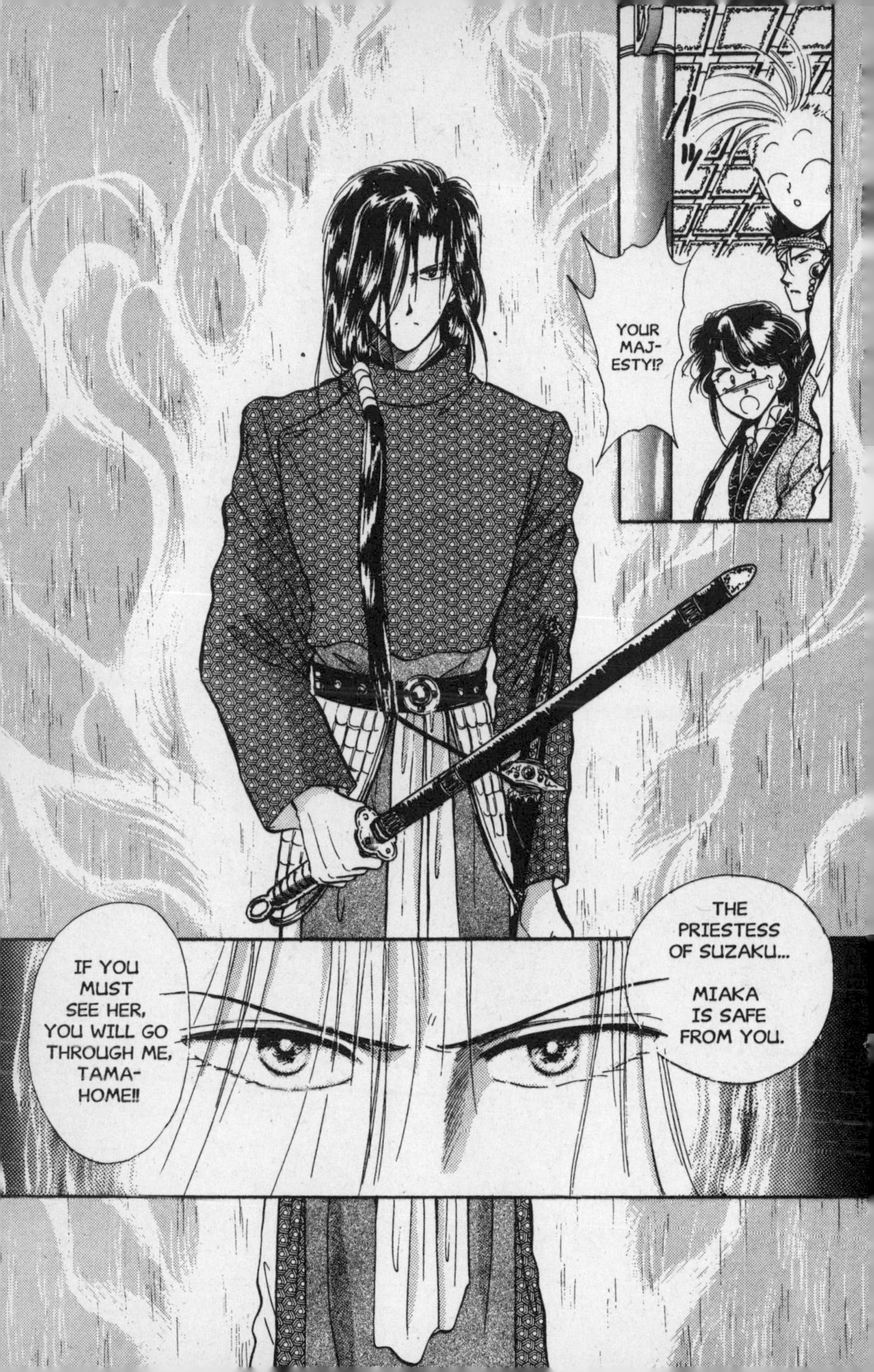
YOUR MAJ-ESTY!?
THE PRIESTESS OF SUZAKU...
MIAKA IS SAFE FROM YOU.
IF YOU MUST SEE HER, YOU WILL GO THROUGH ME, TAMA-HOME!!

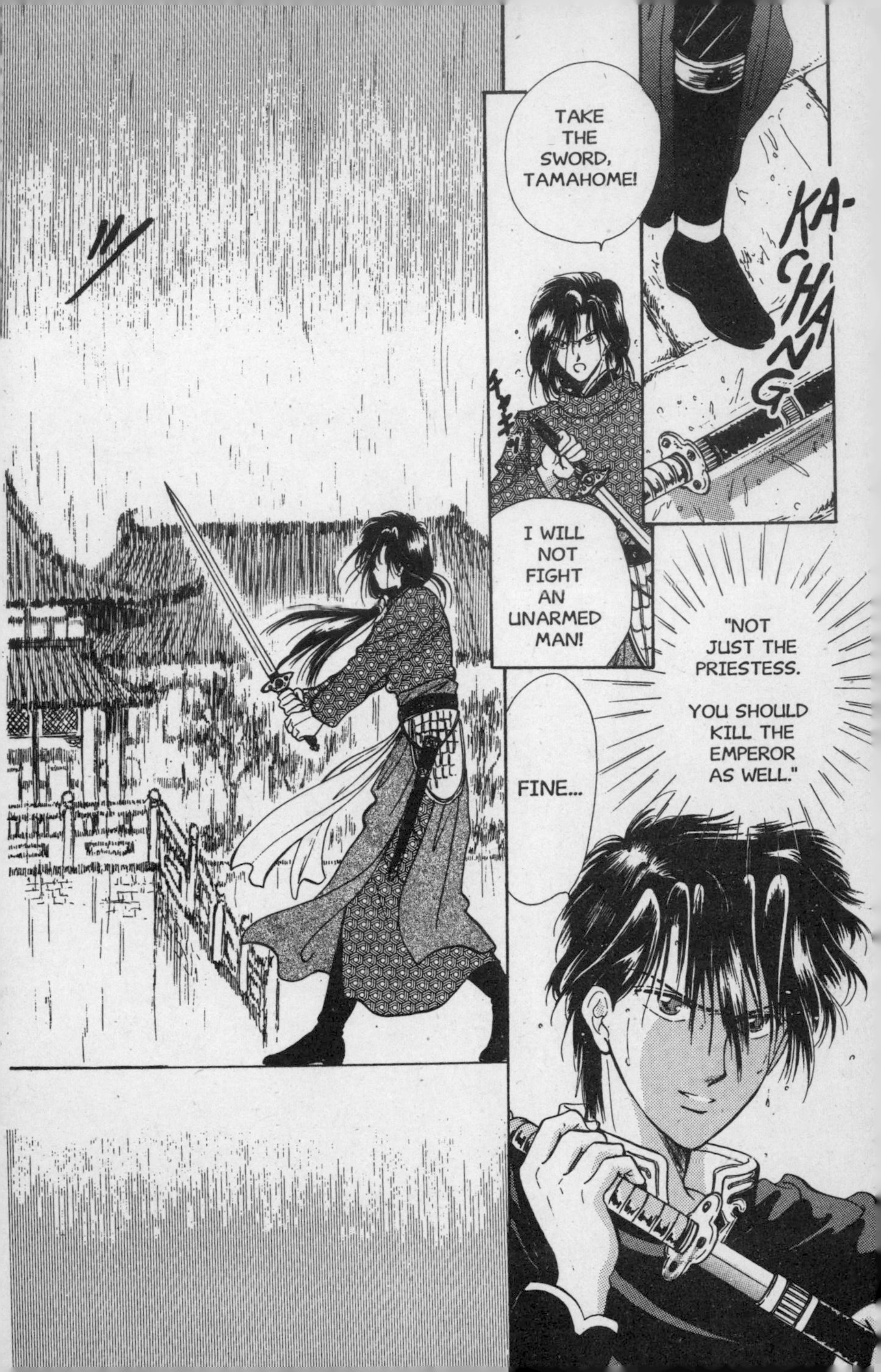
KA-CHANG
TAKE THE SWORD, TAMAHOME!
I WILL NOT FIGHT AN UNARMED MAN!
"NOT JUST THE PRIESTESS.
YOU SHOULD KILL THE EMPEROR AS WELL."
FINE...

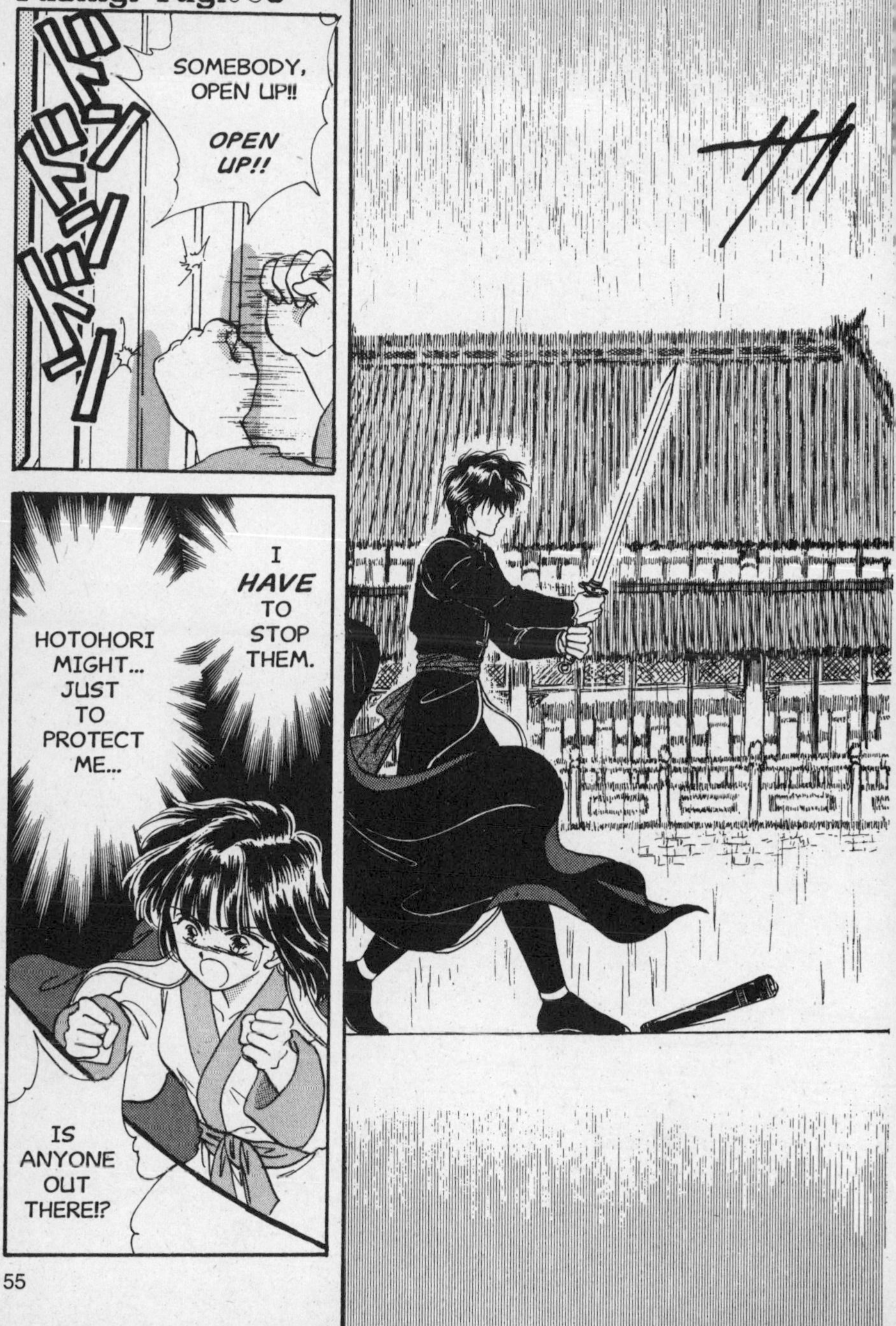
SOMEBODY, OPEN UP!!
OPEN UP!!
I HAVE TO STOP THEM.
HOTOHORI MIGHT... JUST TO PROTECT ME...
IS ANYONE OUT THERE!?

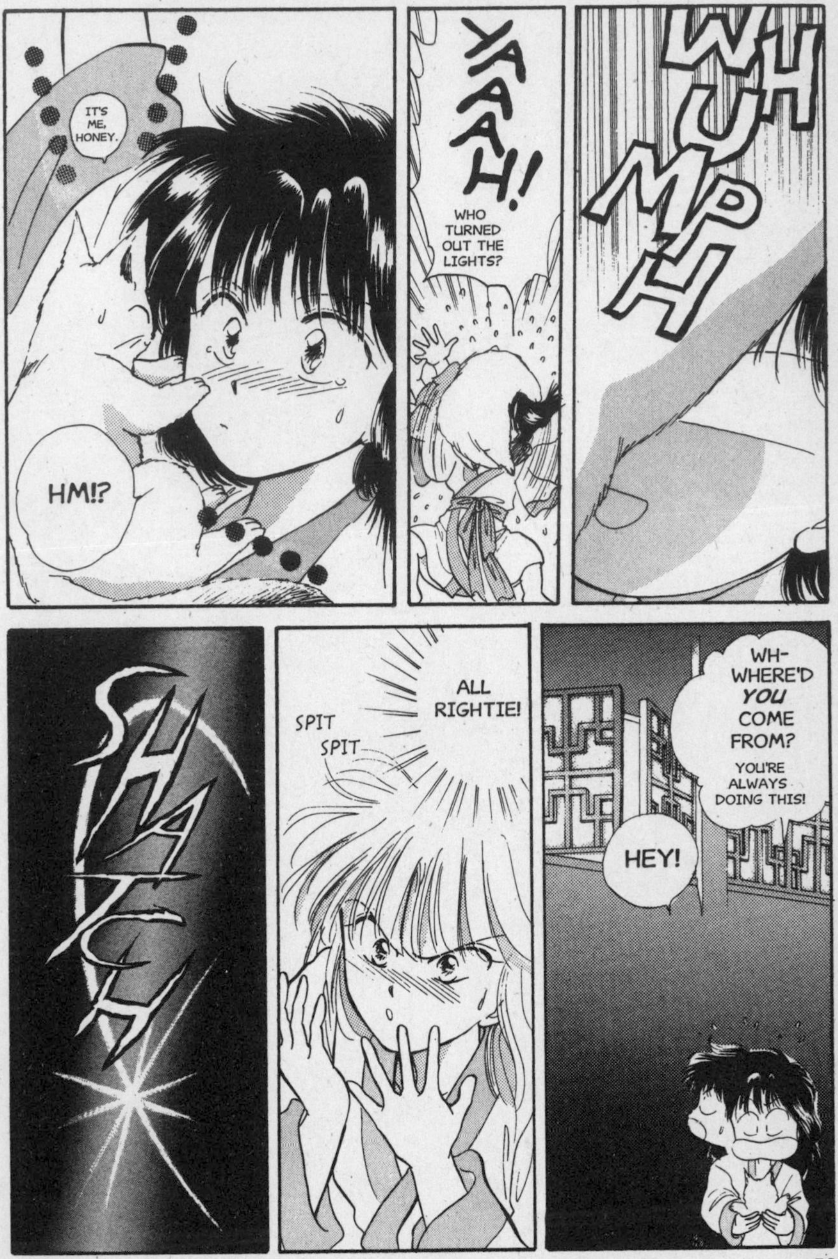
WHUMPH
YAAAH!
WHO TURNED OUT THE LIGHTS?
IT'S ME, HONEY.
HM!?
WH- WHERE'D *YOU* COME FROM? YOU'RE ALWAYS DOING THIS!
HEY!
ALL RIGHTIE!
SPIT SPIT
SHATCH

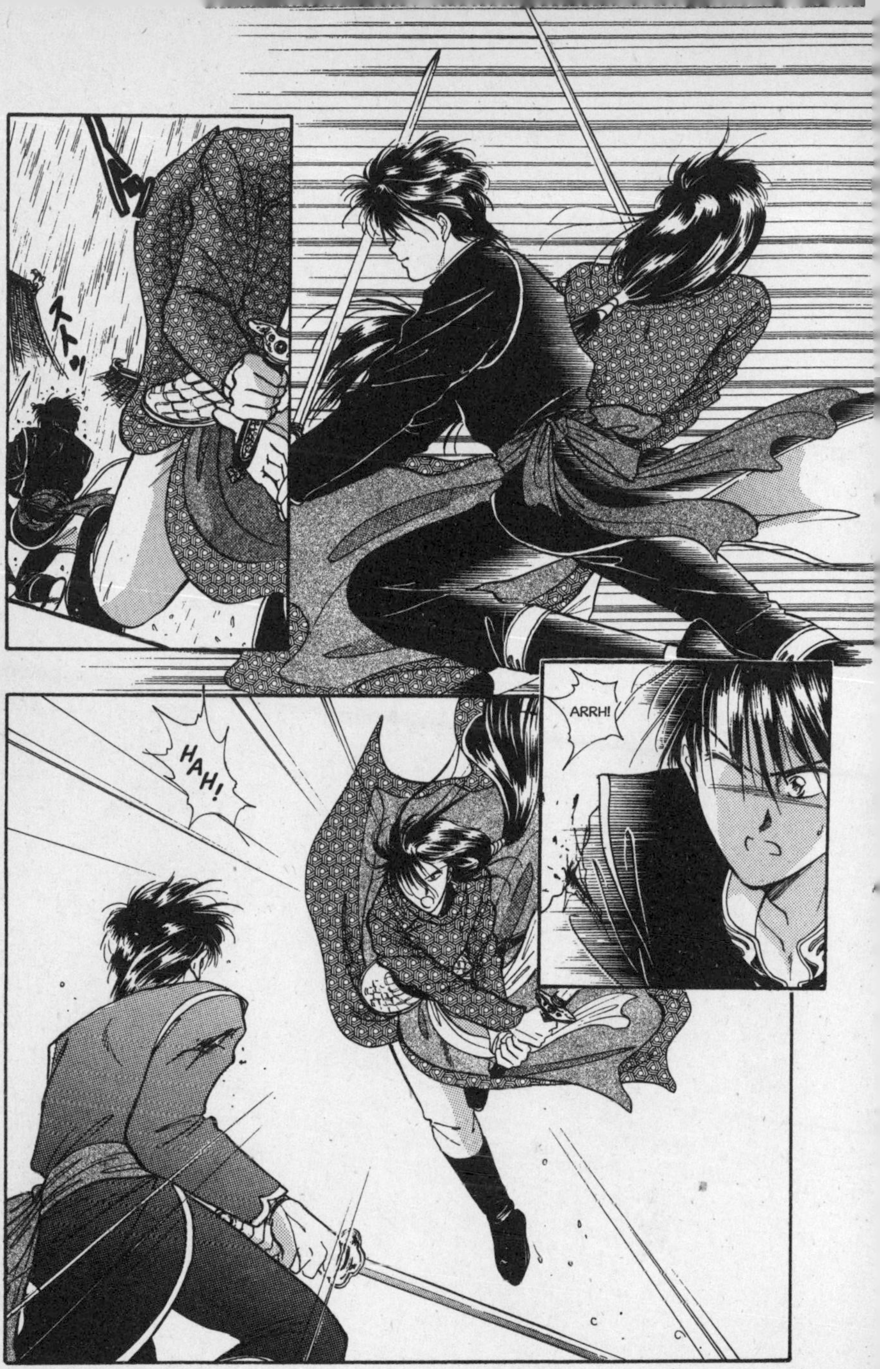
ストッ
ARRH!
HAH!

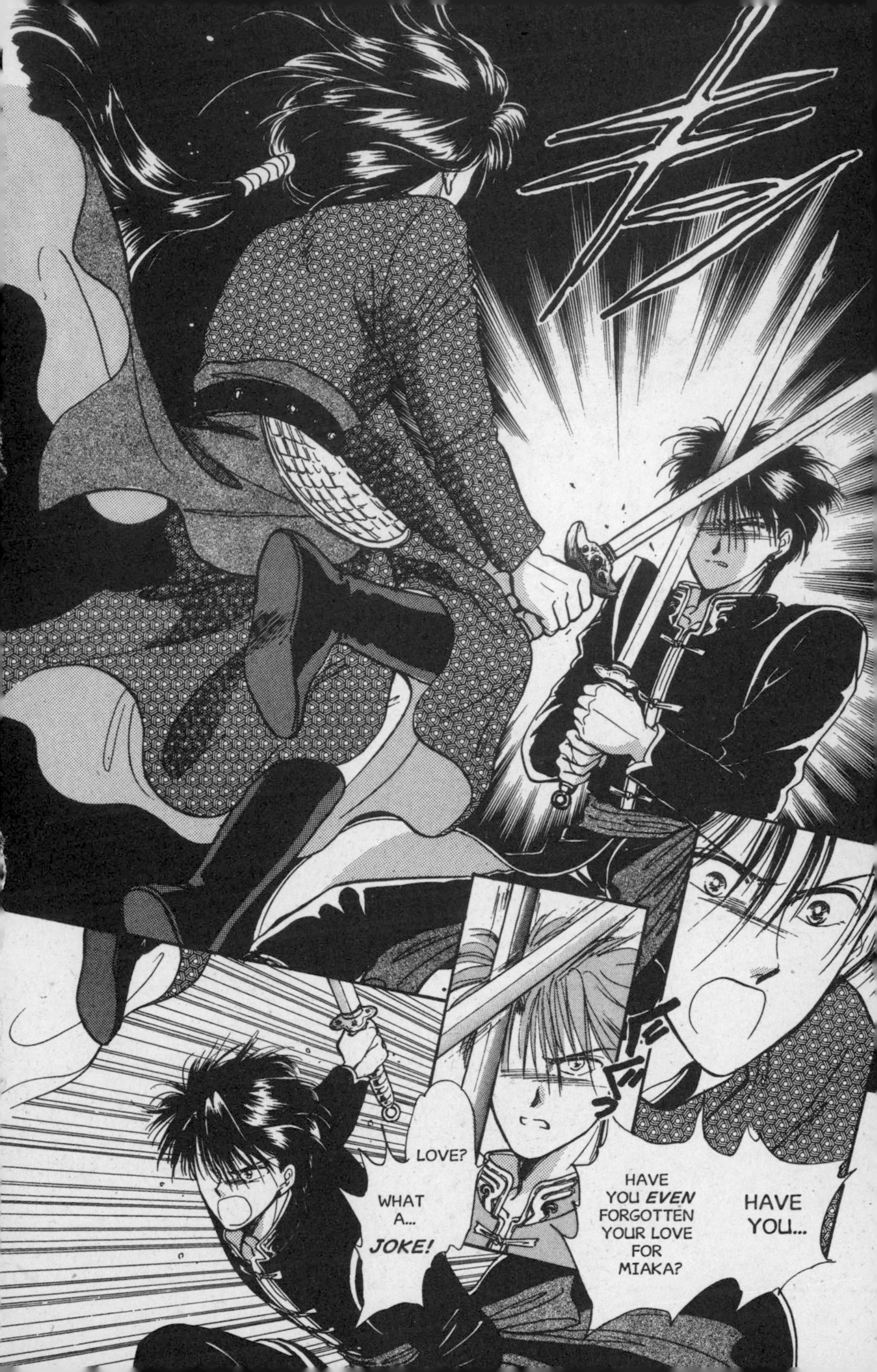
HAVE YOU...
HAVE YOU *EVEN* FORGOTTEN YOUR LOVE FOR MIAKA?
LOVE?
WHAT A... ***JOKE!***

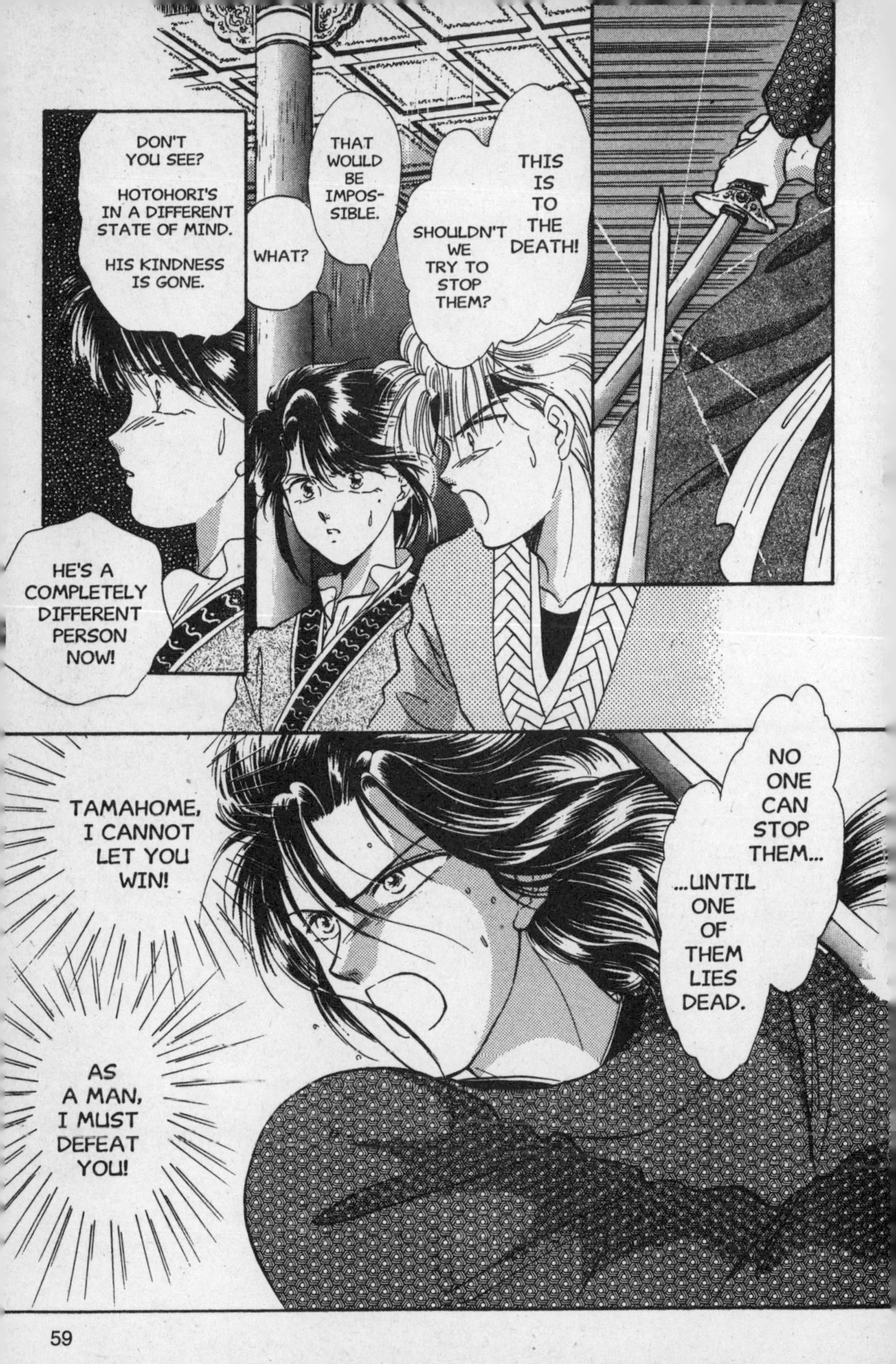
THIS IS TO THE DEATH!
SHOULDN'T WE TRY TO STOP THEM?
THAT WOULD BE IMPOSSIBLE.
WHAT?
DON'T YOU SEE? HOTOHORI'S IN A DIFFERENT STATE OF MIND. HIS KINDNESS IS GONE.
HE'S A COMPLETELY DIFFERENT PERSON NOW!
NO ONE CAN STOP THEM...
...UNTIL ONE OF THEM LIES DEAD.
TAMAHOME, I CANNOT LET YOU WIN!
AS A MAN, I MUST DEFEAT YOU!

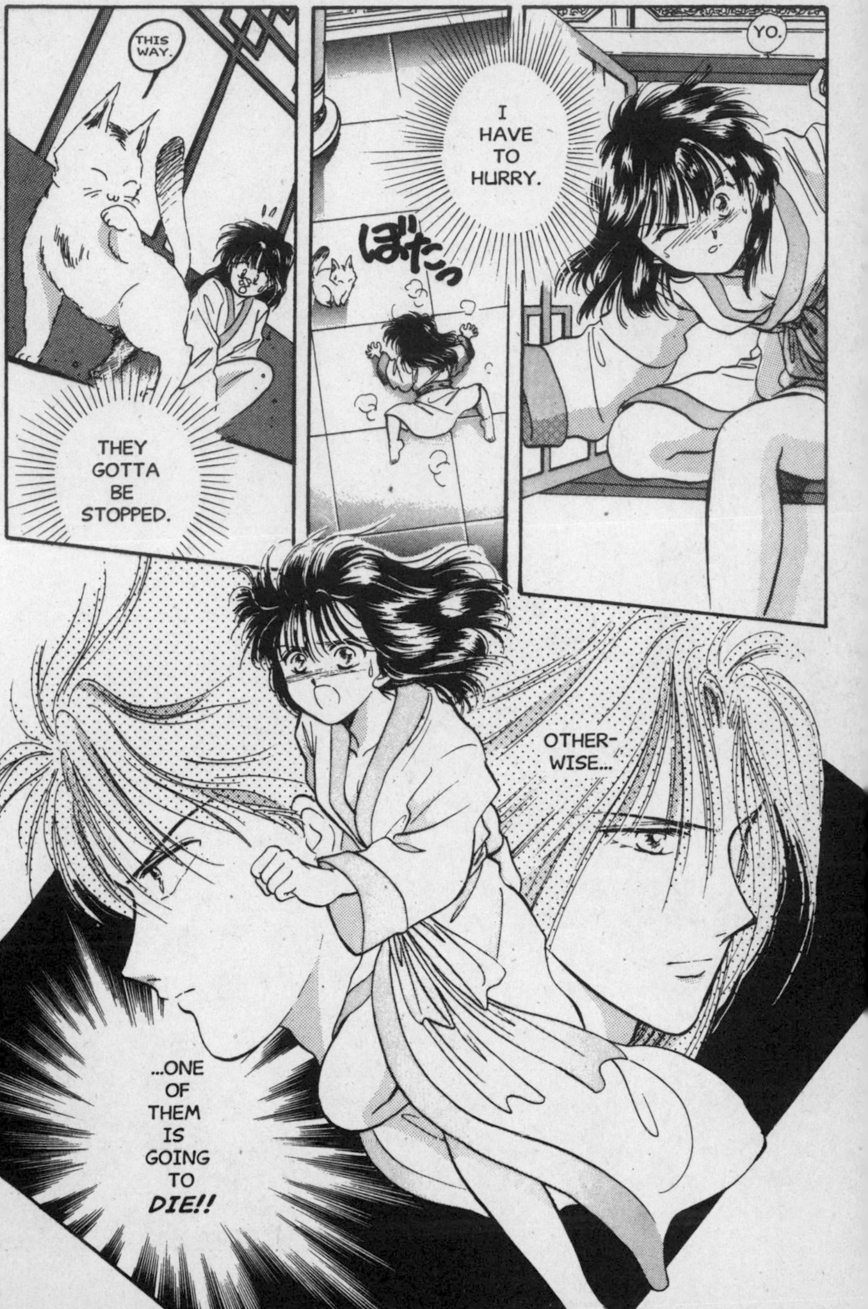
YO.
I HAVE TO HURRY.
ぼたっ
THIS WAY.
THEY GOTTA BE STOPPED.
OTHER-WISE...
...ONE OF THEM IS GOING TO *DIE!!*

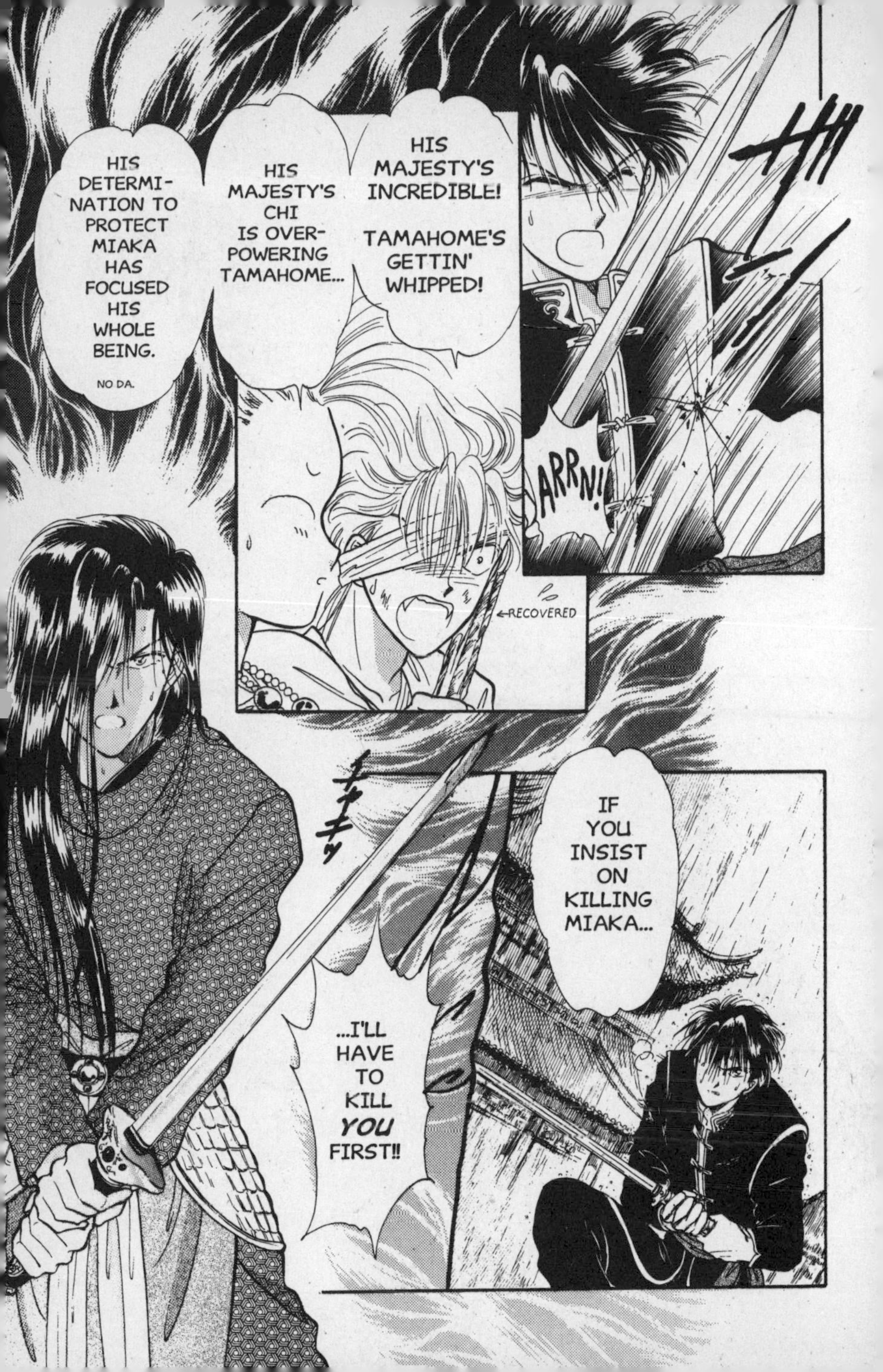
ARRN!
HIS MAJESTY'S INCREDIBLE!
TAMAHOME'S GETTIN' WHIPPED!
HIS MAJESTY'S CHI IS OVER-POWERING TAMAHOME...
HIS DETERMI-NATION TO PROTECT MIAKA HAS FOCUSED HIS WHOLE BEING.
NO DA.
RECOVERED
IF YOU INSIST ON KILLING MIAKA...
...I'LL HAVE TO KILL *YOU* FIRST!!

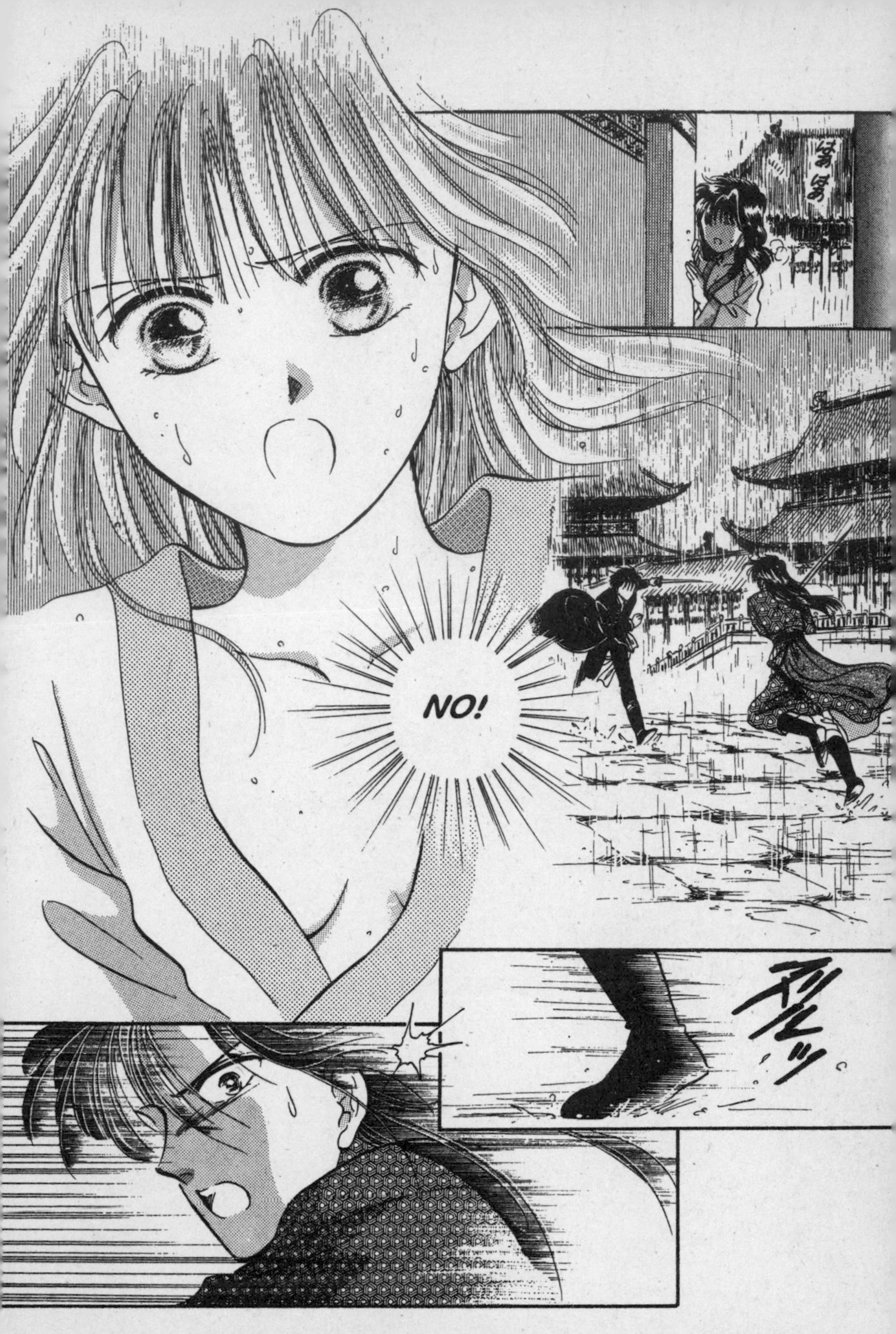
NO!

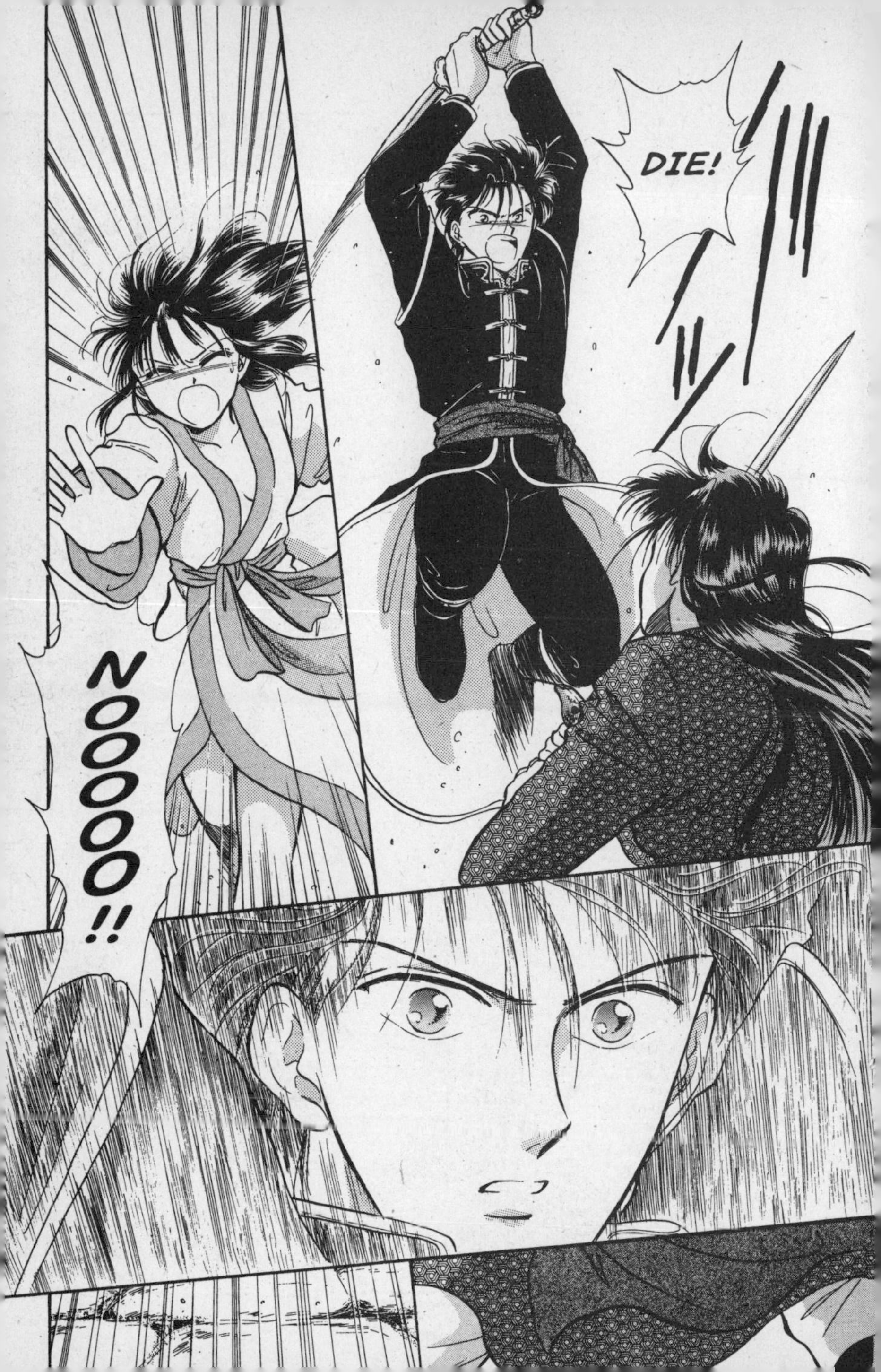
DIE!
NOOOOOO!!

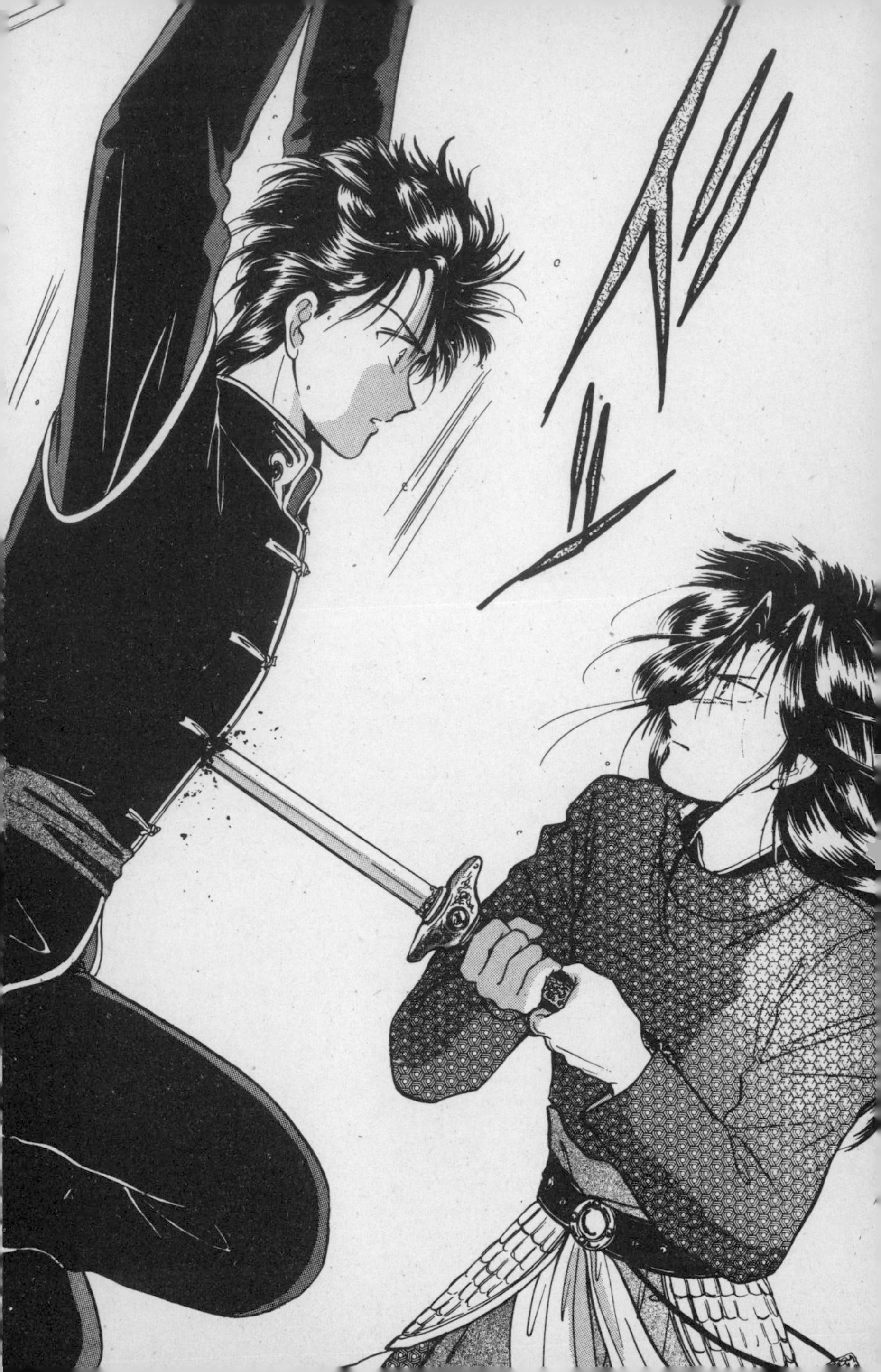

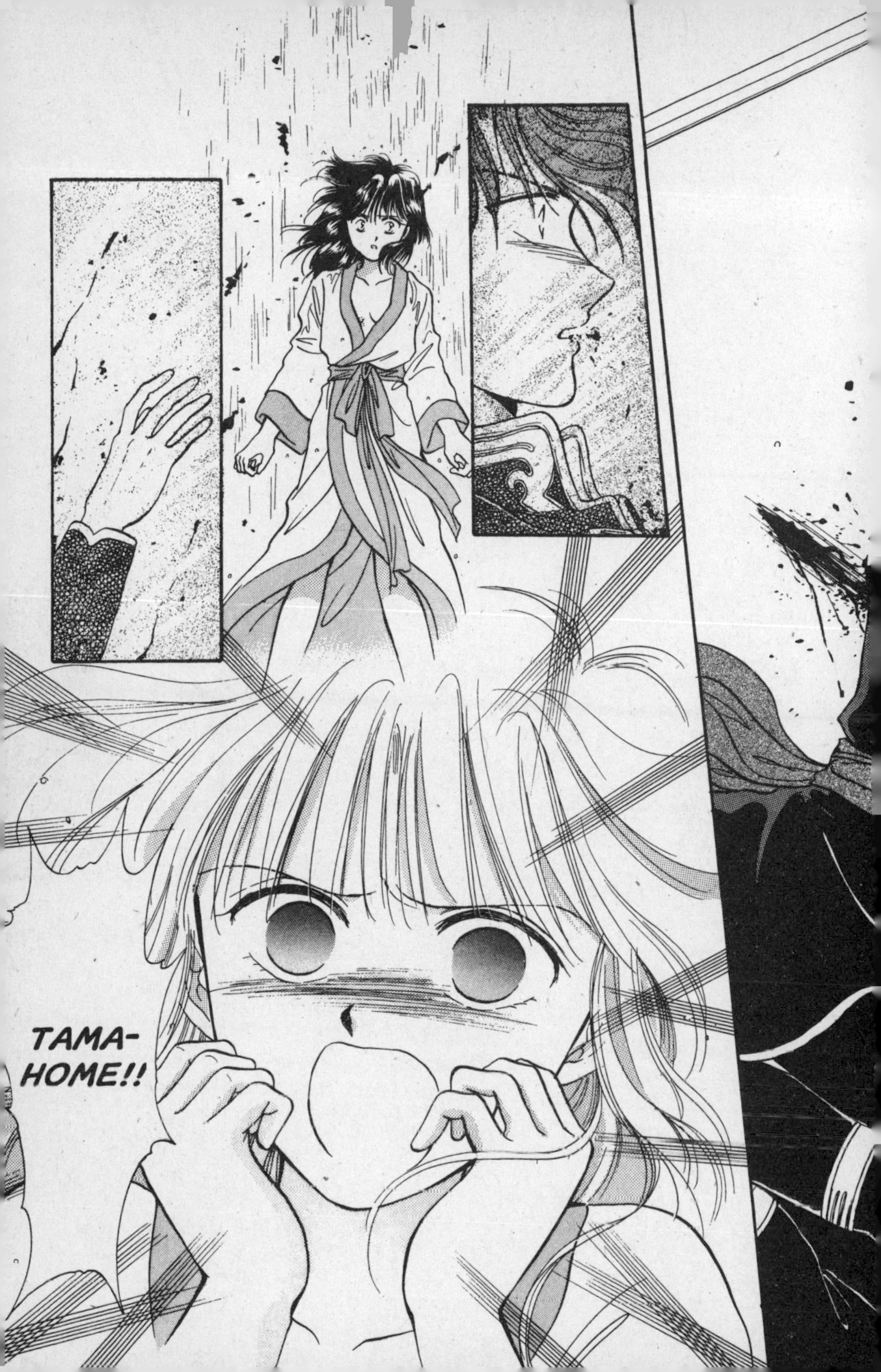
TAMA-
HOME!!

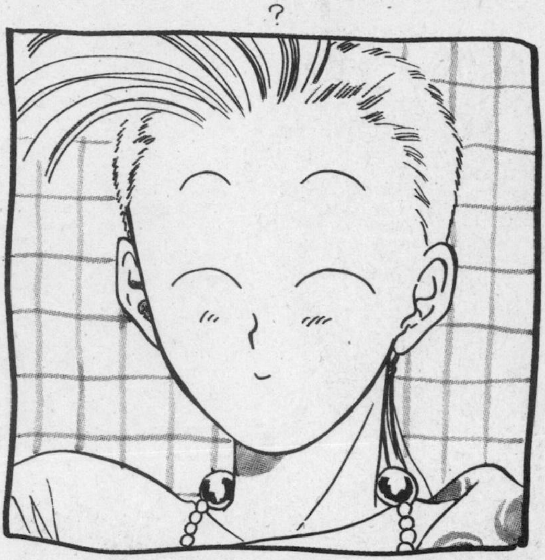

Gemini

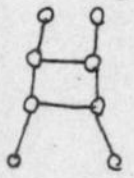

CHICHIRI

- Born in an unknown location.
  He would call himself "a priest," but he isn't really religious.
- Age: 24. ← Everybody is surprised by his age! But at the very beginning, when I asked my assistants, they all were of the opinion that he seemed to be in his twenties. So I went along with that. And his confidence isn't something that's normal for someone in his teens!
- Family: Unknown. In his teens he had a fiancée, but they broke up. (For details, see volume 7.)
- Hobby: Fishing.
- Height: 5' 8". But every now and again, he comes in at under a yard tall.
- Blood Type: Unknown.

An elusive character. A masked man with a seemingly light heart, Chichiri is a mystery. He can turn super-deformed and later be very serious. He's the most neutral character of the seven Celestial Warriors of Suzaku. If Tamahome and Hotohori are the obvious leaders of the warriors, Chichiri is the man manipulating from the shadows. He's the power behind the throne, and he always helps out. (You could also call him the adult who looks after the kids.)
He can use many techniques that Tai Yi-Jun taught him.
He is unconcerned with his own mortality. He has become much like a typical Zen master with his abandonment of earthly desires.

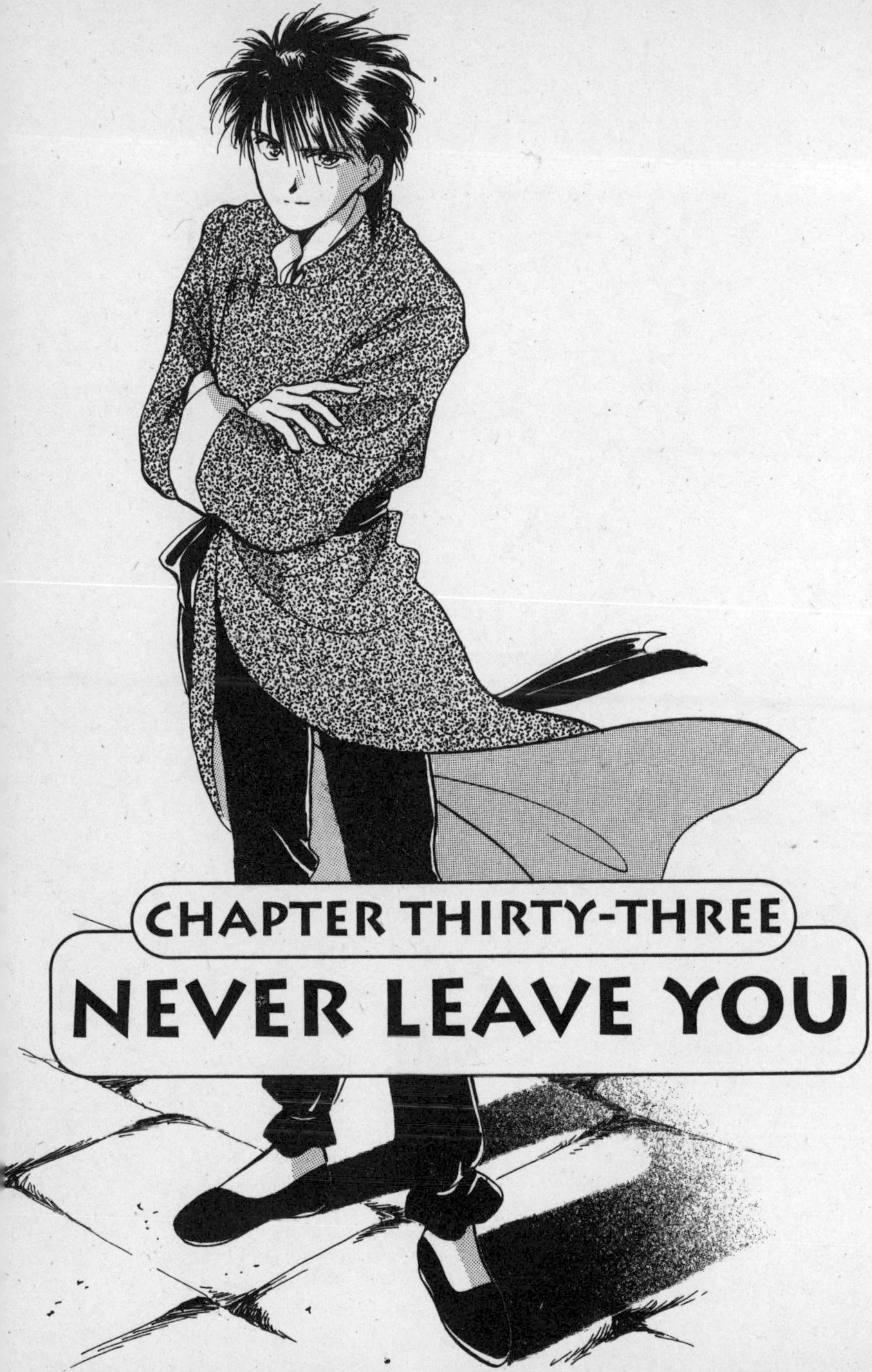
CHAPTER THIRTY-THREE
NEVER LEAVE YOU

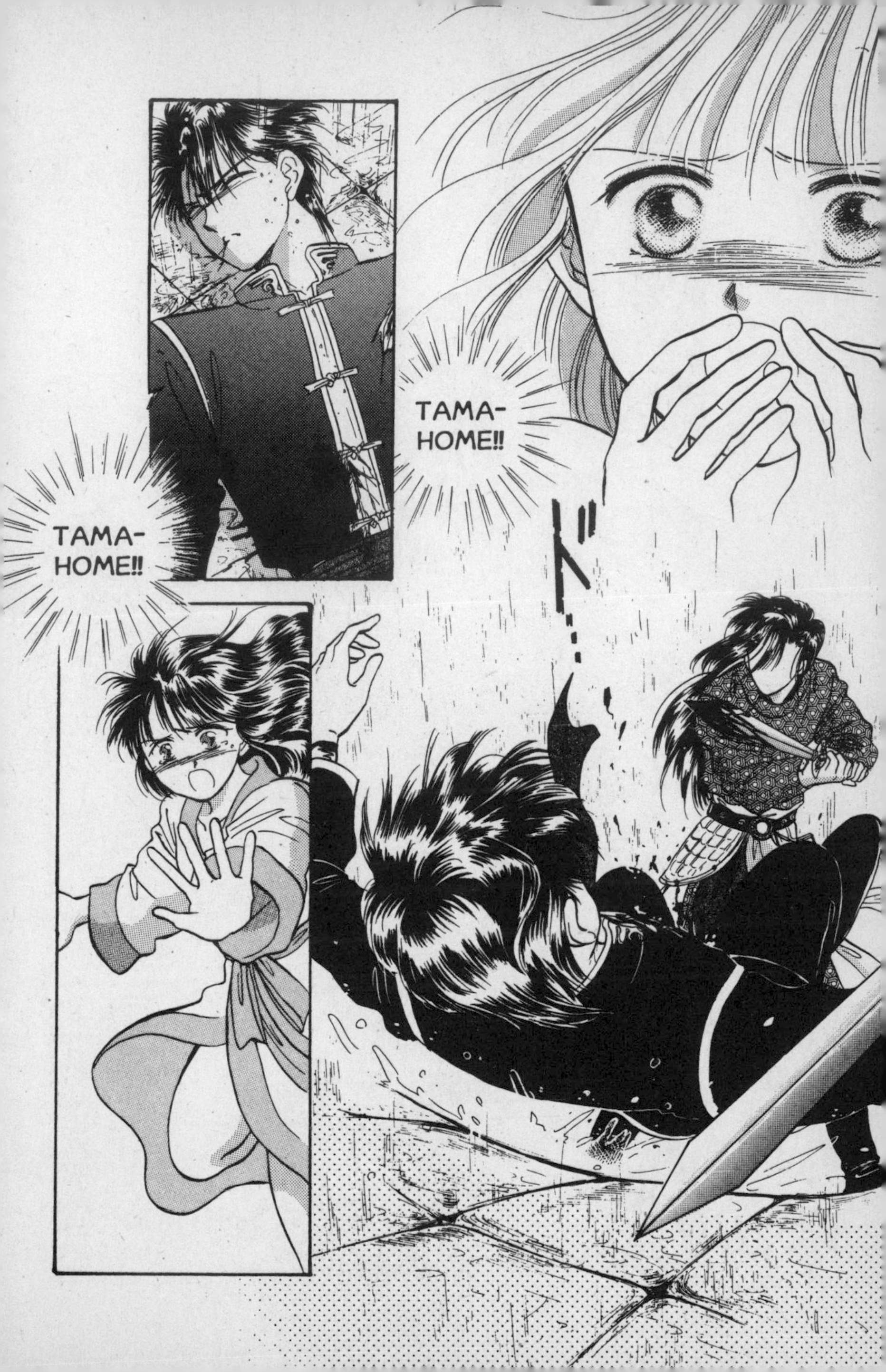
TAMA-
HOME!!
TAMA-
HOME!!
ド

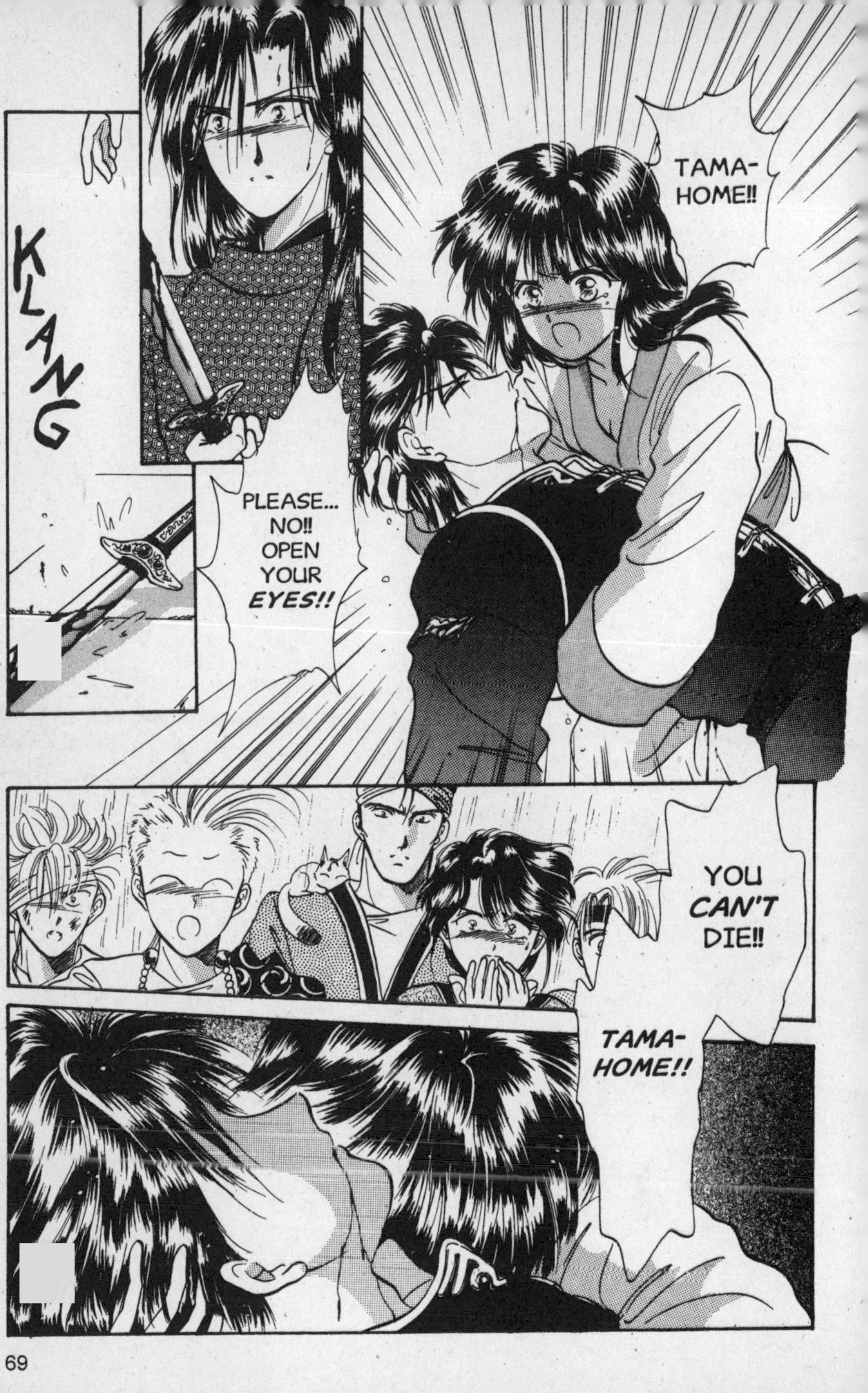
TAMA-HOME!!
PLEASE... NO!! OPEN YOUR *EYES!!*
KLANG
YOU *CAN'T* DIE!!
TAMA-HOME!!

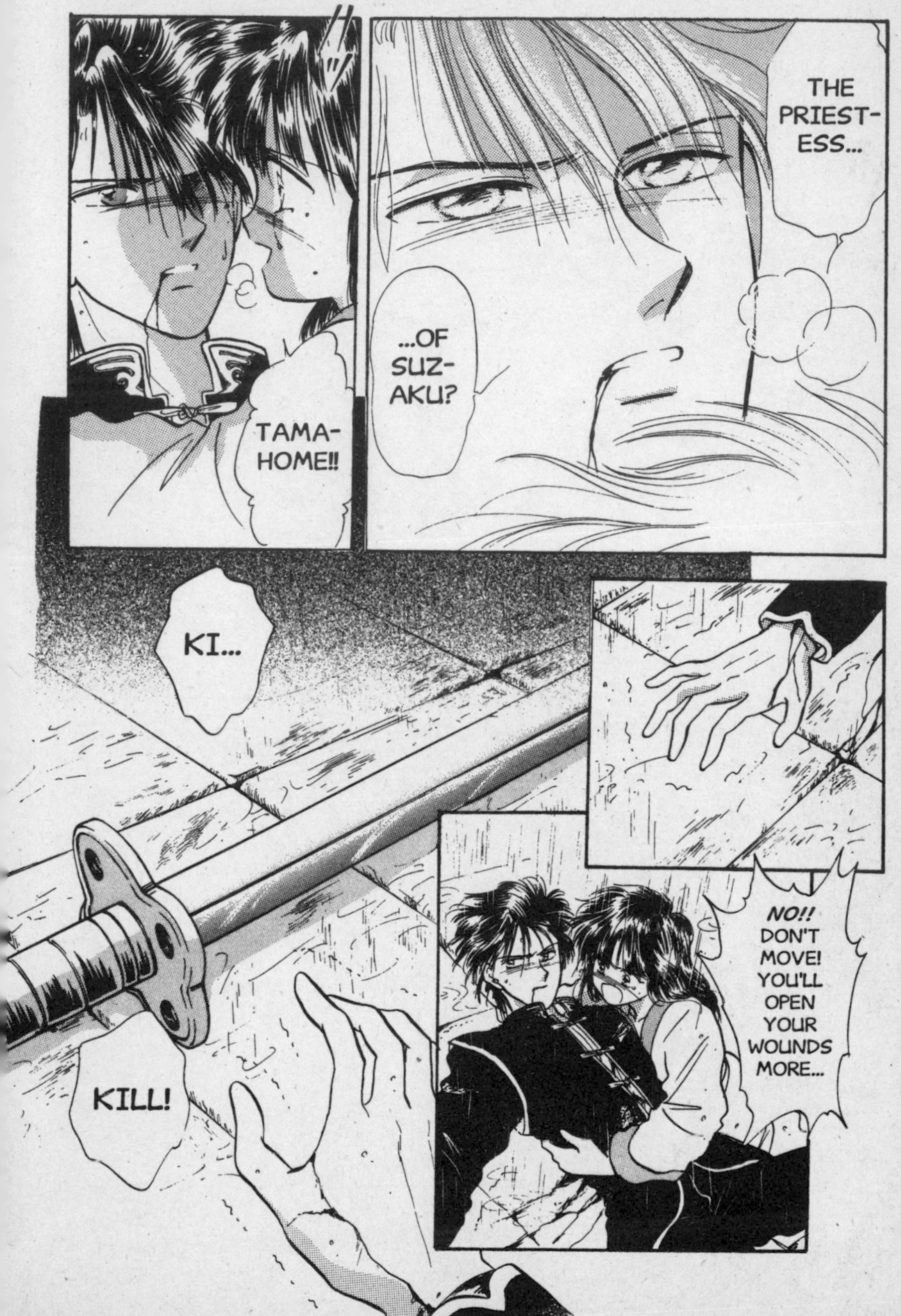
THE PRIEST-ESS...
...OF SUZ-AKU?
TAMA-HOME!!
NO!! DON'T MOVE! YOU'LL OPEN YOUR WOUNDS MORE...
KI...
KILL!

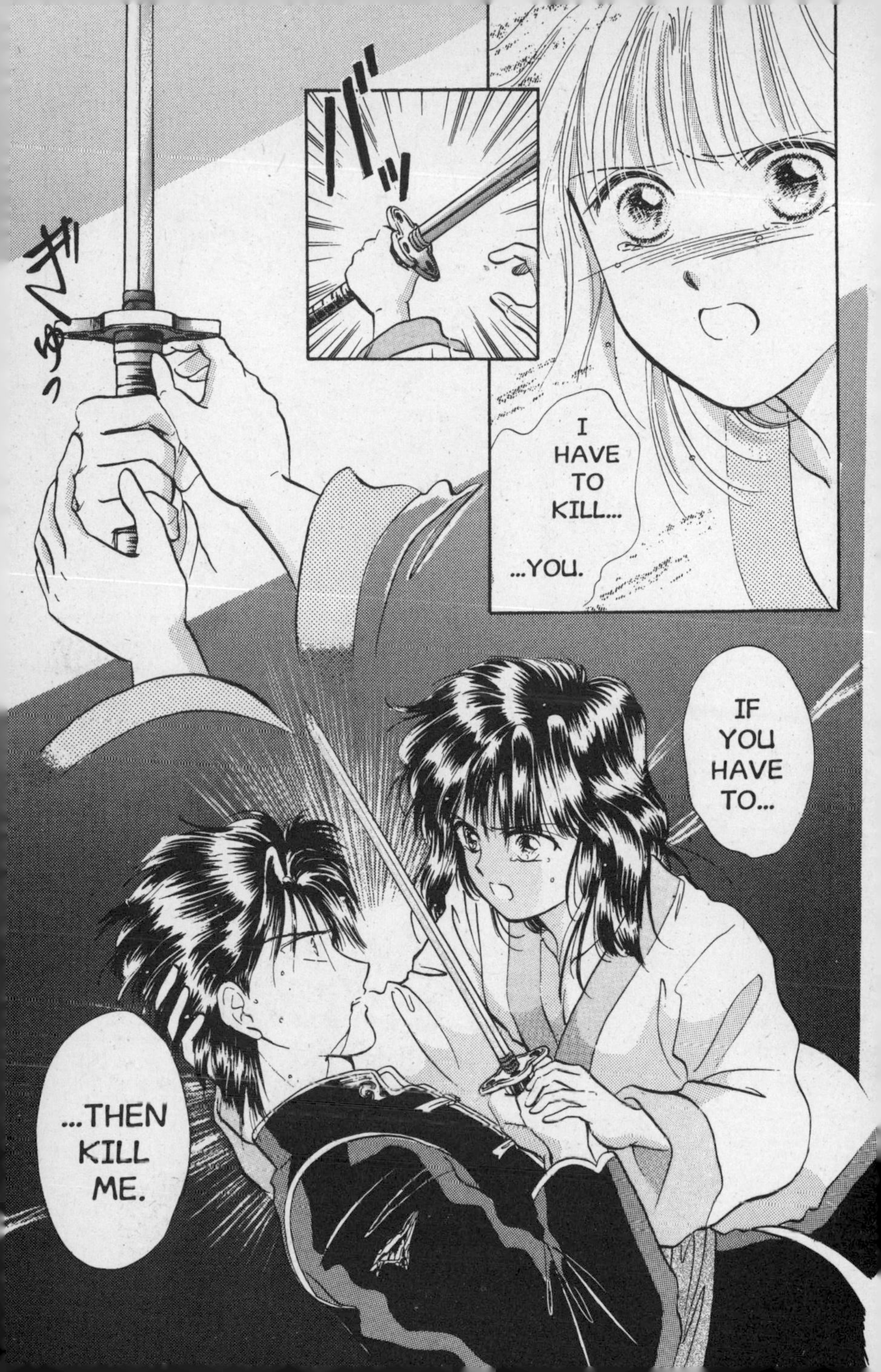
I HAVE TO KILL...
...YOU.
IF YOU HAVE TO...
...THEN KILL ME.

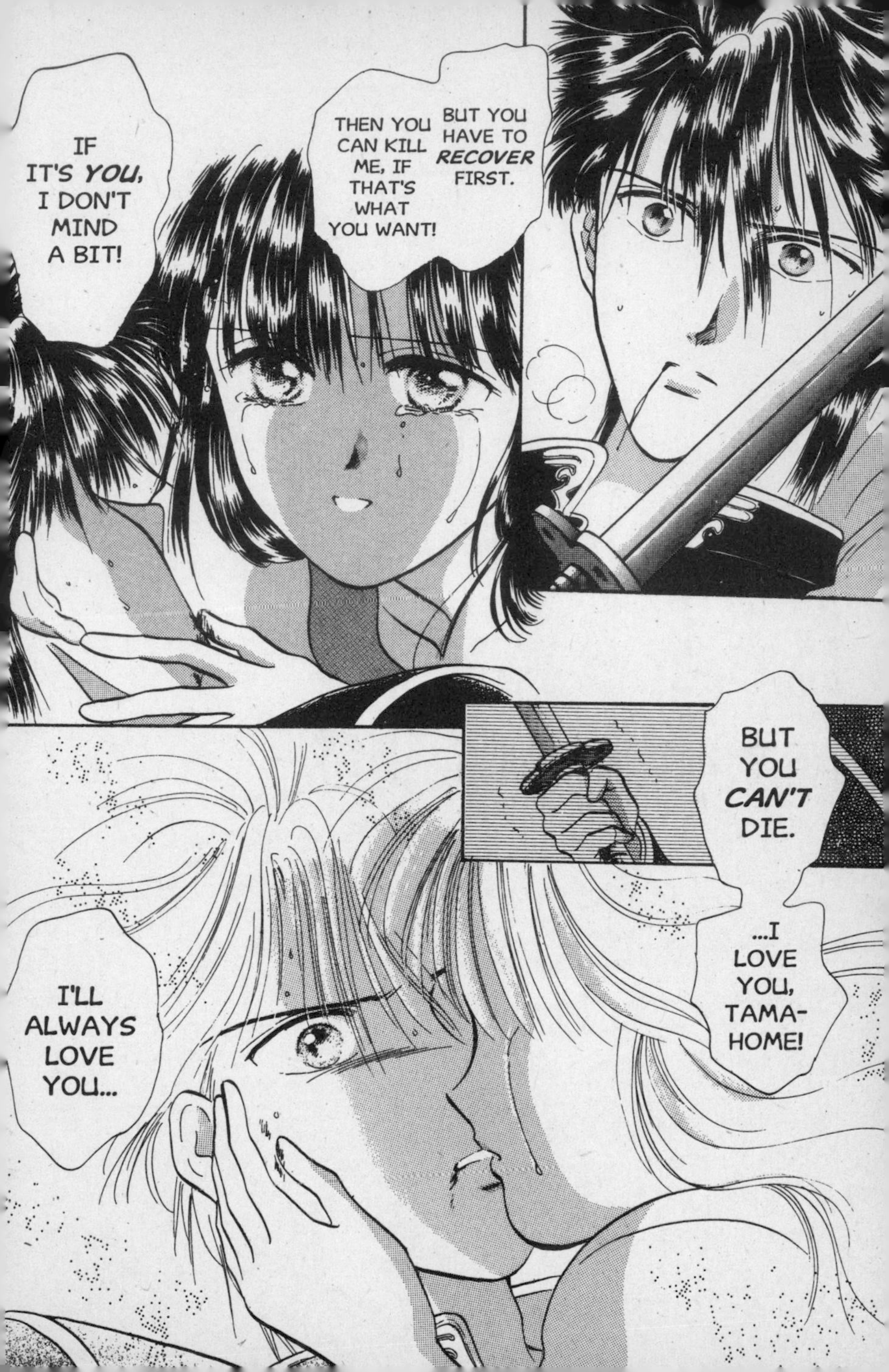
BUT YOU HAVE TO *RECOVER* FIRST.
THEN YOU CAN KILL ME, IF THAT'S WHAT YOU WANT!
IF IT'S *YOU*, I DON'T MIND A BIT!
BUT YOU *CAN'T* DIE.
...I LOVE YOU, TAMA-HOME!
I'LL ALWAYS LOVE YOU...

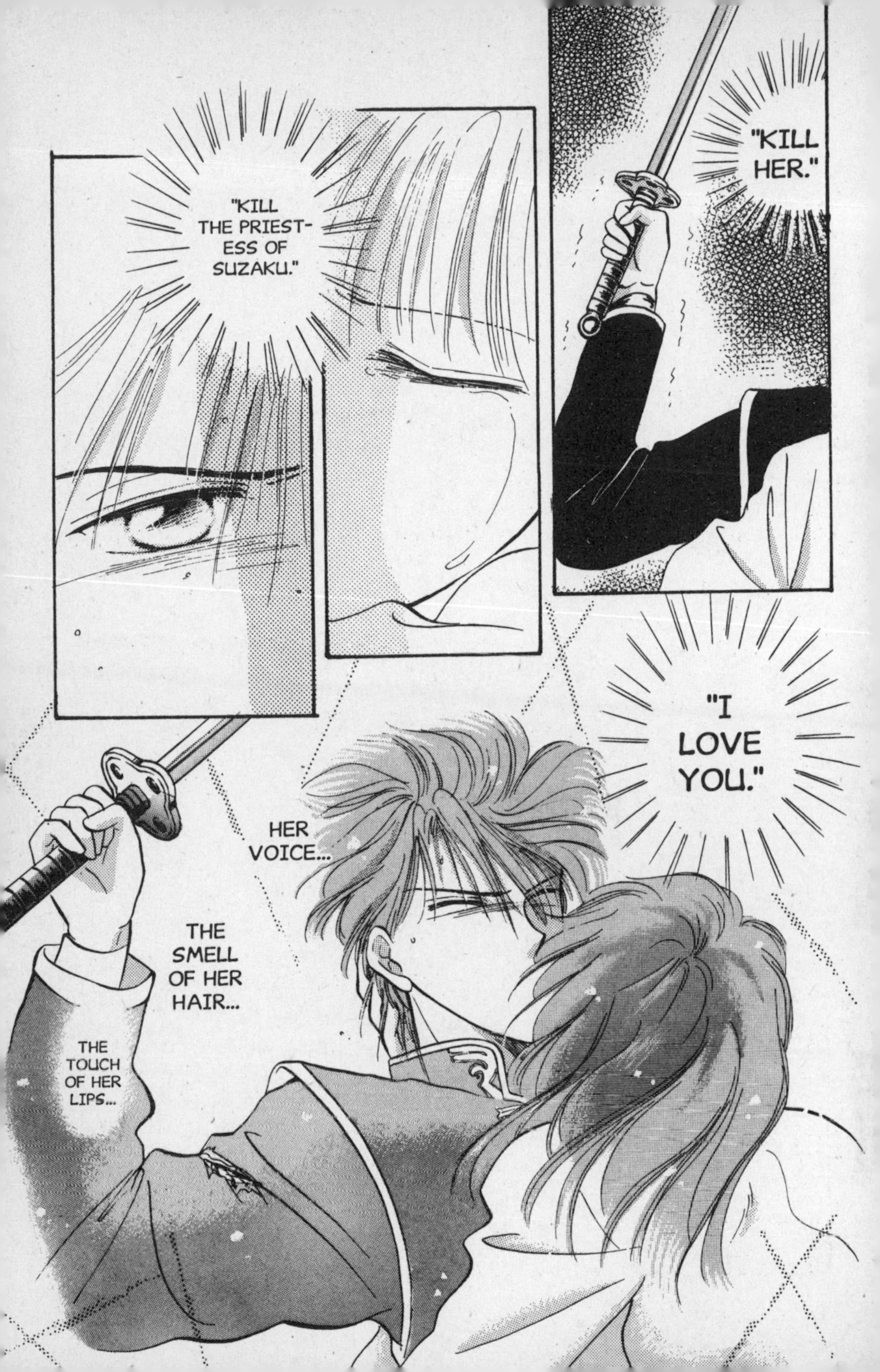
"KILL THE PRIEST-ESS OF SUZAKU."
"KILL HER."
"I LOVE YOU."
HER VOICE...
THE SMELL OF HER HAIR...
THE TOUCH OF HER LIPS...

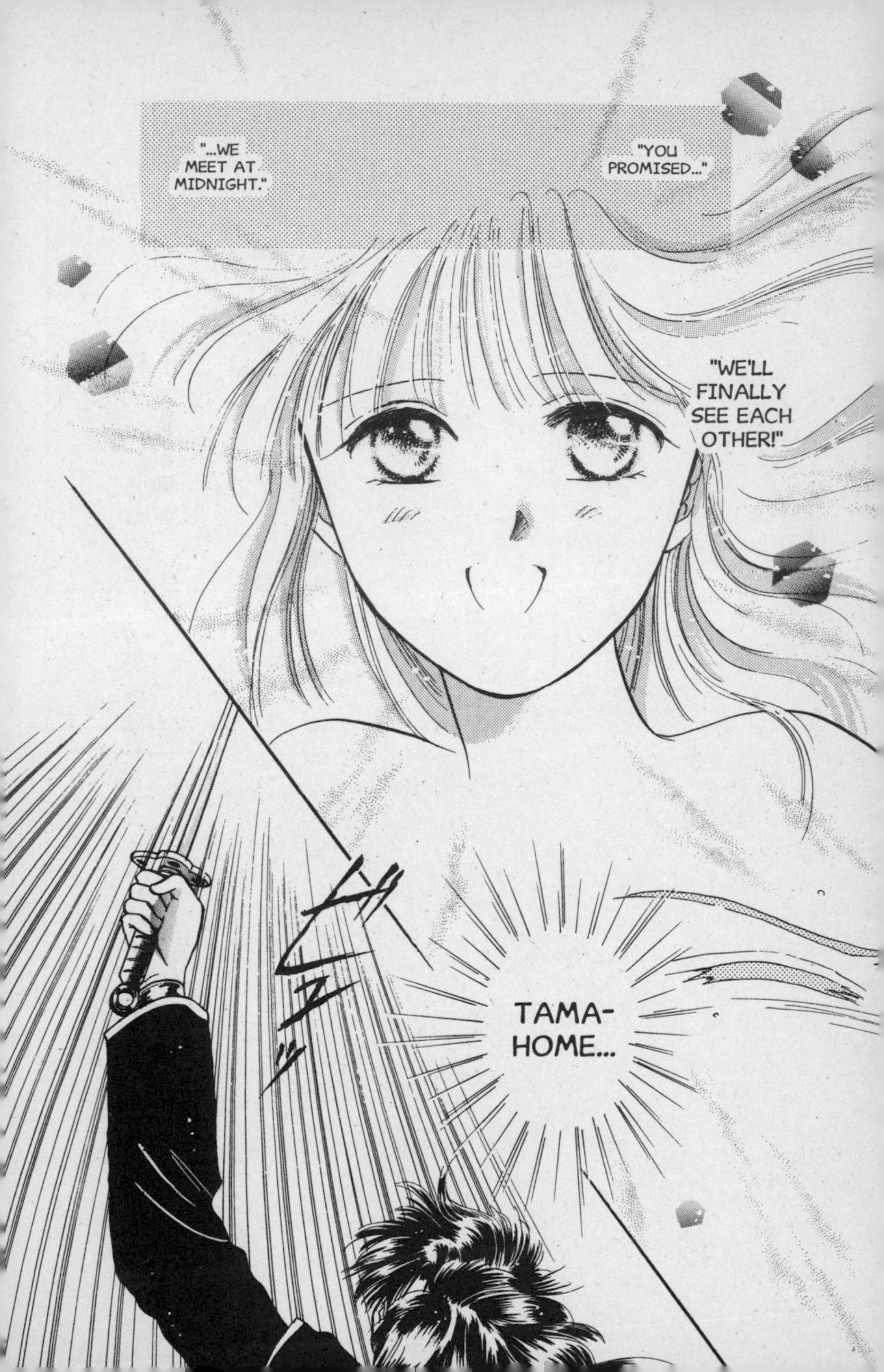
"YOU PROMISED..."
"...WE MEET AT MIDNIGHT."
"WE'LL FINALLY SEE EACH OTHER!"
TAMA-HOME...

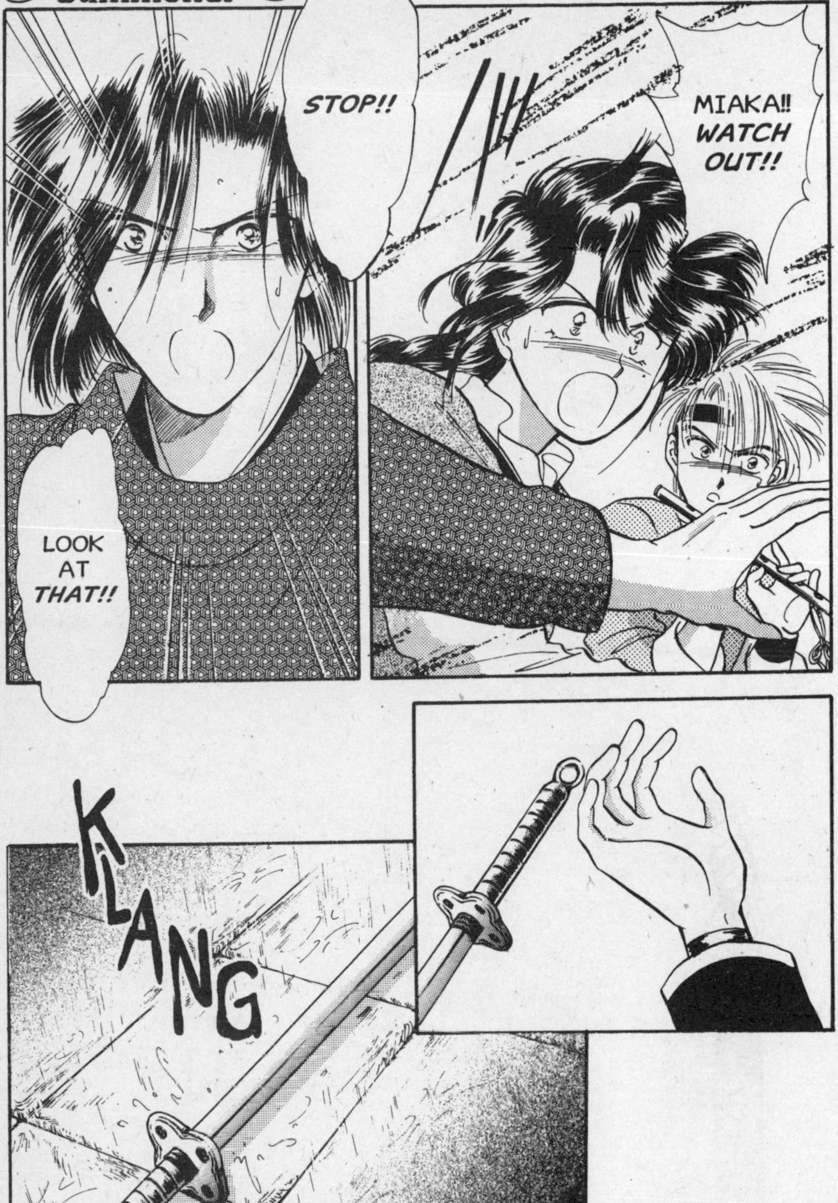
MIAKA!! WATCH OUT!!
STOP!!
LOOK AT THAT!!
KLANG

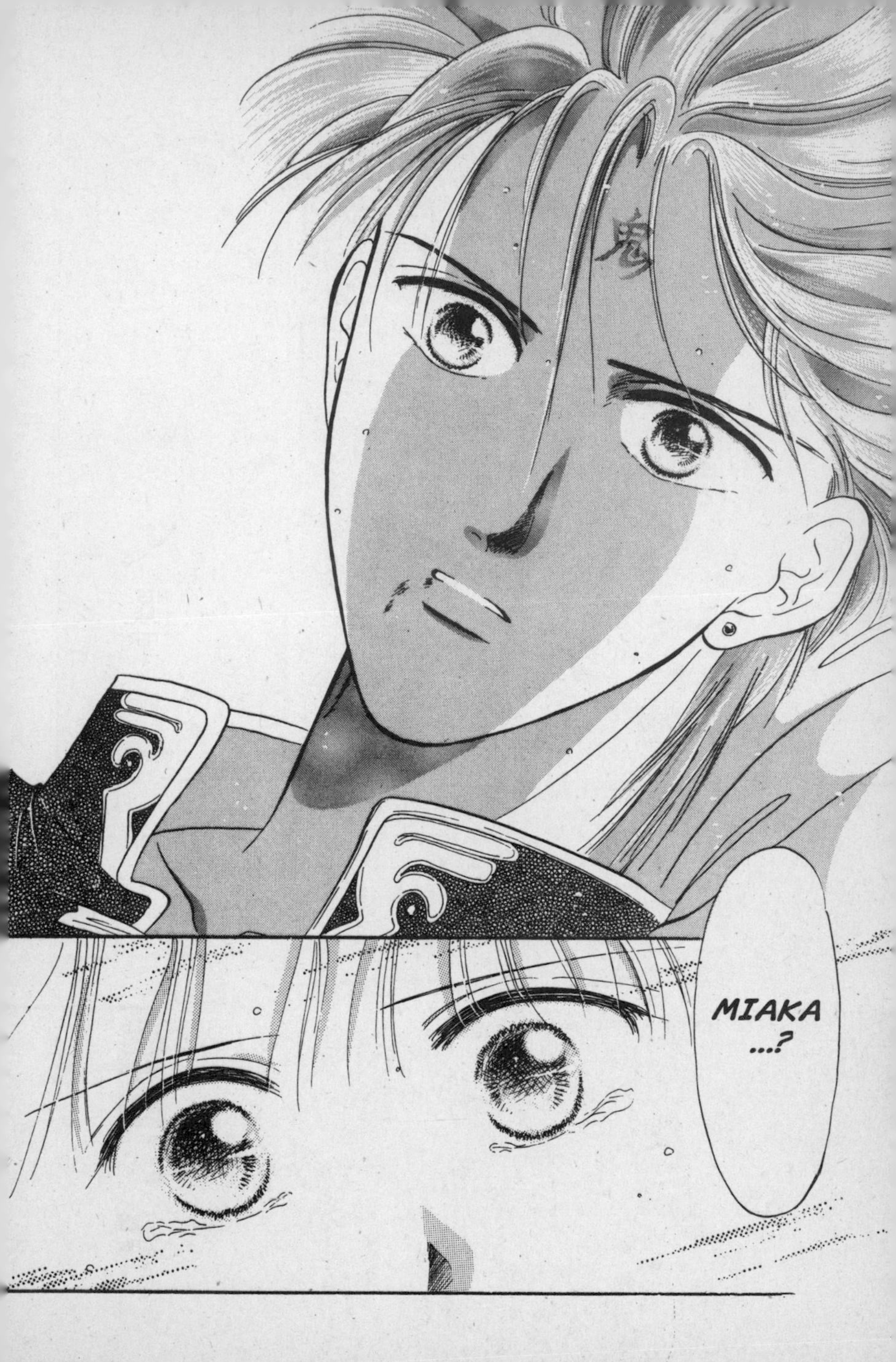
MIAKA ...?

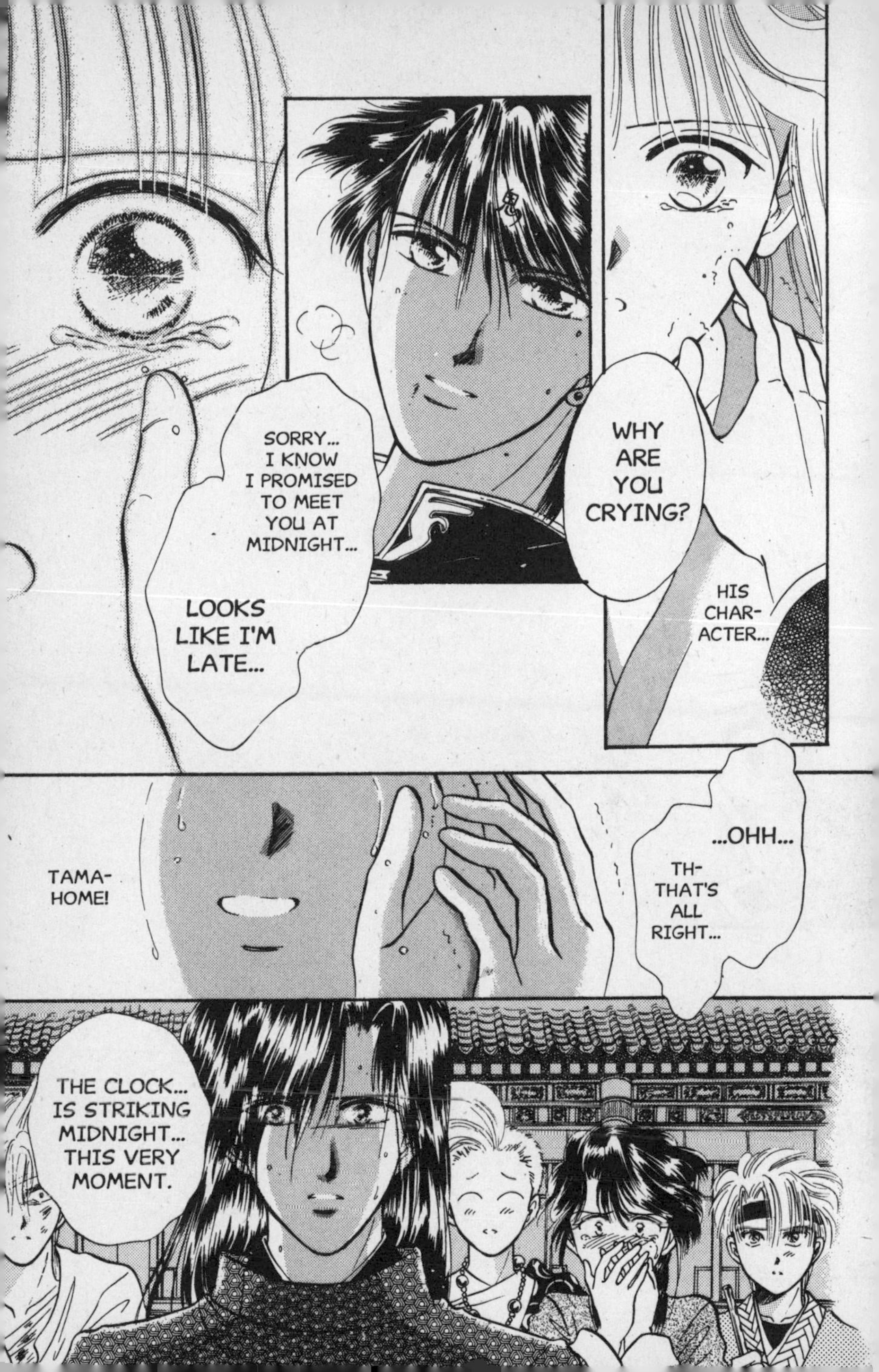
WHY ARE YOU CRYING?
HIS CHAR-ACTER...
SORRY... I KNOW I PROMISED TO MEET YOU AT MIDNIGHT...
LOOKS LIKE I'M LATE...
...OHH...
TH- THAT'S ALL RIGHT...
TAMA-HOME!
THE CLOCK... IS STRIKING MIDNIGHT... THIS VERY MOMENT.

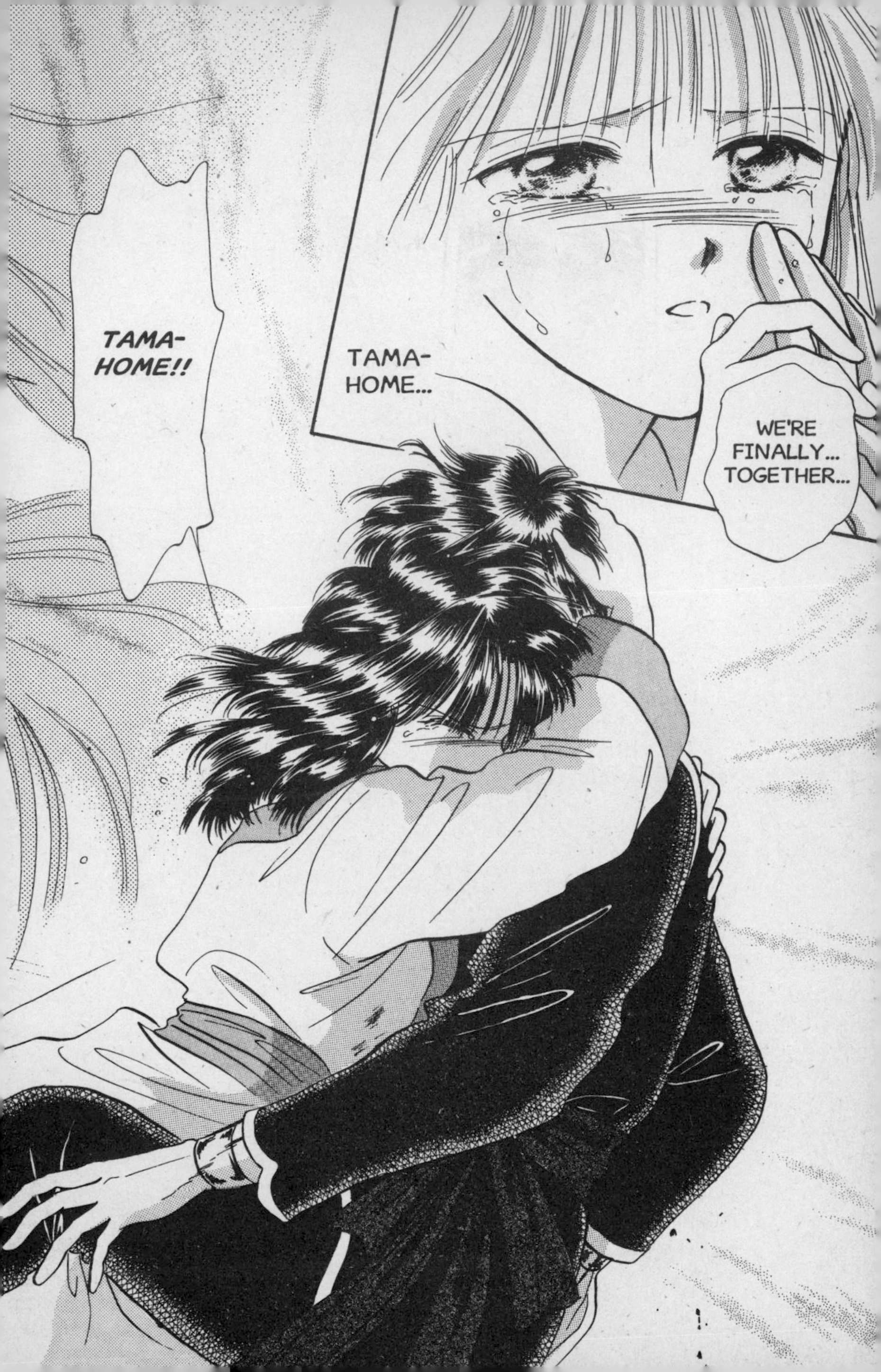
TAMA-HOME...
WE'RE FINALLY... TOGETHER...
TAMA-HOME!!

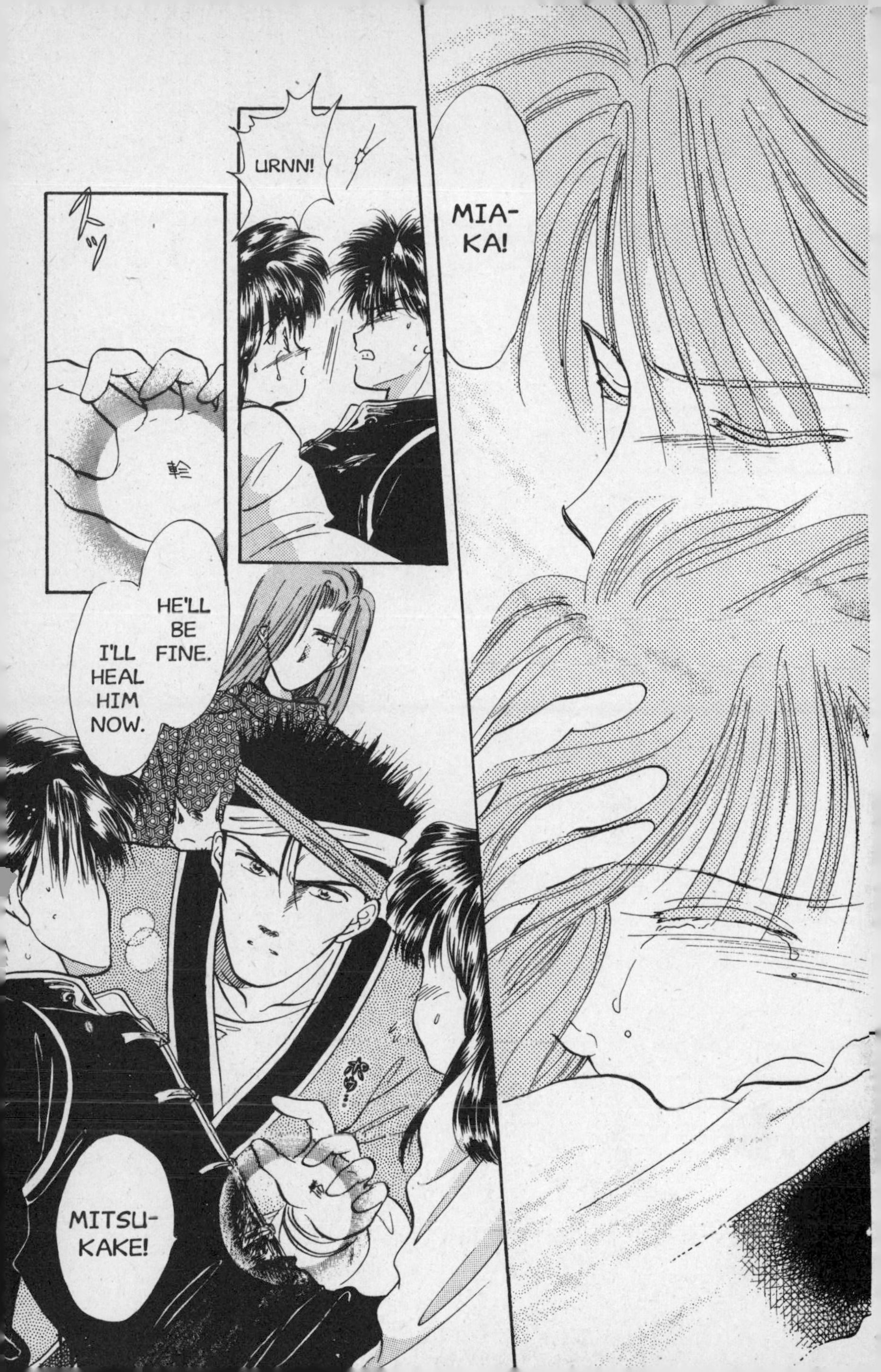
MIA-KA!
URNN!
HE'LL BE FINE. I'LL HEAL HIM NOW.
MITSU-KAKE!

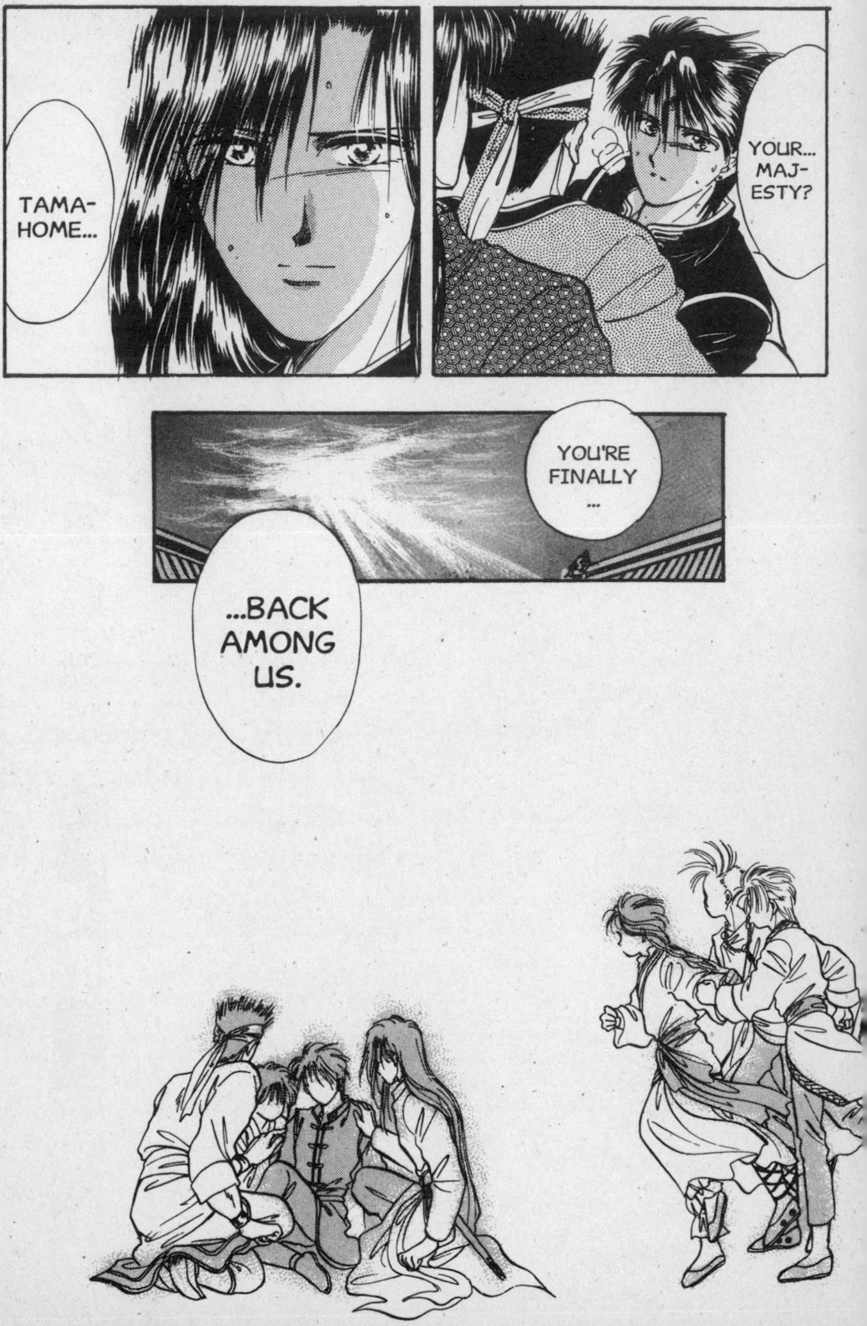
YOUR... MAJ-ESTY?
TAMA-HOME...
YOU'RE FINALLY ...
...BACK AMONG US.

Well, no one died in this house. I never heard the footsteps, but I was up late at night working on a color image and the stereo suddenly shut off. It really surprised me. I started dancing in front of the stereo. I apologized, "I'm sorry, this is part of work, too!!" Just like a husband making excuses to his wife's complaints! And then I went back to work again. The stereo turning off really took me by surprise. I felt like I was being told to go to bed. The TV turned off while my mom was watching it. Then the fan in the bathroom would shut off abruptly (it would start working again when I got mad at it), or the door would open on its own downstairs while we'd be sitting in the living room (this happened all the time). Sleeping next to my parents, I could hear a fourth person breathing beside us. Come to think of it, whatever it was, it liked playing pranks. An interesting thing was that whenever he (she?) walked up or down the creaky old stairs, they would only make light thumping sounds. No living human could have made those sounds! The owner came home, so we moved out of the house after two years. Now we're all fine (?). I wonder what went on there. There really was something dark and murky about the place. Spider webs would form everywhere. It would get moldy. I hear that houses like that are more "prone" to this sort of thing!!

So be careful!

I wasn't afraid though...

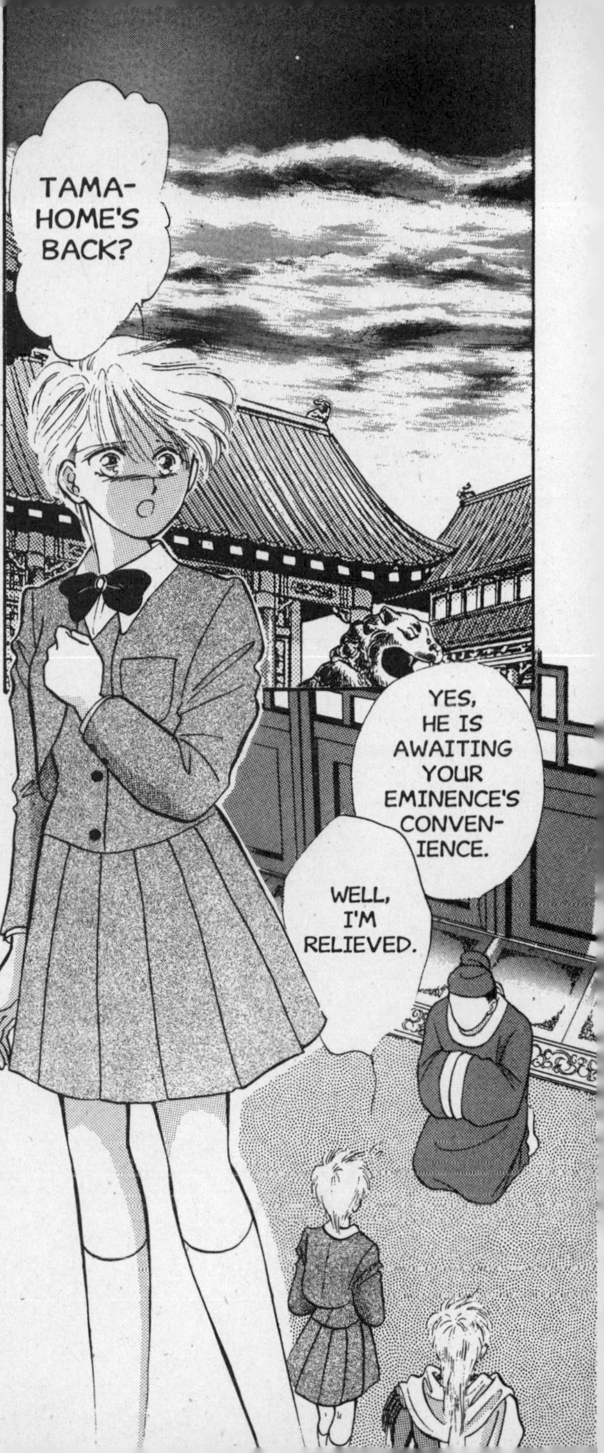
TAMA-HOME'S BACK?
YES, HE IS AWAITING YOUR EMINENCE'S CONVEN-IENCE.
WELL, I'M RELIEVED.

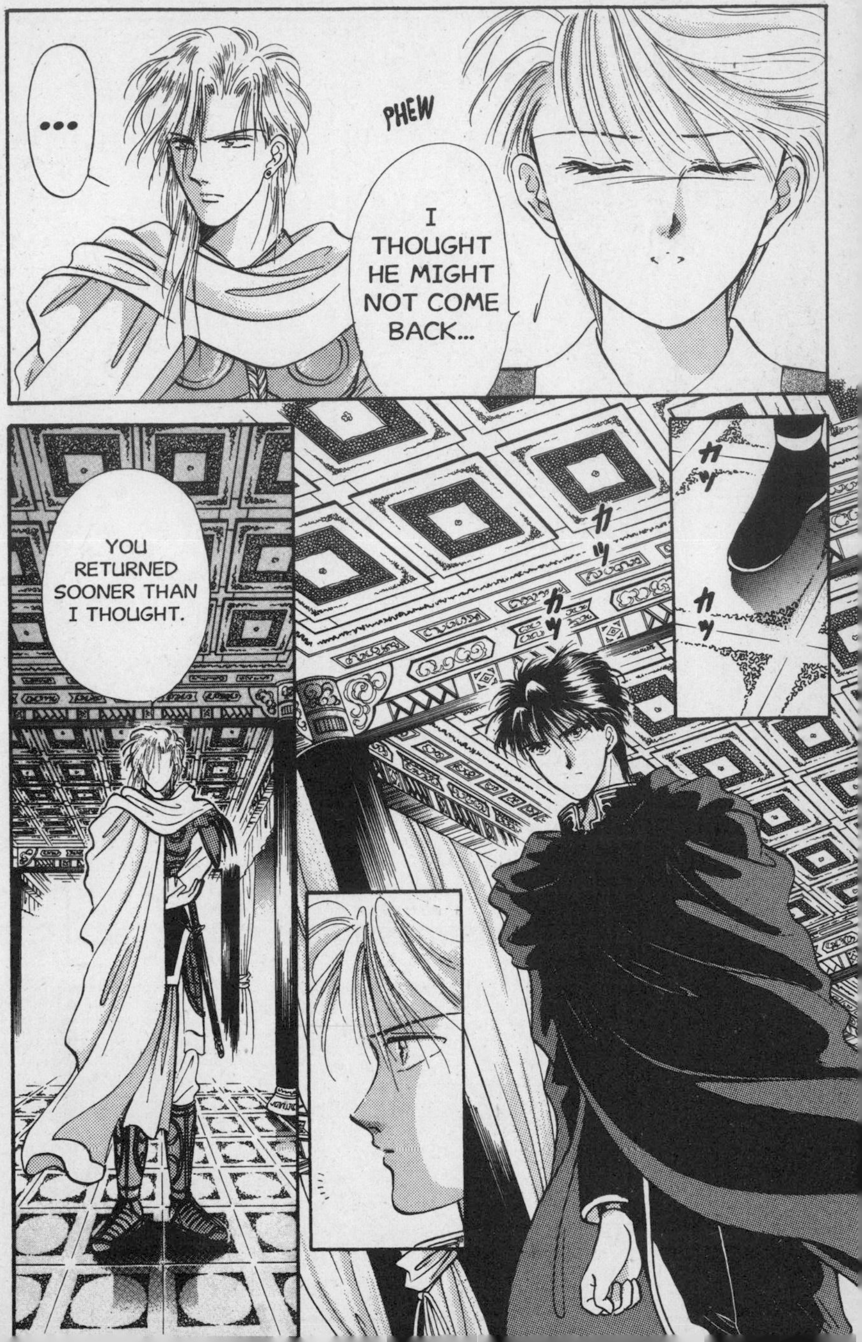
PHEW
I THOUGHT HE MIGHT NOT COME BACK...
...
カッ
カッ
カッ
カッ
YOU RETURNED SOONER THAN I THOUGHT.

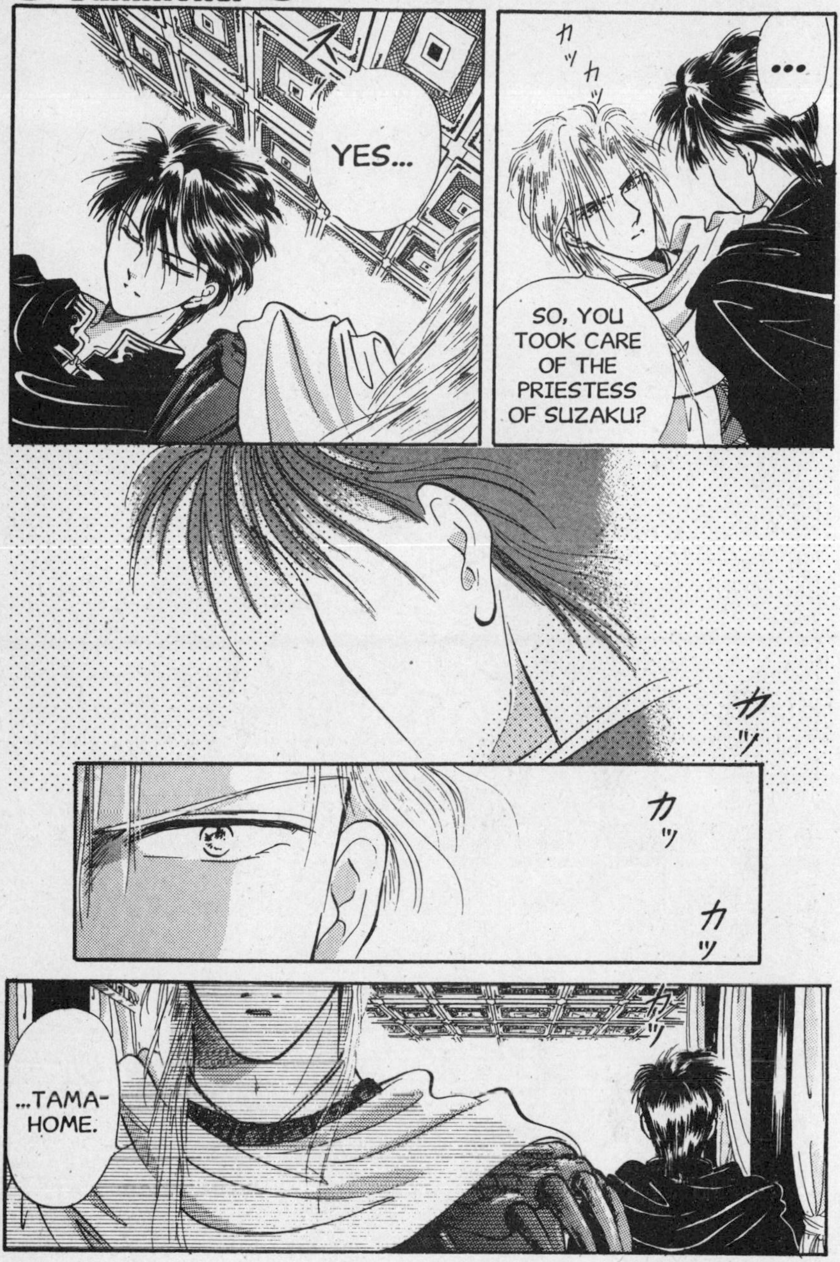
カッ
カッ
...
SO, YOU TOOK CARE OF THE PRIESTESS OF SUZAKU?
ス
YES...
カッ
カッ
カッ
カッ
...TAMA-HOME.

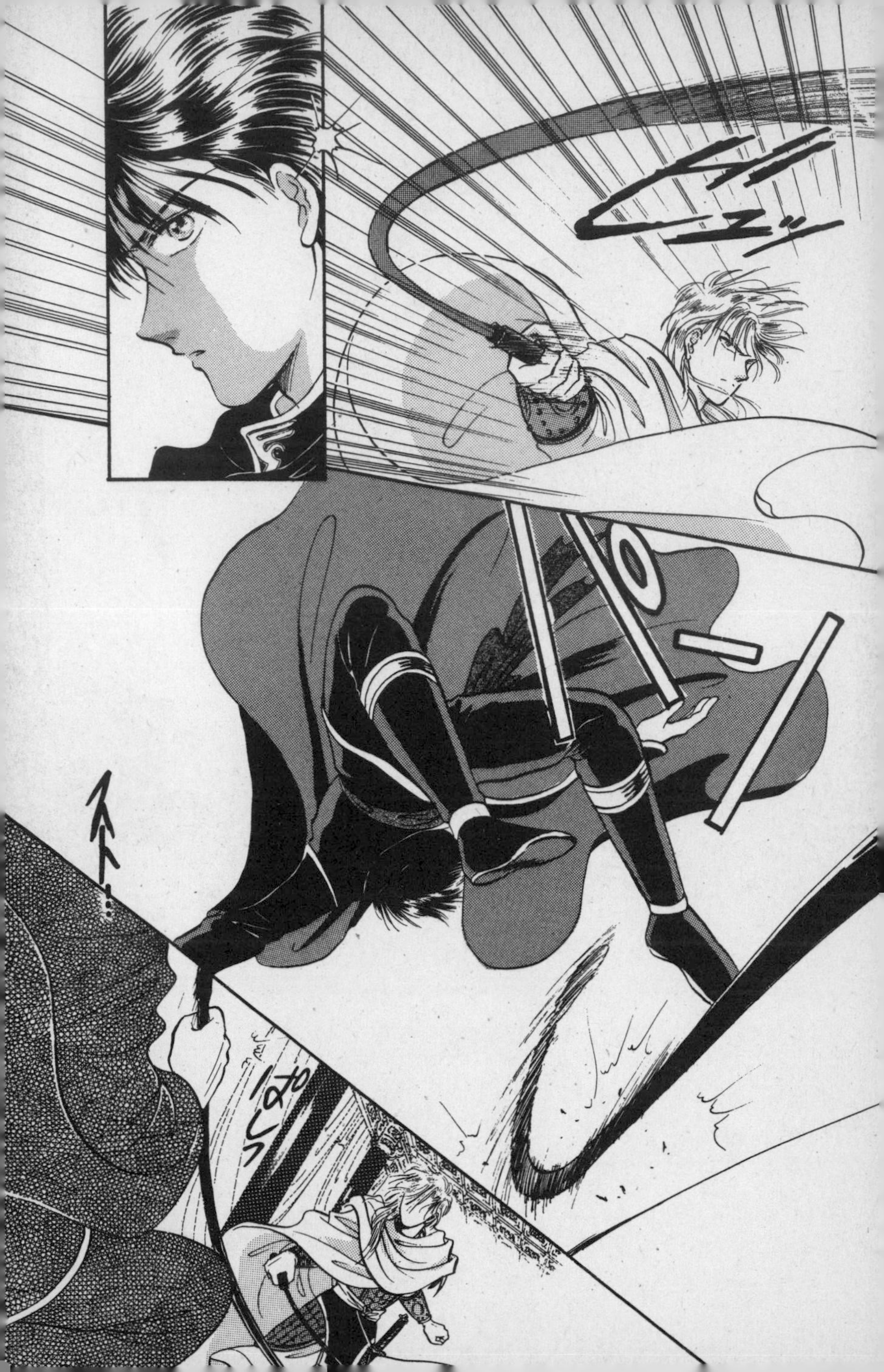
スト…
ぱしっ

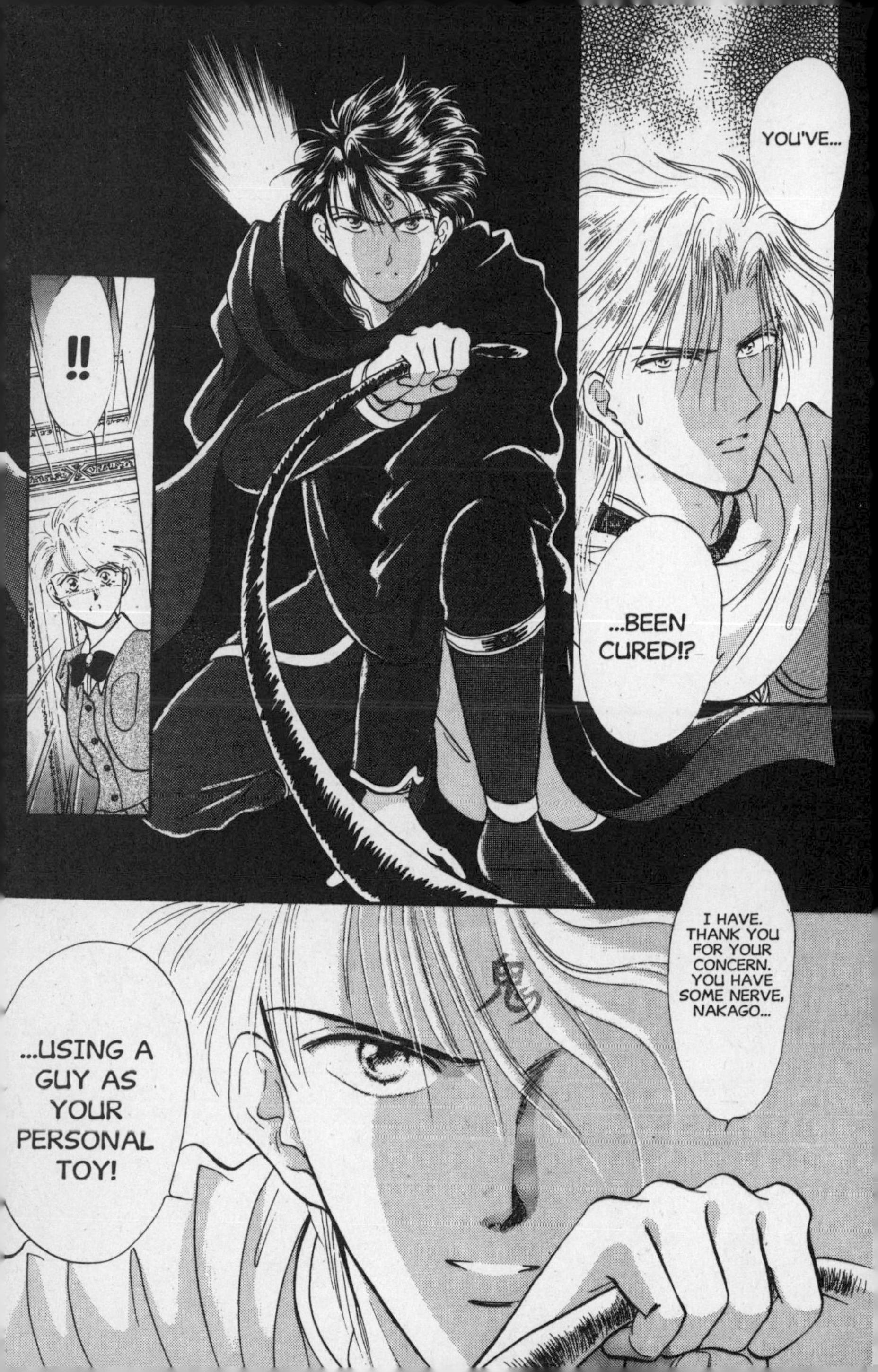
YOU'VE...
...BEEN CURED!?
!!
I HAVE. THANK YOU FOR YOUR CONCERN. YOU HAVE SOME NERVE, NAKAGO...
...USING A GUY AS YOUR PERSONAL TOY!

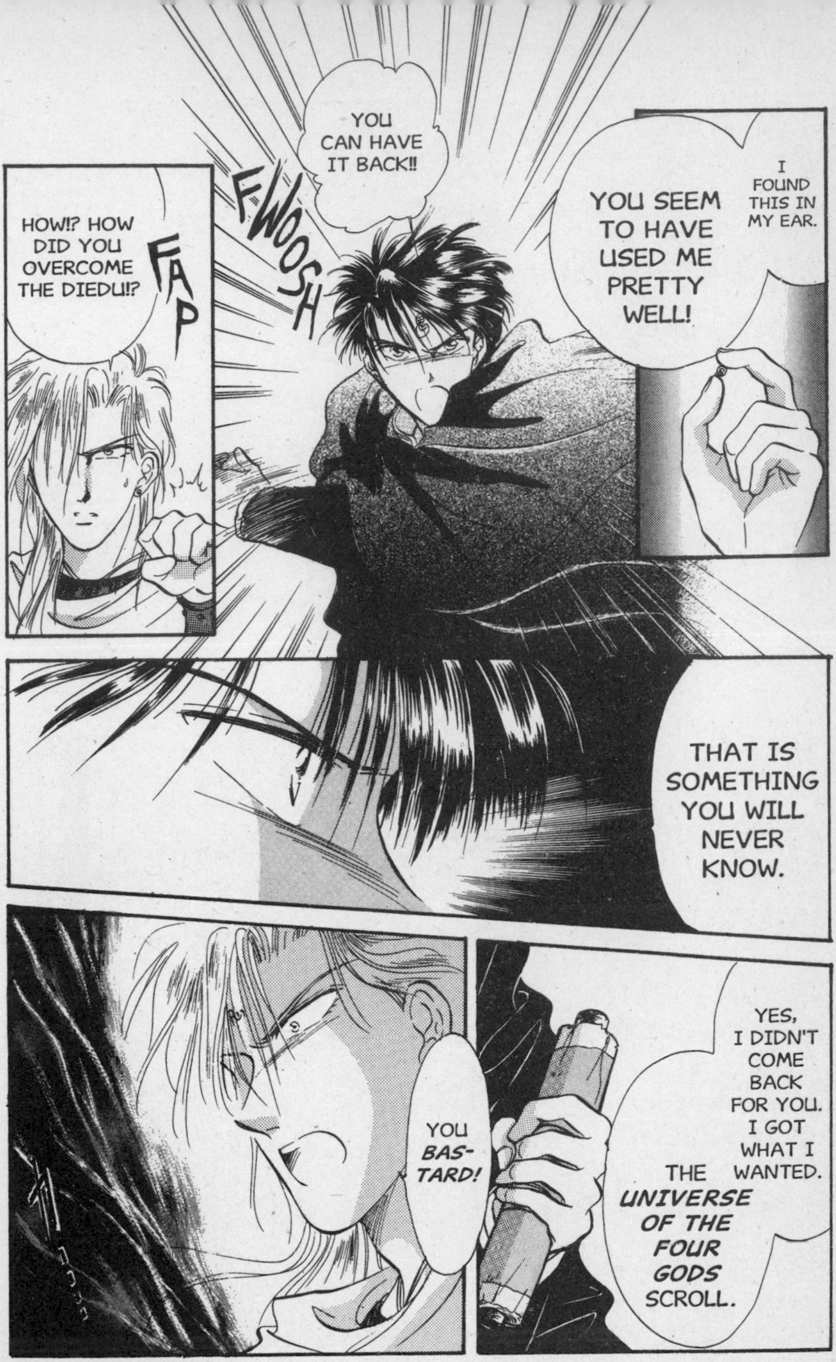
I FOUND THIS IN MY EAR.
YOU SEEM TO HAVE USED ME PRETTY WELL!
YOU CAN HAVE IT BACK!!
FWOOSH
HOW!? HOW DID YOU OVERCOME THE DIEDU!?
FAP
THAT IS SOMETHING YOU WILL NEVER KNOW.
YES, I DIDN'T COME BACK FOR YOU. I GOT WHAT I WANTED. THE *UNIVERSE OF THE FOUR GODS* SCROLL.
YOU *BAS-TARD!*

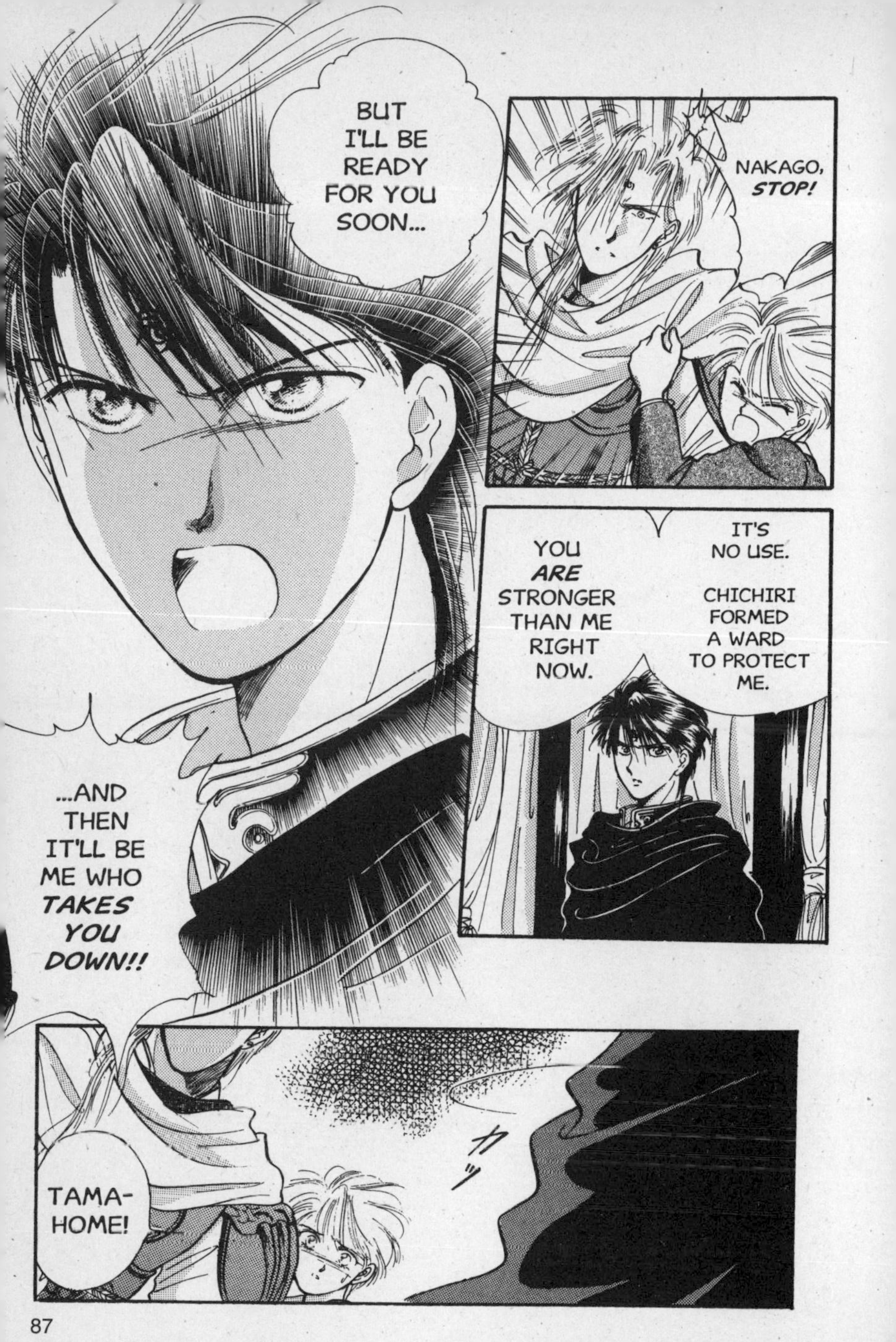
NAKAGO, *STOP!*
IT'S NO USE.
CHICHIRI FORMED A WARD TO PROTECT ME.
YOU *ARE* STRONGER THAN ME RIGHT NOW.
BUT I'LL BE READY FOR YOU SOON...
...AND THEN IT'LL BE ME WHO *TAKES YOU DOWN!!*
TAMA-HOME!
カッ

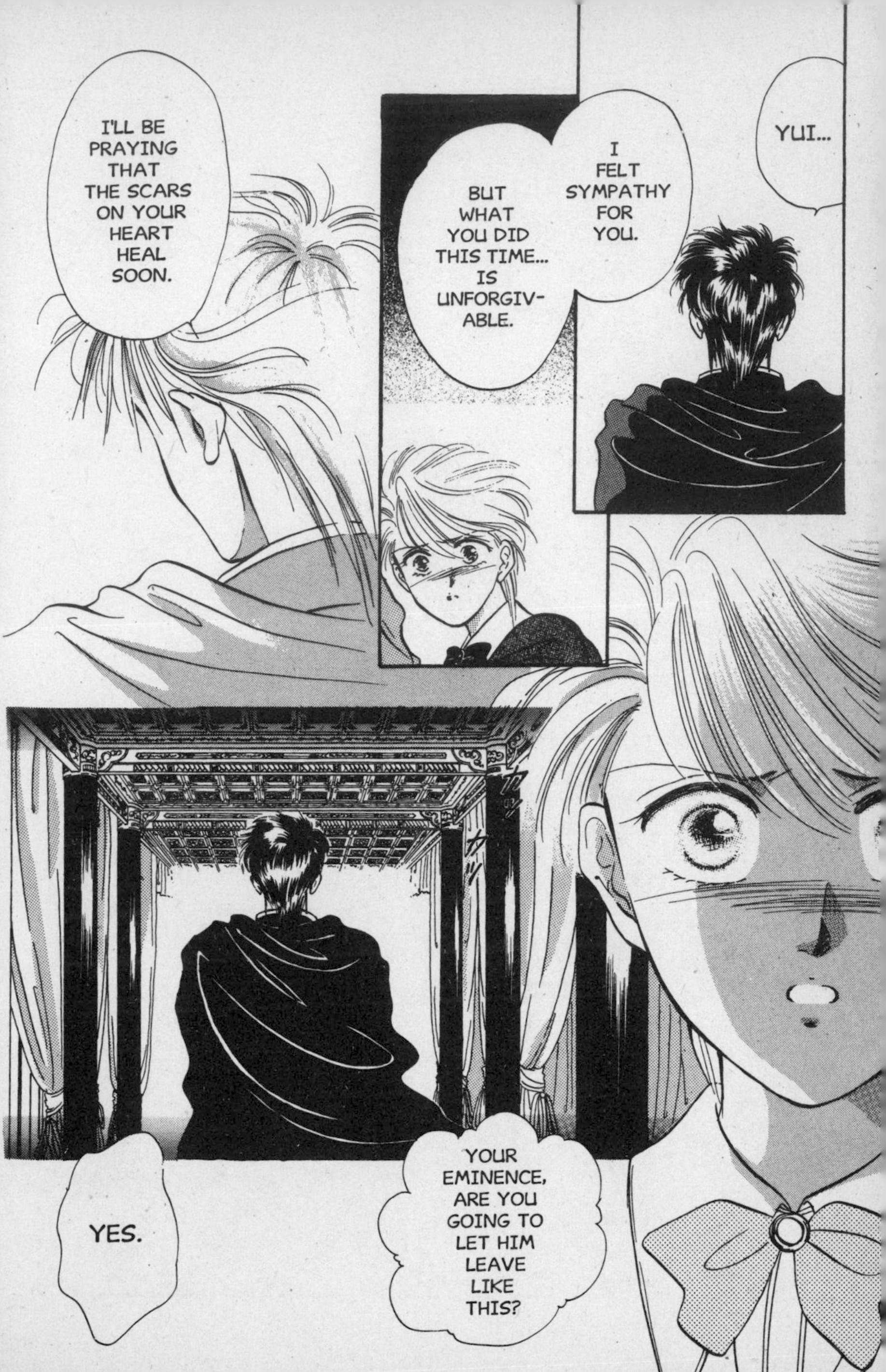
YUI...
I FELT SYMPATHY FOR YOU.
BUT WHAT YOU DID THIS TIME... IS UNFORGIV- ABLE.
I'LL BE PRAYING THAT THE SCARS ON YOUR HEART HEAL SOON.
YOUR EMINENCE, ARE YOU GOING TO LET HIM LEAVE LIKE THIS?
YES.

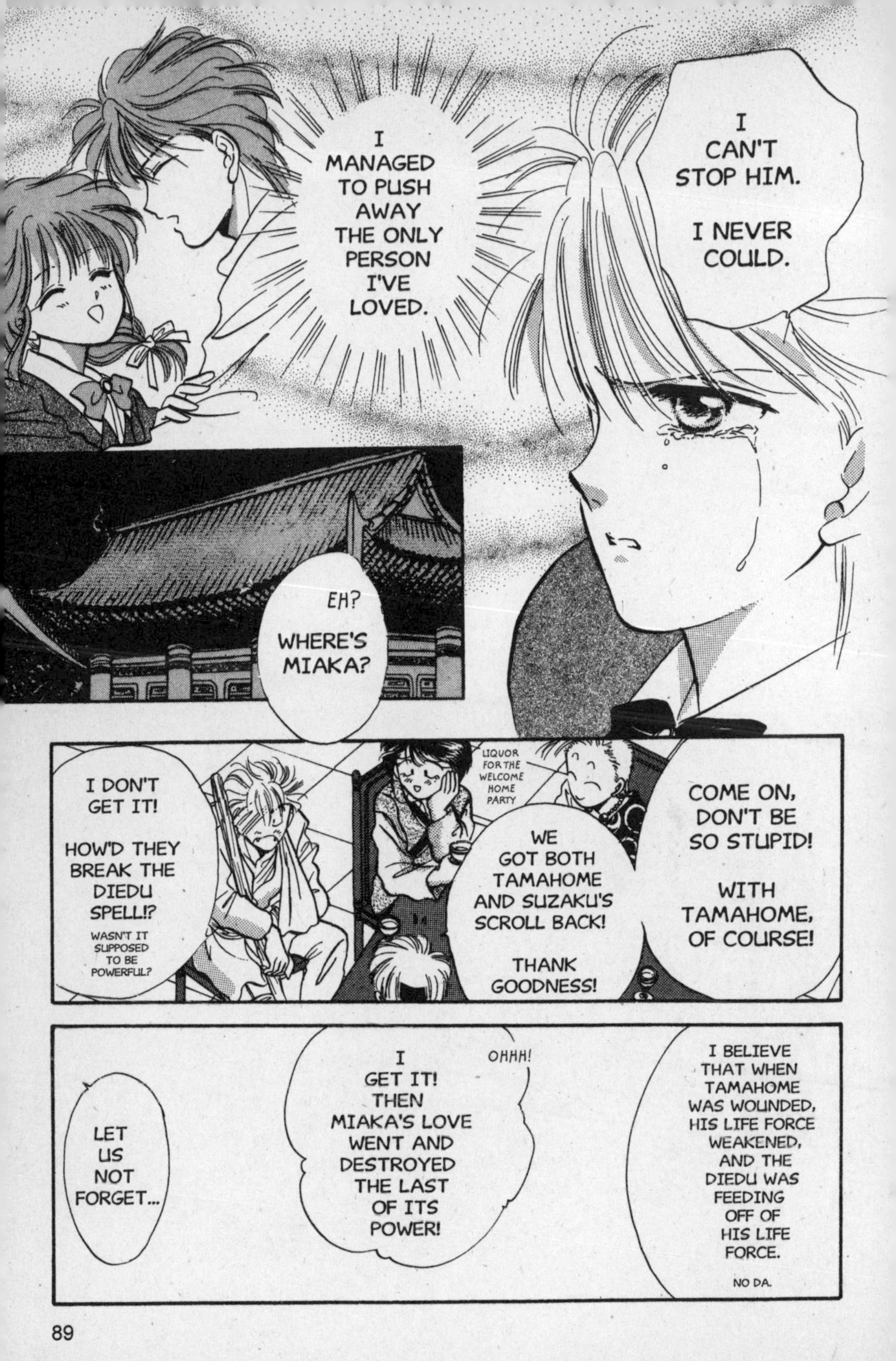
I CAN'T STOP HIM.
I NEVER COULD.
I MANAGED TO PUSH AWAY THE ONLY PERSON I'VE LOVED.
EH?
WHERE'S MIAKA?
COME ON, DON'T BE SO STUPID!
WITH TAMAHOME, OF COURSE!
LIQUOR FOR THE WELCOME HOME PARTY
WE GOT BOTH TAMAHOME AND SUZAKU'S SCROLL BACK!
THANK GOODNESS!
I DON'T GET IT!
HOW'D THEY BREAK THE DIEDU SPELL!?
WASN'T IT SUPPOSED TO BE POWERFUL?
I BELIEVE THAT WHEN TAMAHOME WAS WOUNDED, HIS LIFE FORCE WEAKENED, AND THE DIEDU WAS FEEDING OFF OF HIS LIFE FORCE.
NO DA.
OHHH!
I GET IT! THEN MIAKA'S LOVE WENT AND DESTROYED THE LAST OF ITS POWER!
LET US NOT FORGET...

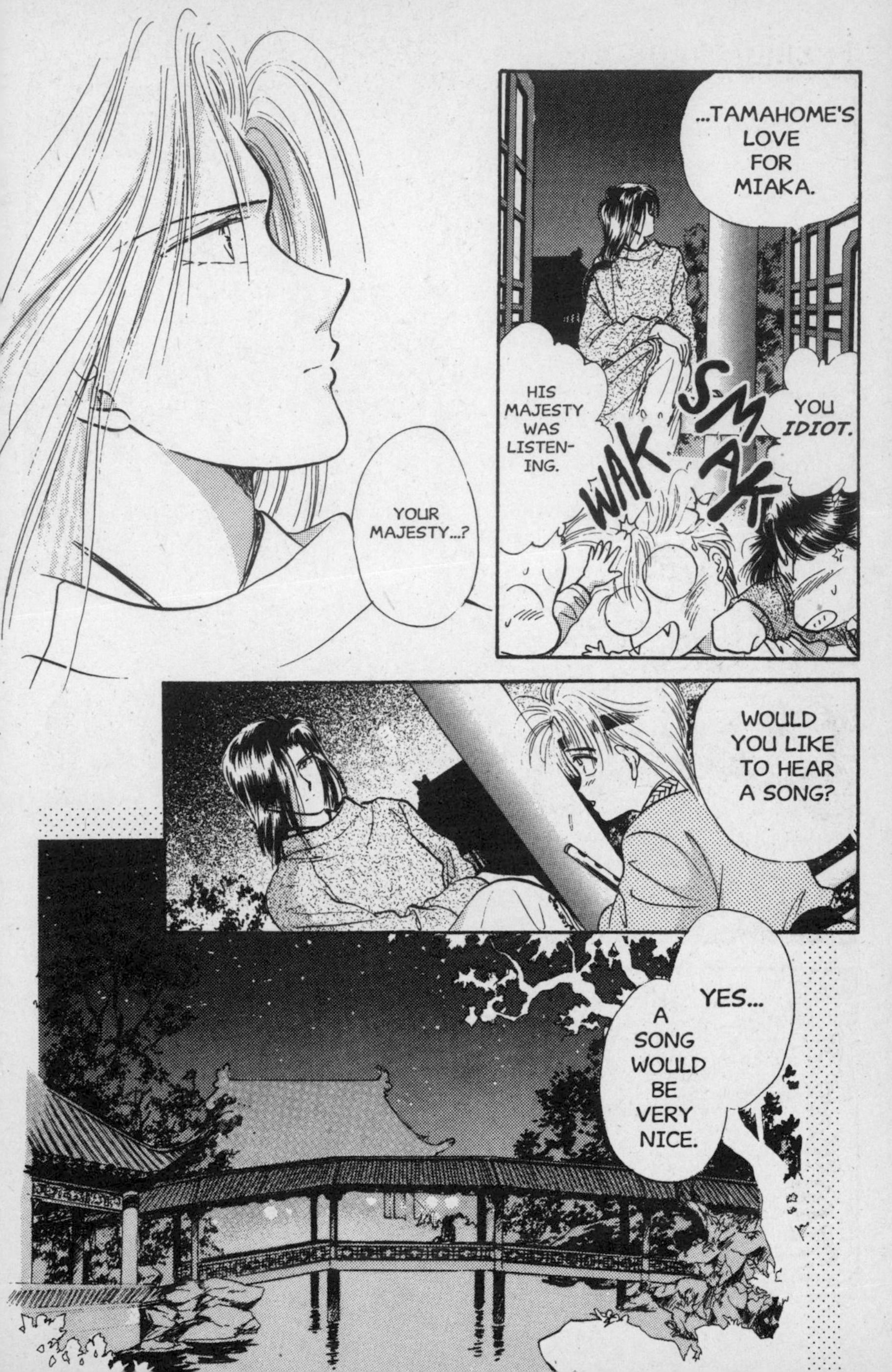
...TAMAHOME'S LOVE FOR MIAKA.
YOU *IDIOT.*
SMAK
HIS MAJESTY WAS LISTEN-ING.
WAK
YOUR MAJESTY...?
WOULD YOU LIKE TO HEAR A SONG?
YES...
A SONG WOULD BE VERY NICE.

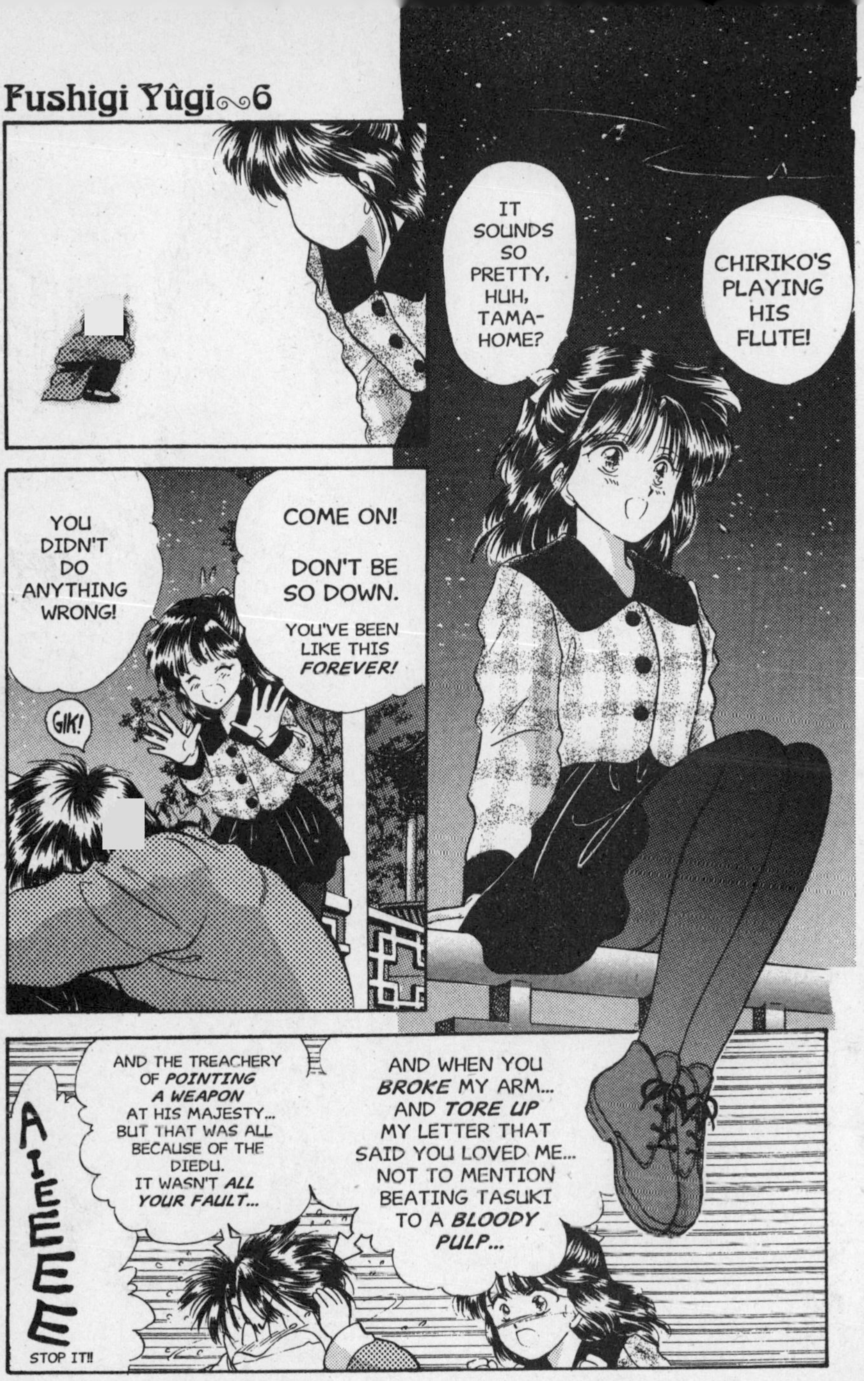
CHIRIKO'S PLAYING HIS FLUTE!
IT SOUNDS SO PRETTY, HUH, TAMA-HOME?
COME ON! DON'T BE SO DOWN. YOU'VE BEEN LIKE THIS FOREVER!
YOU DIDN'T DO ANYTHING WRONG!
GIK!
AND WHEN YOU BROKE MY ARM... AND TORE UP MY LETTER THAT SAID YOU LOVED ME... NOT TO MENTION BEATING TASUKI TO A BLOODY PULP...
AND THE TREACHERY OF POINTING A WEAPON AT HIS MAJESTY... BUT THAT WAS ALL BECAUSE OF THE DIEDU. IT WASN'T ALL YOUR FAULT...
AIEEEEE
STOP IT!!

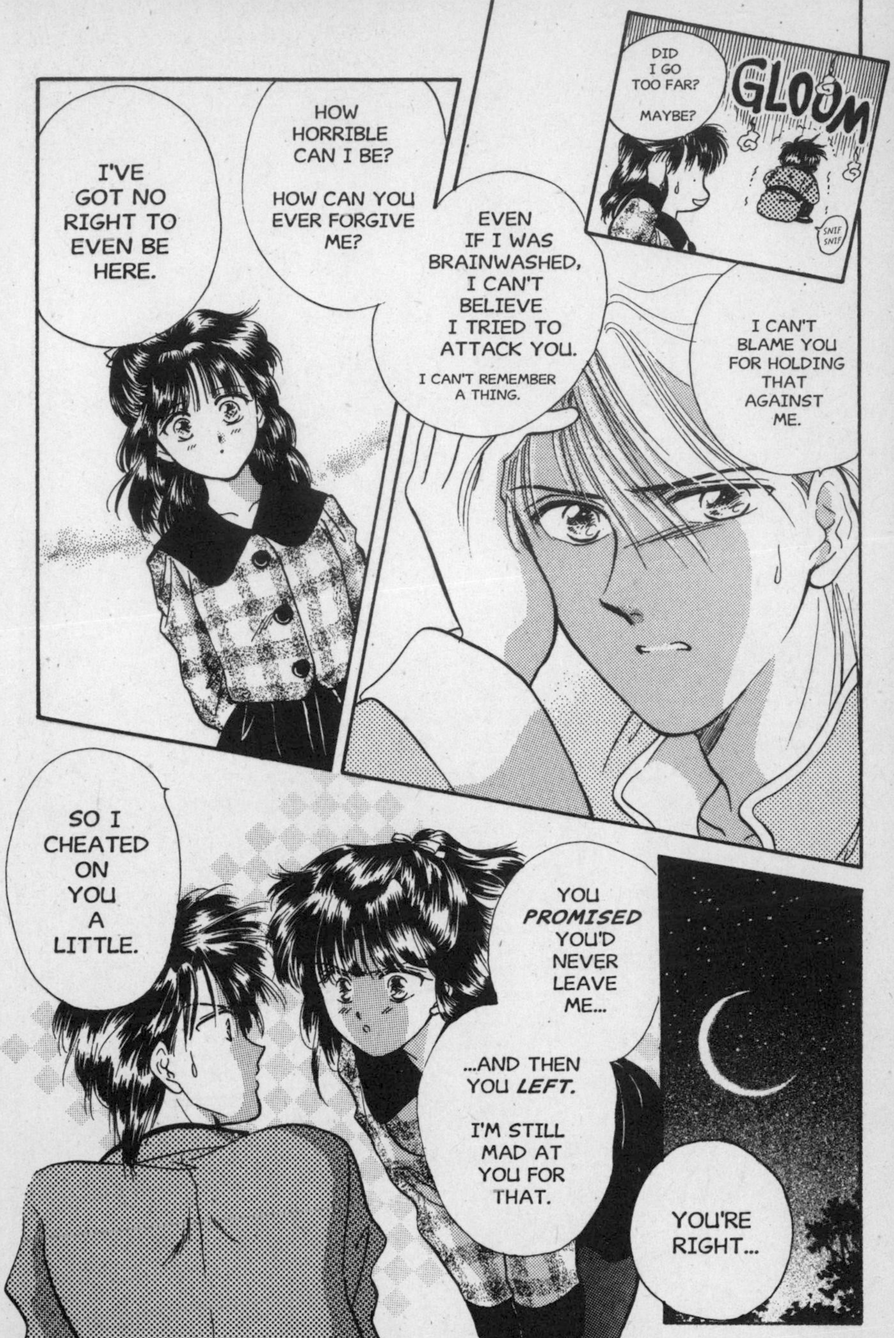
EVEN IF I WAS BRAINWASHED, I CAN'T BELIEVE I TRIED TO ATTACK YOU.
I CAN'T REMEMBER A THING.
I CAN'T BLAME YOU FOR HOLDING THAT AGAINST ME.
HOW HORRIBLE CAN I BE?
HOW CAN YOU EVER FORGIVE ME?
I'VE GOT NO RIGHT TO EVEN BE HERE.
DID I GO TOO FAR?
MAYBE?
GLOOM
SNIF SNIF
YOU *PROMISED* YOU'D NEVER LEAVE ME...
...AND THEN YOU *LEFT.*
I'M STILL MAD AT YOU FOR THAT.
YOU'RE RIGHT...
SO I CHEATED ON YOU A LITTLE.

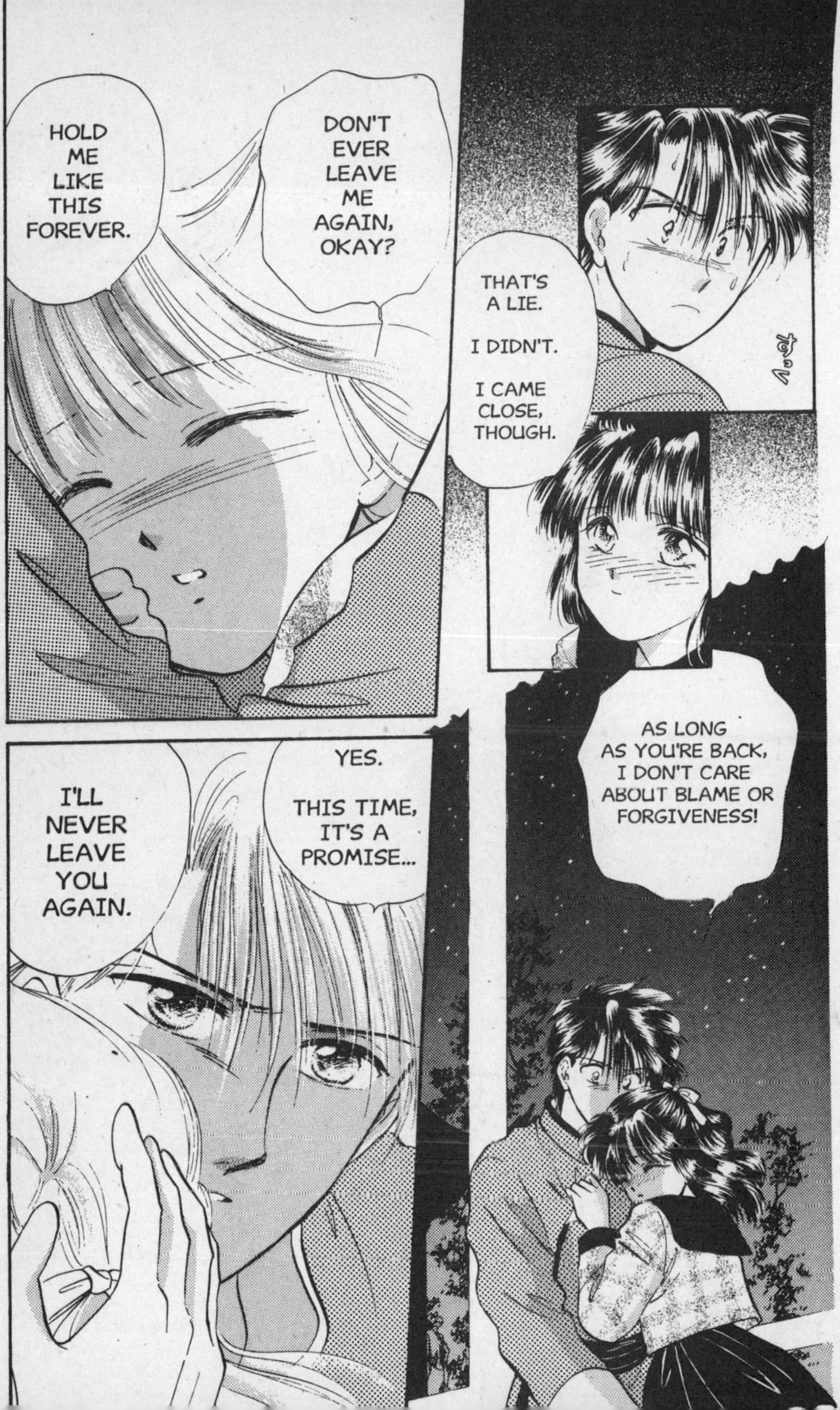
THAT'S A LIE.
I DIDN'T.
I CAME CLOSE, THOUGH.
DON'T EVER LEAVE ME AGAIN, OKAY?
HOLD ME LIKE THIS FOREVER.
AS LONG AS YOU'RE BACK, I DON'T CARE ABOUT BLAME OR FORGIVENESS!
YES.
THIS TIME, IT'S A PROMISE...
I'LL NEVER LEAVE YOU AGAIN.

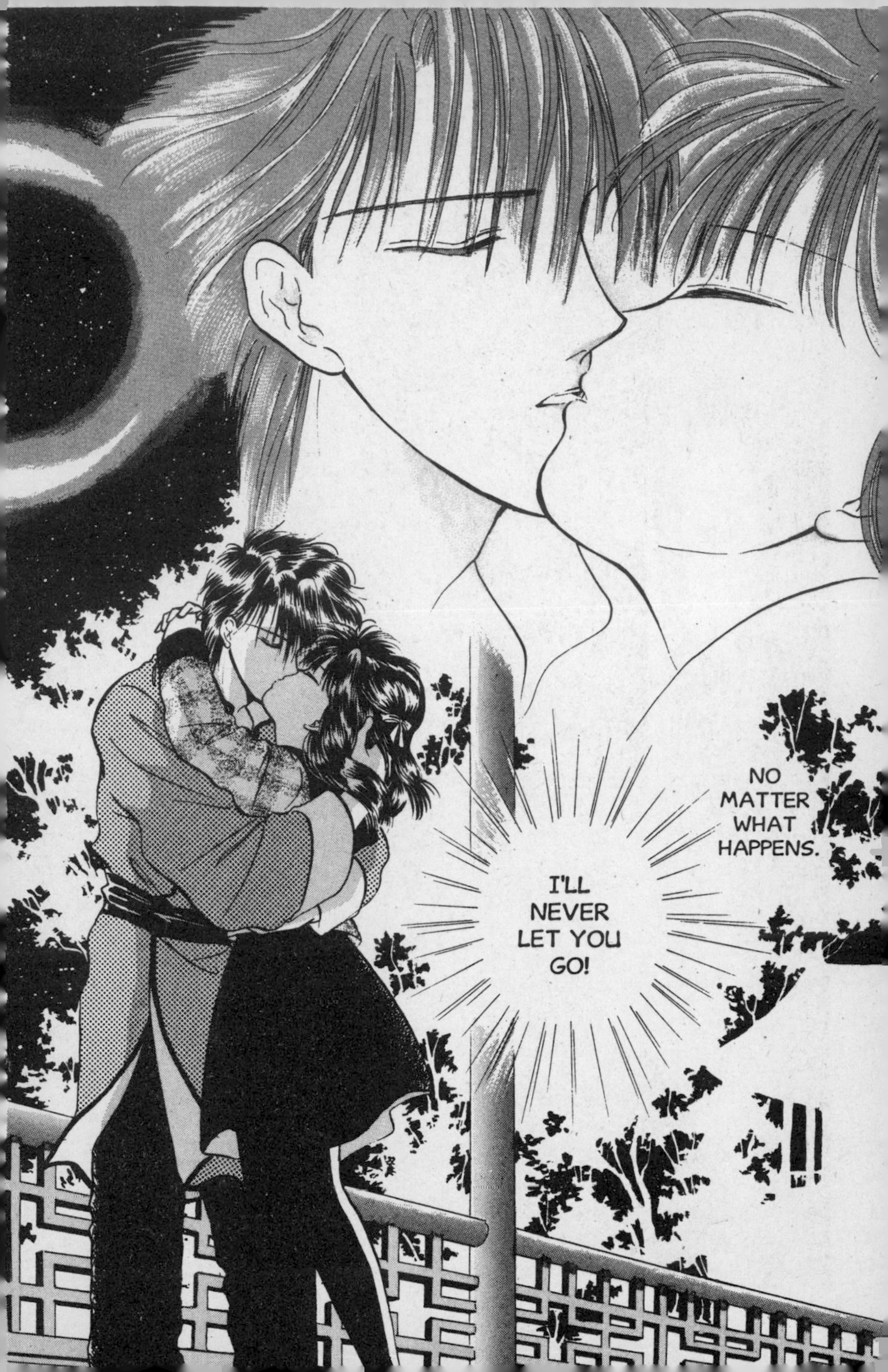
NO MATTER WHAT HAPPENS.
I'LL NEVER LET YOU GO!
!!

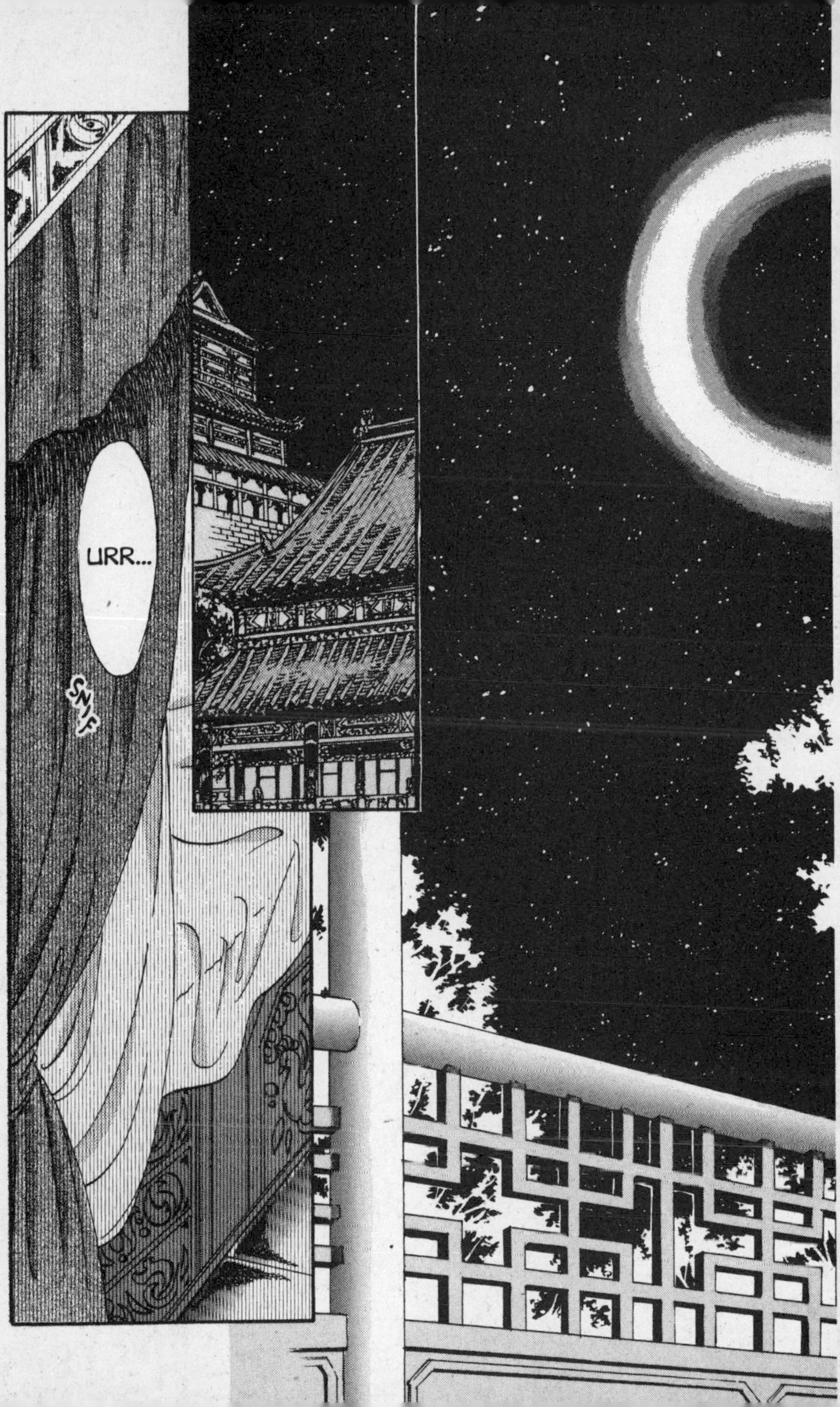
URR...
SNYF

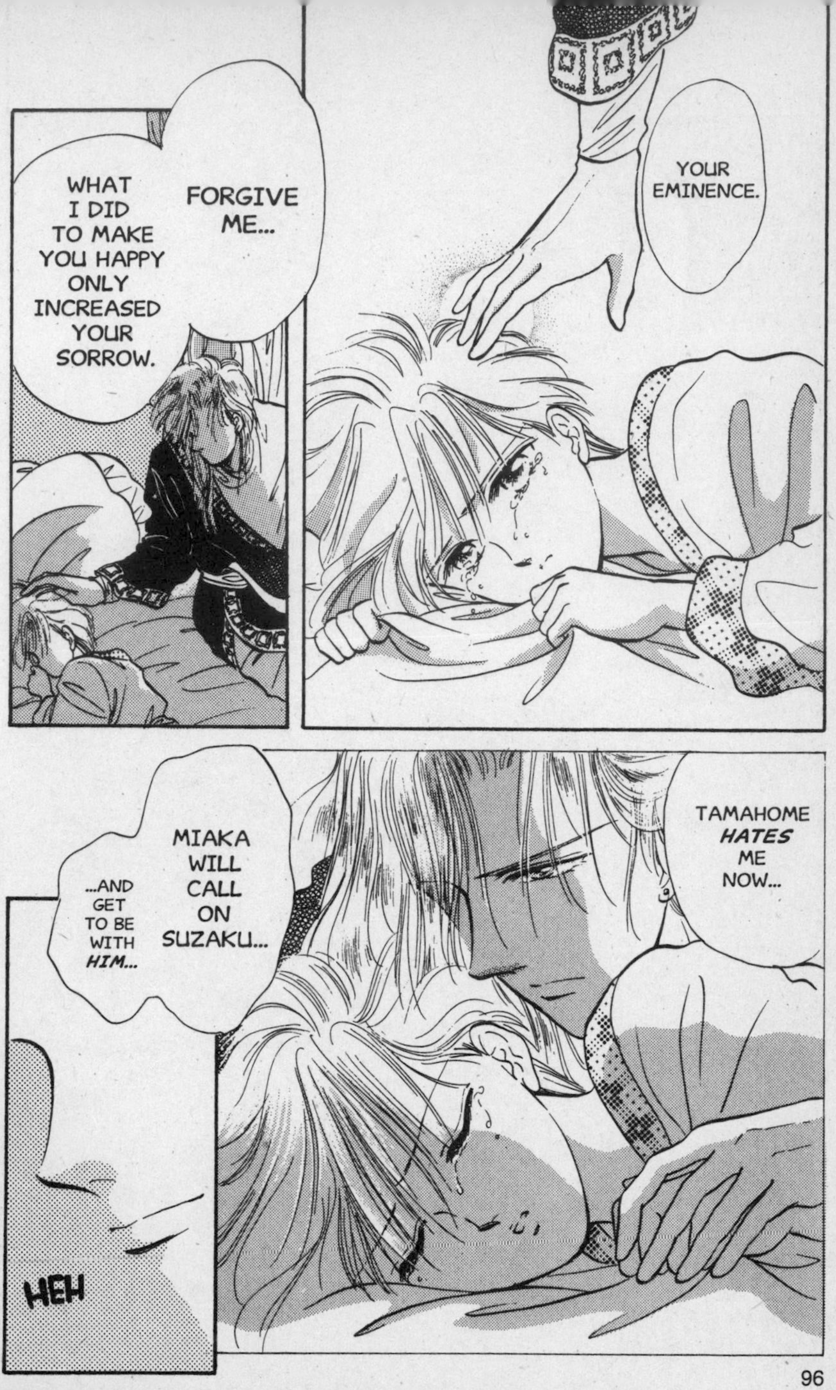
YOUR EMINENCE.
FORGIVE ME...
WHAT I DID TO MAKE YOU HAPPY ONLY INCREASED YOUR SORROW.
TAMAHOME *HATES* ME NOW...
MIAKA WILL CALL ON SUZAKU...
...AND GET TO BE WITH *HIM*...
HEH

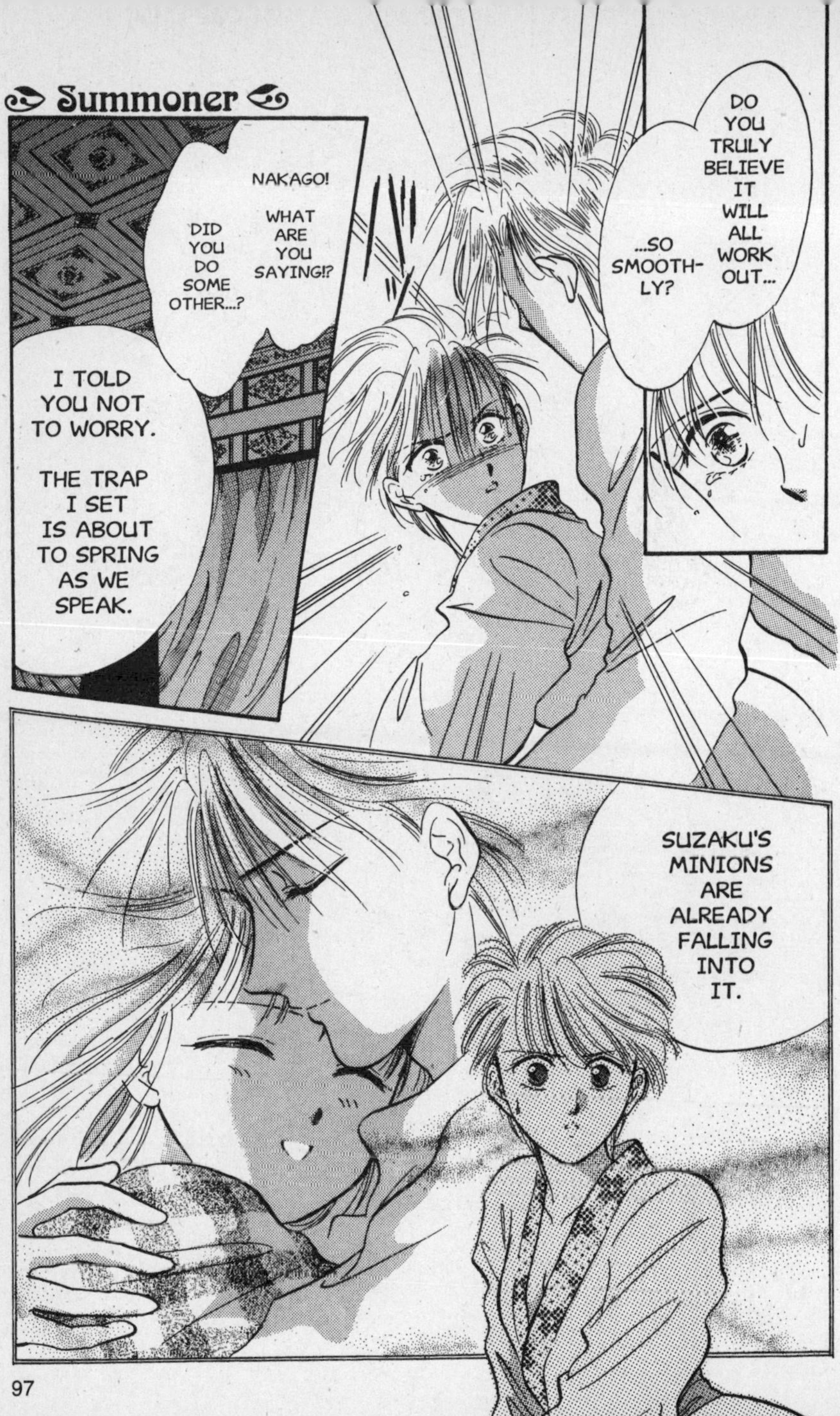
DO YOU TRULY BELIEVE IT WILL ALL WORK OUT...
...SO SMOOTHLY?
NAKAGO!
WHAT ARE YOU SAYING!?
DID YOU DO SOME OTHER...?
I TOLD YOU NOT TO WORRY.
THE TRAP I SET IS ABOUT TO SPRING AS WE SPEAK.
SUZAKU'S MINIONS ARE ALREADY FALLING INTO IT.

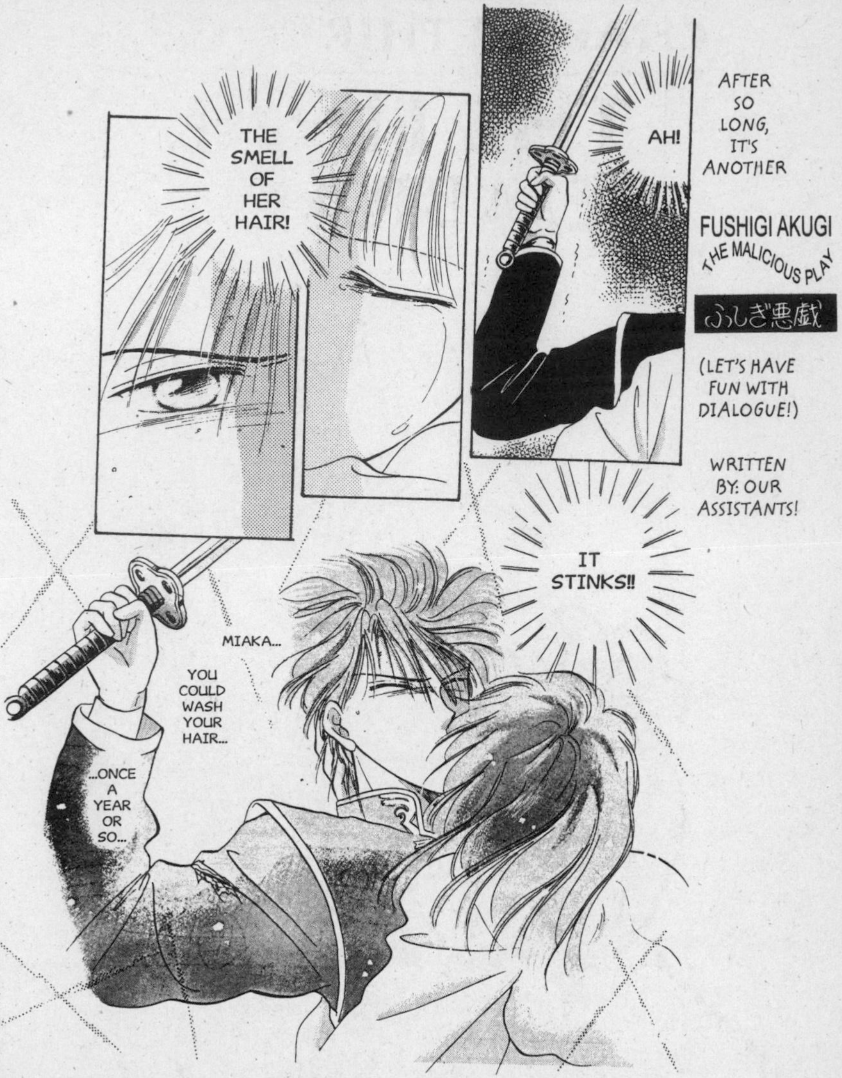
AFTER SO LONG, IT'S ANOTHER
FUSHIGI AKUGI
THE MALICIOUS PLAY
ふしぎ悪戯
(LET'S HAVE FUN WITH DIALOGUE!)
WRITTEN BY: OUR ASSISTANTS!
AH!
THE SMELL OF HER HAIR!
IT STINKS!!
MIAKA...
YOU COULD WASH YOUR HAIR...
...ONCE A YEAR OR SO...

I got a lot of suggestions for this section from readers. I collected them, put them safely aside, then promptly forgot them! (I'm an idiot!)(And I'LL do the drawing here, thank you very much.) The scene where the evil Tama goes to hit Miaka with the nunchucks... (By the way, they're actually a weapon called a "tasekkon"!) They're NOT nunchucks!
Well, there were loads of suggestions where he hit himself instead.
When I wrote this, I patted myself on the back for coming up with an angle nobody else came up with.

What was I trying to do with this corner?

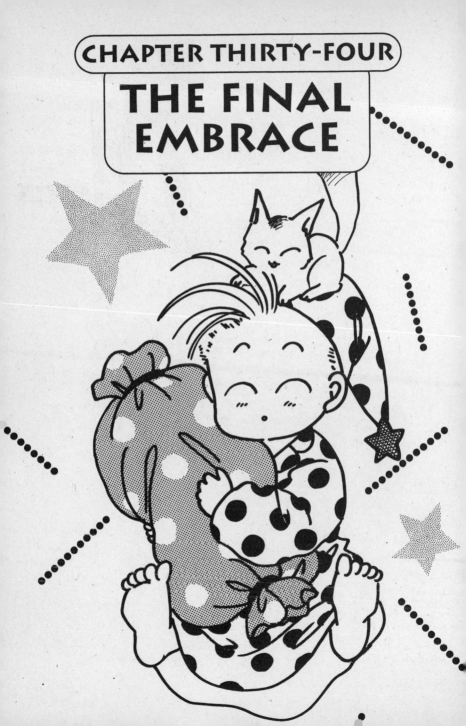

CHAPTER THIRTY-FOUR

THE FINAL EMBRACE

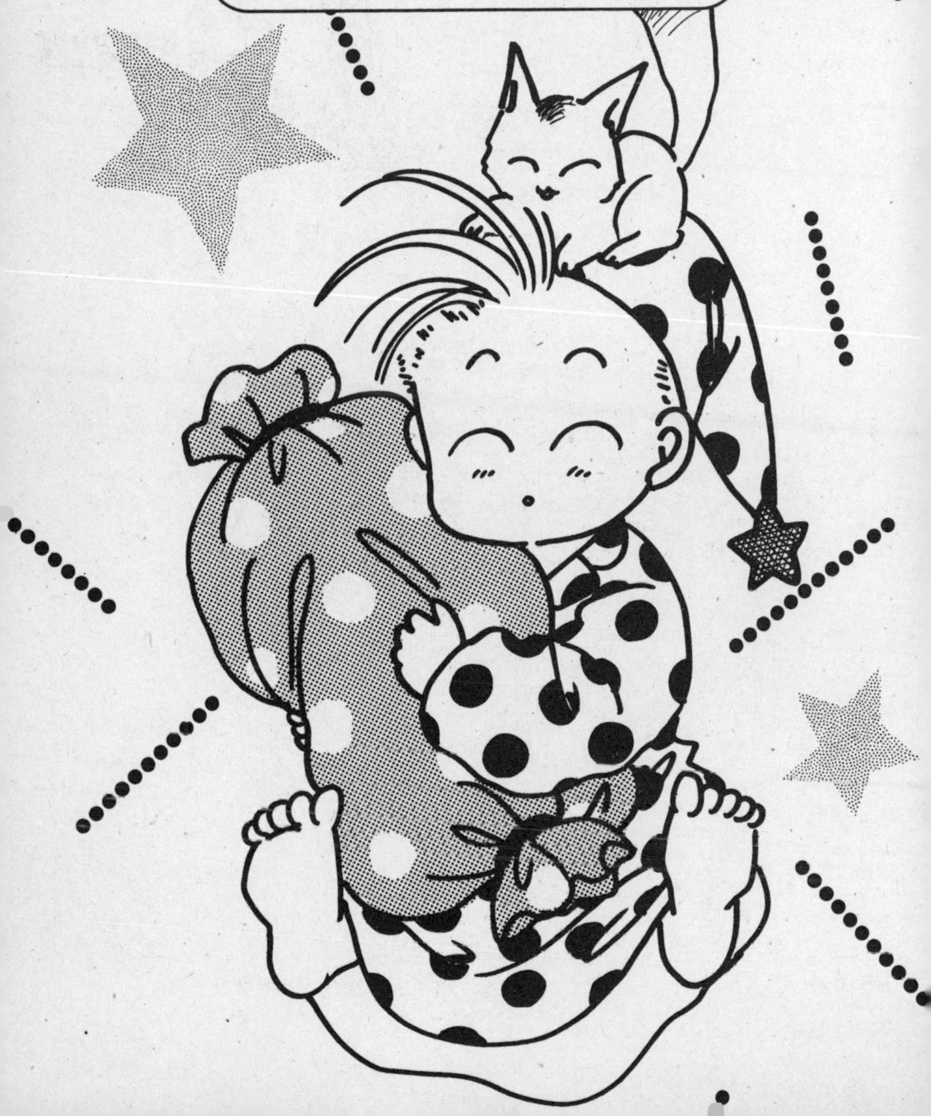

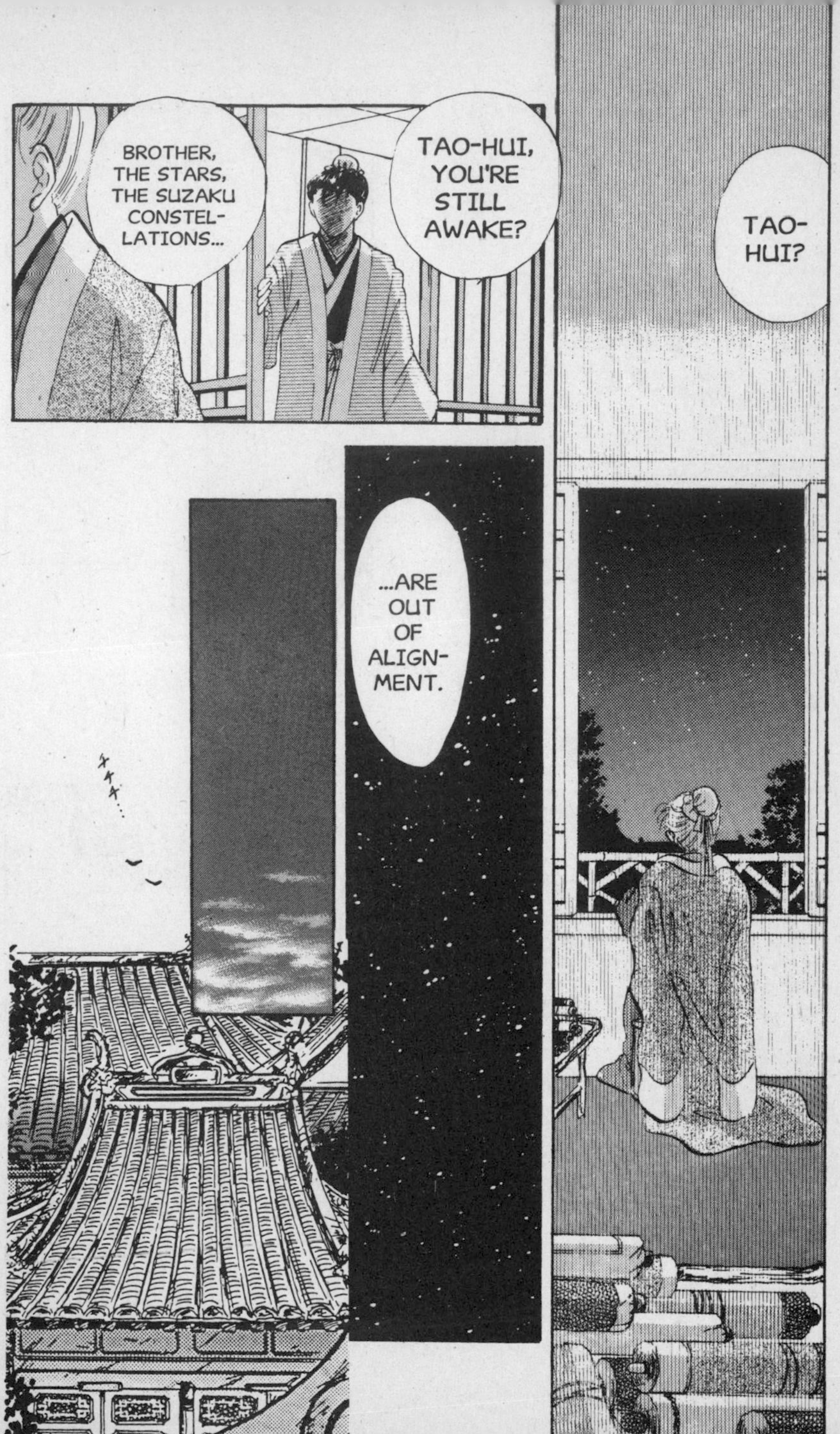
TAO-HUI?
TAO-HUI, YOU'RE STILL AWAKE?
BROTHER, THE STARS, THE SUZAKU CONSTEL-LATIONS...
...ARE OUT OF ALIGNMENT.

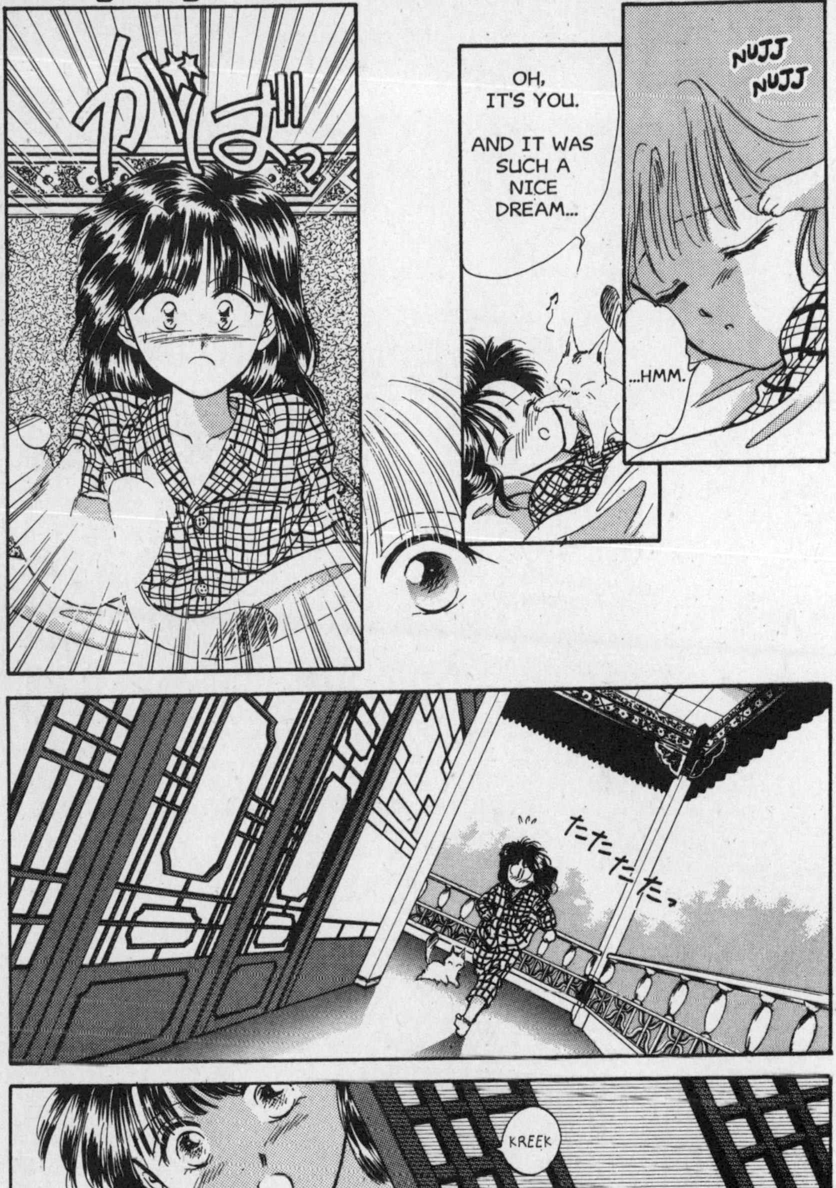
NUJJ NUJJ
...HMM.
OH, IT'S YOU.
AND IT WAS SUCH A NICE DREAM...
がばっ
たたたたっ
KREEK

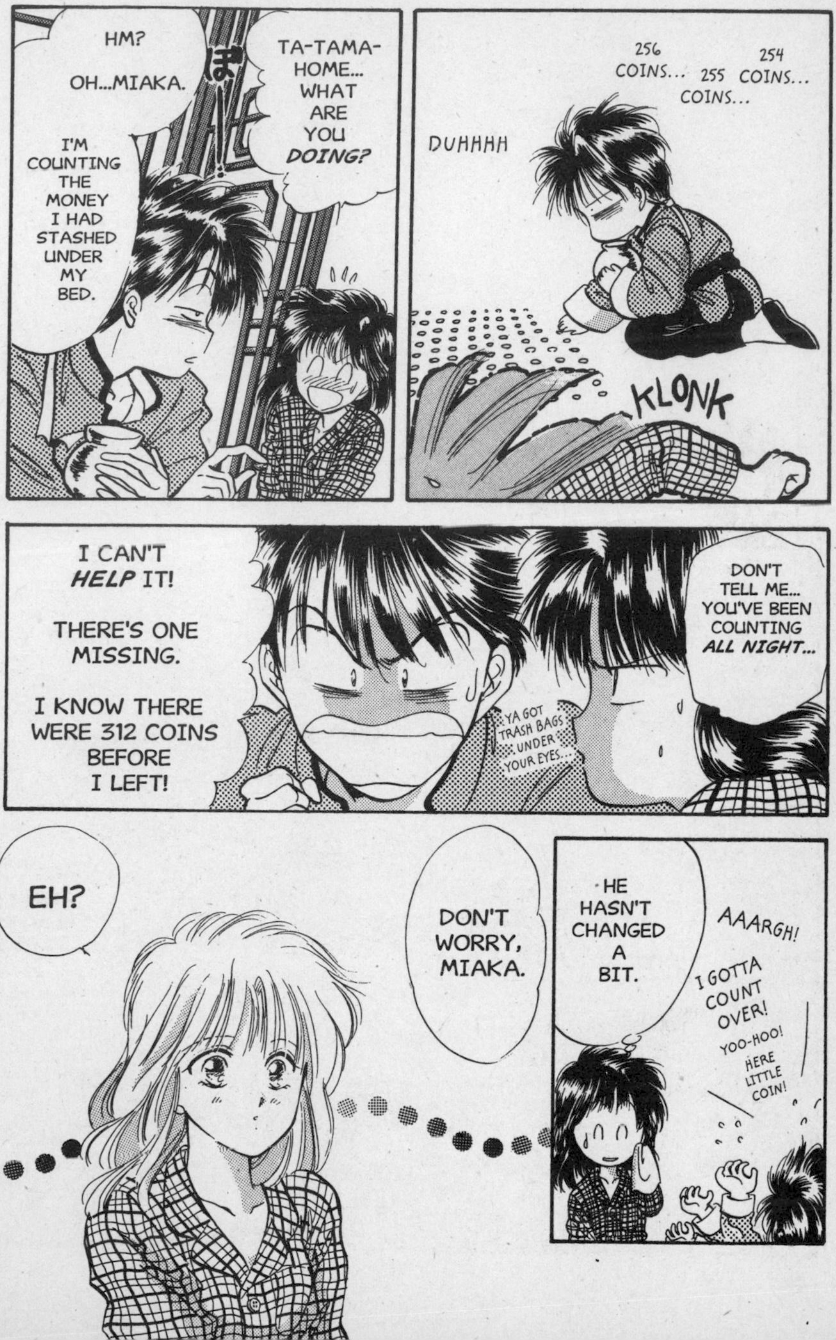
254 COINS... 255 COINS... 256 COINS...
DUHHHH
KLONK
TA-TAMA-HOME... WHAT ARE YOU *DOING?*
HM? OH...MIAKA.
I'M COUNTING THE MONEY I HAD STASHED UNDER MY BED.
DON'T TELL ME... YOU'VE BEEN COUNTING *ALL NIGHT...*
YA GOT TRASH BAGS UNDER YOUR EYES...
I CAN'T *HELP* IT!
THERE'S ONE MISSING.
I KNOW THERE WERE 312 COINS BEFORE I LEFT!
AAARGH!
HE HASN'T CHANGED A BIT.
I GOTTA COUNT OVER!
YOO-HOO! HERE LITTLE COIN!
DON'T WORRY, MIAKA.
EH?

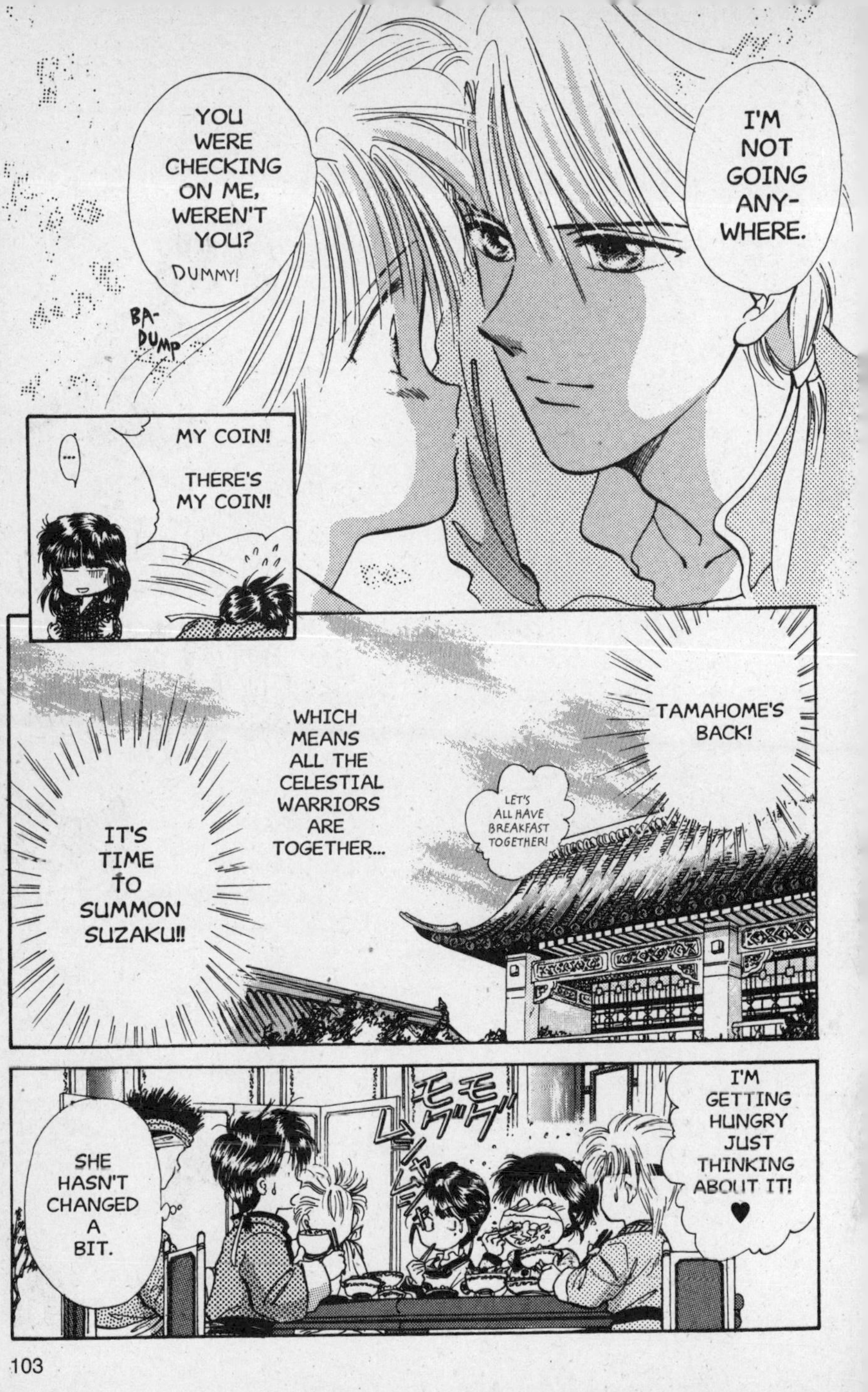
I'M NOT GOING ANY-WHERE.
YOU WERE CHECKING ON ME, WEREN'T YOU?
DUMMY!
BA-DUMP
MY COIN!
THERE'S MY COIN!
...
TAMAHOME'S BACK!
LET'S ALL HAVE BREAKFAST TOGETHER!
WHICH MEANS ALL THE CELESTIAL WARRIORS ARE TOGETHER...
IT'S TIME TO SUMMON SUZAKU!!
I'M GETTING HUNGRY JUST THINKING ABOUT IT! ♥
SHE HASN'T CHANGED A BIT.

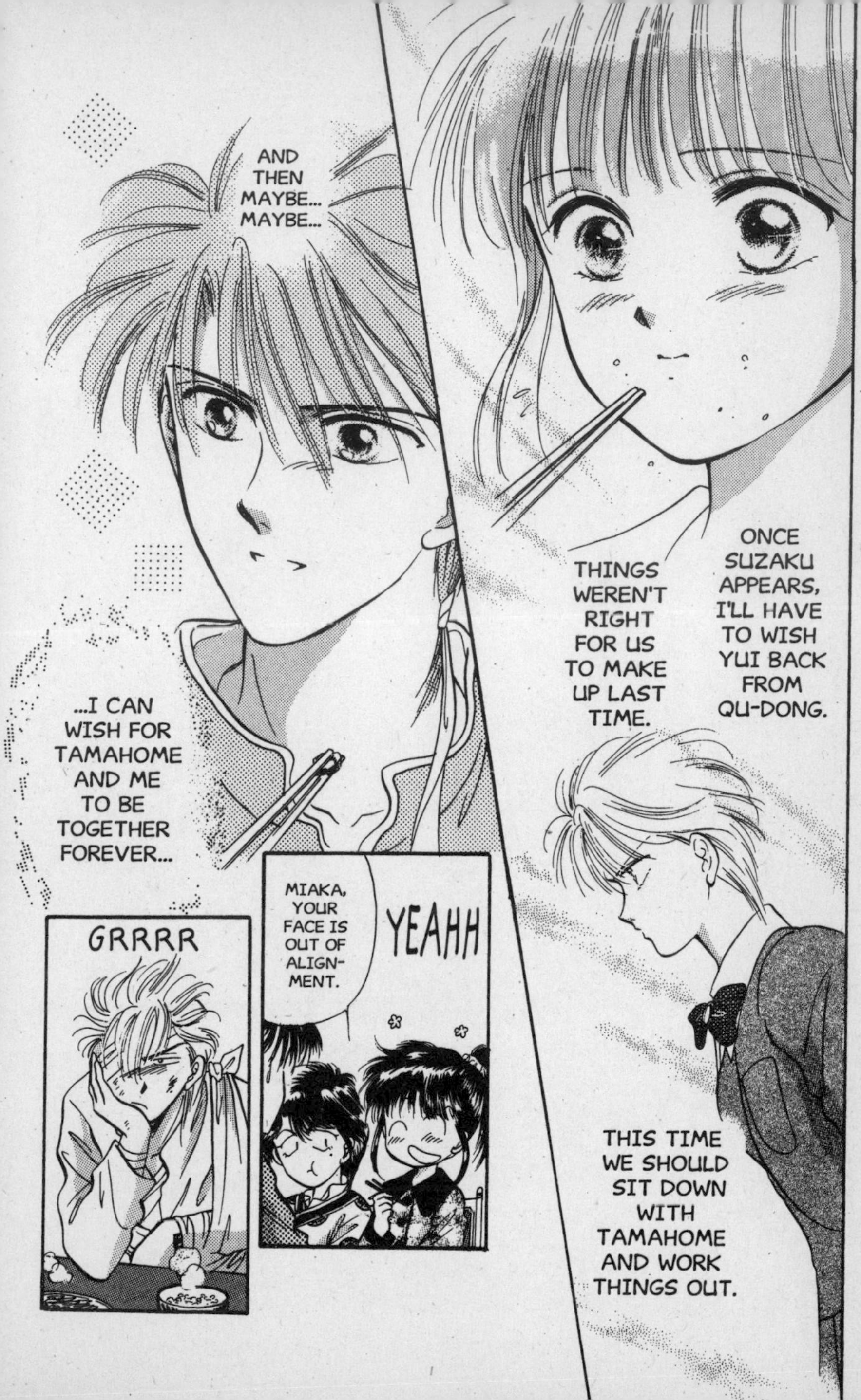
ONCE SUZAKU APPEARS, I'LL HAVE TO WISH YUI BACK FROM QU-DONG.
THINGS WEREN'T RIGHT FOR US TO MAKE UP LAST TIME.
THIS TIME WE SHOULD SIT DOWN WITH TAMAHOME AND WORK THINGS OUT.
AND THEN MAYBE... MAYBE...
...I CAN WISH FOR TAMAHOME AND ME TO BE TOGETHER FOREVER...
YEAHH
MIAKA, YOUR FACE IS OUT OF ALIGN-MENT.
GRRRR

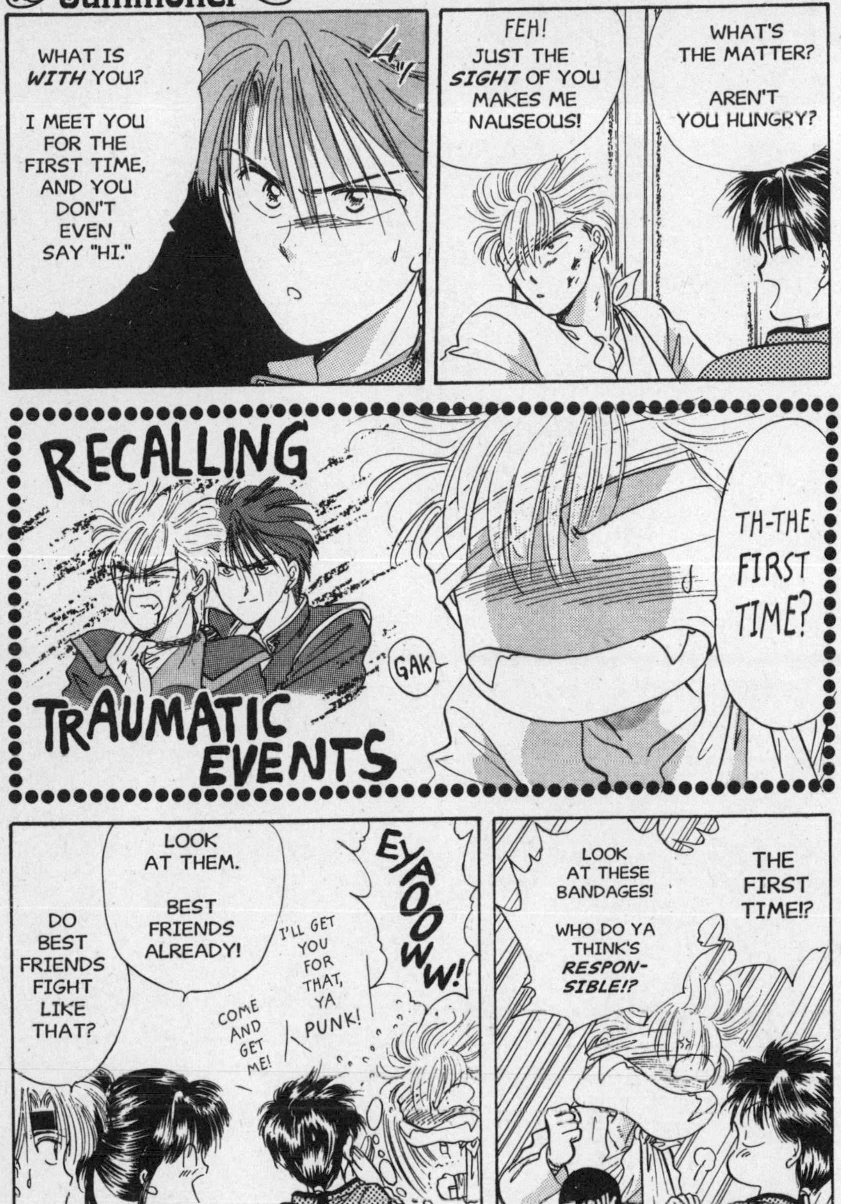
WHAT'S THE MATTER? AREN'T YOU HUNGRY?
FEH! JUST THE SIGHT OF YOU MAKES ME NAUSEOUS!
WHAT IS WITH YOU? I MEET YOU FOR THE FIRST TIME, AND YOU DON'T EVEN SAY "HI."
TH-THE FIRST TIME?
GAK
RECALLING TRAUMATIC EVENTS
THE FIRST TIME!?
LOOK AT THESE BANDAGES! WHO DO YA THINK'S RESPONSIBLE!?
THONK
EYAOOOWW!
I'LL GET YOU FOR THAT, YA PUNK!
COME AND GET ME!
LOOK AT THEM. BEST FRIENDS ALREADY!
DO BEST FRIENDS FIGHT LIKE THAT?

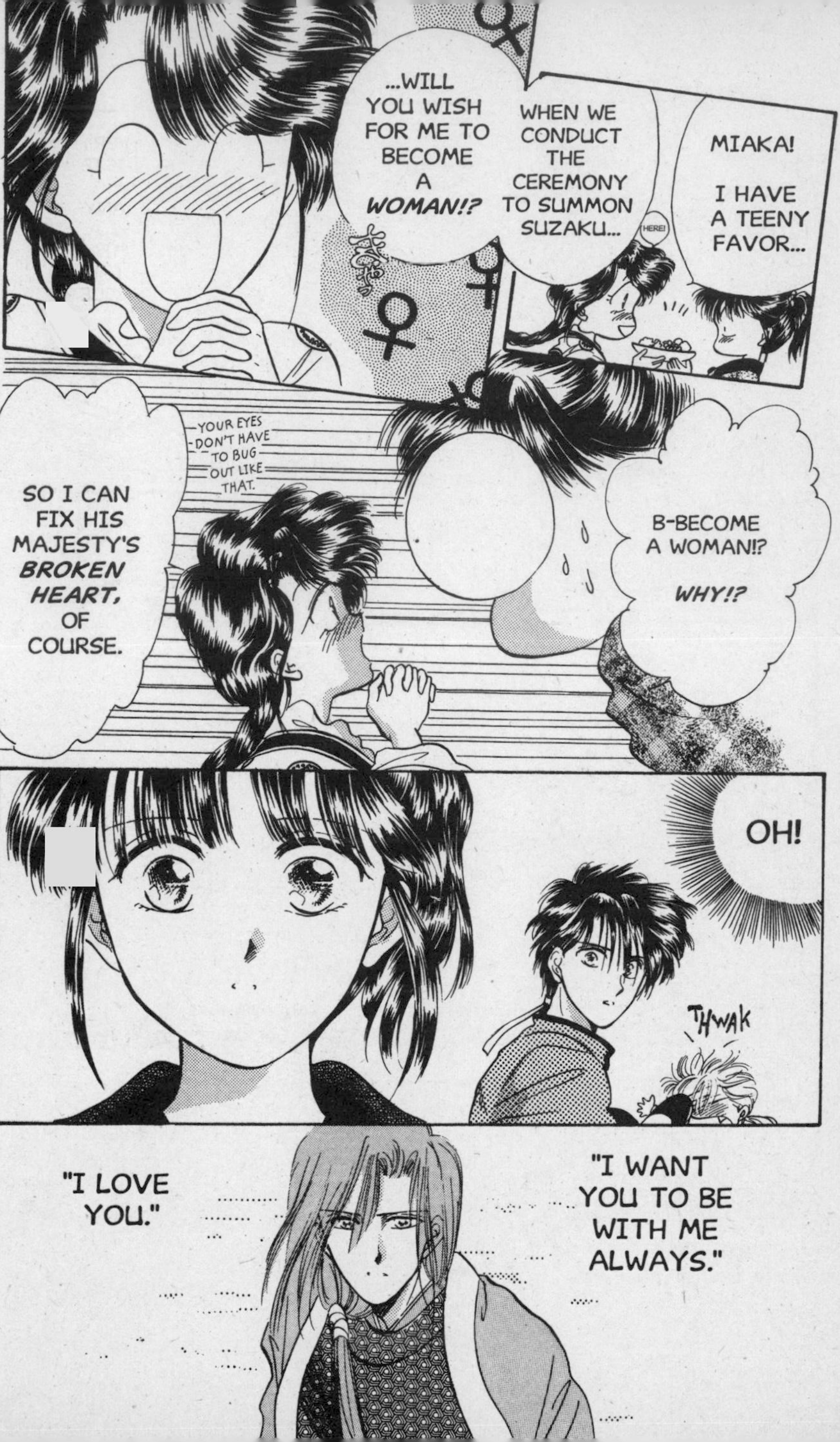
MIAKA! I HAVE A TEENY FAVOR...
HERE!
WHEN WE CONDUCT THE CEREMONY TO SUMMON SUZAKU...
...WILL YOU WISH FOR ME TO BECOME A WOMAN!?
B-BECOME A WOMAN!? WHY!?
YOUR EYES DON'T HAVE TO BUG OUT LIKE THAT.
SO I CAN FIX HIS MAJESTY'S BROKEN HEART, OF COURSE.
OH!
THWAK
"I WANT YOU TO BE WITH ME ALWAYS."
"I LOVE YOU."

Now, to completely change the subject, we have two new members in my household. One is a Yūsen (cable radio) hookup, and the other is a five-month-old Yorkshire Terrier puppy. I got Yūsen so I can listen to all 440 audio channels at work. (There must be a lot of homes that have Yūsen now.) I can pick Japanese pop songs, jazz, classical, or simulcasts ("Disco Tokyo" and other areas), and get "Juliana Tokyo" Yeaaahhh! or "Maharaja" Yeaaahhh! (At night they have live broadcasts!) They even have karaoke and movie soundtracks, etc. There's so much that it's really fun, but the funniest programs are "Taking Care of Business" (recordings of shopkeepers inviting pedestrians into their shops, store announcements at closing time, etc.), "Battleship March," "Applause" (the never-ending sound of applause), "Soroban" (abacus sounds that go on endlessly), "Alibi" (you can use the noise of pachinko parlors and bars to lie about where you are), "Telephone Booth on the Street," and many more! But I'm so serious, I'd never pull a prank like that. The scary ones are called "Spiritual Music," "Wish Fulfillment," "Subliminal Power Enhancement," and "Spiritual Healing." What the heck is this stuff!? There's one called "Hypnosis," where you hear some guy counting sheep endlessly. There's "Heart Beat" for children. It's a little scary and strange. I mean we're talking about the heartbeat a fetus hears in the womb. A baby might feel secure, but for an adult like me it's kinda creepy.

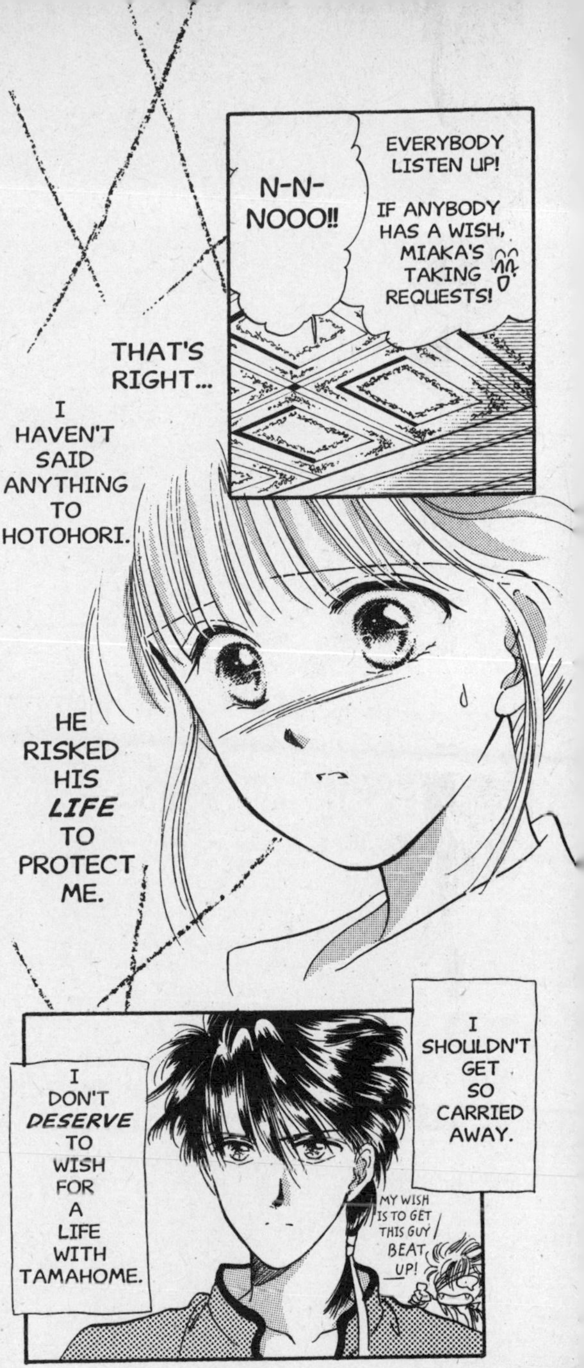
EVERYBODY LISTEN UP!
IF ANYBODY HAS A WISH, MIAKA'S TAKING REQUESTS!
N-N-NOOO!!
THAT'S RIGHT...
I HAVEN'T SAID ANYTHING TO HOTOHORI.
HE RISKED HIS LIFE TO PROTECT ME.
I SHOULDN'T GET SO CARRIED AWAY.
MY WISH IS TO GET THIS GUY BEAT UP!
I DON'T DESERVE TO WISH FOR A LIFE WITH TAMAHOME.

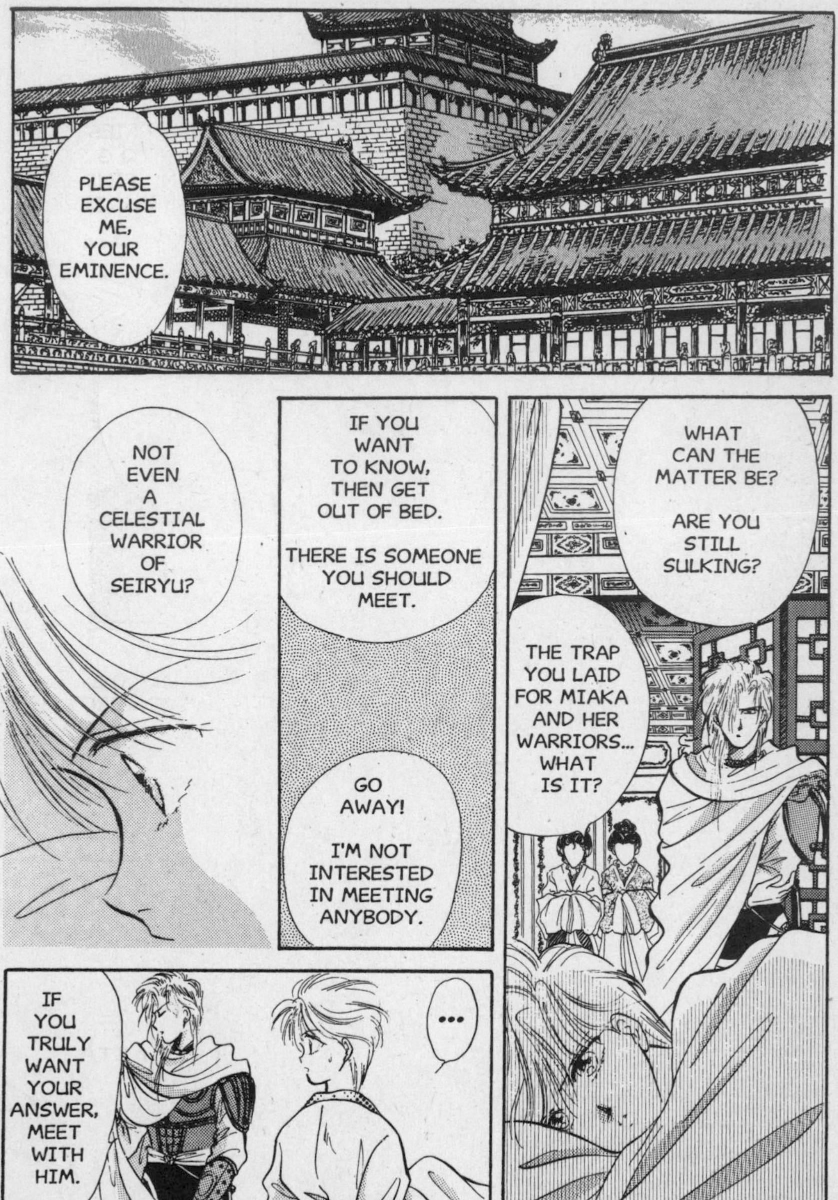
PLEASE EXCUSE ME, YOUR EMINENCE.
WHAT CAN THE MATTER BE? ARE YOU STILL SULKING?
THE TRAP YOU LAID FOR MIAKA AND HER WARRIORS... WHAT IS IT?
IF YOU WANT TO KNOW, THEN GET OUT OF BED. THERE IS SOMEONE YOU SHOULD MEET.
GO AWAY! I'M NOT INTERESTED IN MEETING ANYBODY.
NOT EVEN A CELESTIAL WARRIOR OF SEIRYU?
...
IF YOU TRULY WANT YOUR ANSWER, MEET WITH HIM.

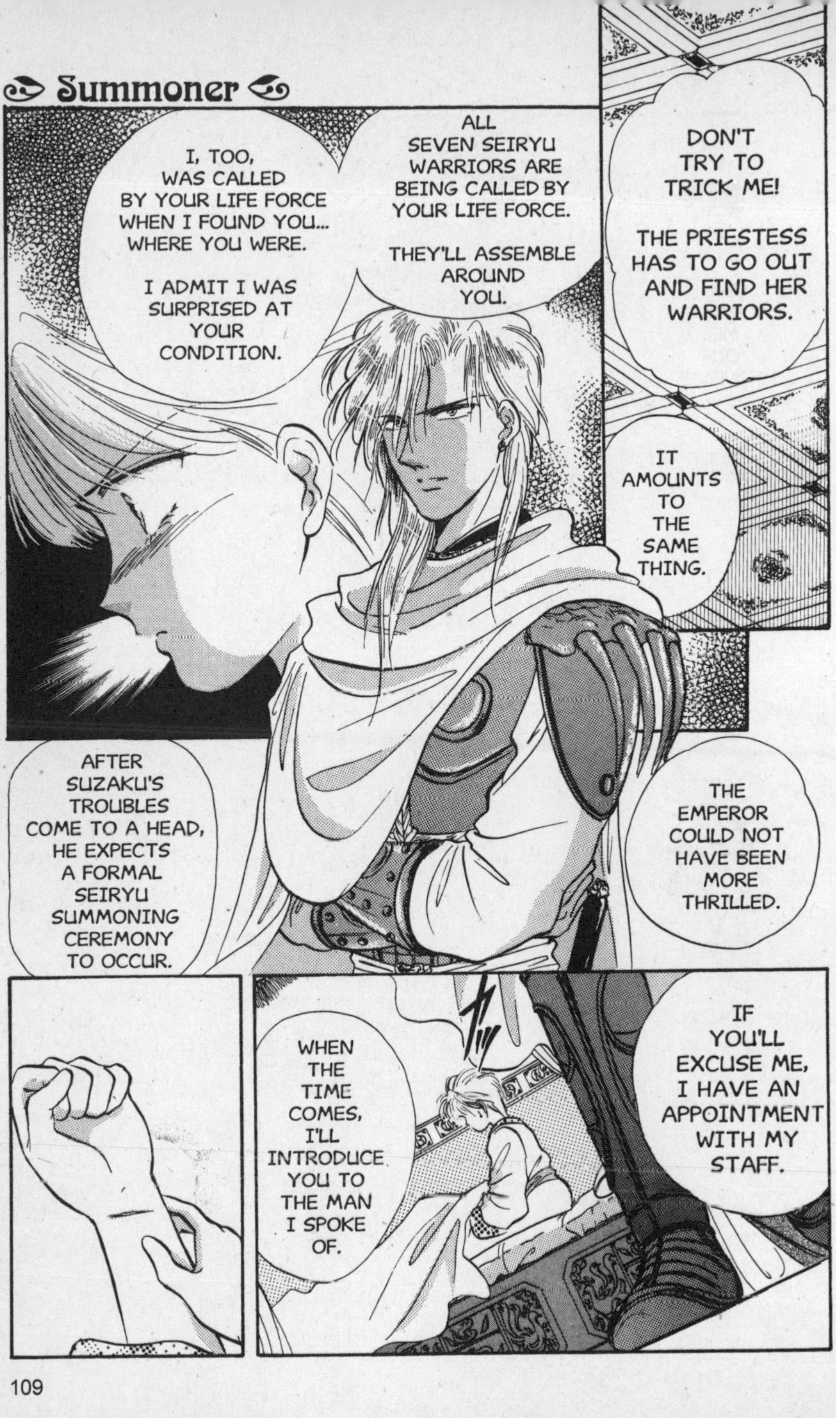
I, TOO, WAS CALLED BY YOUR LIFE FORCE WHEN I FOUND YOU... WHERE YOU WERE.
I ADMIT I WAS SURPRISED AT YOUR CONDITION.
ALL SEVEN SEIRYU WARRIORS ARE BEING CALLED BY YOUR LIFE FORCE.
THEY'LL ASSEMBLE AROUND YOU.
DON'T TRY TO TRICK ME!
THE PRIESTESS HAS TO GO OUT AND FIND HER WARRIORS.
IT AMOUNTS TO THE SAME THING.
AFTER SUZAKU'S TROUBLES COME TO A HEAD, HE EXPECTS A FORMAL SEIRYU SUMMONING CEREMONY TO OCCUR.
THE EMPEROR COULD NOT HAVE BEEN MORE THRILLED.
WHEN THE TIME COMES, I'LL INTRODUCE YOU TO THE MAN I SPOKE OF.
IF YOU'LL EXCUSE ME, I HAVE AN APPOINTMENT WITH MY STAFF.

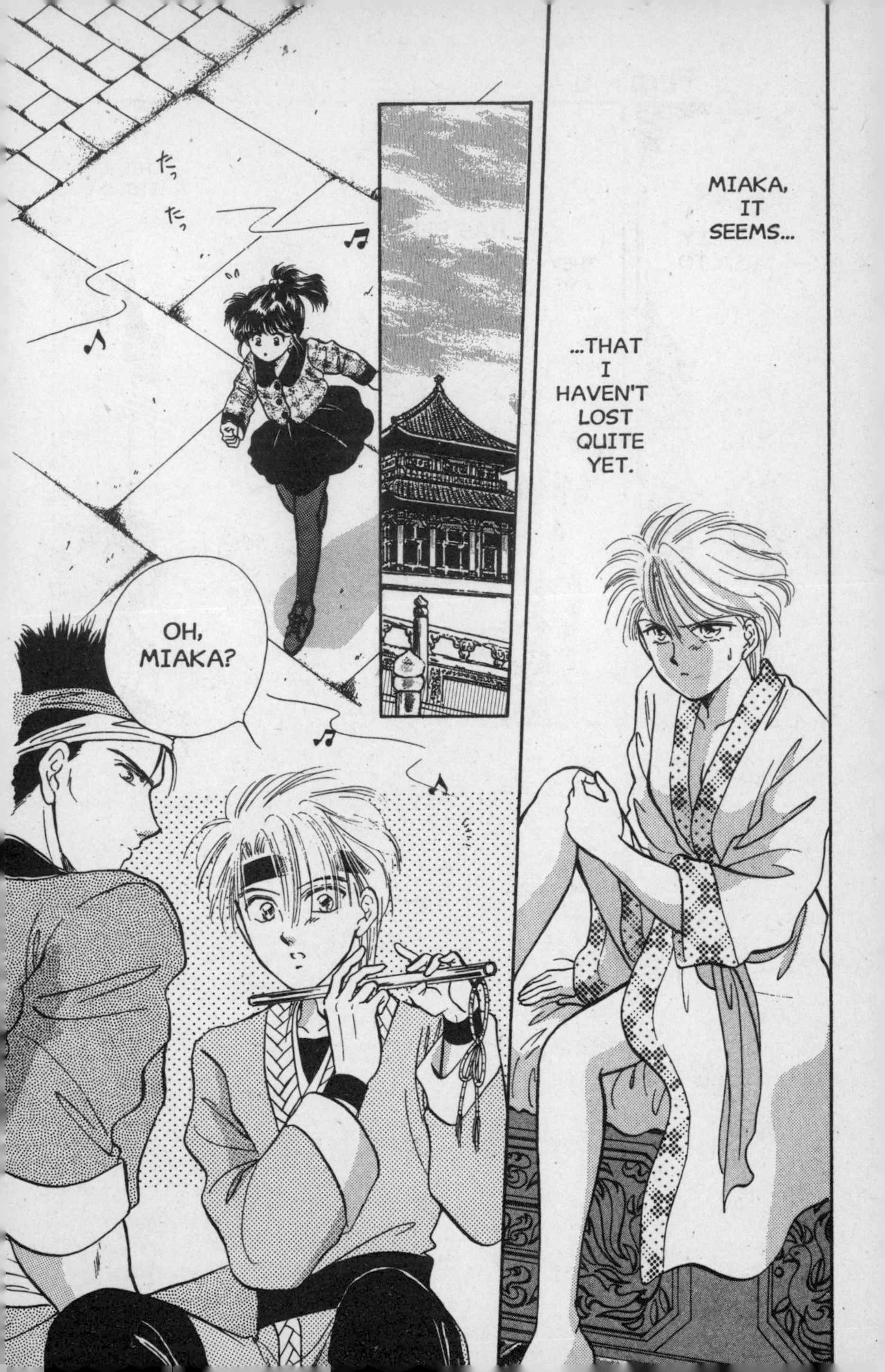
MIAKA, IT SEEMS...
...THAT I HAVEN'T LOST QUITE YET.
たっ
たっ
OH, MIAKA?

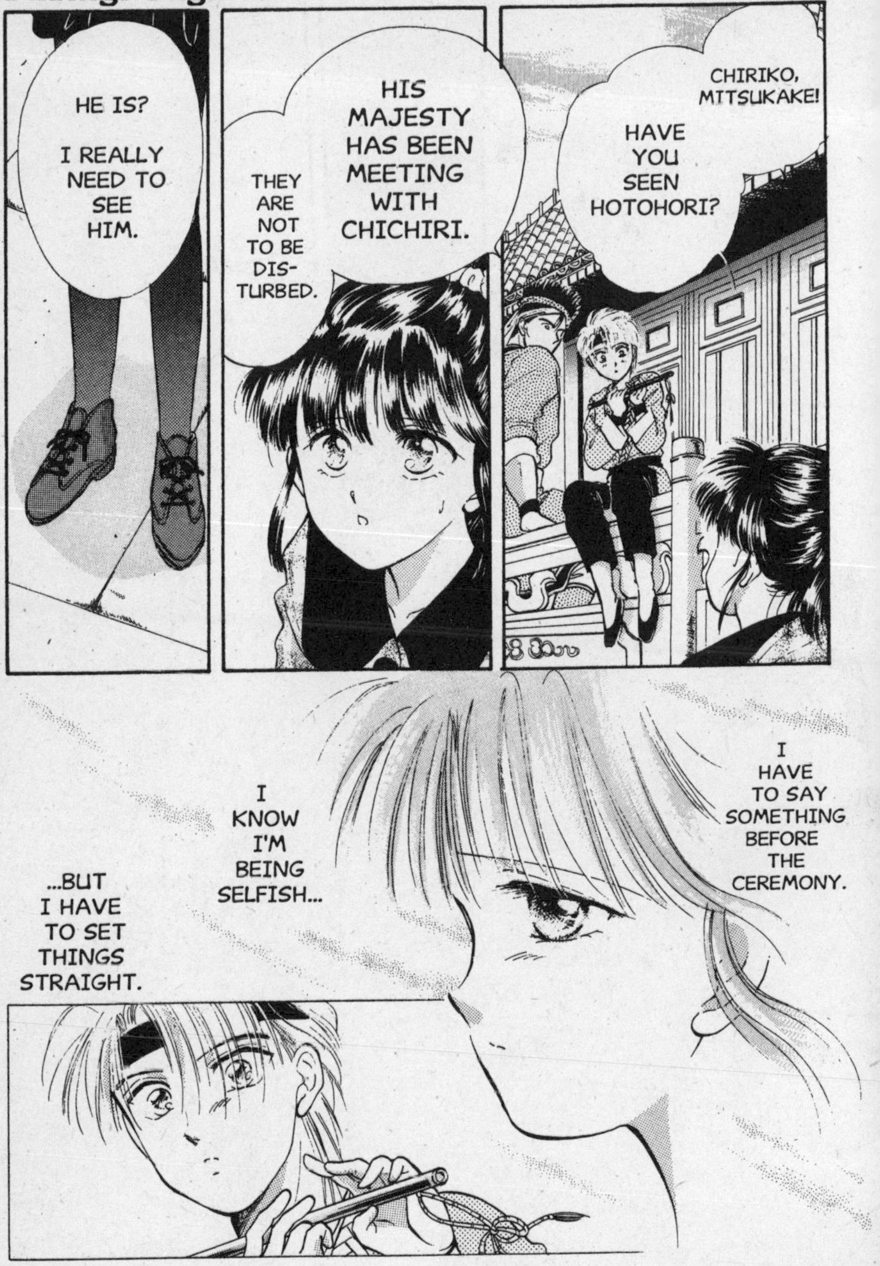
CHIRIKO, MITSUKAKE!
HAVE YOU SEEN HOTOHORI?
HIS MAJESTY HAS BEEN MEETING WITH CHICHIRI.
THEY ARE NOT TO BE DIS-TURBED.
HE IS?
I REALLY NEED TO SEE HIM.
I HAVE TO SAY SOMETHING BEFORE THE CEREMONY.
I KNOW I'M BEING SELFISH...
...BUT I HAVE TO SET THINGS STRAIGHT.

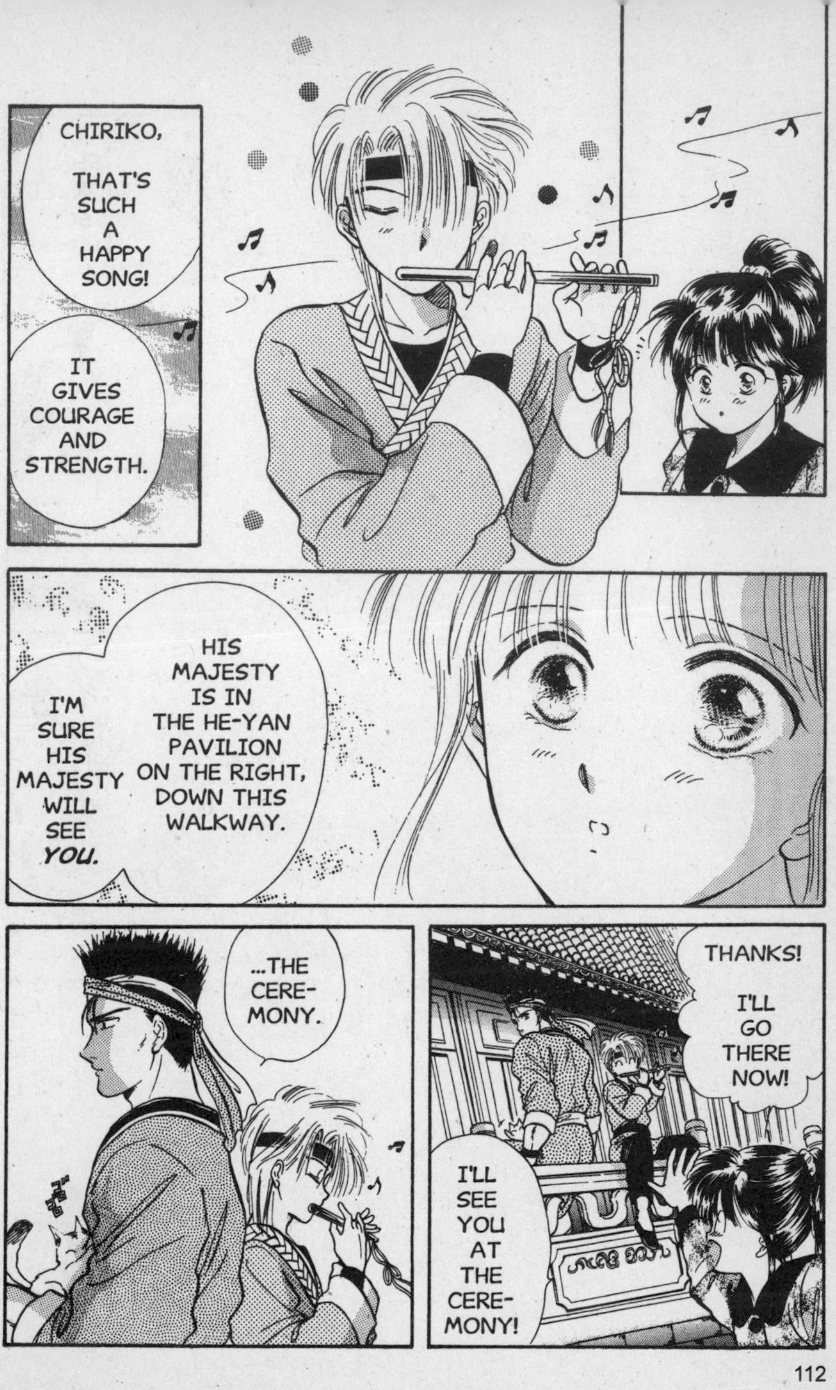
CHIRIKO, THAT'S SUCH A HAPPY SONG!
IT GIVES COURAGE AND STRENGTH.
HIS MAJESTY IS IN THE HE-YAN PAVILION ON THE RIGHT, DOWN THIS WALKWAY.
I'M SURE HIS MAJESTY WILL SEE *YOU.*
THANKS! I'LL GO THERE NOW!
I'LL SEE YOU AT THE CERE-MONY!
...THE CERE-MONY.

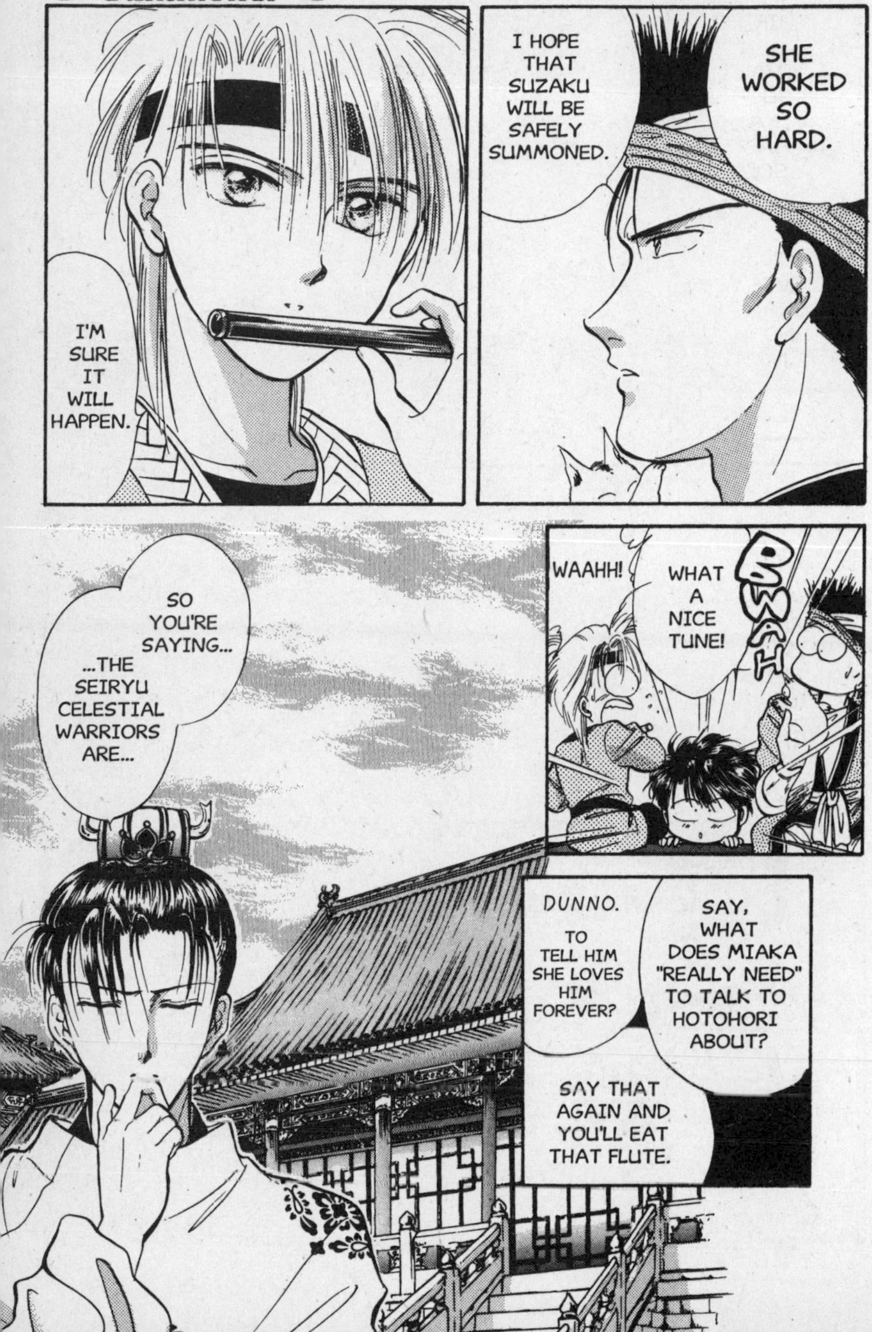
SHE WORKED SO HARD.
I HOPE THAT SUZAKU WILL BE SAFELY SUMMONED.
I'M SURE IT WILL HAPPEN.
WHAT A NICE TUNE!
WAAHH!
BWAH
SAY, WHAT DOES MIAKA "REALLY NEED" TO TALK TO HOTOHORI ABOUT?
DUNNO.
TO TELL HIM SHE LOVES HIM FOREVER?
SAY THAT AGAIN AND YOU'LL EAT THAT FLUTE.
SO YOU'RE SAYING...
...THE SEIRYU CELESTIAL WARRIORS ARE...

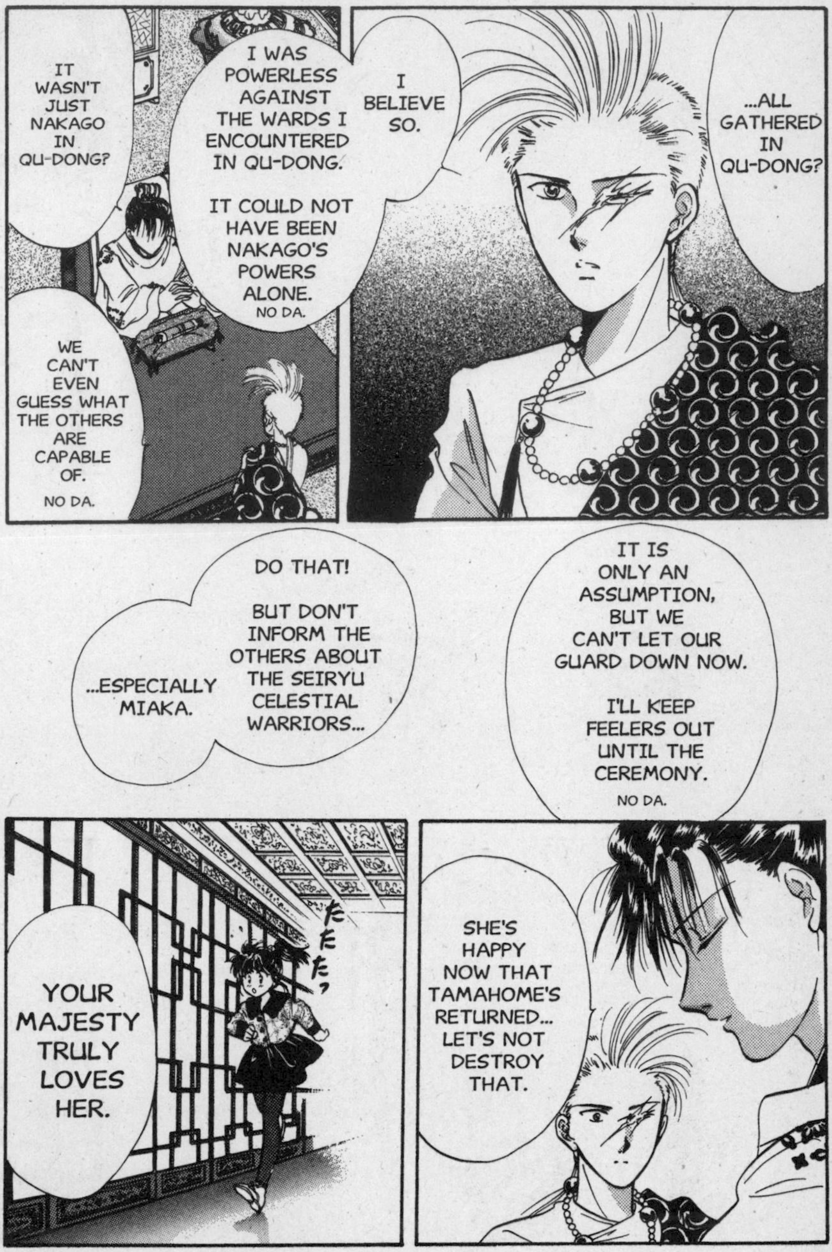
...ALL GATHERED IN QU-DONG?
I BELIEVE SO.
I WAS POWERLESS AGAINST THE WARDS I ENCOUNTERED IN QU-DONG. IT COULD NOT HAVE BEEN NAKAGO'S POWERS ALONE. NO DA.
IT WASN'T JUST NAKAGO IN QU-DONG?
WE CAN'T EVEN GUESS WHAT THE OTHERS ARE CAPABLE OF. NO DA.
IT IS ONLY AN ASSUMPTION, BUT WE CAN'T LET OUR GUARD DOWN NOW. I'LL KEEP FEELERS OUT UNTIL THE CEREMONY. NO DA.
DO THAT! BUT DON'T INFORM THE OTHERS ABOUT THE SEIRYU CELESTIAL WARRIORS...
...ESPECIALLY MIAKA.
SHE'S HAPPY NOW THAT TAMAHOME'S RETURNED... LET'S NOT DESTROY THAT.
たたたっ
YOUR MAJESTY TRULY LOVES HER.

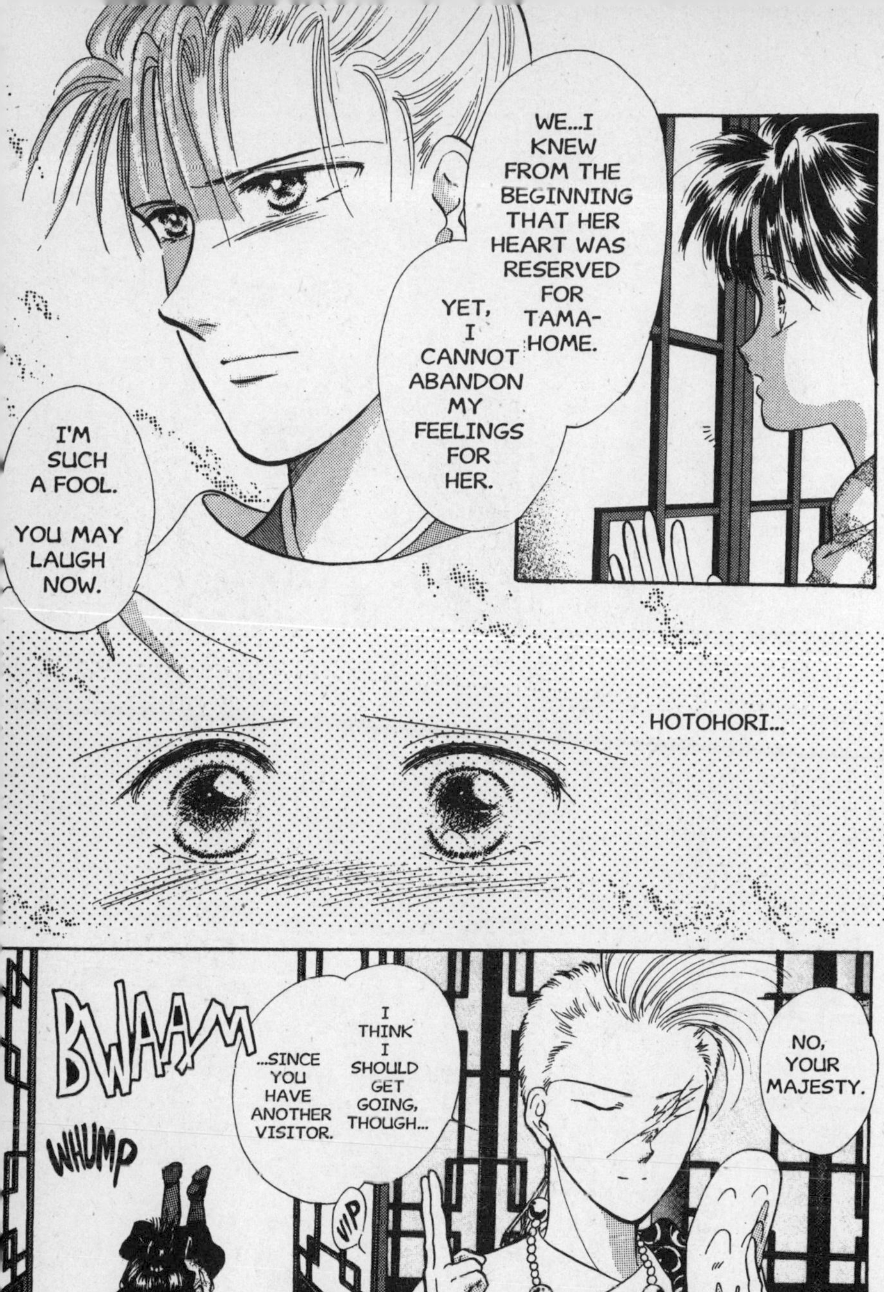
WE...I KNEW FROM THE BEGINNING THAT HER HEART WAS RESERVED FOR TAMA-HOME.
YET, I CANNOT ABANDON MY FEELINGS FOR HER.
I'M SUCH A FOOL.
YOU MAY LAUGH NOW.
HOTOHORI...
NO, YOUR MAJESTY.
I THINK I SHOULD GET GOING, THOUGH...
...SINCE YOU HAVE ANOTHER VISITOR.
YIP
BWAAM
WHUMP

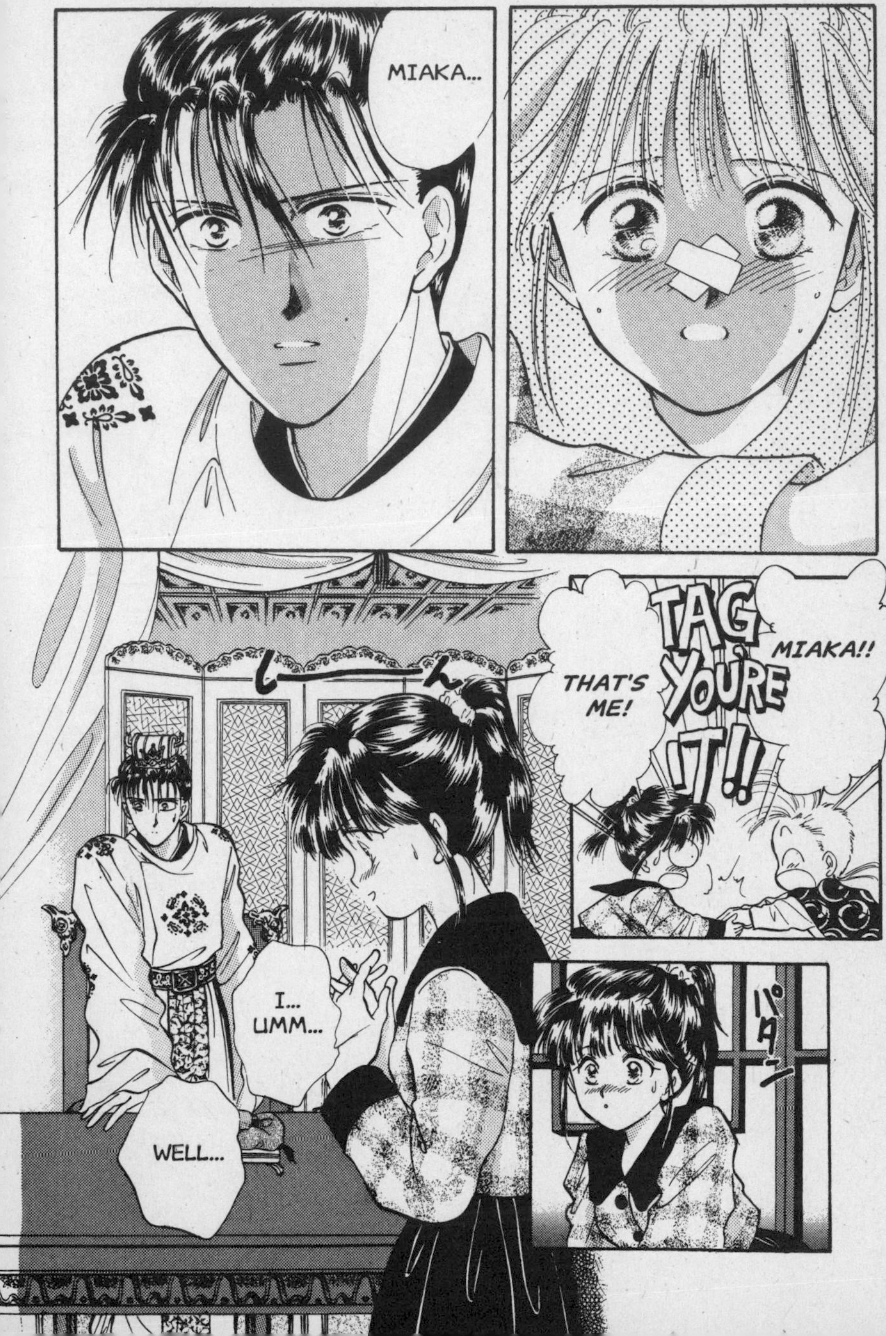
MIAKA...
MIAKA!!
TAG YOU'RE IT!!
THAT'S ME!
パタン
しーん
I... UMM...
WELL...

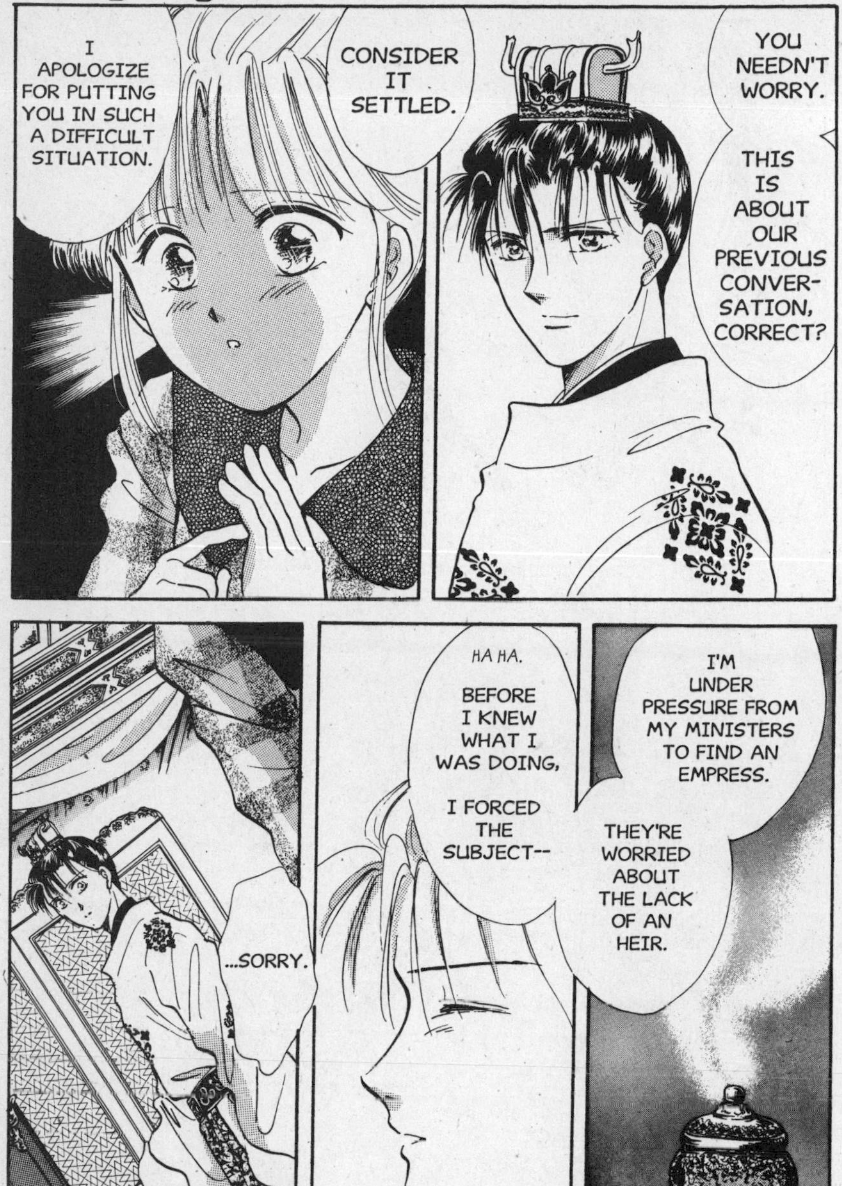
YOU NEEDN'T WORRY.
THIS IS ABOUT OUR PREVIOUS CONVERSATION, CORRECT?
CONSIDER IT SETTLED.
I APOLOGIZE FOR PUTTING YOU IN SUCH A DIFFICULT SITUATION.
I'M UNDER PRESSURE FROM MY MINISTERS TO FIND AN EMPRESS.
THEY'RE WORRIED ABOUT THE LACK OF AN HEIR.
HA HA.
BEFORE I KNEW WHAT I WAS DOING,
I FORCED THE SUBJECT--
...SORRY.

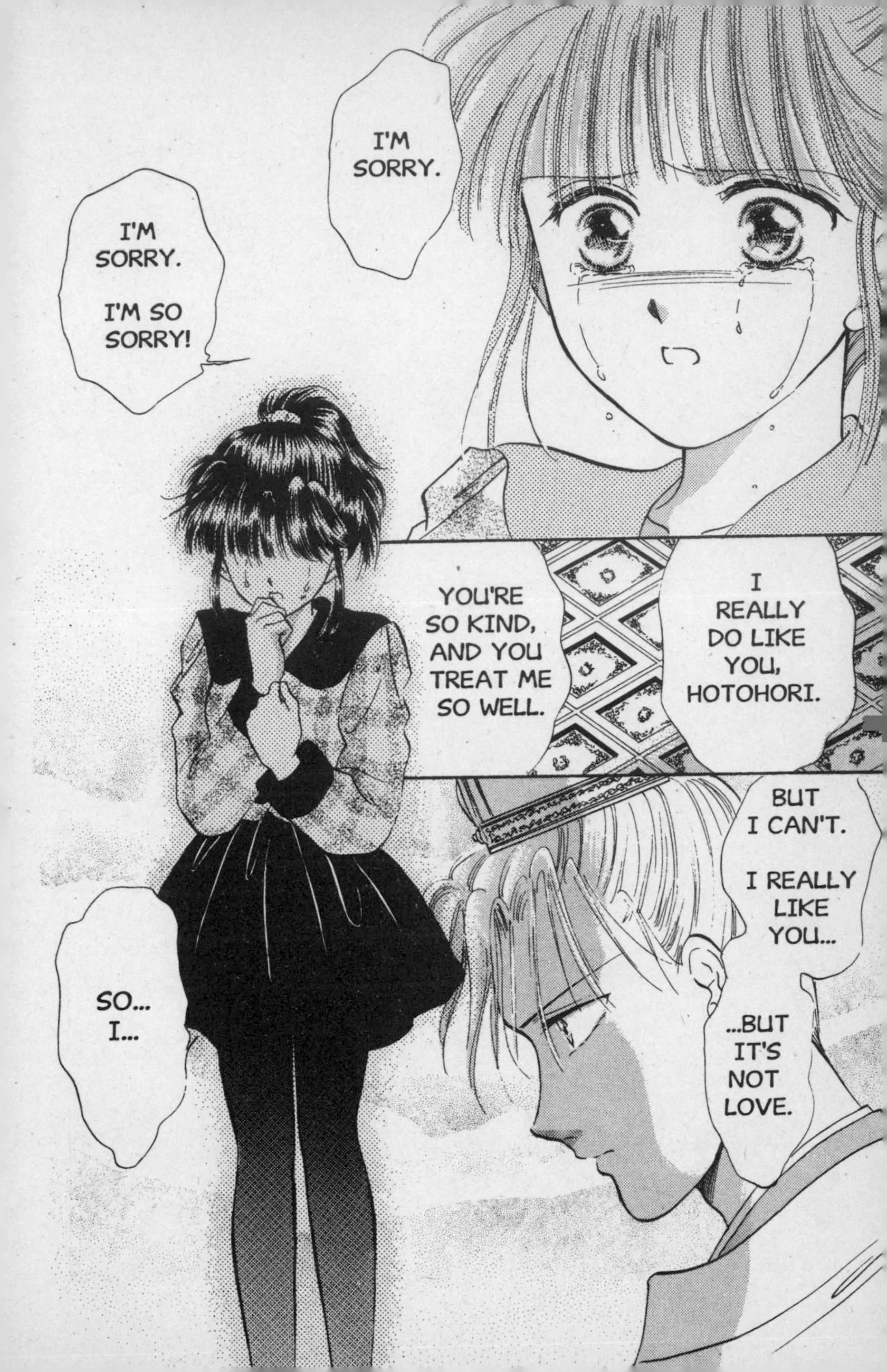
I'M SORRY.
I'M SORRY. I'M SO SORRY!
I REALLY DO LIKE YOU, HOTOHORI.
YOU'RE SO KIND, AND YOU TREAT ME SO WELL.
BUT I CAN'T. I REALLY LIKE YOU...
...BUT IT'S NOT LOVE.
SO... I...

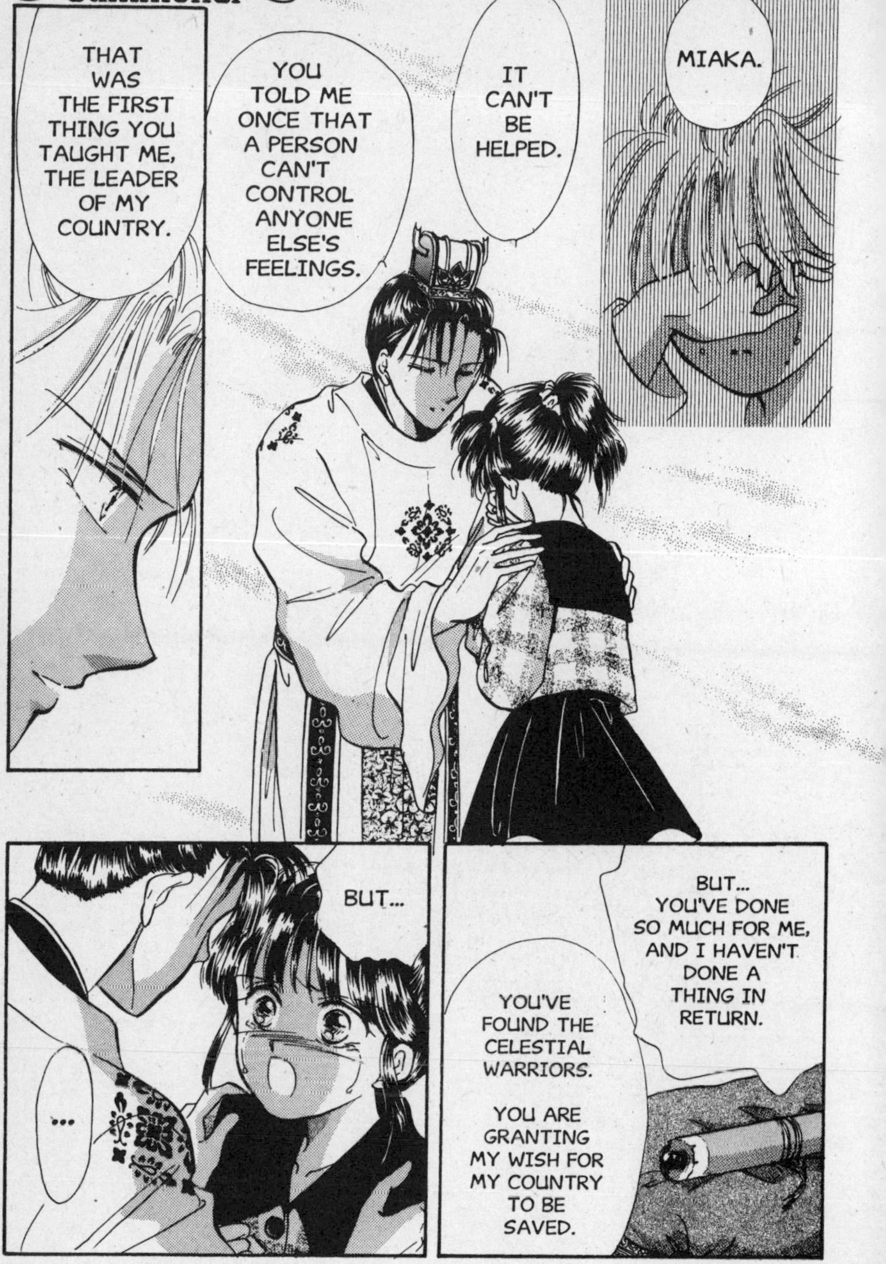
MIAKA.
IT CAN'T BE HELPED.
YOU TOLD ME ONCE THAT A PERSON CAN'T CONTROL ANYONE ELSE'S FEELINGS.
THAT WAS THE FIRST THING YOU TAUGHT ME, THE LEADER OF MY COUNTRY.
BUT... YOU'VE DONE SO MUCH FOR ME, AND I HAVEN'T DONE A THING IN RETURN.
YOU'VE FOUND THE CELESTIAL WARRIORS.
YOU ARE GRANTING MY WISH FOR MY COUNTRY TO BE SAVED.
BUT...
...

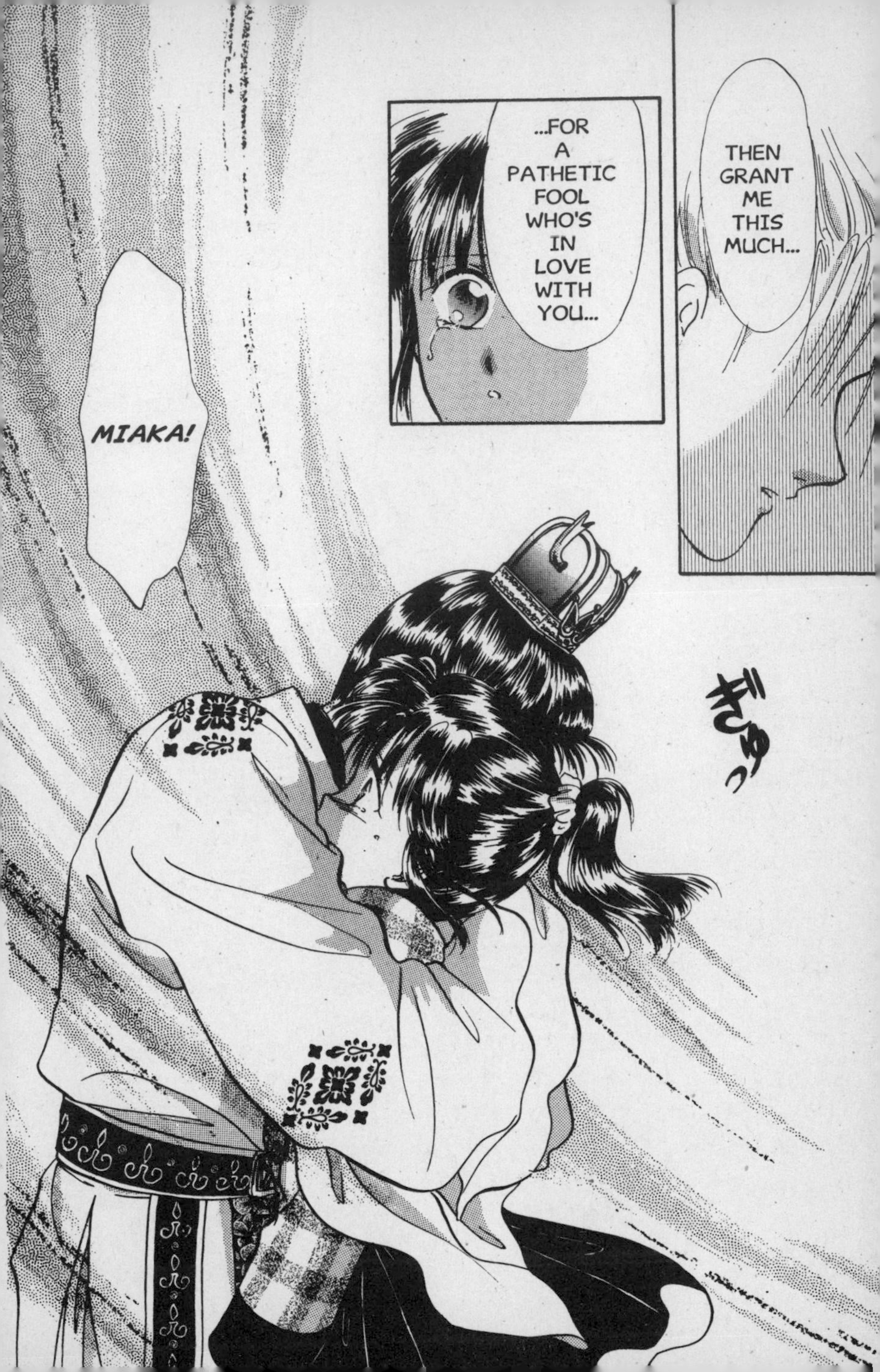
THEN GRANT ME THIS MUCH...
...FOR A PATHETIC FOOL WHO'S IN LOVE WITH YOU...
MIAKA!
ぎゅっ

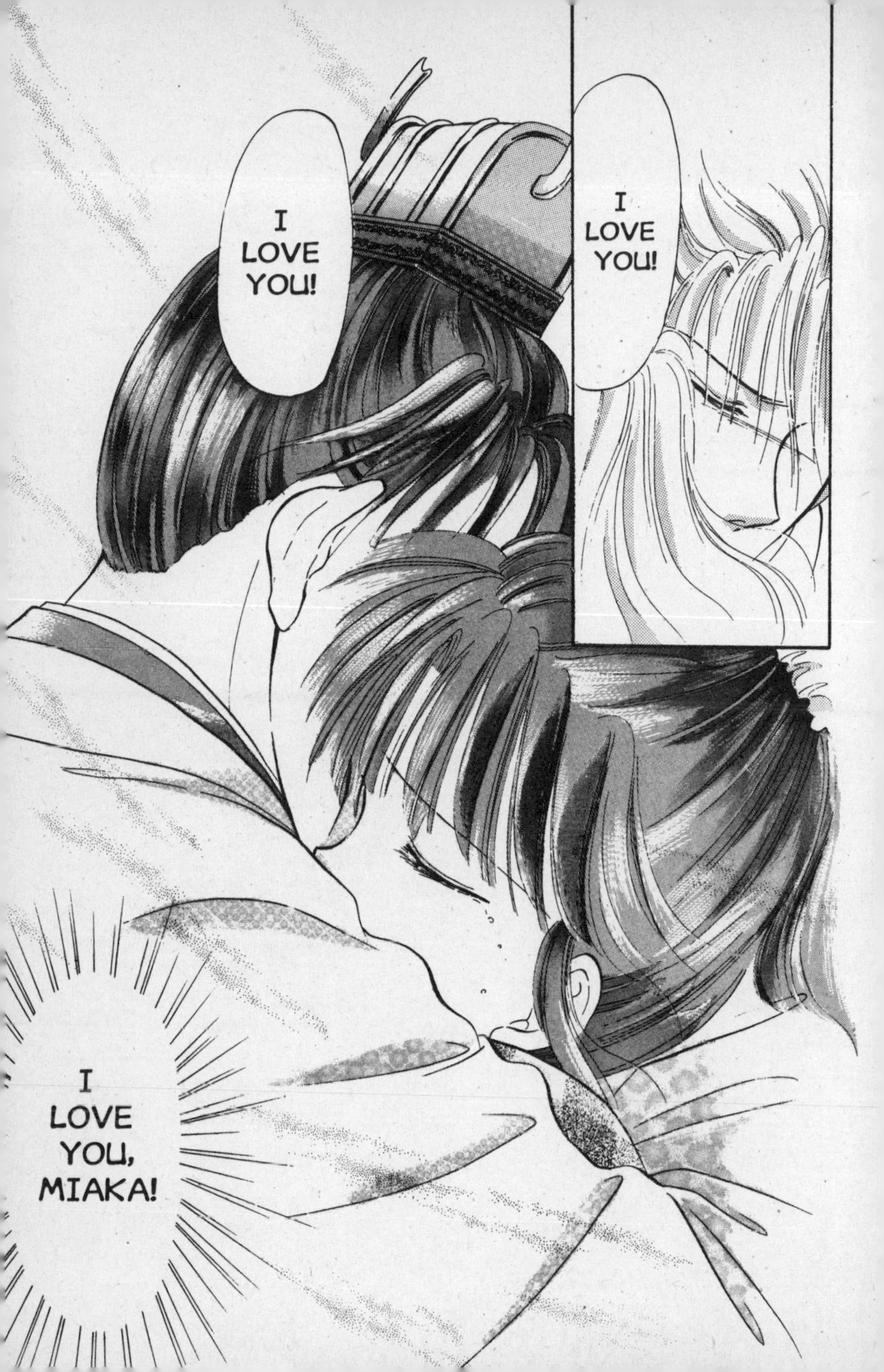
I LOVE YOU!
I LOVE YOU!
I LOVE YOU, MIAKA!

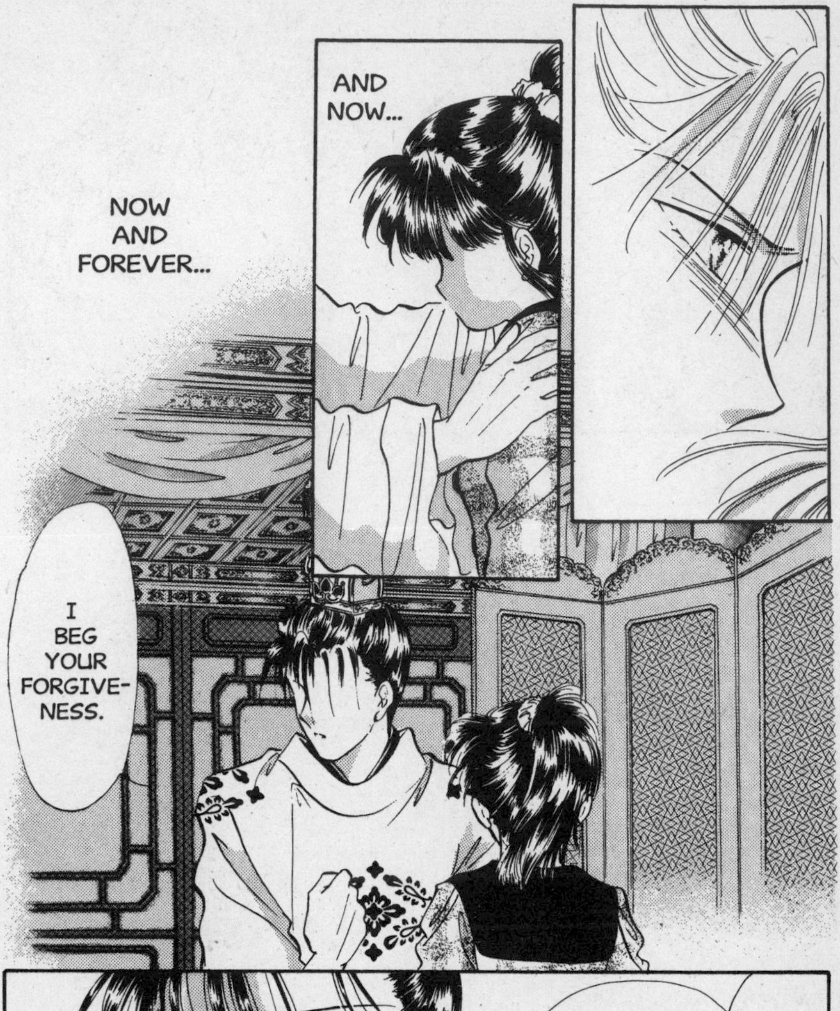
AND NOW...
NOW AND FOREVER...
I BEG YOUR FORGIVENESS.
PLEASE...
THE TIME OF THE CEREMONY IS APPROACHING.
GO JOIN TAMAHOME AND THE OTHERS AT THE SUZAKU SHRINE.

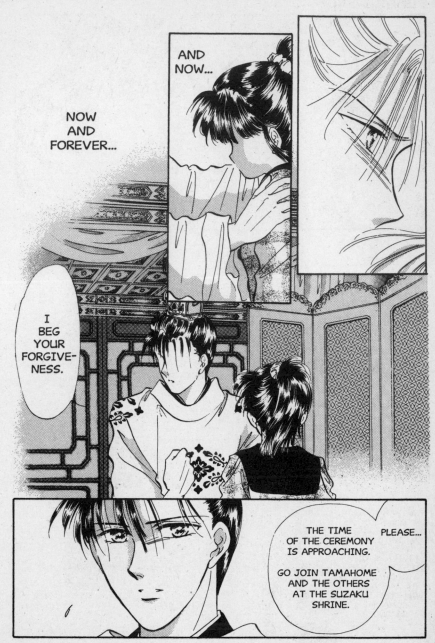

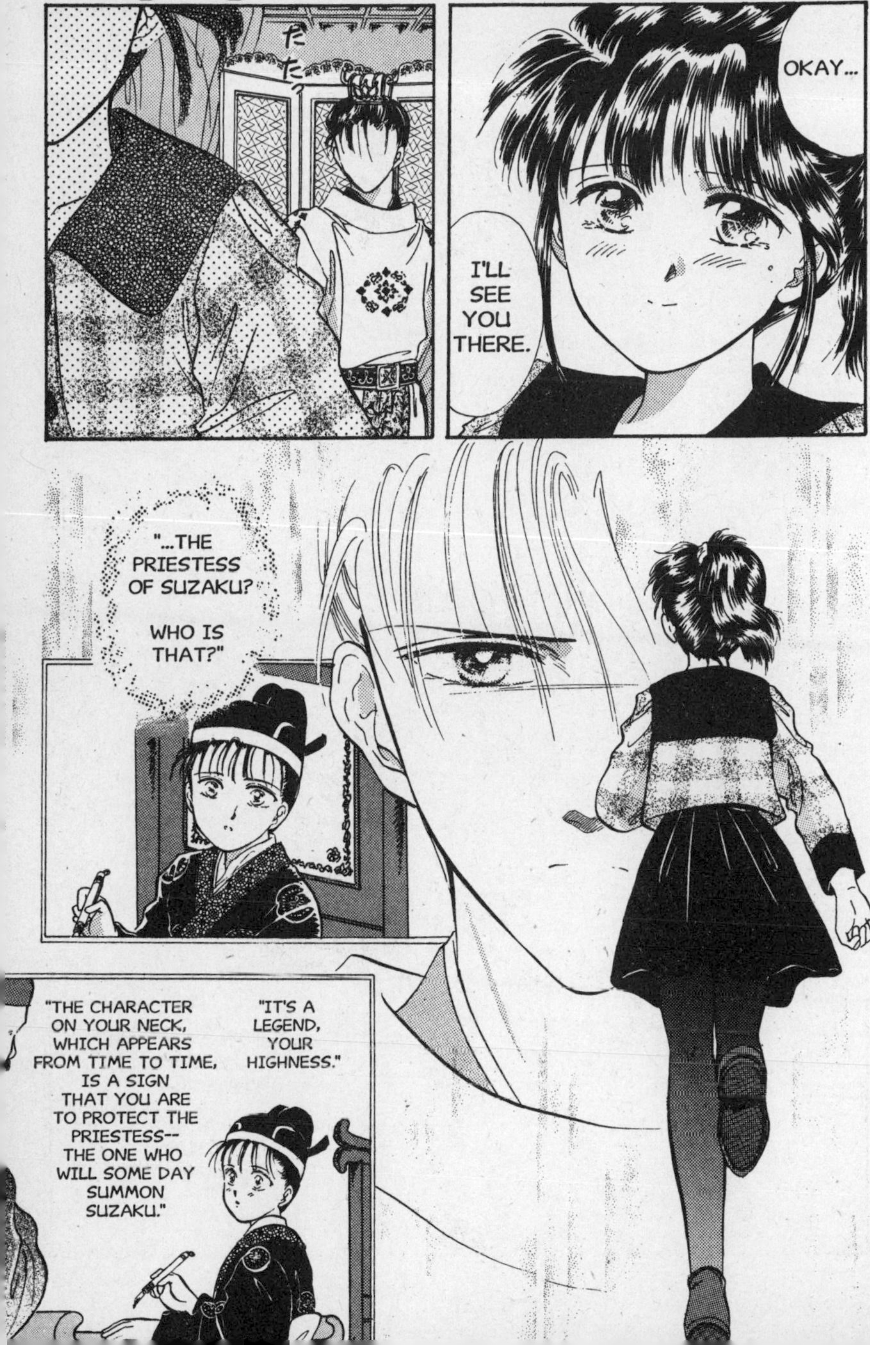
OKAY...
I'LL SEE YOU THERE.
たたっ
"...THE PRIESTESS OF SUZAKU?
WHO IS THAT?"
"IT'S A LEGEND, YOUR HIGHNESS."
"THE CHARACTER ON YOUR NECK, WHICH APPEARS FROM TIME TO TIME, IS A SIGN THAT YOU ARE TO PROTECT THE PRIESTESS-- THE ONE WHO WILL SOME DAY SUMMON SUZAKU."

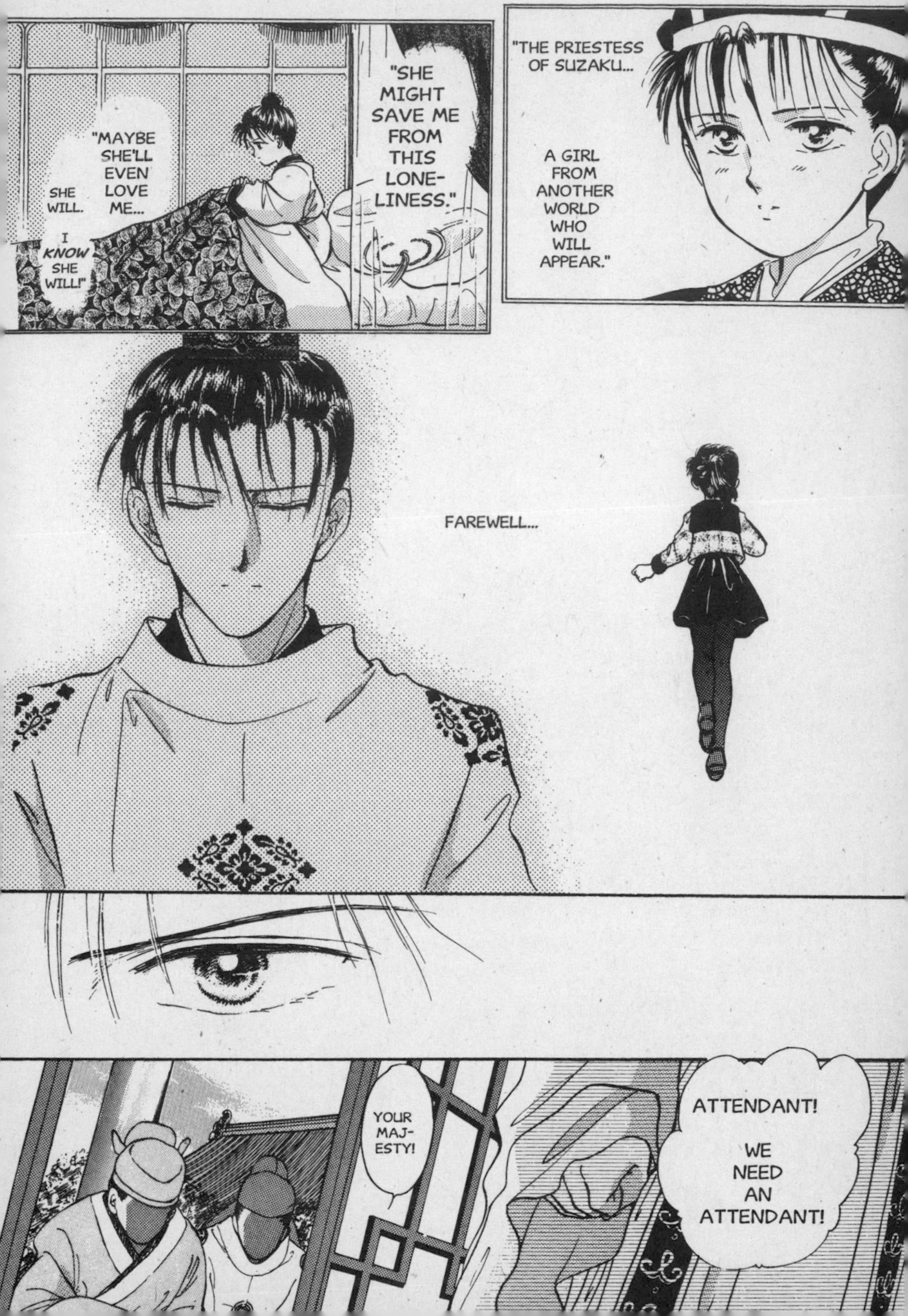
"THE PRIESTESS OF SUZAKU...
A GIRL FROM ANOTHER WORLD WHO WILL APPEAR."
"SHE MIGHT SAVE ME FROM THIS LONE-LINESS."
"MAYBE SHE'LL EVEN LOVE ME...
SHE WILL.
I *KNOW* SHE WILL!"
FAREWELL...
ATTENDANT!
WE NEED AN ATTENDANT!
YOUR MAJ-ESTY!

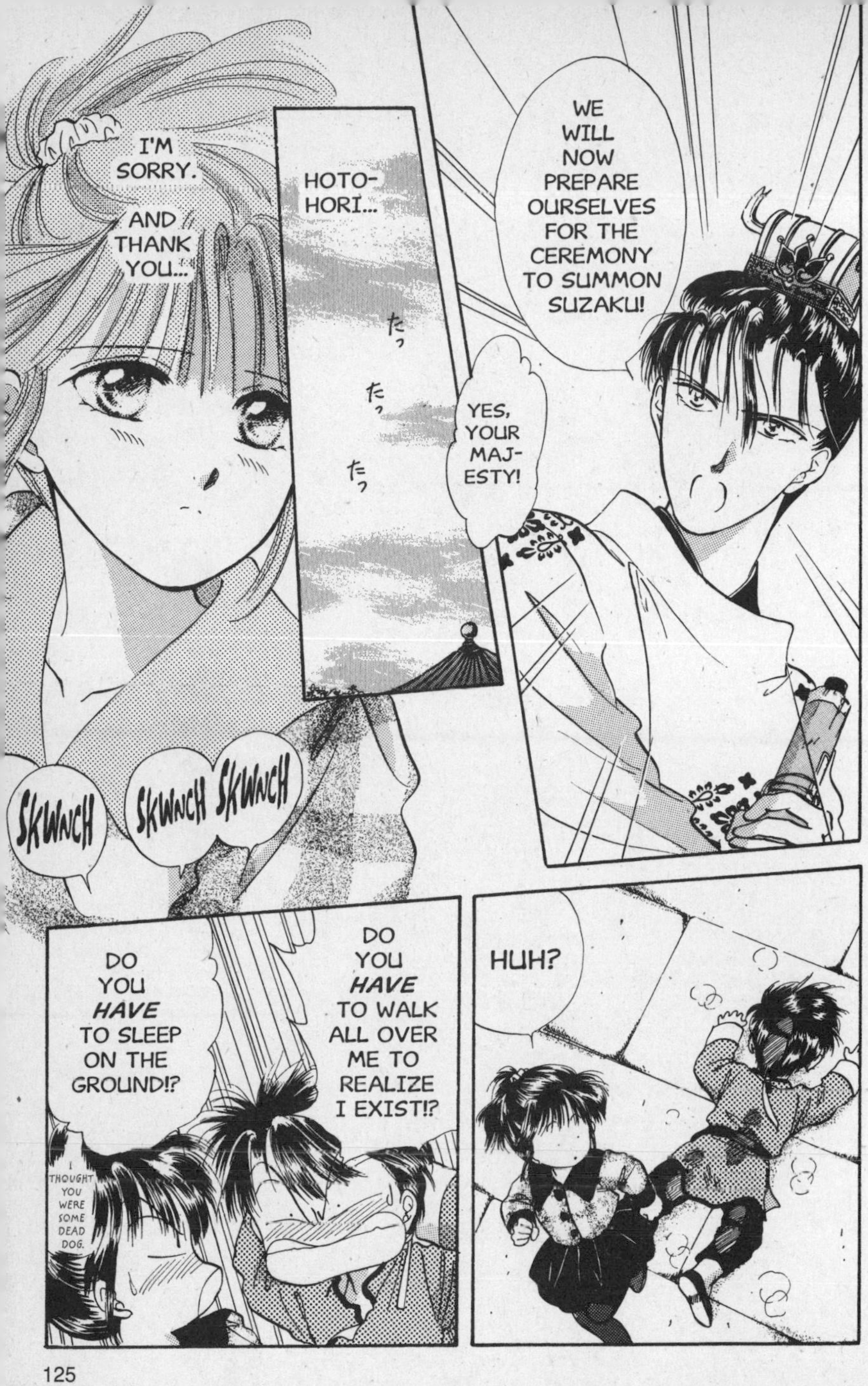
WE WILL NOW PREPARE OURSELVES FOR THE CEREMONY TO SUMMON SUZAKU!
YES, YOUR MAJ-ESTY!
HOTO-HORI...
たっ
たっ
たっ
I'M SORRY.
AND THANK YOU...
SKWNCH
SKWNCH
SKWNCH
HUH?
DO YOU *HAVE* TO WALK ALL OVER ME TO REALIZE I EXIST!?
DO YOU *HAVE* TO SLEEP ON THE GROUND!?
I THOUGHT YOU WERE SOME DEAD DOG.

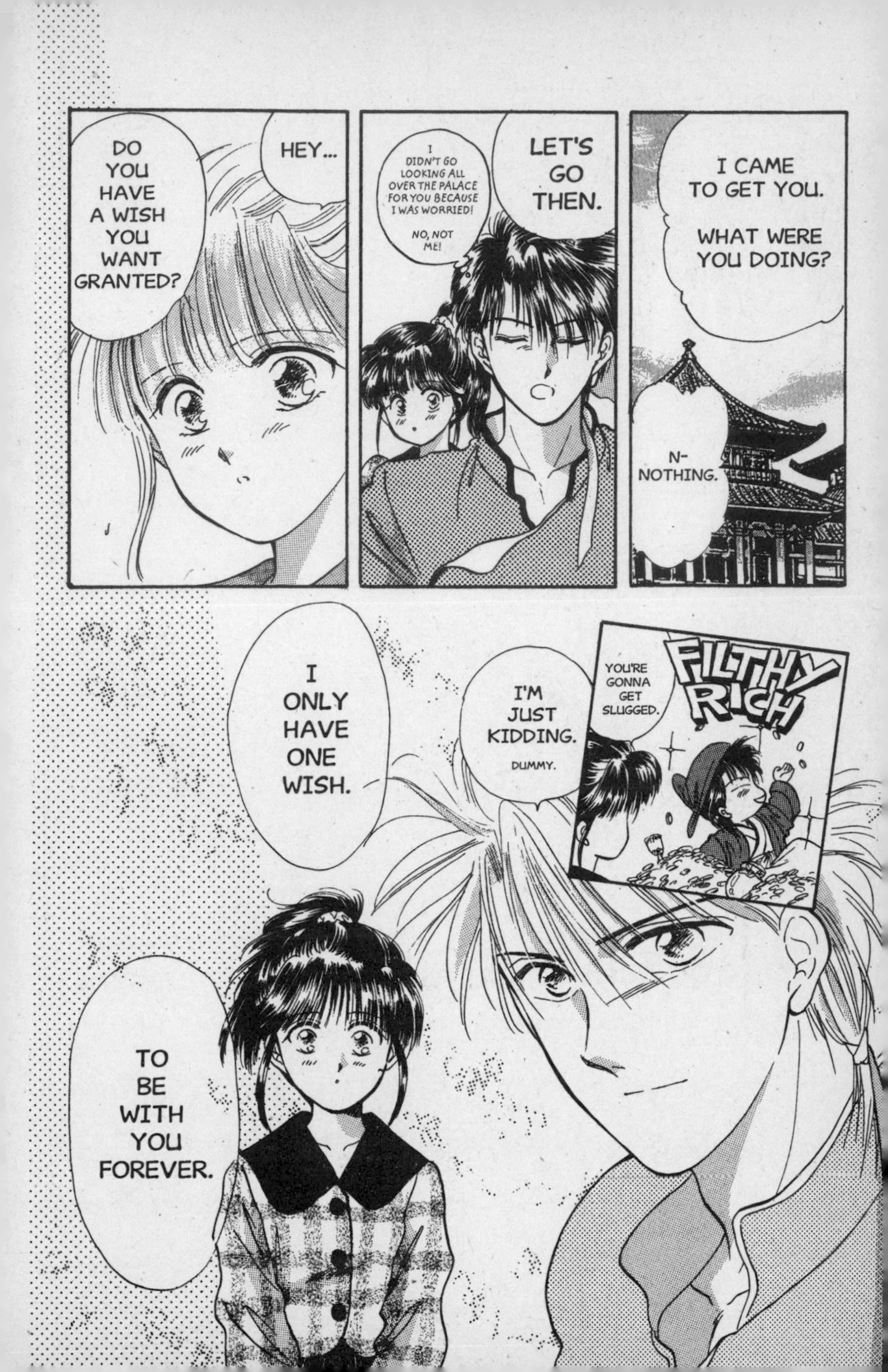
I CAME TO GET YOU.
WHAT WERE YOU DOING?
N-NOTHING.
LET'S GO THEN.
I DIDN'T GO LOOKING ALL OVER THE PALACE FOR YOU BECAUSE I WAS WORRIED!
NO, NOT ME!
HEY...
DO YOU HAVE A WISH YOU WANT GRANTED?
FILTHY RICH
YOU'RE GONNA GET SLUGGED.
I'M JUST KIDDING.
DUMMY.
I ONLY HAVE ONE WISH.
TO BE WITH YOU FOREVER.

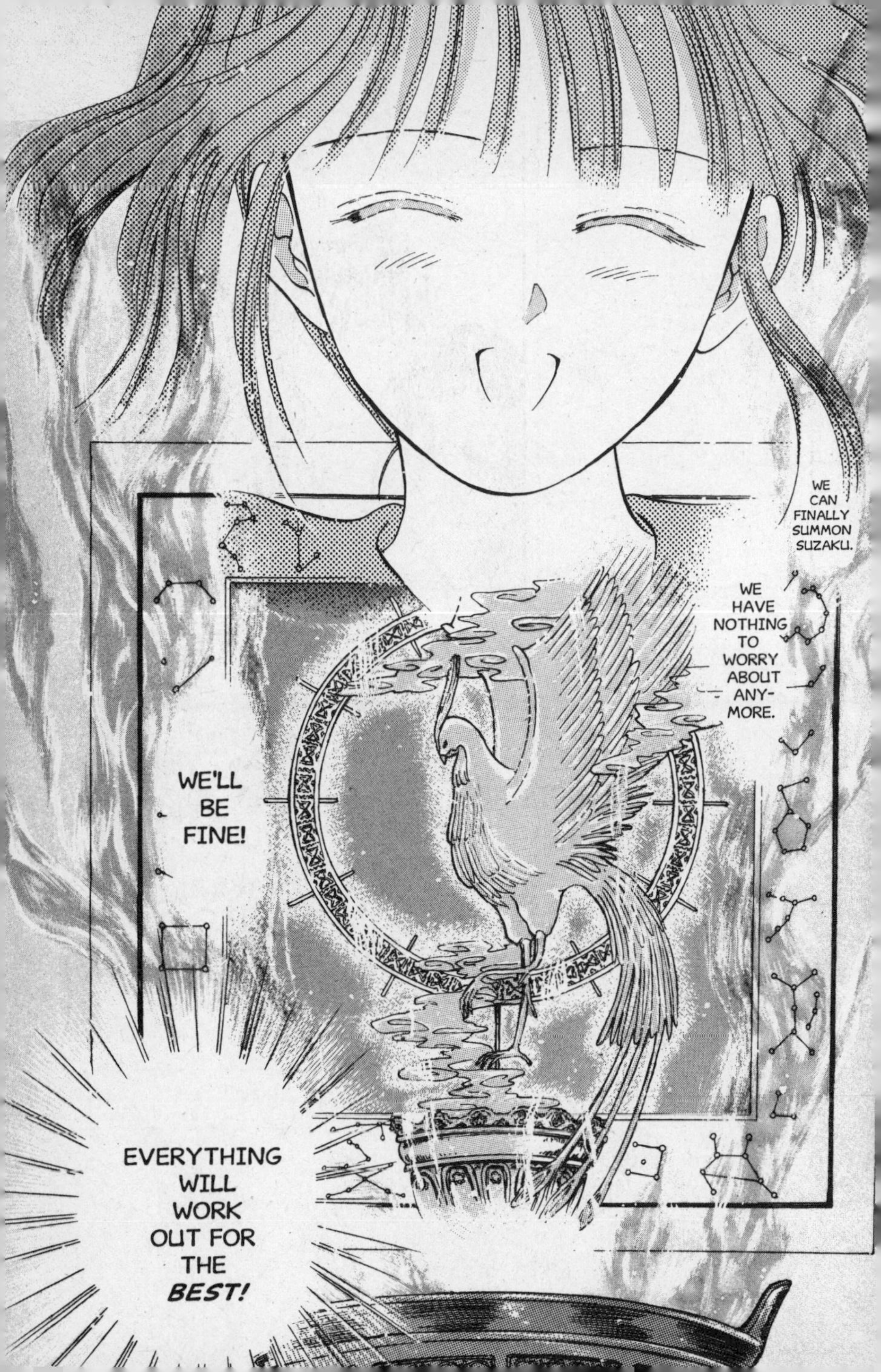
WE CAN FINALLY SUMMON SUZAKU.
WE HAVE NOTHING TO WORRY ABOUT ANY-MORE.
WE'LL BE FINE!
EVERYTHING WILL WORK OUT FOR THE *BEST!*

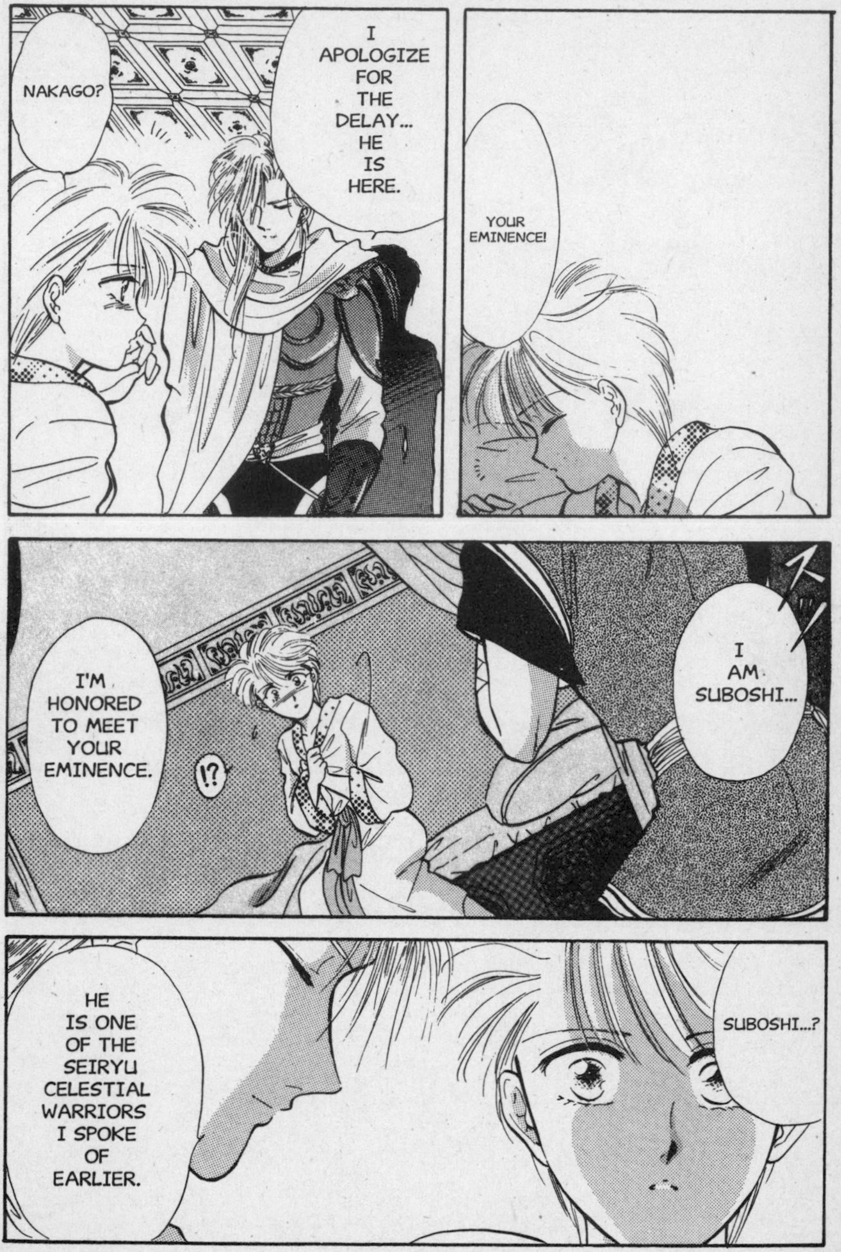
NAKAGO?
I APOLOGIZE FOR THE DELAY... HE IS HERE.
YOUR EMINENCE!
I'M HONORED TO MEET YOUR EMINENCE.
!?
I AM SUBOSHI...
HE IS ONE OF THE SEIRYU CELESTIAL WARRIORS I SPOKE OF EARLIER.
SUBOSHI...?

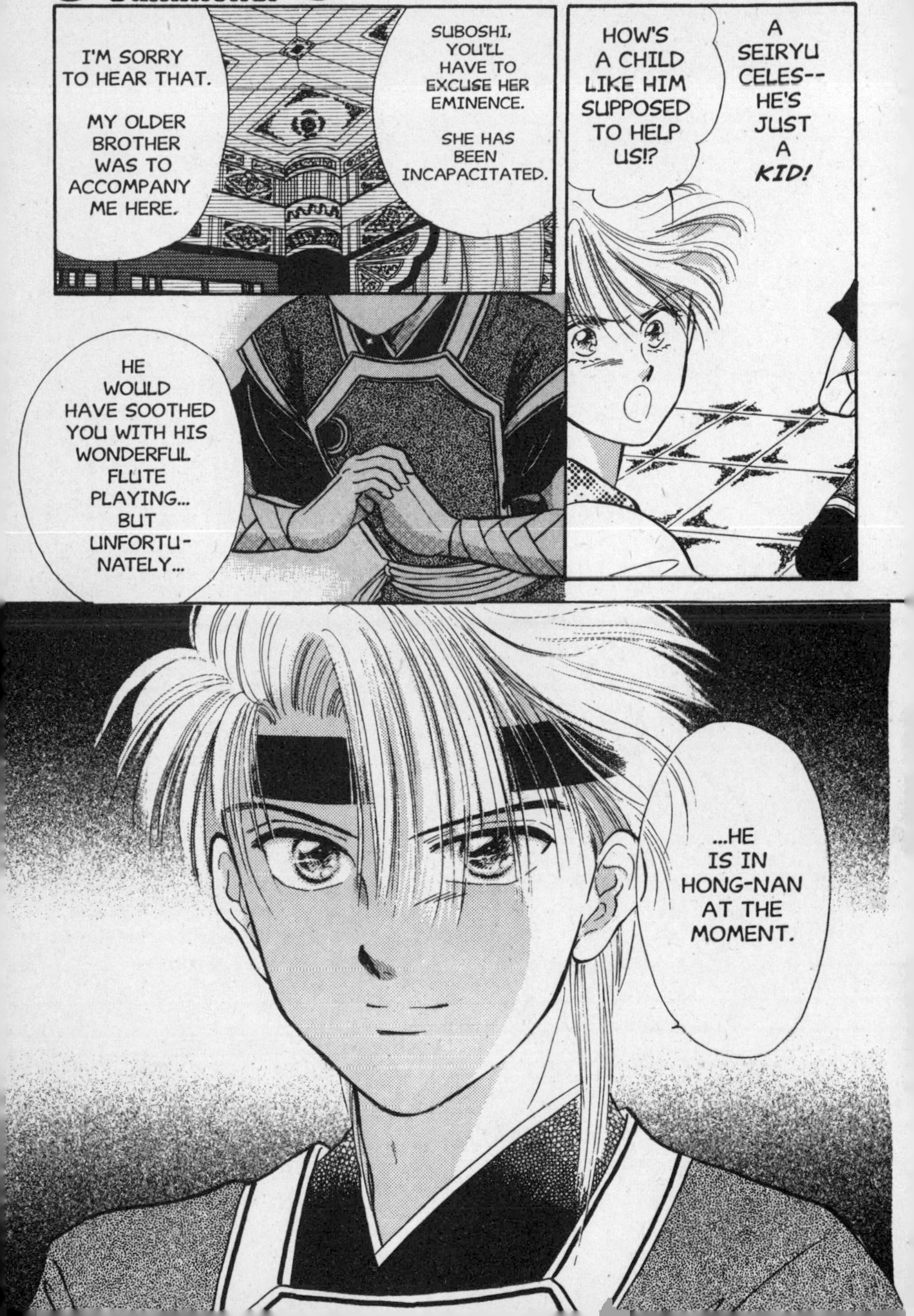
A SEIRYU CELES-- HE'S JUST A KID!
HOW'S A CHILD LIKE HIM SUPPOSED TO HELP US!?
SUBOSHI, YOU'LL HAVE TO EXCUSE HER EMINENCE. SHE HAS BEEN INCAPACITATED.
I'M SORRY TO HEAR THAT. MY OLDER BROTHER WAS TO ACCOMPANY ME HERE.
HE WOULD HAVE SOOTHED YOU WITH HIS WONDERFUL FLUTE PLAYING... BUT UNFORTU-NATELY...
...HE IS IN HONG-NAN AT THE MOMENT.

HOU CHUN YU HUAN LANG

侯俊宇（幻狼）

WHOOPS! I DREW THE KANJI IN BOLD! AWW, WHO'LL EVER NOTICE?

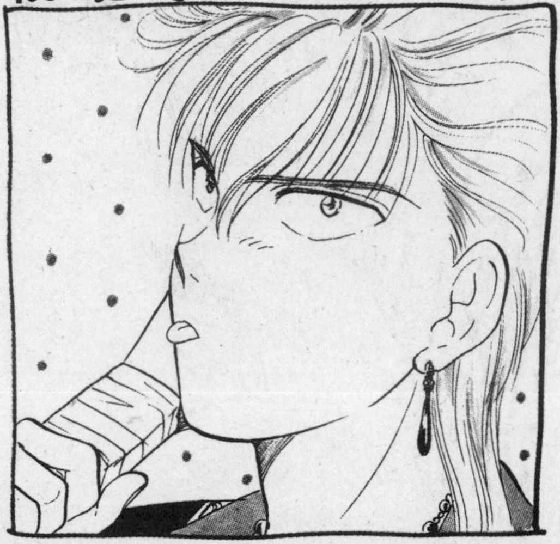

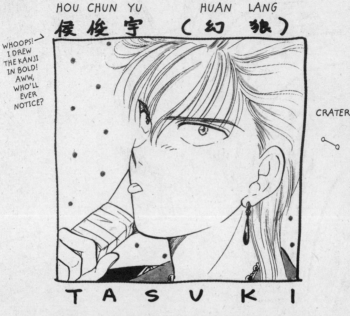

CRATER

SOMETHING OF A MYSTERY.

TASUKI

- Born in the town of Tai-Tou at the foot of Ligé-San Mountain in the prefecture of Ko.
- Age: 17.
- Family: Parents and five sisters--a house dominated by women. (It's thought that this is where his woman-hating tendencies started.)
- Hobby: Picking fights.
- Height: 5' 10". • Blood Type: B (naturally!).
- He's like a little boy who got bigger but no more mature. As a child he wasn't very brave. But when the chief bandit of Ligé-San Mountain took Tasuki under his wing, Tasuki found his calling. He started to improve his martial skills in order to be like--and carry on after--his mentor as the bandit leader. He also learned the use of the iron harisen. Now that he's left his close friend Knei-Gong as the bandit leader, Tasuki's gone off to help Miaka in her quests. Tasuki is too straightforward, simpleminded, and quick to pick a fight. Despite that, he is bound by chivalry, gets emotional easily, and is surprisingly shy. He puts on an overly macho act and will beat up on people, but he's probably the most "manly" of the group.

Umm... Rui-Ni hid in the shadows and listened while Tasuki learned the use of the iron harisen, and that's why he was able to use it. But nowadays, Tasuki is the only person in the world that can use it. It's so heavy!!

KNEI-GONG (19 years old) Knei-Gong took Tasuki's place as the bandit leader. In a way, he's something of a Tasuki hero-worshipper.

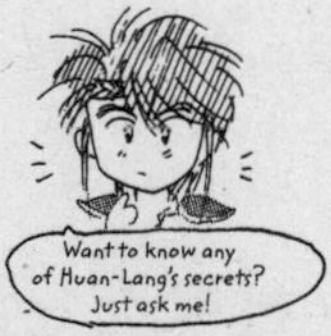
Want to know any of Huan-Lang's secrets? Just ask me!

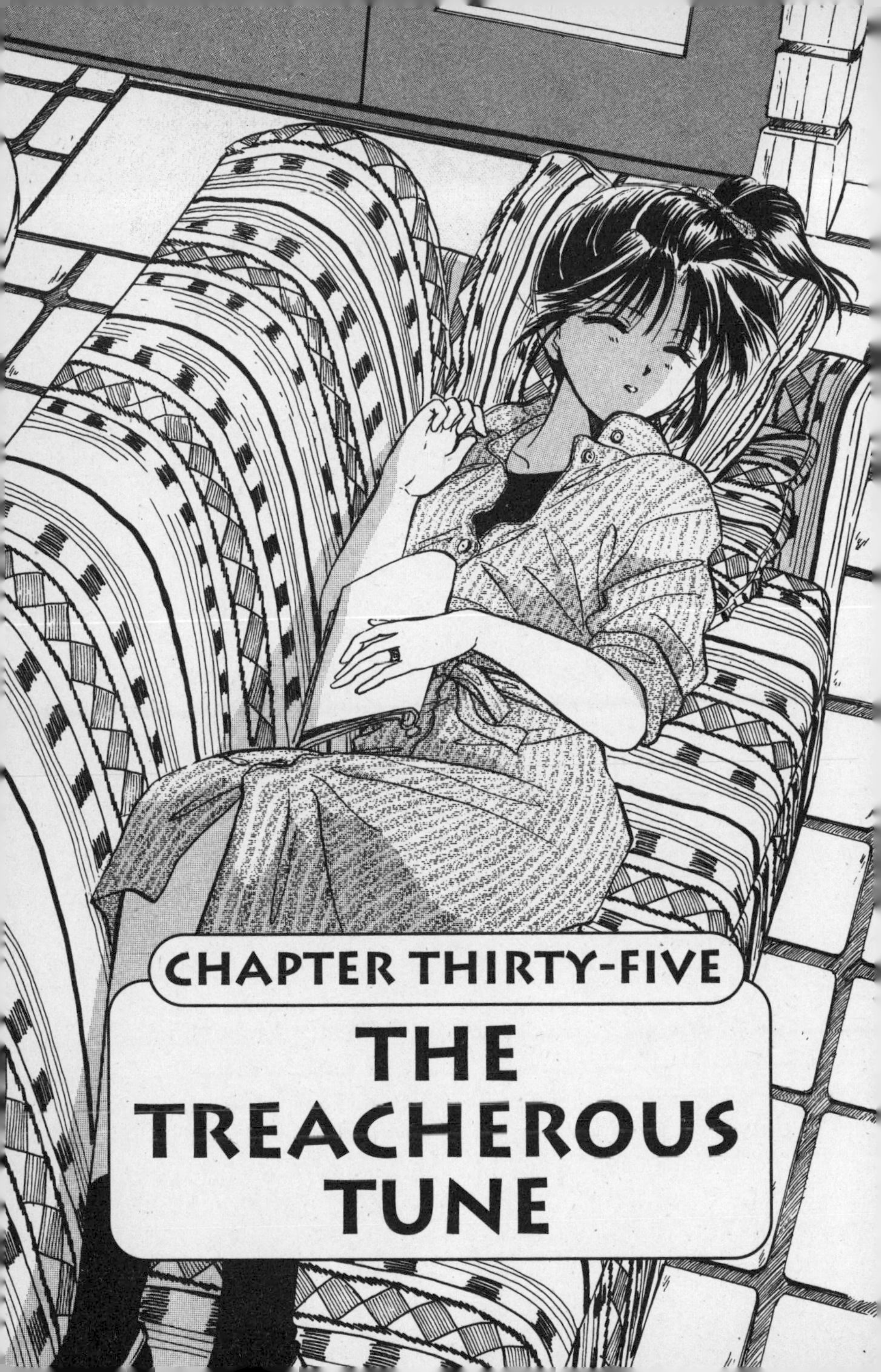
CHAPTER THIRTY-FIVE
THE TREACHEROUS TUNE

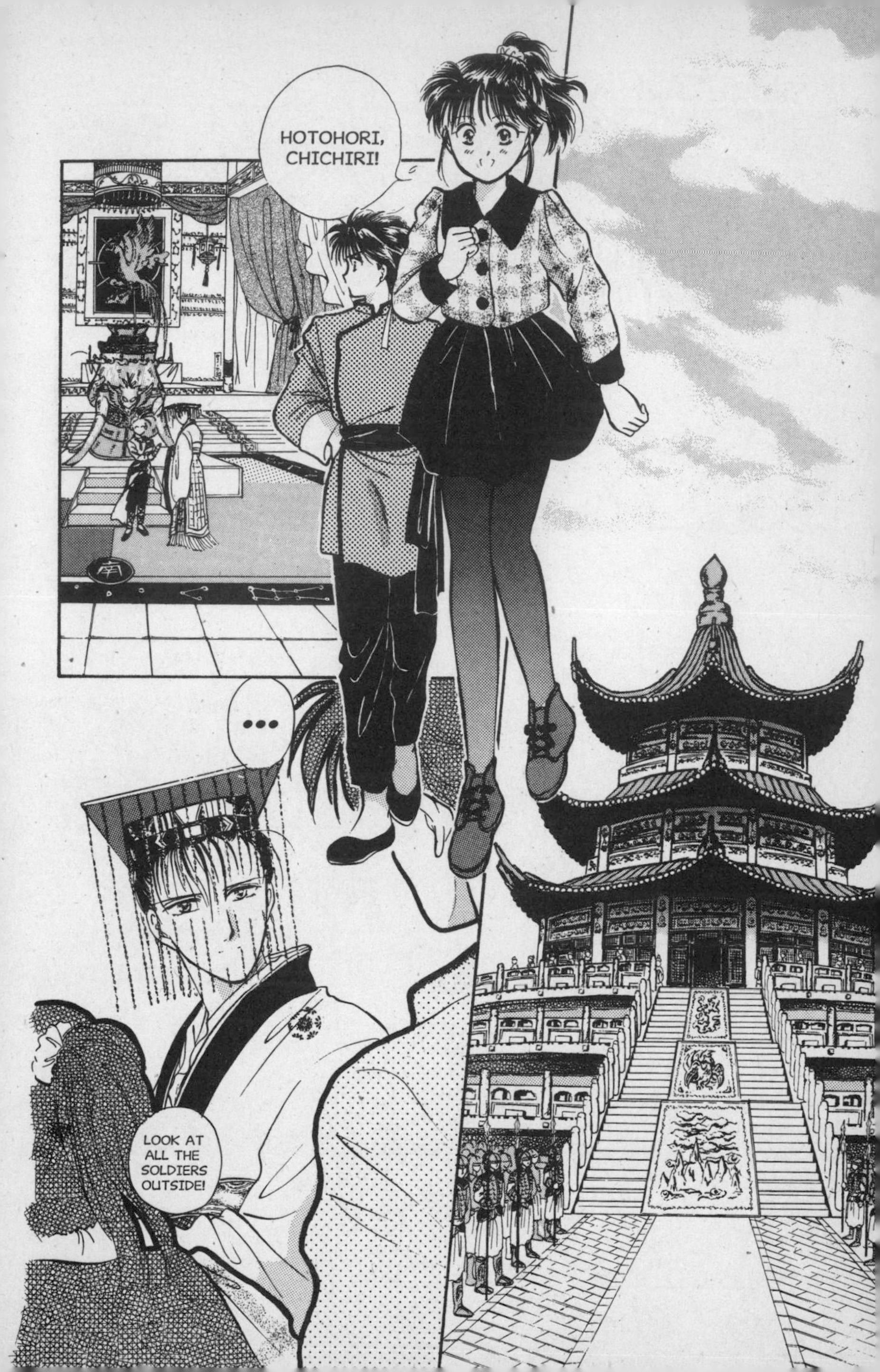
HOTOHORI, CHICHIRI!
...
LOOK AT ALL THE SOLDIERS OUTSIDE!

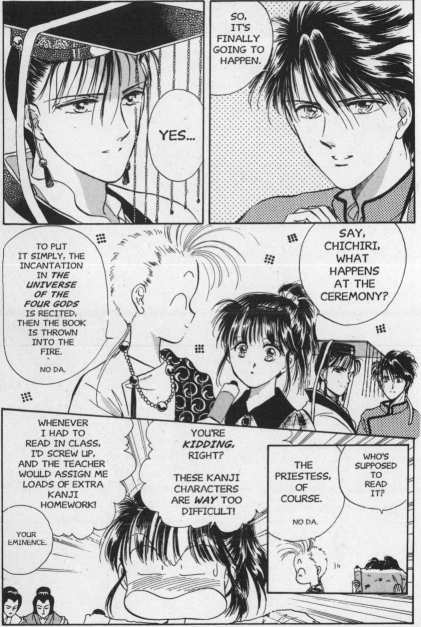

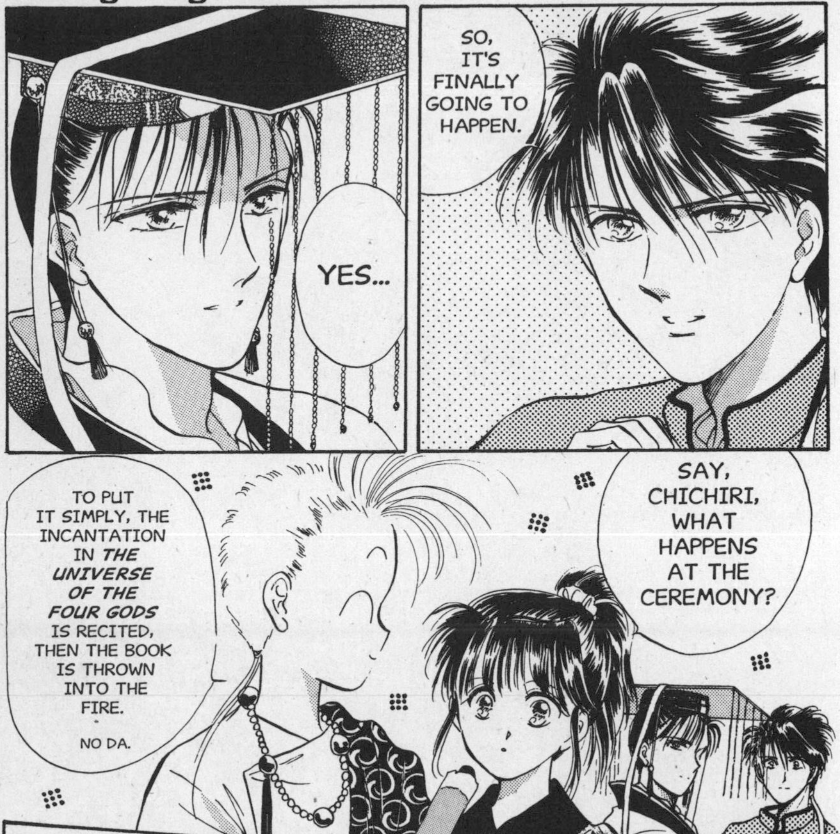
SO, IT'S FINALLY GOING TO HAPPEN.
YES...
SAY, CHICHIRI, WHAT HAPPENS AT THE CEREMONY?
TO PUT IT SIMPLY, THE INCANTATION IN *THE UNIVERSE OF THE FOUR GODS* IS RECITED, THEN THE BOOK IS THROWN INTO THE FIRE.
NO DA.
WHO'S SUPPOSED TO READ IT?
THE PRIESTESS, OF COURSE.
NO DA.
YOU'RE *KIDDING,* RIGHT?
THESE KANJI CHARACTERS ARE *WAY* TOO DIFFICULT!
WHENEVER I HAD TO READ IN CLASS, I'D SCREW UP, AND THE TEACHER WOULD ASSIGN ME LOADS OF EXTRA KANJI HOMEWORK!
YOUR EMINENCE.

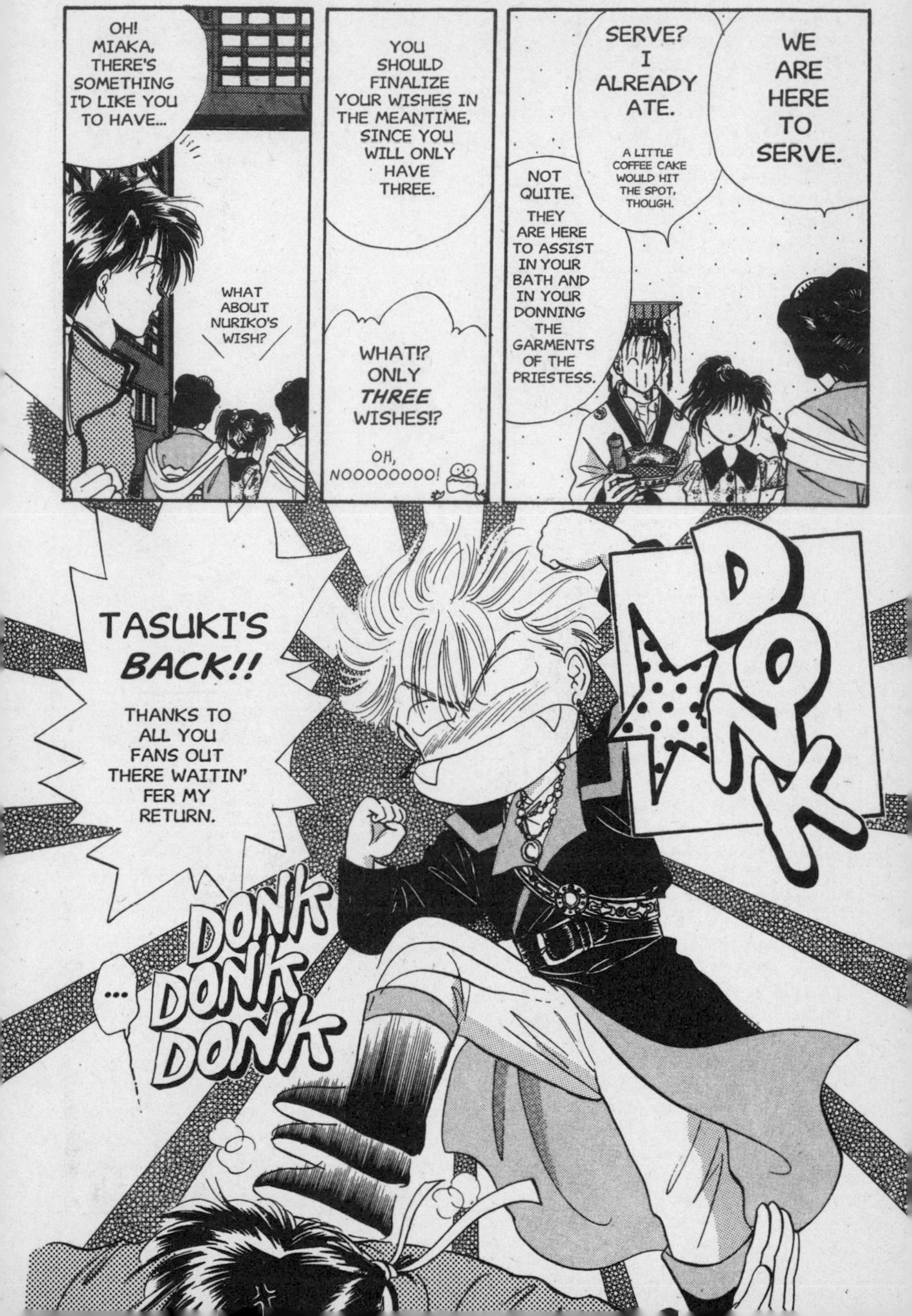
WE ARE HERE TO SERVE.
SERVE? I ALREADY ATE.
A LITTLE COFFEE CAKE WOULD HIT THE SPOT, THOUGH.
NOT QUITE.
THEY ARE HERE TO ASSIST IN YOUR BATH AND IN YOUR DONNING THE GARMENTS OF THE PRIESTESS.
YOU SHOULD FINALIZE YOUR WISHES IN THE MEANTIME, SINCE YOU WILL ONLY HAVE THREE.
WHAT!? ONLY *THREE* WISHES!?
OH, NOOOOOOOO!
OH! MIAKA, THERE'S SOMETHING I'D LIKE YOU TO HAVE...
WHAT ABOUT NURIKO'S WISH?
DONK
TASUKI'S *BACK!!*
THANKS TO ALL YOU FANS OUT THERE WAITIN' FER MY RETURN.
DONK DONK DONK
...

Summoner

So what have I been listening to on the Yūsen cable radio? "Music of Fear." It's the kind of music you'd hear in a horror movie, one tune right after the next. Oh, no! Some girl's crying! It's too creepy, so I'll change the channel. And just to create a mood for the manga, I changed it to the "Traditional Chinese Music Channel." LA LA LA! I'd like to talk about my Yorkshire terrier, but I don't have enough space to describe how immensely cute he is! So I'll save it for later. He's soooo cute! It's been a while since I answered my fan mail. I thought I'd get this question when the serial began, but I didn't, and so finally now someone asks, "How can Miaka and Tamahome speak to each other?" It's simple. This "Universe of the Four Gods" is a Japanese translation! Some of the store signs and such haven't been translated. So Tamahome and the others are all speaking Japanese. Let's just leave it at that. Also, this world might be based on China, but it's not really China. However, I had to use "Wo ai ni" because I just loved the sound of the expression. I'll also answer the question, "In Chapter 10, Tamahome and Hotohori give blood to Miaka, but how could they all have the same blood type?" That wasn't real blood but blood energy. Also, "Why is it that Miaka can communicate with Yui, but she can't with her brother?" Hmmm. Very perceptive. To be continued...

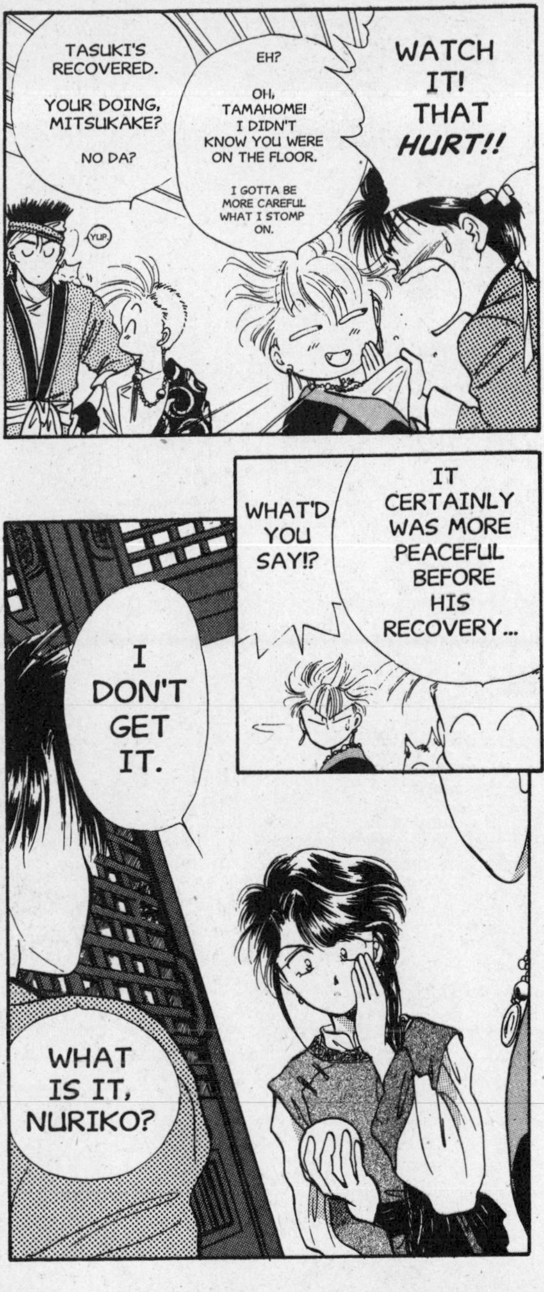
WATCH IT! THAT *HURT!!*
EH?
OH, TAMAHOME! I DIDN'T KNOW YOU WERE ON THE FLOOR.
I GOTTA BE MORE CAREFUL WHAT I STOMP ON.
TASUKI'S RECOVERED.
YOUR DOING, MITSUKAKE?
NO DA?
YUP.
IT CERTAINLY WAS MORE PEACEFUL BEFORE HIS RECOVERY...
WHAT'D YOU SAY!?
I DON'T GET IT.
WHAT IS IT, NURIKO?

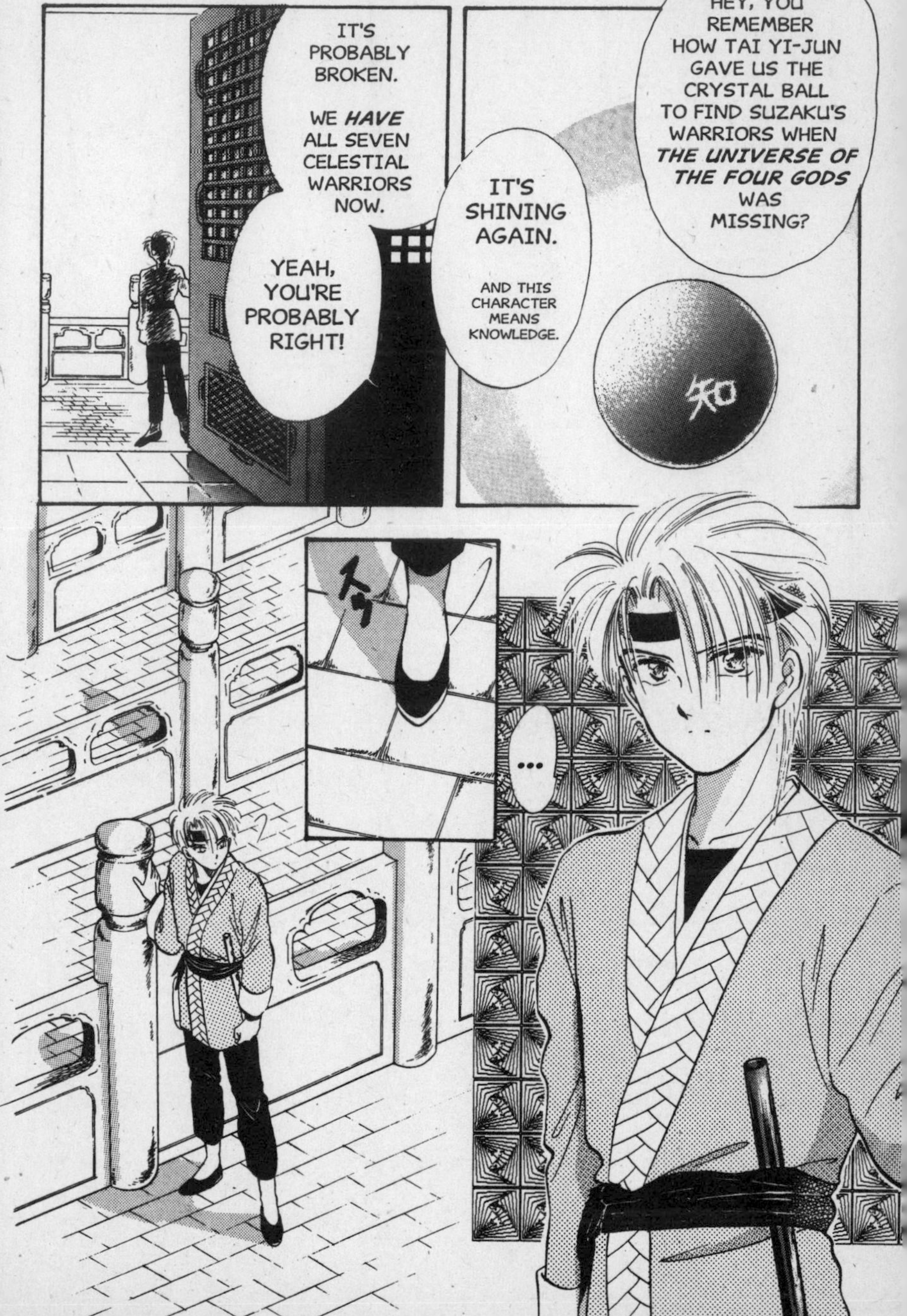
HEY, YOU REMEMBER HOW TAI YI-JUN GAVE US THE CRYSTAL BALL TO FIND SUZAKU'S WARRIORS WHEN *THE UNIVERSE OF THE FOUR GODS* WAS MISSING?
IT'S SHINING AGAIN.
AND THIS CHARACTER MEANS KNOWLEDGE.
知
IT'S PROBABLY BROKEN.
WE *HAVE* ALL SEVEN CELESTIAL WARRIORS NOW.
YEAH, YOU'RE PROBABLY RIGHT!
...

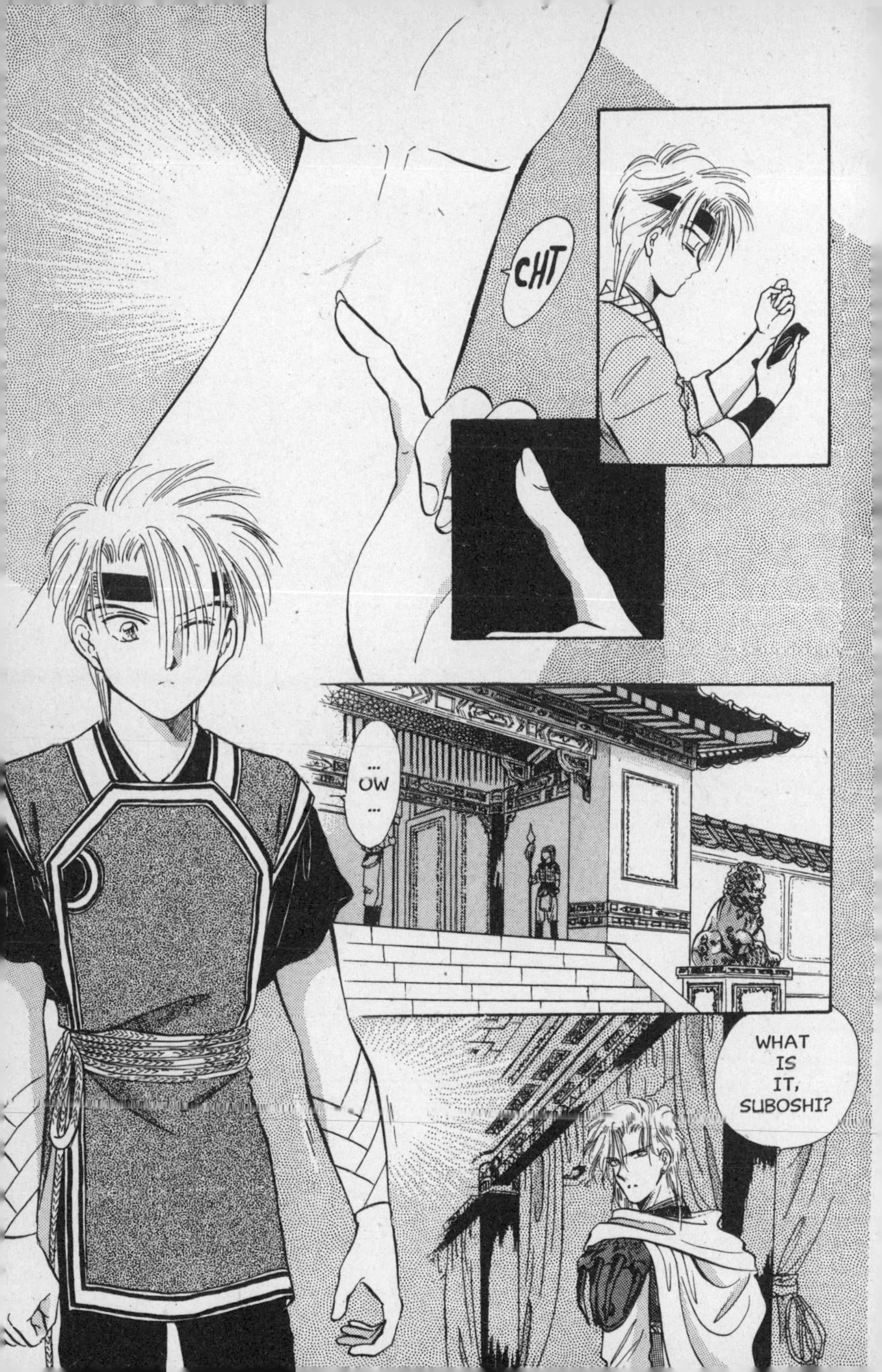
CHT
... OW ...
WHAT IS IT, SUBOSHI?

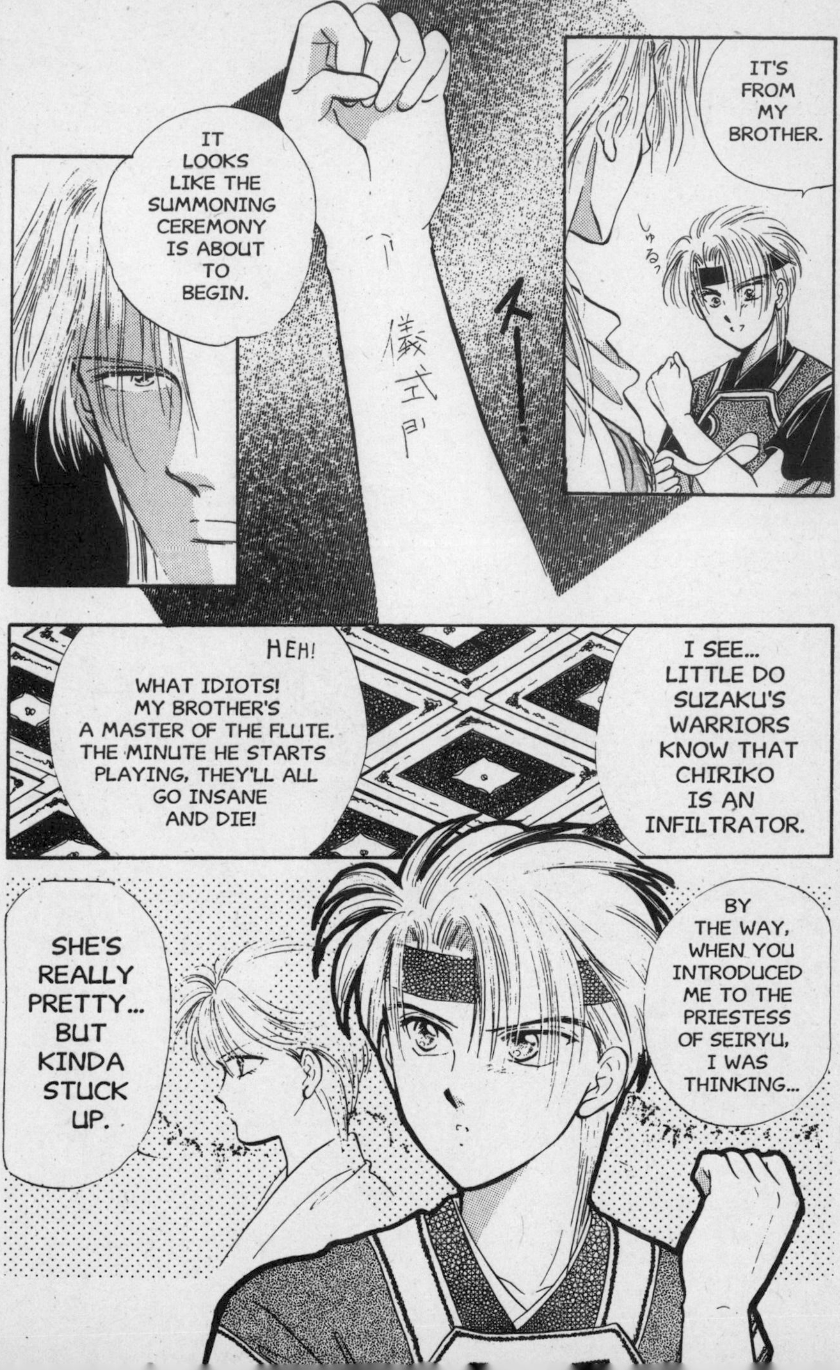
IT'S FROM MY BROTHER.
しゅるっ
IT LOOKS LIKE THE SUMMONING CEREMONY IS ABOUT TO BEGIN.
I SEE... LITTLE DO SUZAKU'S WARRIORS KNOW THAT CHIRIKO IS AN INFILTRATOR.
HEH!
WHAT IDIOTS! MY BROTHER'S A MASTER OF THE FLUTE. THE MINUTE HE STARTS PLAYING, THEY'LL ALL GO INSANE AND DIE!
BY THE WAY, WHEN YOU INTRODUCED ME TO THE PRIESTESS OF SEIRYU, I WAS THINKING...
SHE'S REALLY PRETTY... BUT KINDA STUCK UP.

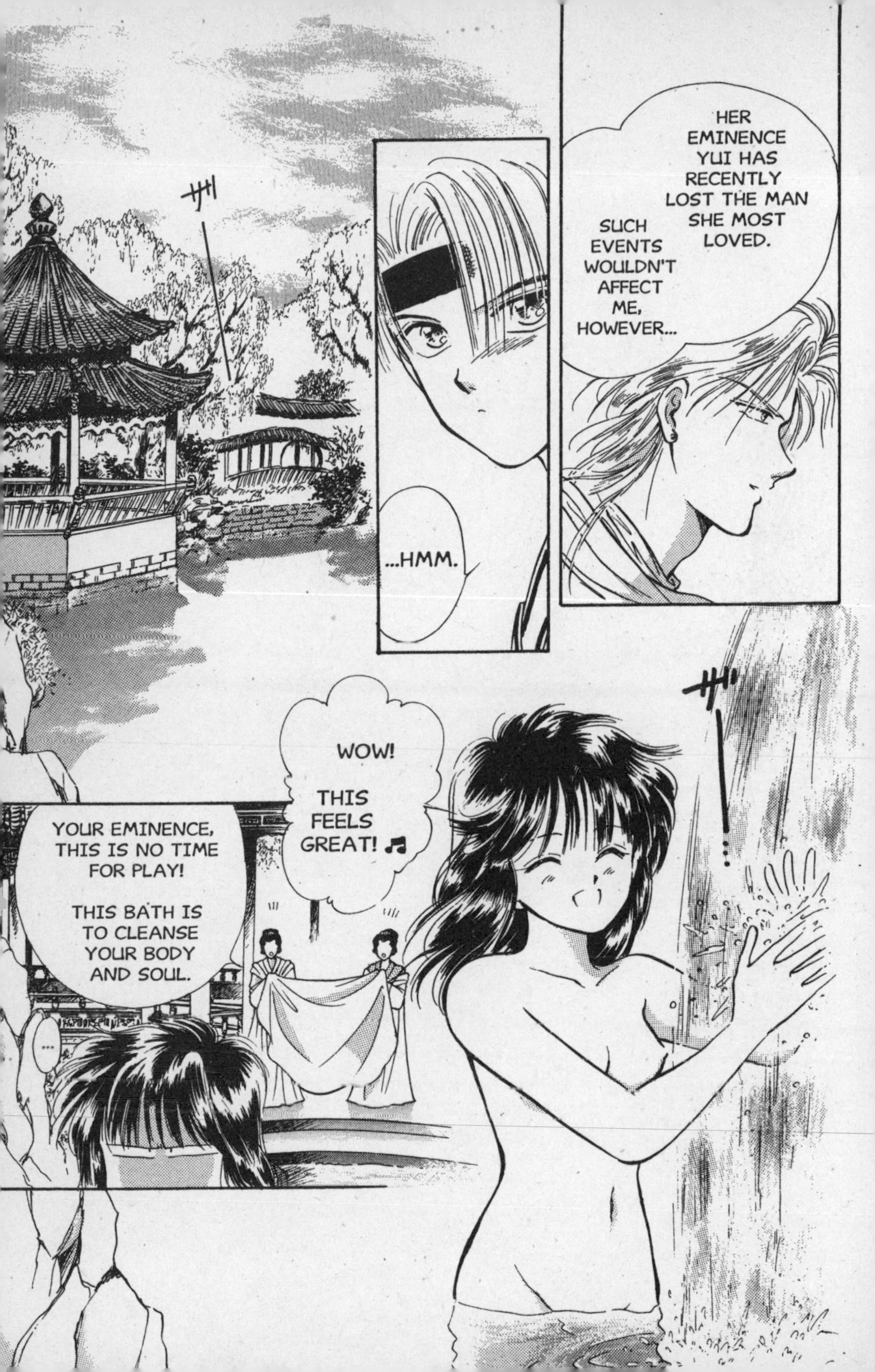
HER EMINENCE YUI HAS RECENTLY LOST THE MAN SHE MOST LOVED.
SUCH EVENTS WOULDN'T AFFECT ME, HOWEVER...
...HMM.
WOW! THIS FEELS GREAT! ♫
YOUR EMINENCE, THIS IS NO TIME FOR PLAY! THIS BATH IS TO CLEANSE YOUR BODY AND SOUL.
...

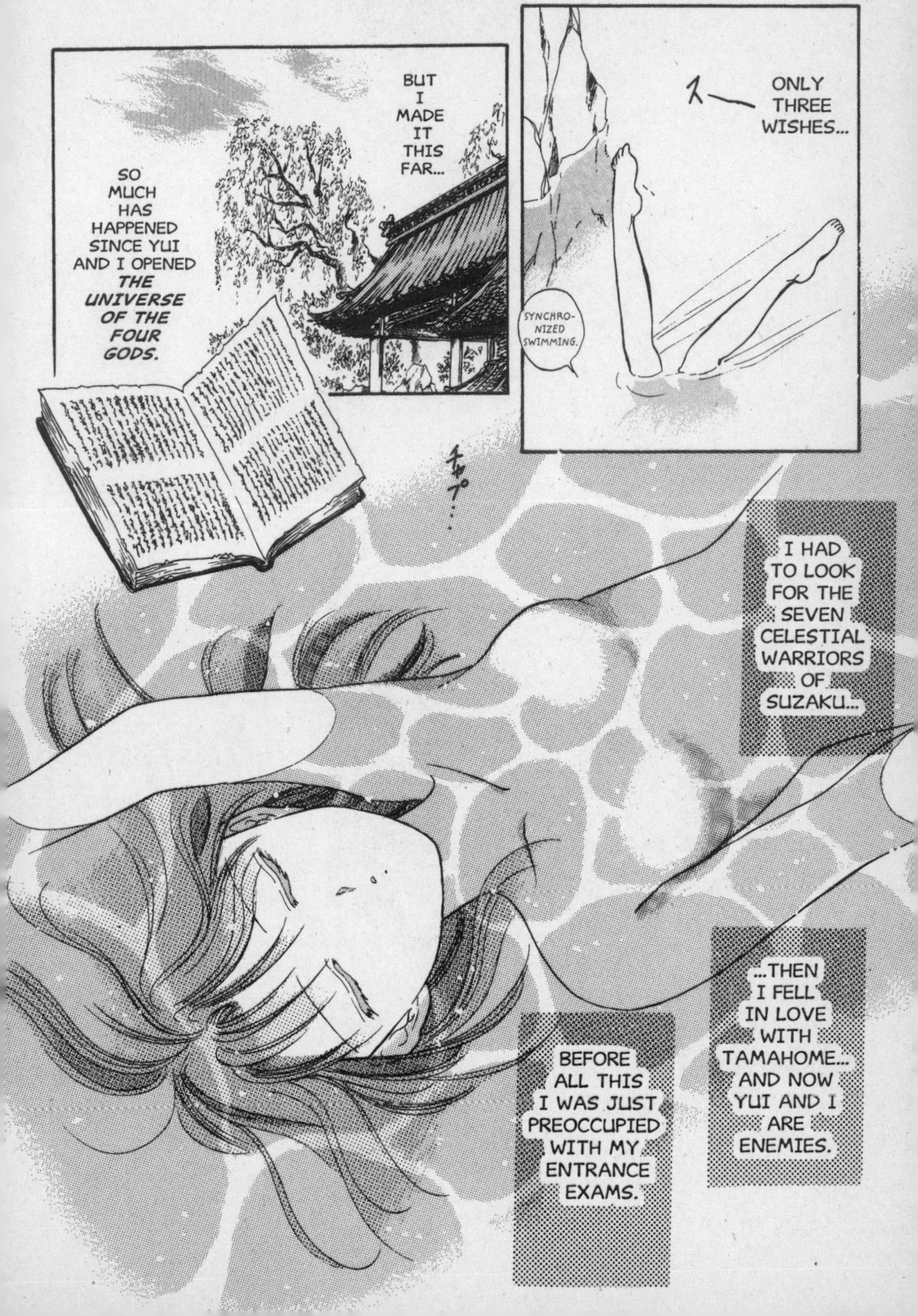
ス—
ONLY THREE WISHES...
SYNCHRONIZED SWIMMING.
BUT I MADE IT THIS FAR...
SO MUCH HAS HAPPENED SINCE YUI AND I OPENED ***THE UNIVERSE OF THE FOUR GODS.***
チャプ...
I HAD TO LOOK FOR THE SEVEN CELESTIAL WARRIORS OF SUZAKU...
...THEN I FELL IN LOVE WITH TAMAHOME... AND NOW YUI AND I ARE ENEMIES.
BEFORE ALL THIS I WAS JUST PREOCCUPIED WITH MY ENTRANCE EXAMS.

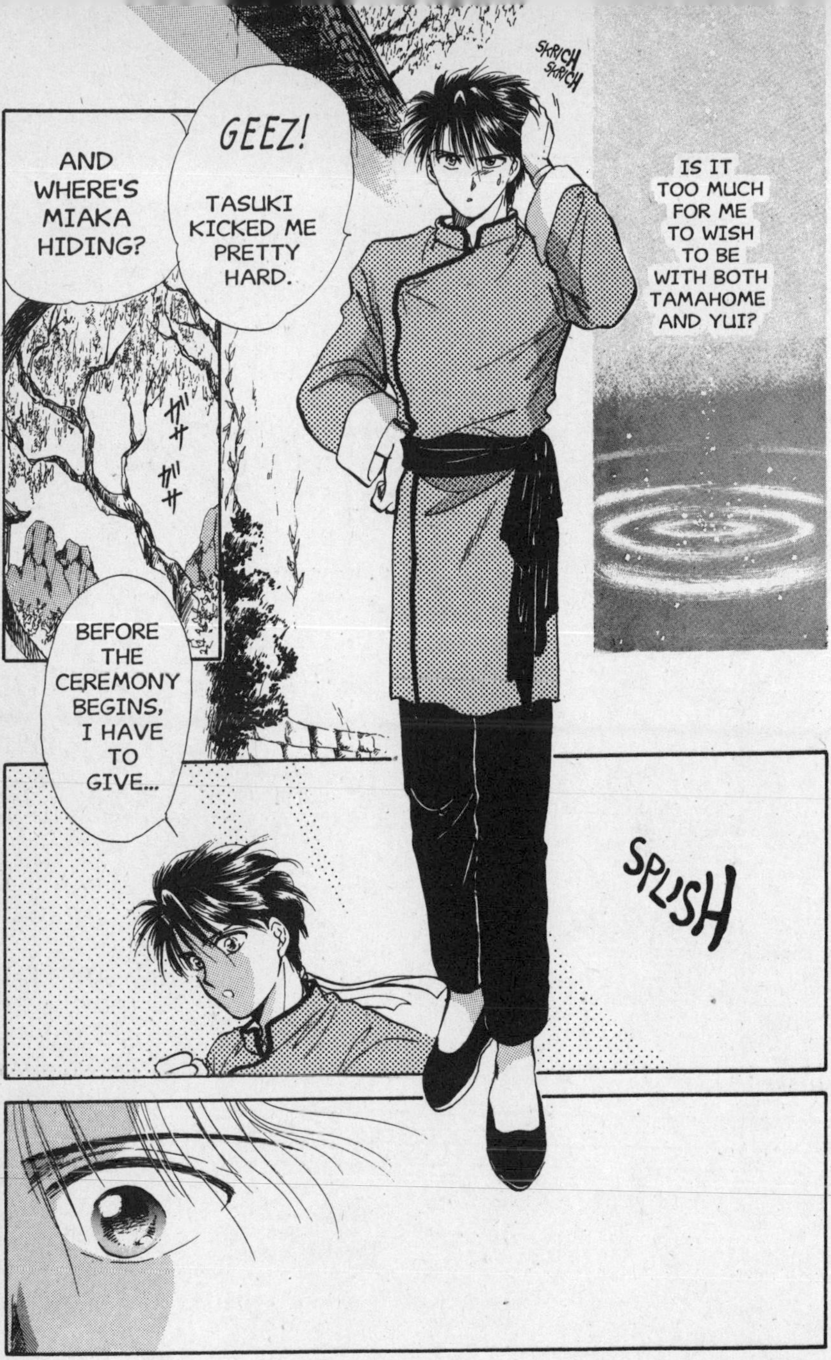
IS IT TOO MUCH FOR ME TO WISH TO BE WITH BOTH TAMAHOME AND YUI?
SKRICH SKRICH
GEEZ!
TASUKI KICKED ME PRETTY HARD.
AND WHERE'S MIAKA HIDING?
ガサ ガサ
BEFORE THE CEREMONY BEGINS, I HAVE TO GIVE...
SPLISH

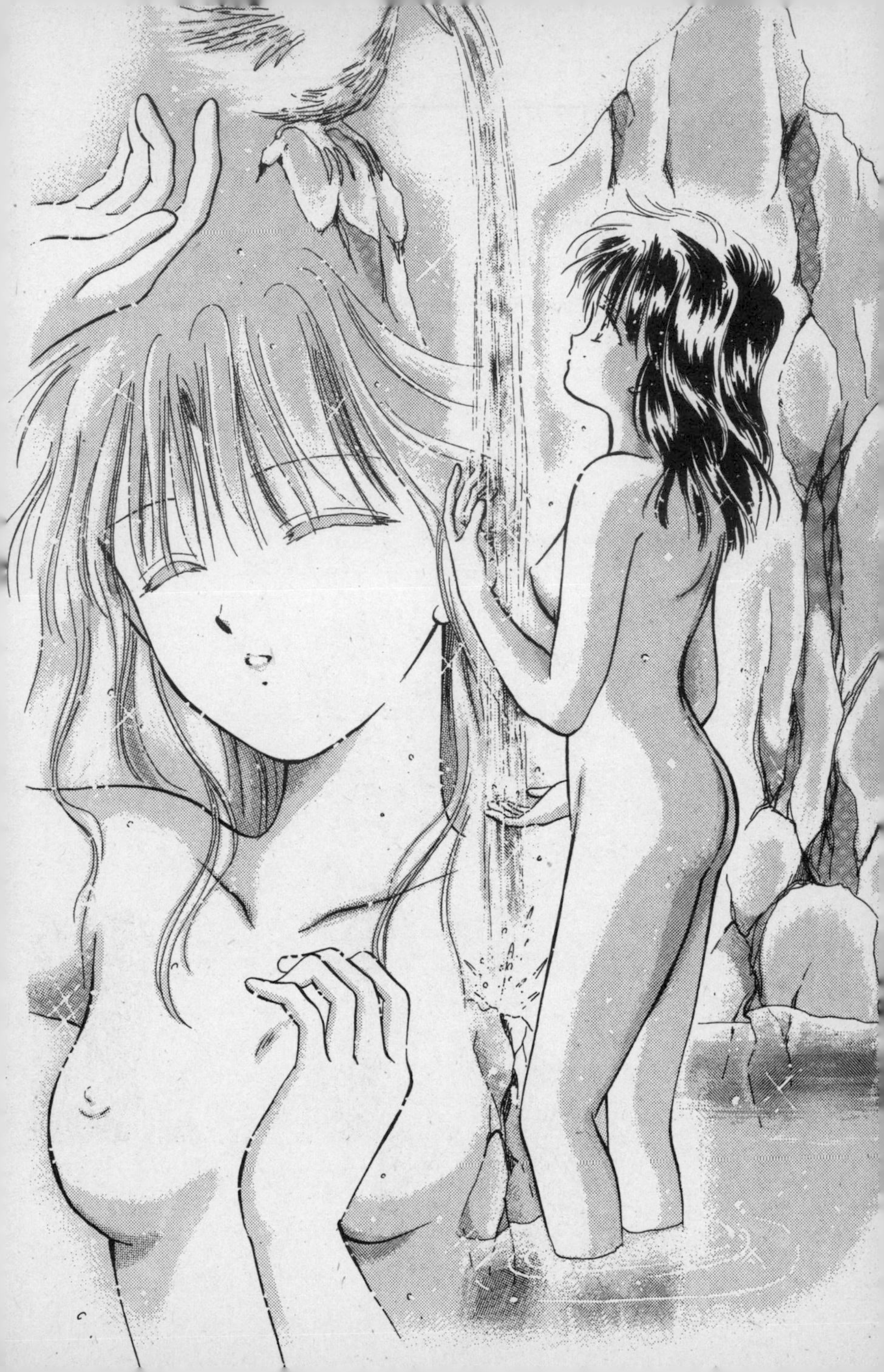

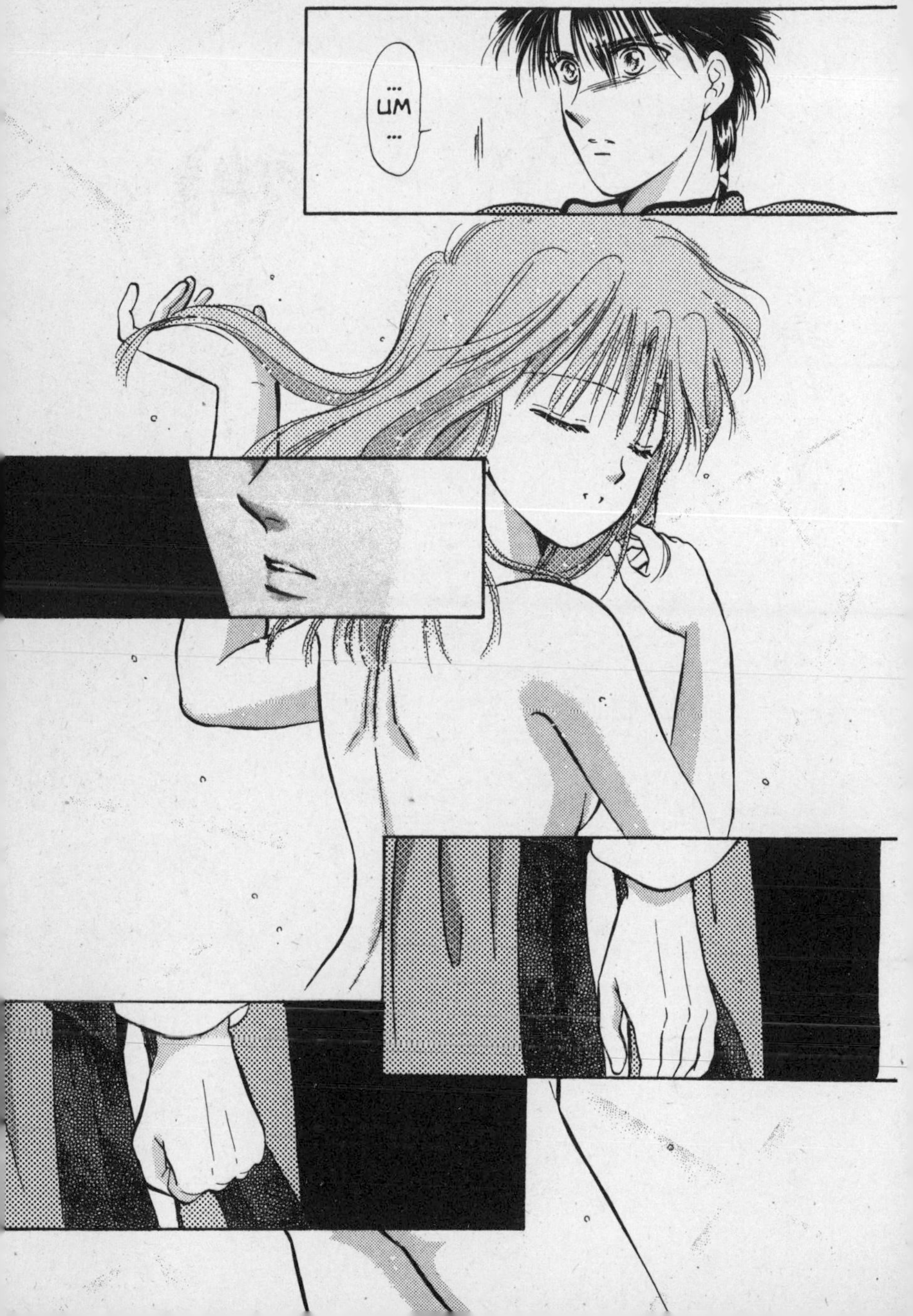
... UM ...

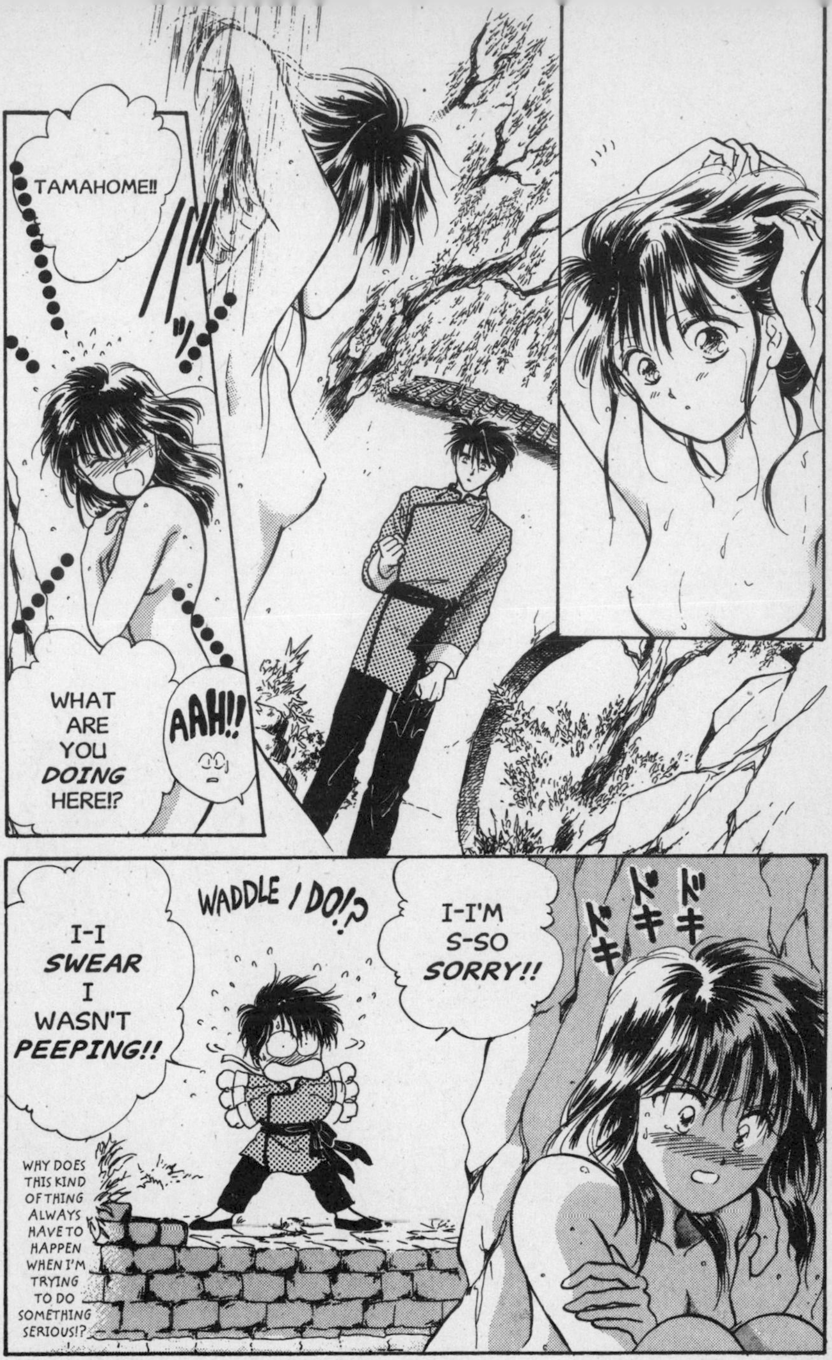
TAMAHOME!!
AAH!!
WHAT ARE YOU DOING HERE!?
ドキドキドキ
I-I'M S-SO SORRY!!
WADDLE I DO!?
I-I SWEAR I WASN'T PEEPING!!
WHY DOES THIS KIND OF THING ALWAYS HAVE TO HAPPEN WHEN I'M TRYING TO DO SOMETHING SERIOUS!?

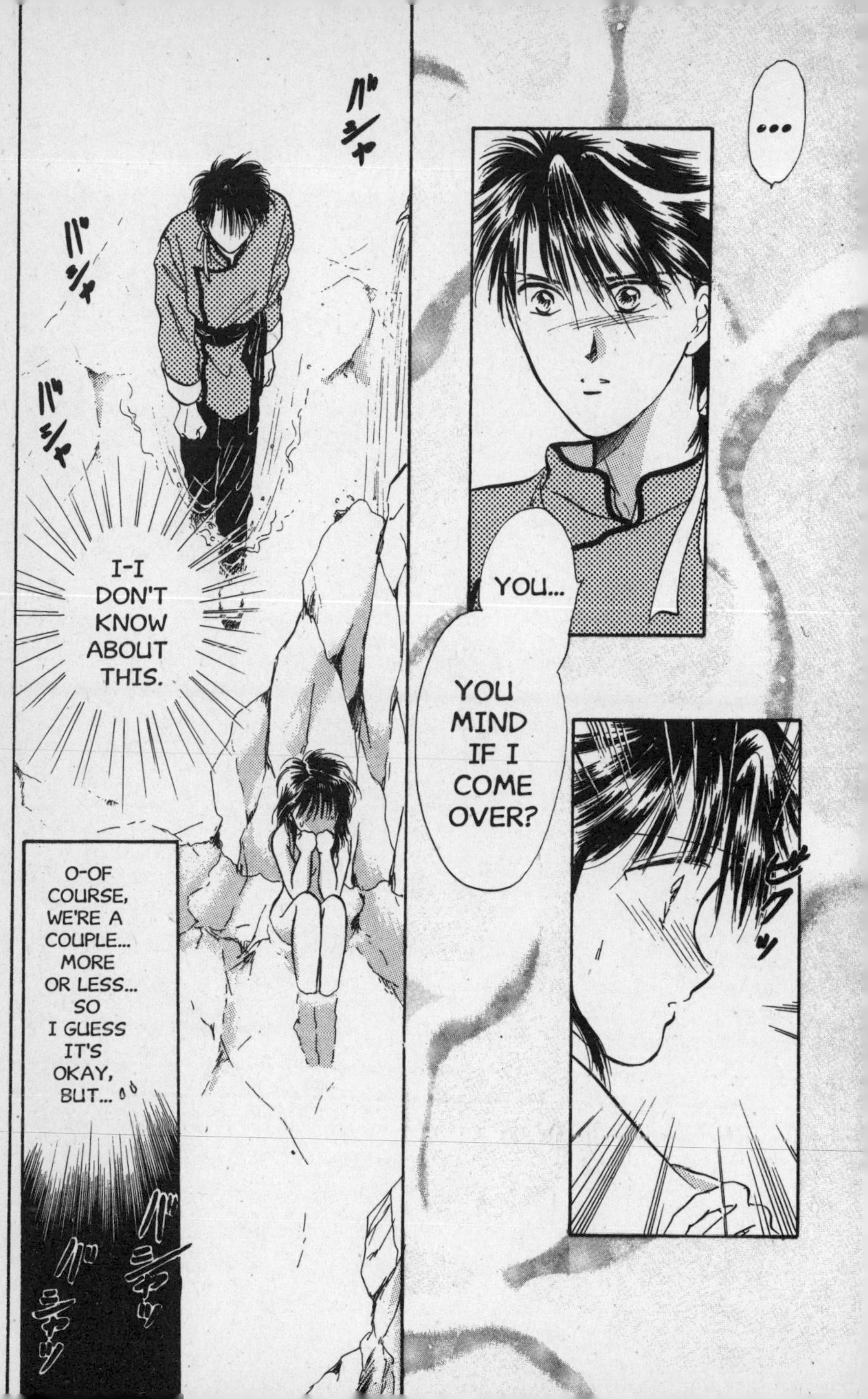
...
YOU...
YOU MIND IF I COME OVER?
I-I DON'T KNOW ABOUT THIS.
O-OF COURSE, WE'RE A COUPLE... MORE OR LESS... SO I GUESS IT'S OKAY, BUT...

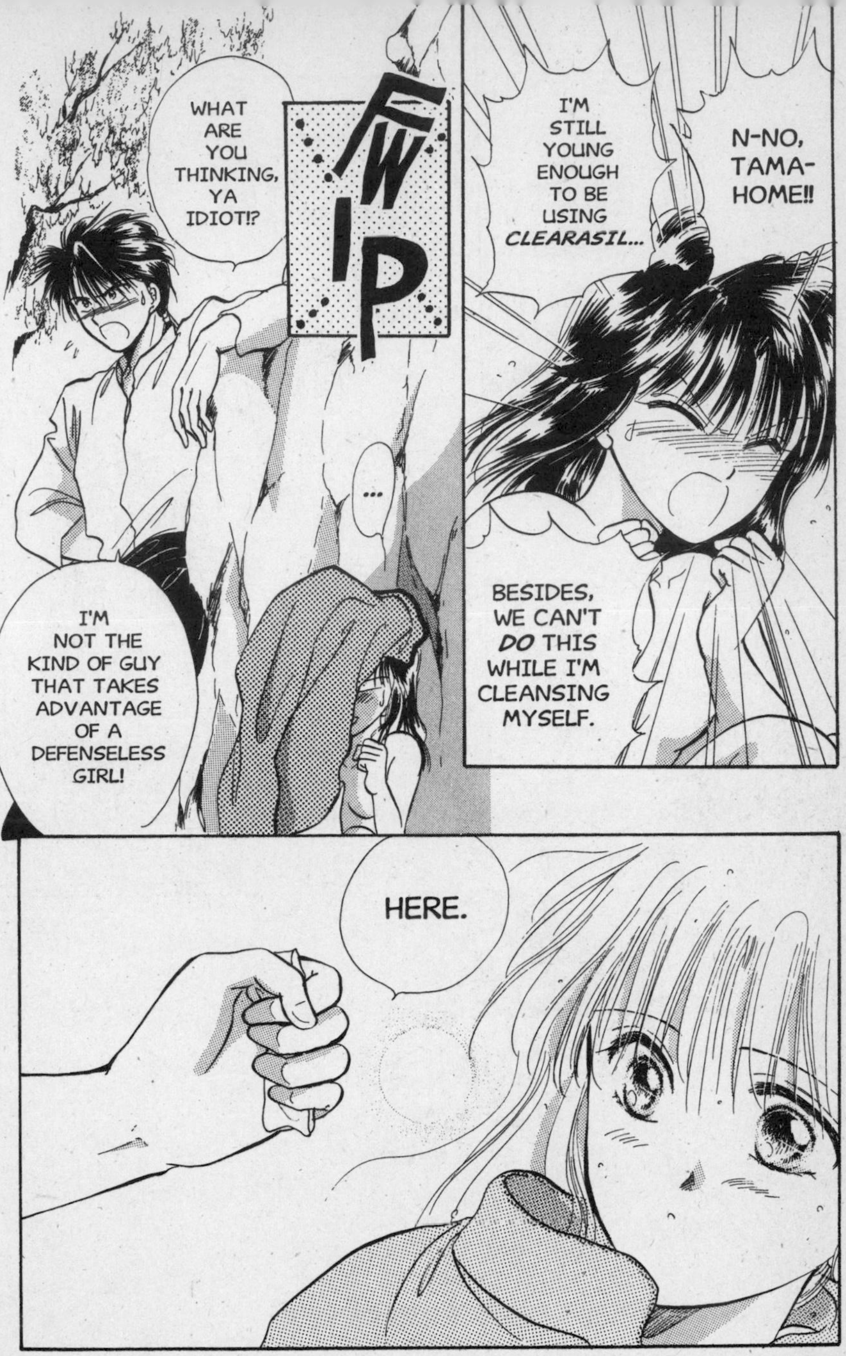
N-NO, TAMA-HOME!!
I'M STILL YOUNG ENOUGH TO BE USING *CLEARASIL*...
BESIDES, WE CAN'T *DO* THIS WHILE I'M CLEANSING MYSELF.
FWIP
WHAT ARE YOU THINKING, YA IDIOT!?
...
I'M NOT THE KIND OF GUY THAT TAKES ADVANTAGE OF A DEFENSELESS GIRL!
HERE.

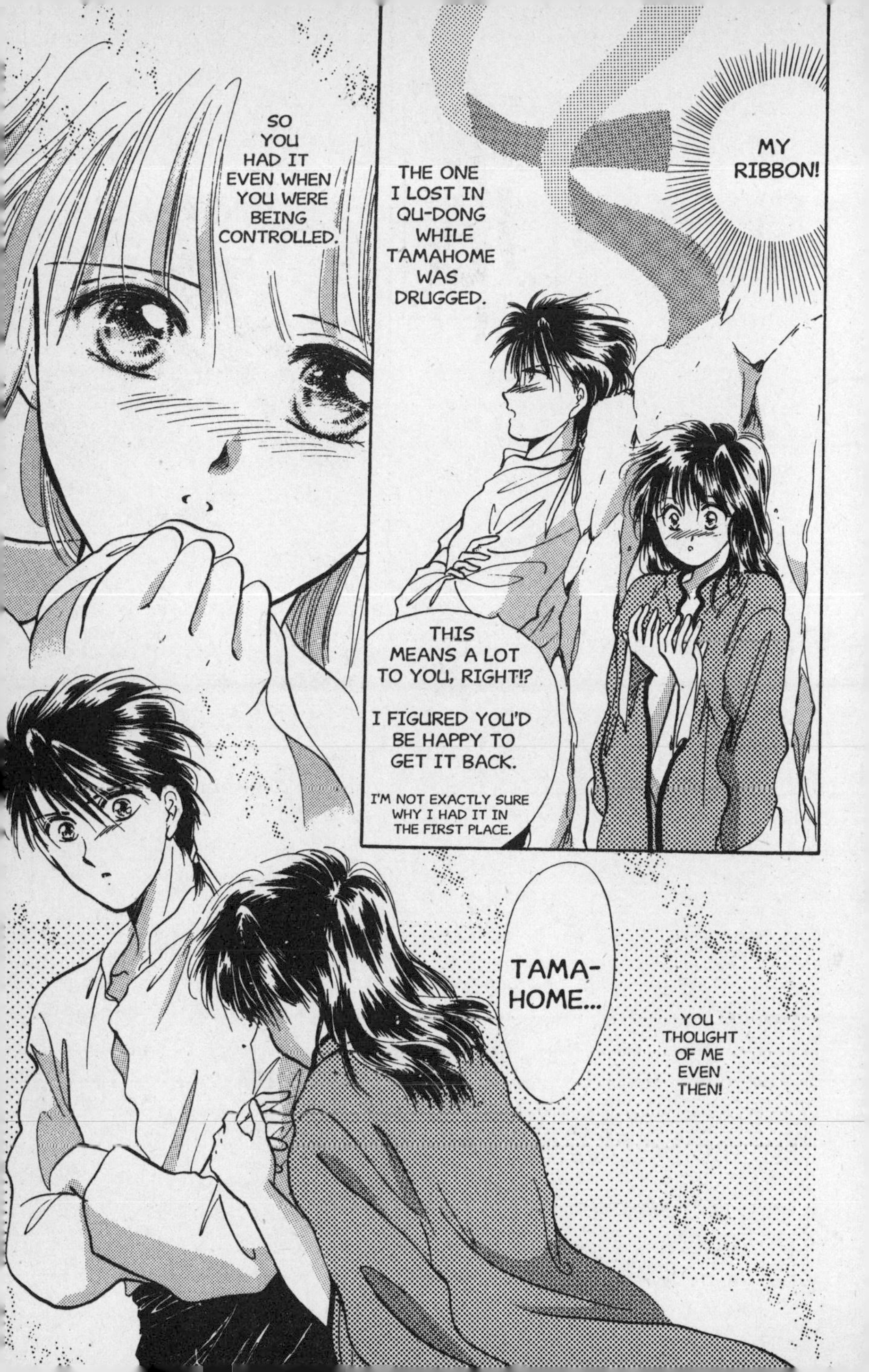
MY RIBBON!
THE ONE I LOST IN QU-DONG WHILE TAMAHOME WAS DRUGGED.
THIS MEANS A LOT TO YOU, RIGHT!? I FIGURED YOU'D BE HAPPY TO GET IT BACK.
I'M NOT EXACTLY SURE WHY I HAD IT IN THE FIRST PLACE.
SO YOU HAD IT EVEN WHEN YOU WERE BEING CONTROLLED.
TAMA-HOME...
YOU THOUGHT OF ME EVEN THEN!

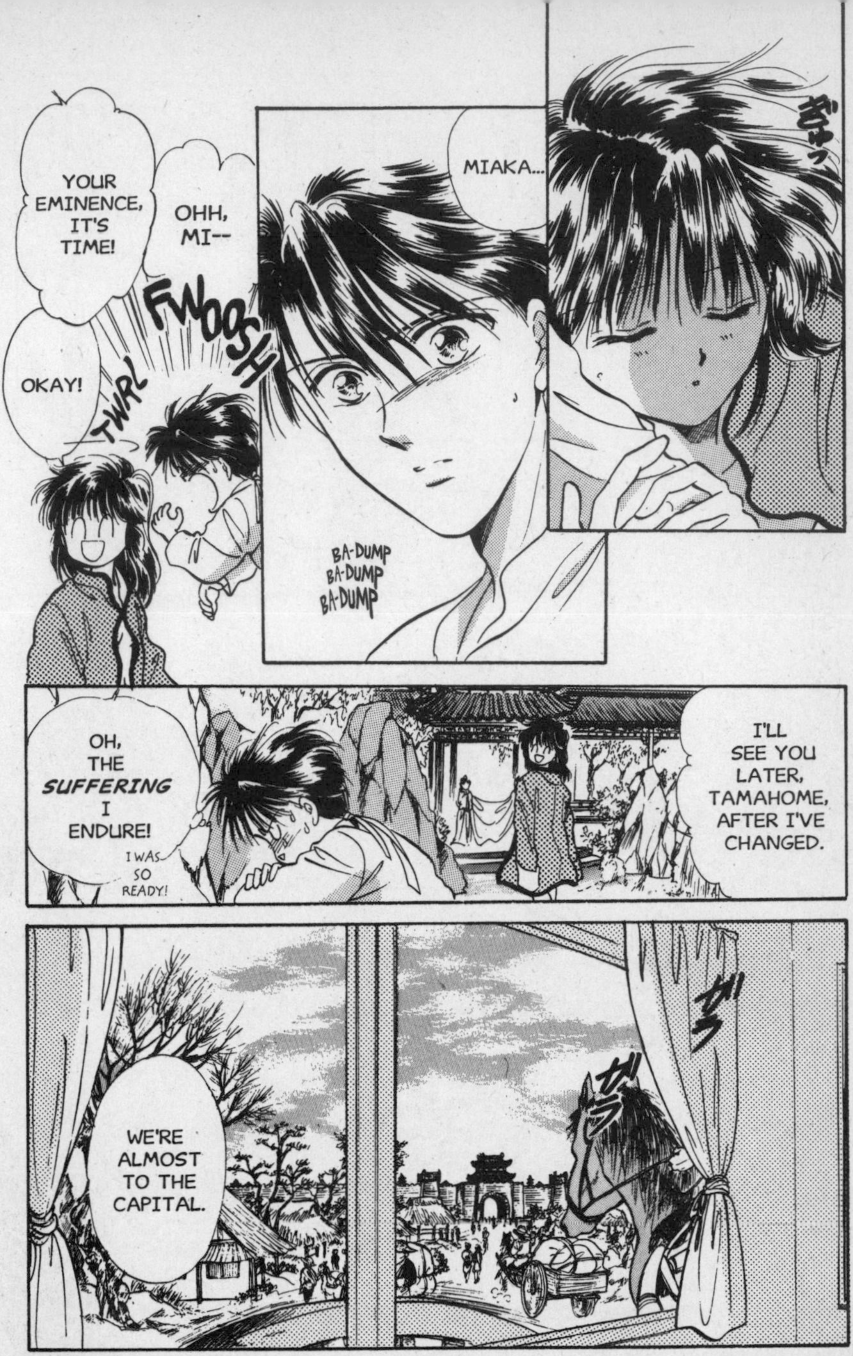
MIAKA...
BA-DUMP BA-DUMP BA-DUMP
OHH, MI--
YOUR EMINENCE, IT'S TIME!
FWOOSH
OKAY!
TWRL
I'LL SEE YOU LATER, TAMAHOME, AFTER I'VE CHANGED.
OH, THE *SUFFERING* I ENDURE!
I WAS SO READY!
WE'RE ALMOST TO THE CAPITAL.

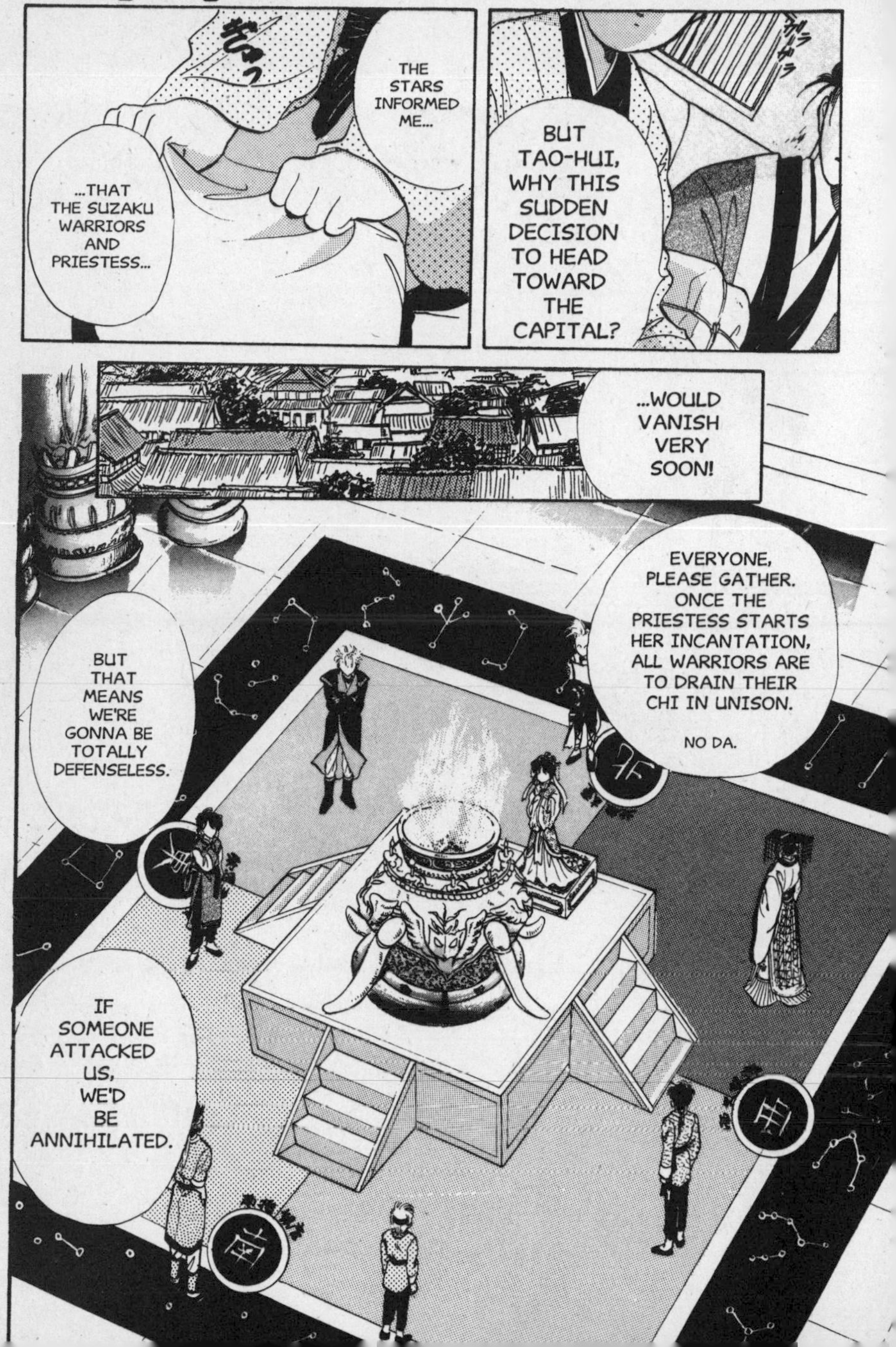
BUT TAO-HUI, WHY THIS SUDDEN DECISION TO HEAD TOWARD THE CAPITAL?
THE STARS INFORMED ME...
...THAT THE SUZAKU WARRIORS AND PRIESTESS...
...WOULD VANISH VERY SOON!
EVERYONE, PLEASE GATHER. ONCE THE PRIESTESS STARTS HER INCANTATION, ALL WARRIORS ARE TO DRAIN THEIR CHI IN UNISON.
NO DA.
BUT THAT MEANS WE'RE GONNA BE TOTALLY DEFENSELESS.
IF SOMEONE ATTACKED US, WE'D BE ANNIHILATED.

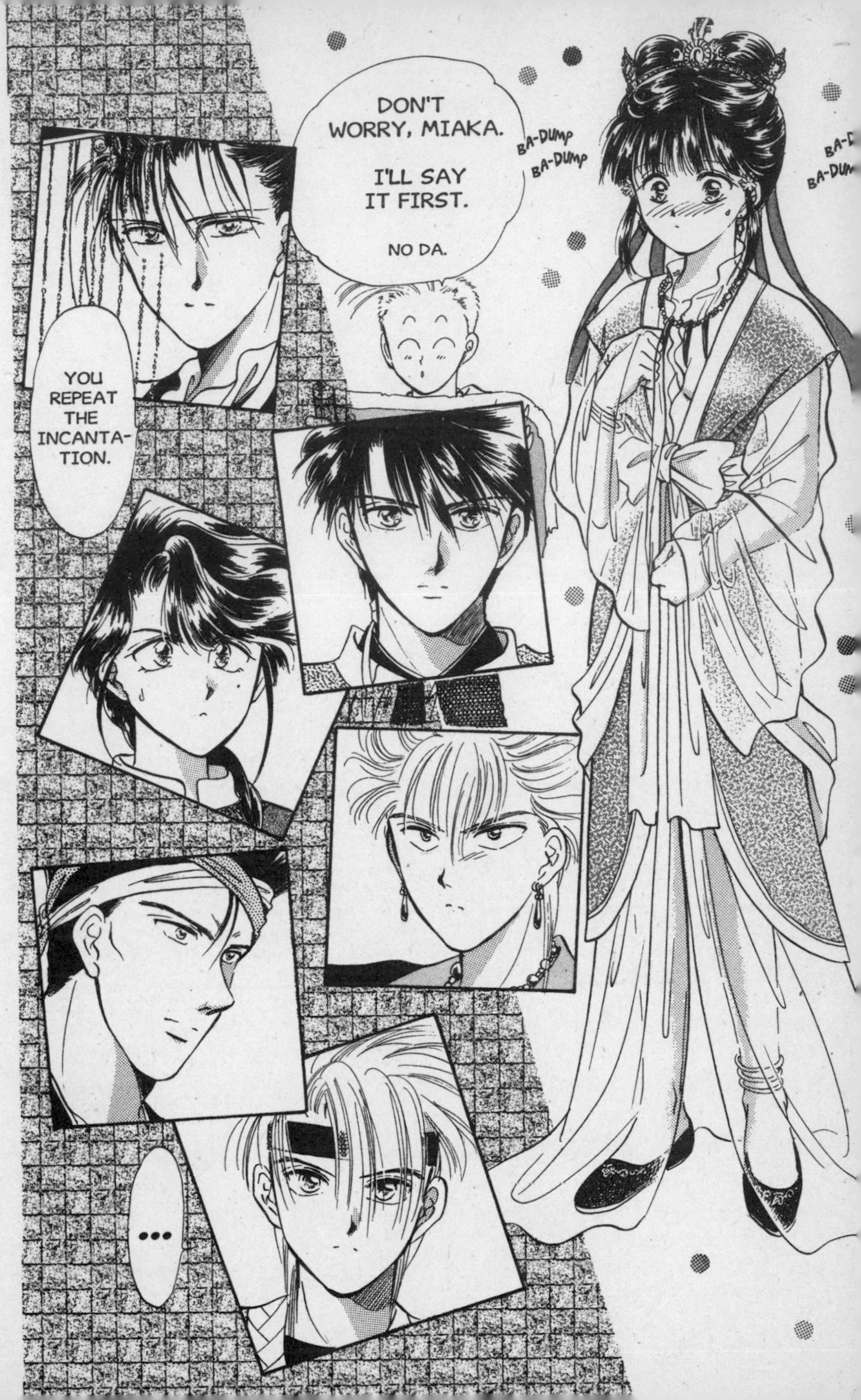
BA-DUMP
BA-DUMP
BA-DUMP
BA-DUMP
DON'T WORRY, MIAKA. I'LL SAY IT FIRST. NO DA.
YOU REPEAT THE INCANTATION.
...

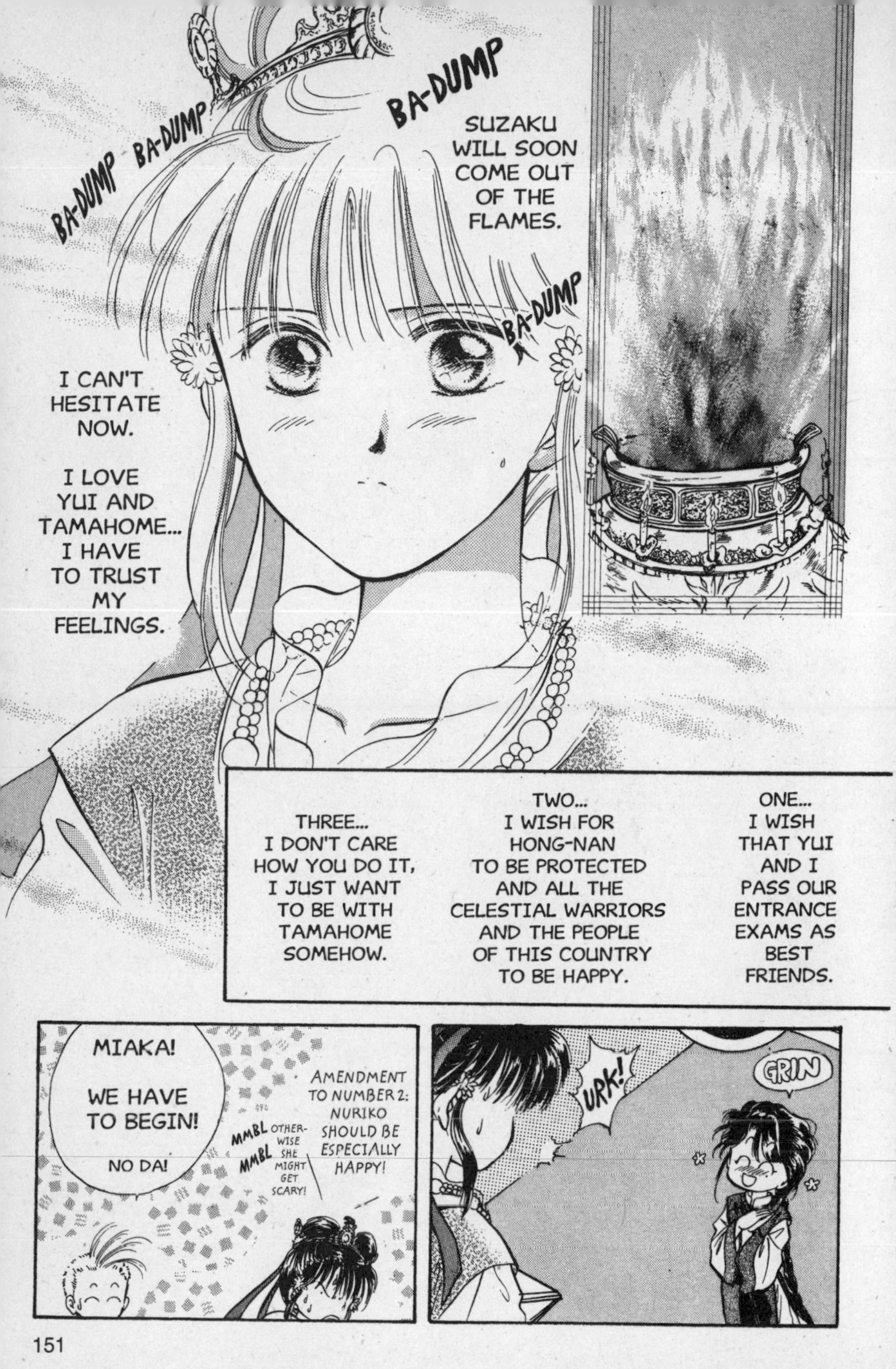
BA-DUMP BA-DUMP
BA-DUMP
SUZAKU WILL SOON COME OUT OF THE FLAMES.
BA-DUMP
I CAN'T HESITATE NOW.
I LOVE YUI AND TAMAHOME... I HAVE TO TRUST MY FEELINGS.
THREE... I DON'T CARE HOW YOU DO IT, I JUST WANT TO BE WITH TAMAHOME SOMEHOW.
TWO... I WISH FOR HONG-NAN TO BE PROTECTED AND ALL THE CELESTIAL WARRIORS AND THE PEOPLE OF THIS COUNTRY TO BE HAPPY.
ONE... I WISH THAT YUI AND I PASS OUR ENTRANCE EXAMS AS BEST FRIENDS.
MIAKA! WE HAVE TO BEGIN! NO DA!
MMBL MMBL
OTHER-WISE SHE MIGHT GET SCARY!
AMENDMENT TO NUMBER 2: NURIKO SHOULD BE ESPECIALLY HAPPY!
URK!
GRIN

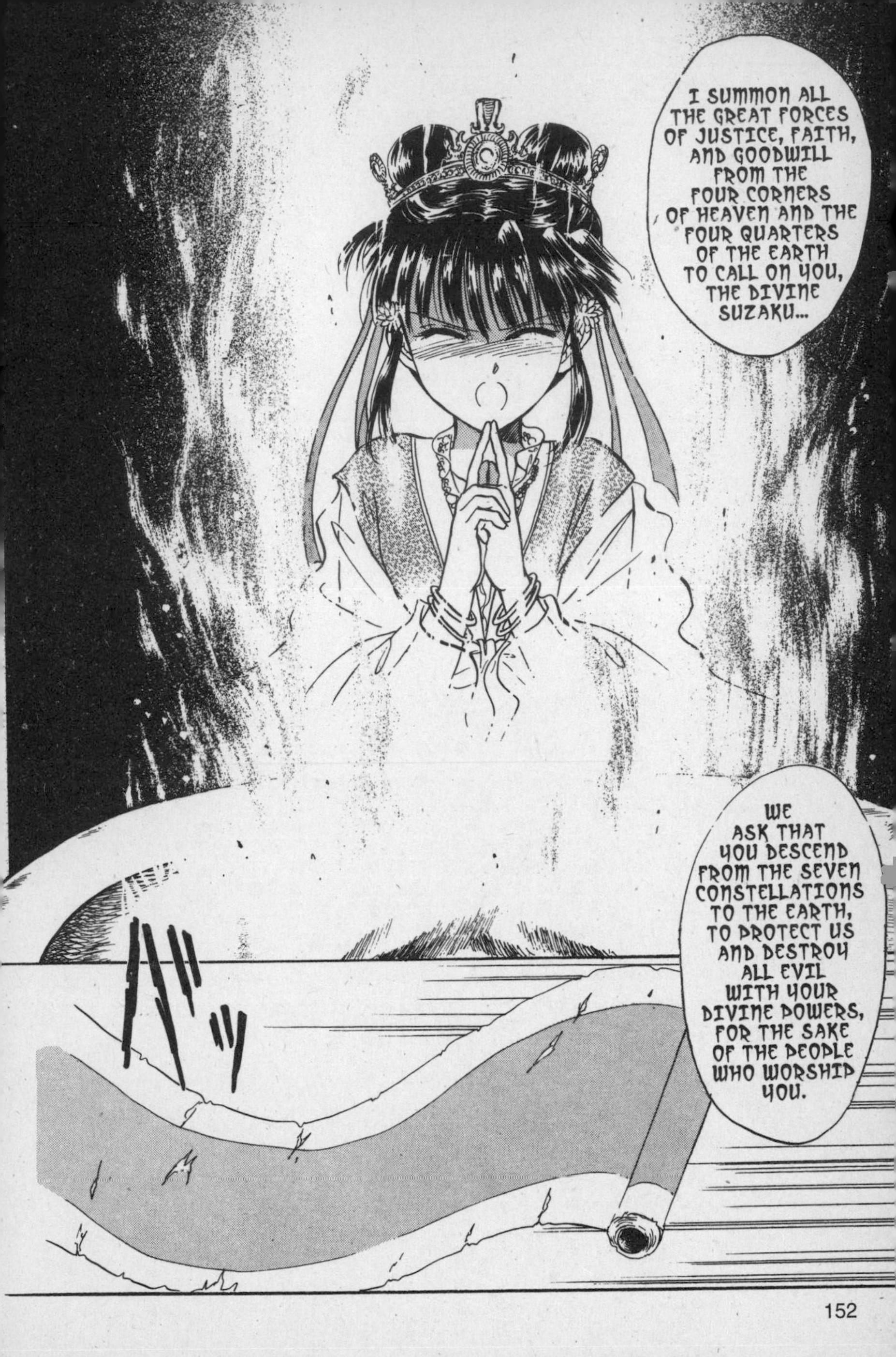
I SUMMON ALL THE GREAT FORCES OF JUSTICE, FAITH, AND GOODWILL FROM THE FOUR CORNERS OF HEAVEN AND THE FOUR QUARTERS OF THE EARTH TO CALL ON YOU, THE DIVINE SUZAKU...
WE ASK THAT YOU DESCEND FROM THE SEVEN CONSTELLATIONS TO THE EARTH, TO PROTECT US AND DESTROY ALL EVIL WITH YOUR DIVINE POWERS, FOR THE SAKE OF THE PEOPLE WHO WORSHIP YOU.
バッ

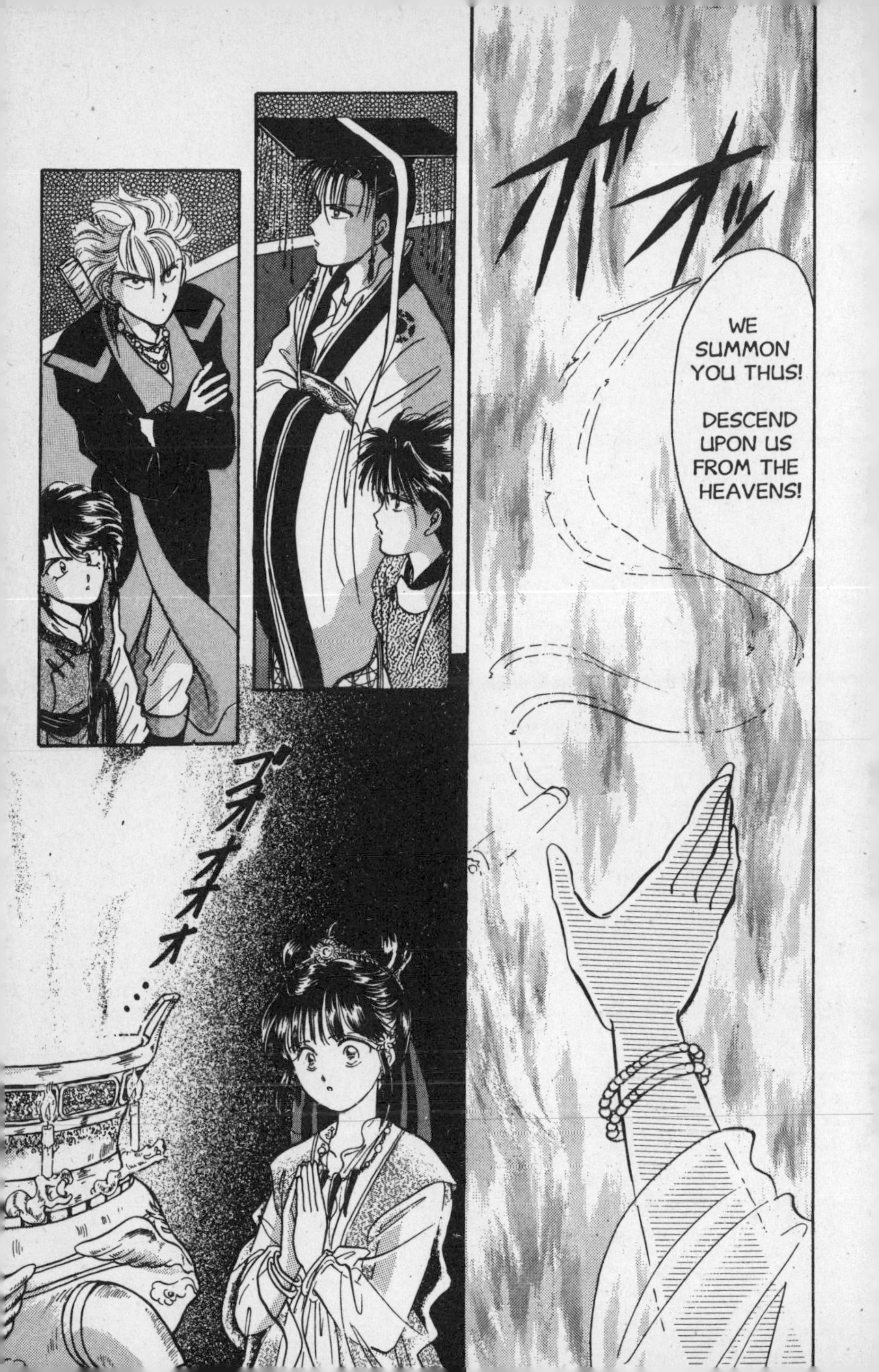
WE SUMMON YOU THUS!
DESCEND UPON US FROM THE HEAVENS!

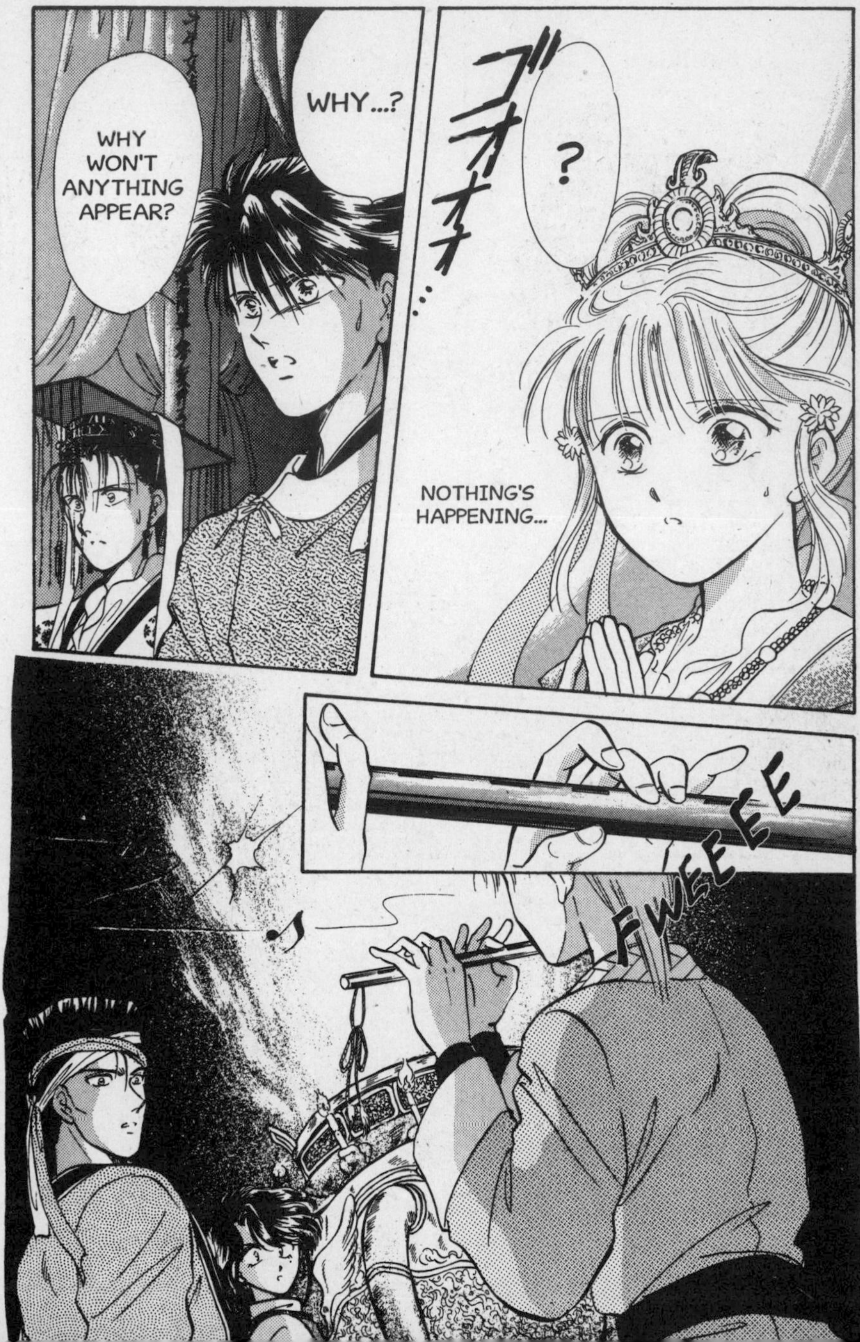
?
ゴオオオ…
NOTHING'S HAPPENING...
WHY...?
WHY WON'T ANYTHING APPEAR?
FWEEEE

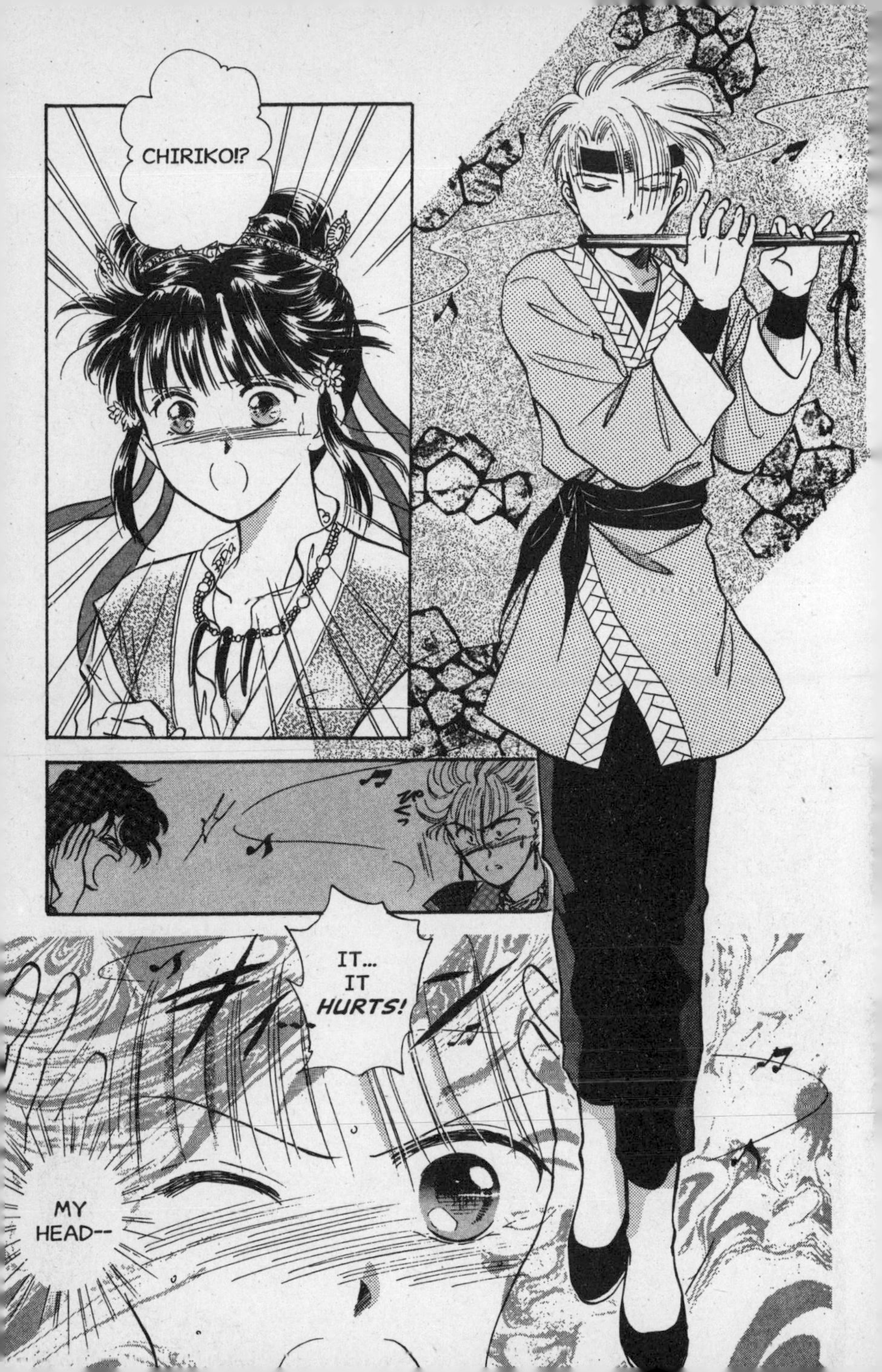
CHIRIKO!?
IT... IT HURTS!
MY HEAD--

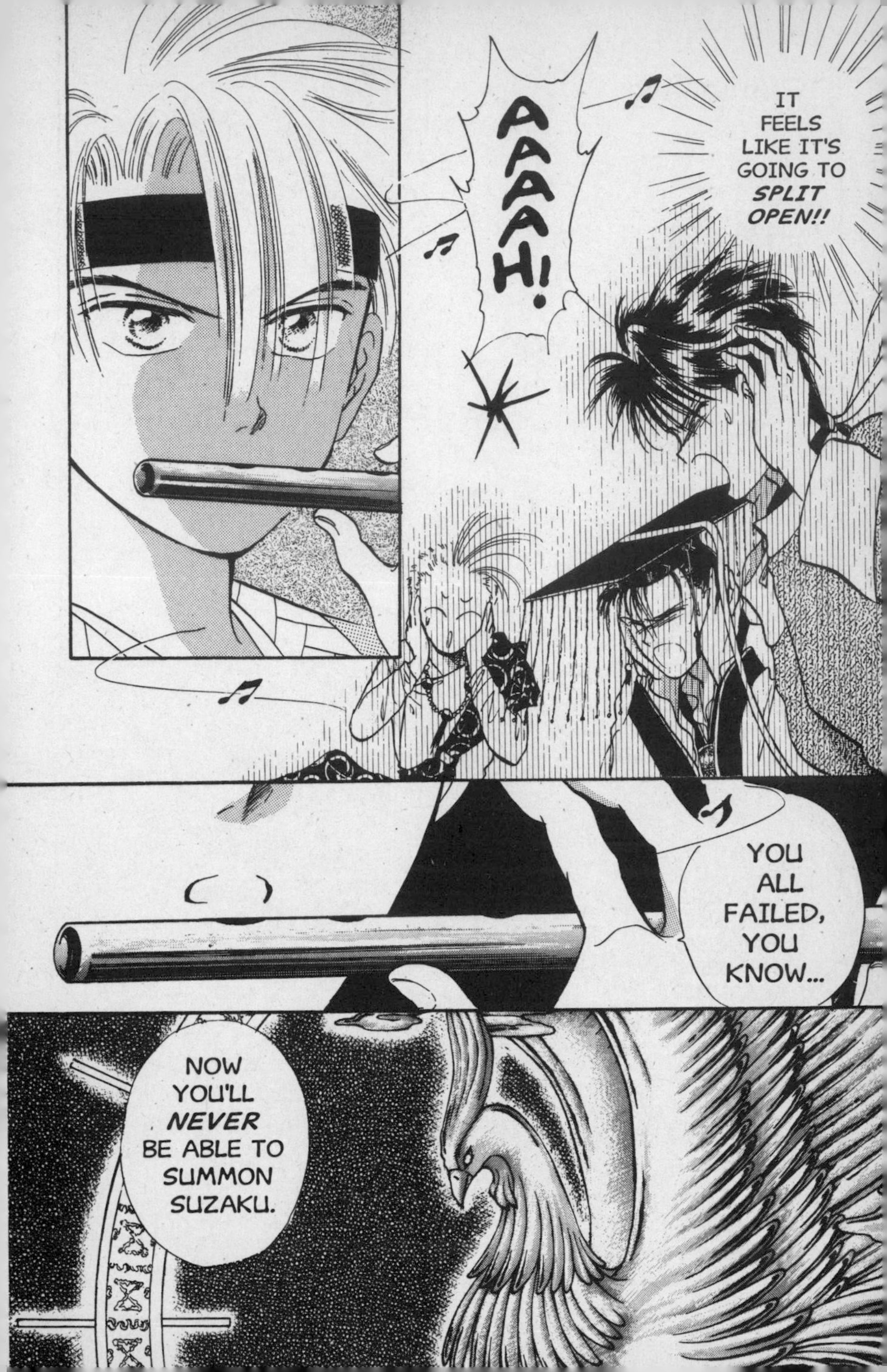
IT FEELS LIKE IT'S GOING TO *SPLIT OPEN!!*
AAAAH!
YOU ALL FAILED, YOU KNOW...
NOW YOU'LL ***NEVER*** BE ABLE TO SUMMON SUZAKU.

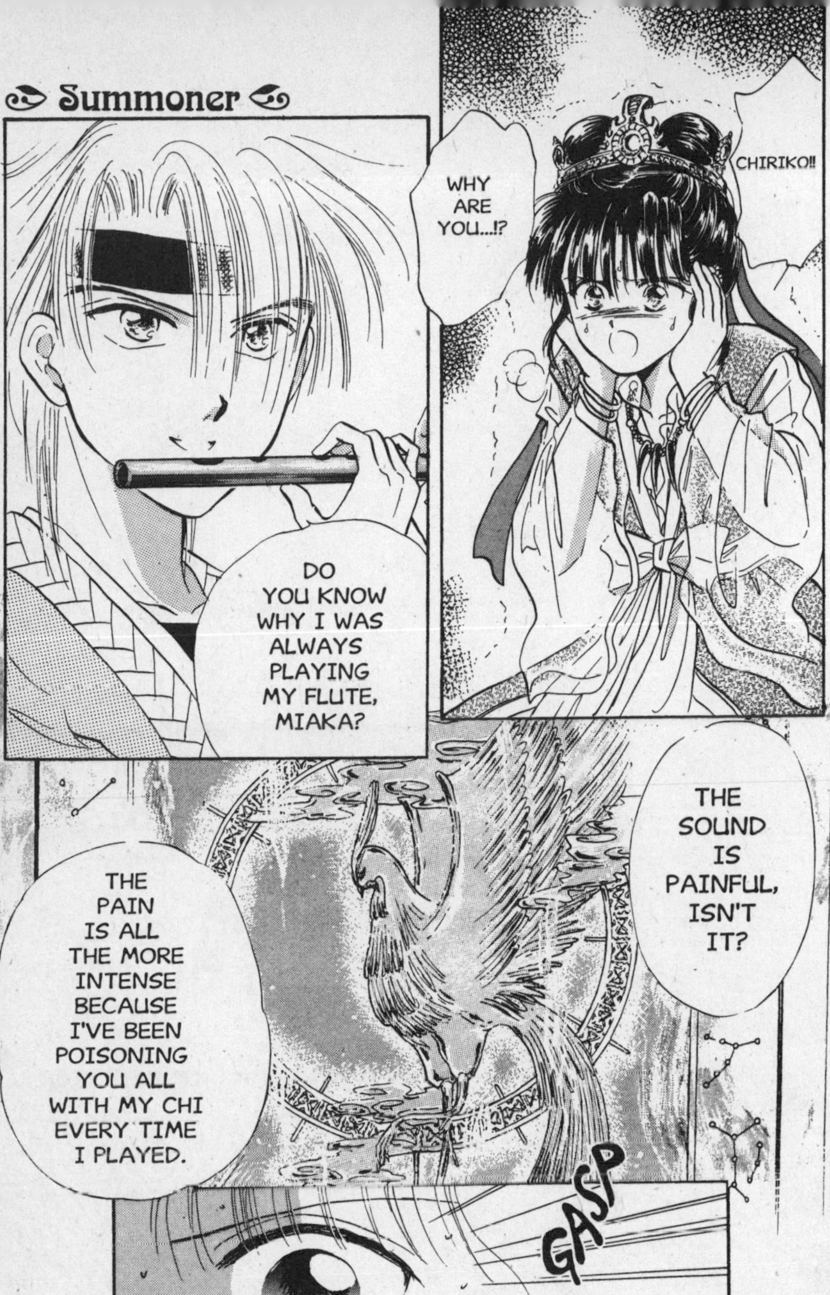
CHIRIKO!!
WHY ARE YOU...!?
DO YOU KNOW WHY I WAS ALWAYS PLAYING MY FLUTE, MIAKA?
THE SOUND IS PAINFUL, ISN'T IT?
THE PAIN IS ALL THE MORE INTENSE BECAUSE I'VE BEEN POISONING YOU ALL WITH MY CHI EVERY TIME I PLAYED.
GASP

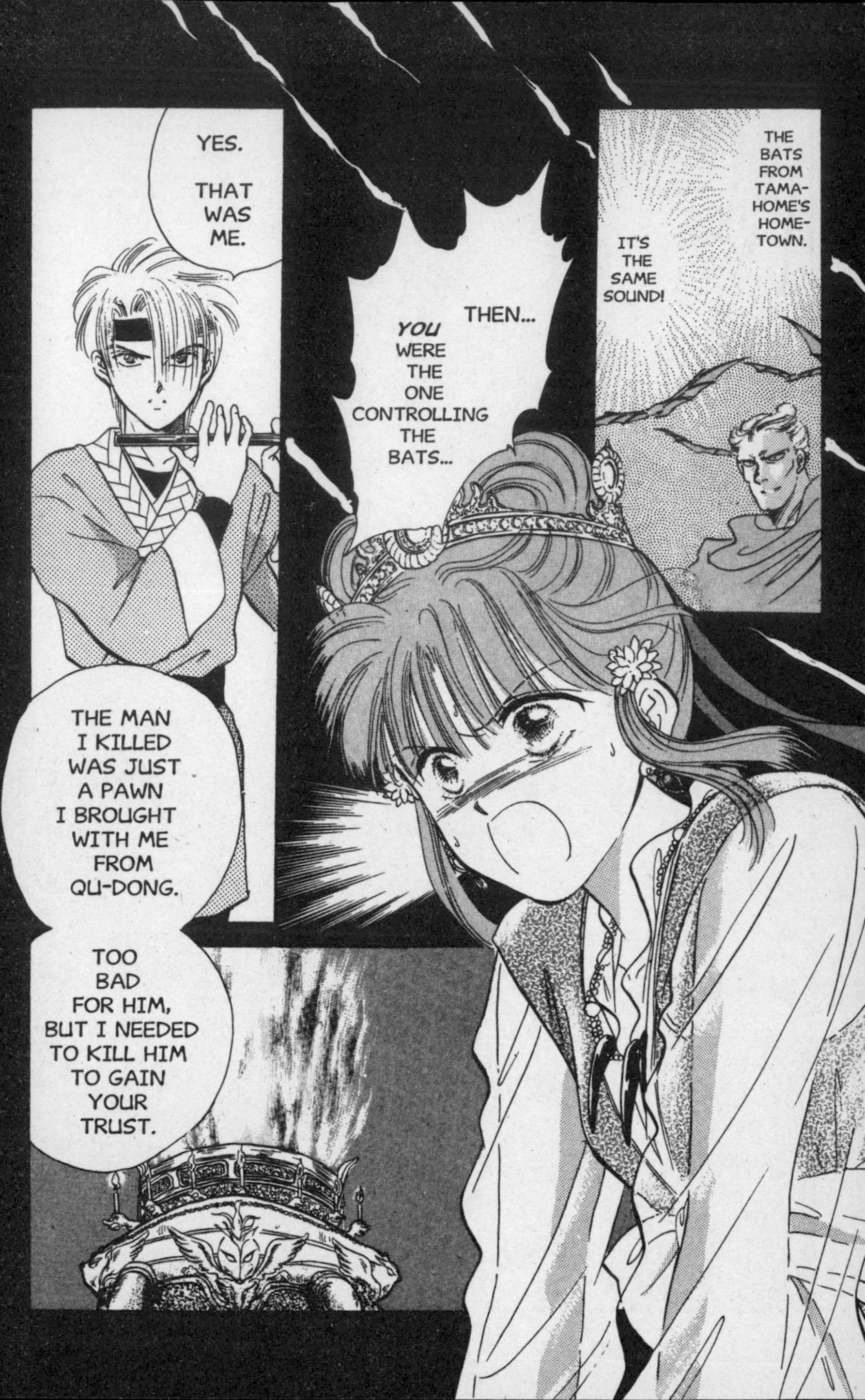
THE BATS FROM TAMA-HOME'S HOME-TOWN.
IT'S THE SAME SOUND!
THEN...
YOU WERE THE ONE CONTROLLING THE BATS...
YES.
THAT WAS ME.
THE MAN I KILLED WAS JUST A PAWN I BROUGHT WITH ME FROM QU-DONG.
TOO BAD FOR HIM, BUT I NEEDED TO KILL HIM TO GAIN YOUR TRUST.

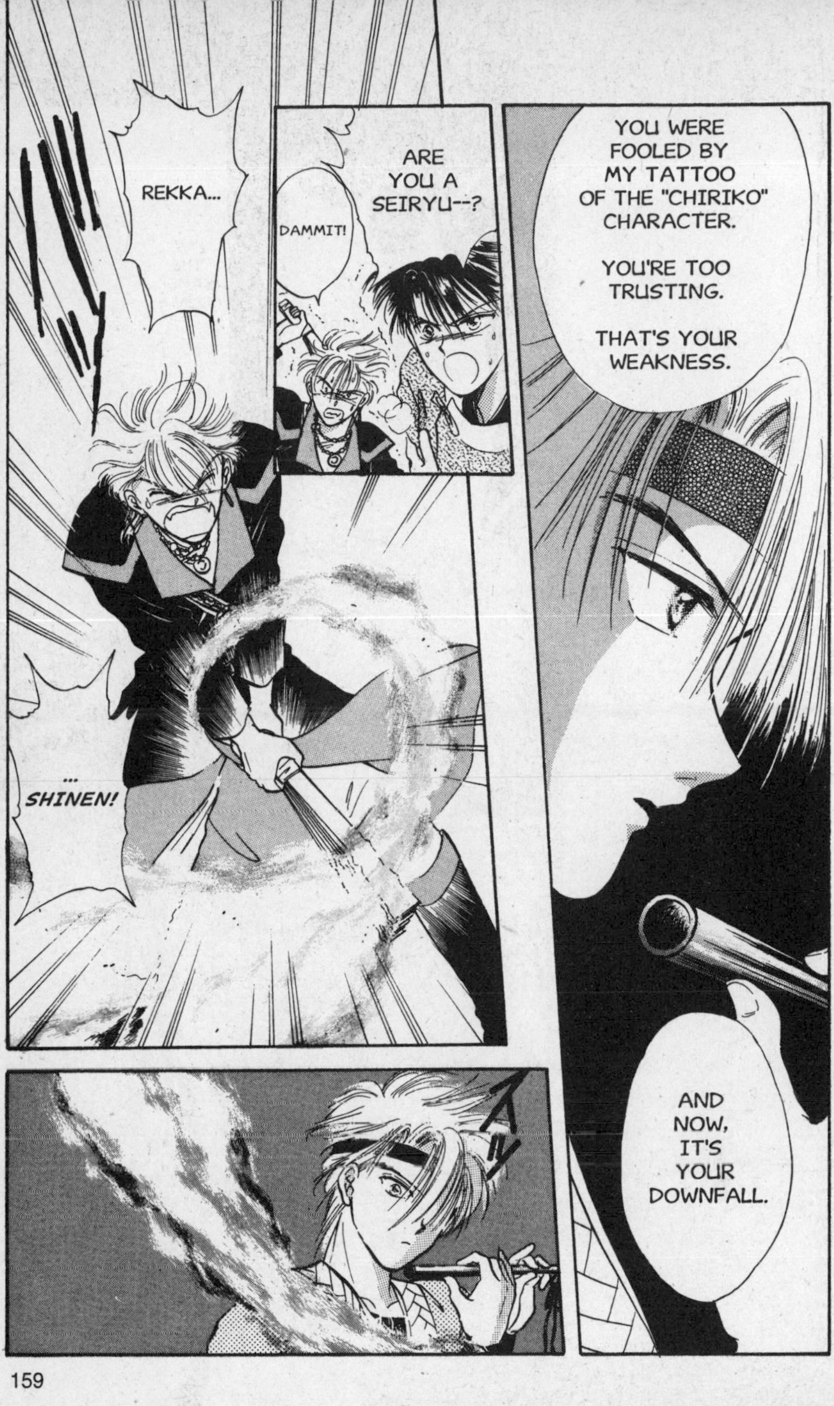
YOU WERE FOOLED BY MY TATTOO OF THE "CHIRIKO" CHARACTER.
YOU'RE TOO TRUSTING.
THAT'S YOUR WEAKNESS.
AND NOW, IT'S YOUR DOWNFALL.
ARE YOU A SEIRYU--?
DAMMIT!
REKKA...
... SHINEN!

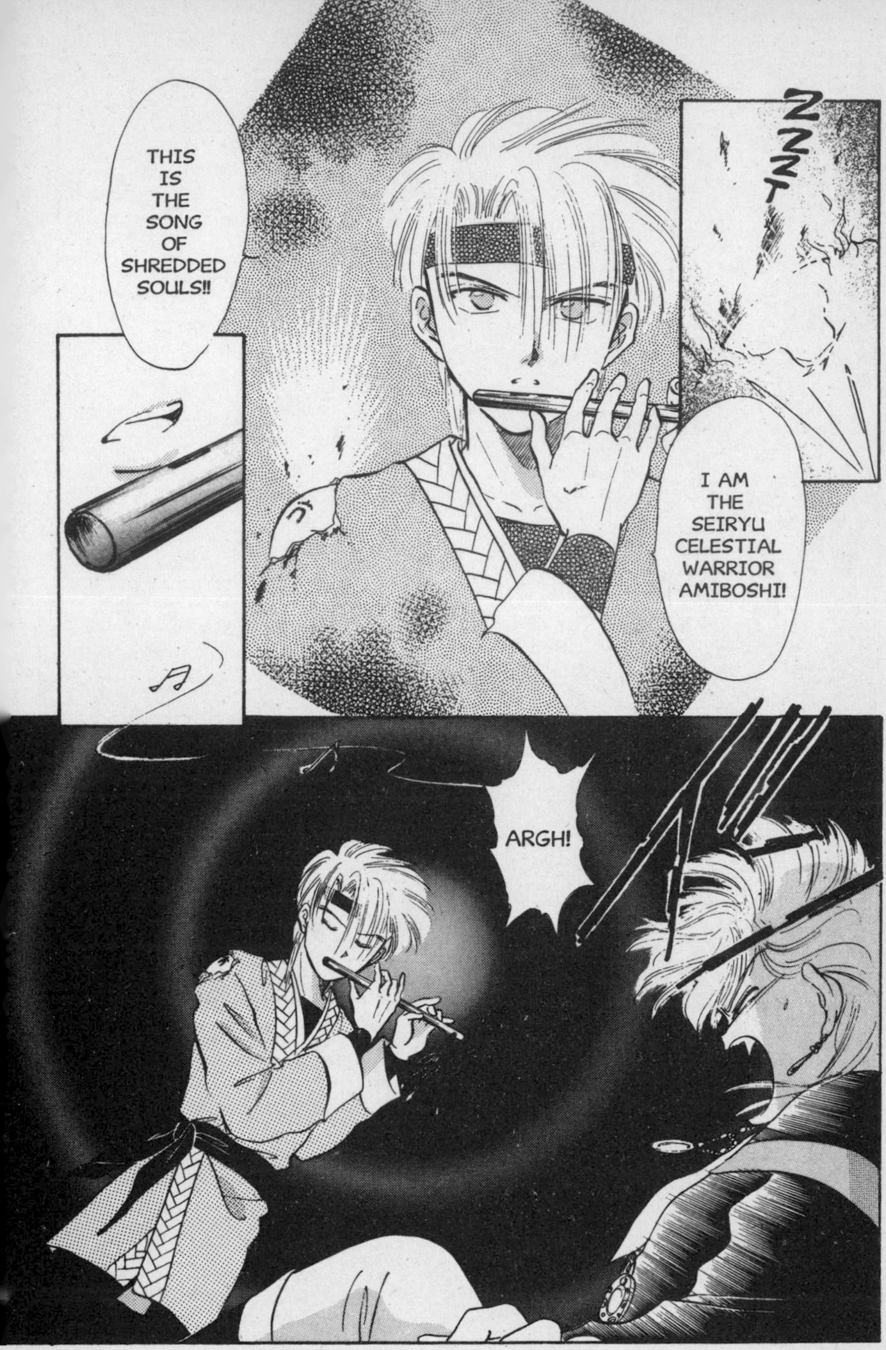
ZZZT
I AM THE SEIRYU CELESTIAL WARRIOR AMIBOSHI!
THIS IS THE SONG OF SHREDDED SOULS!!
ARGH!

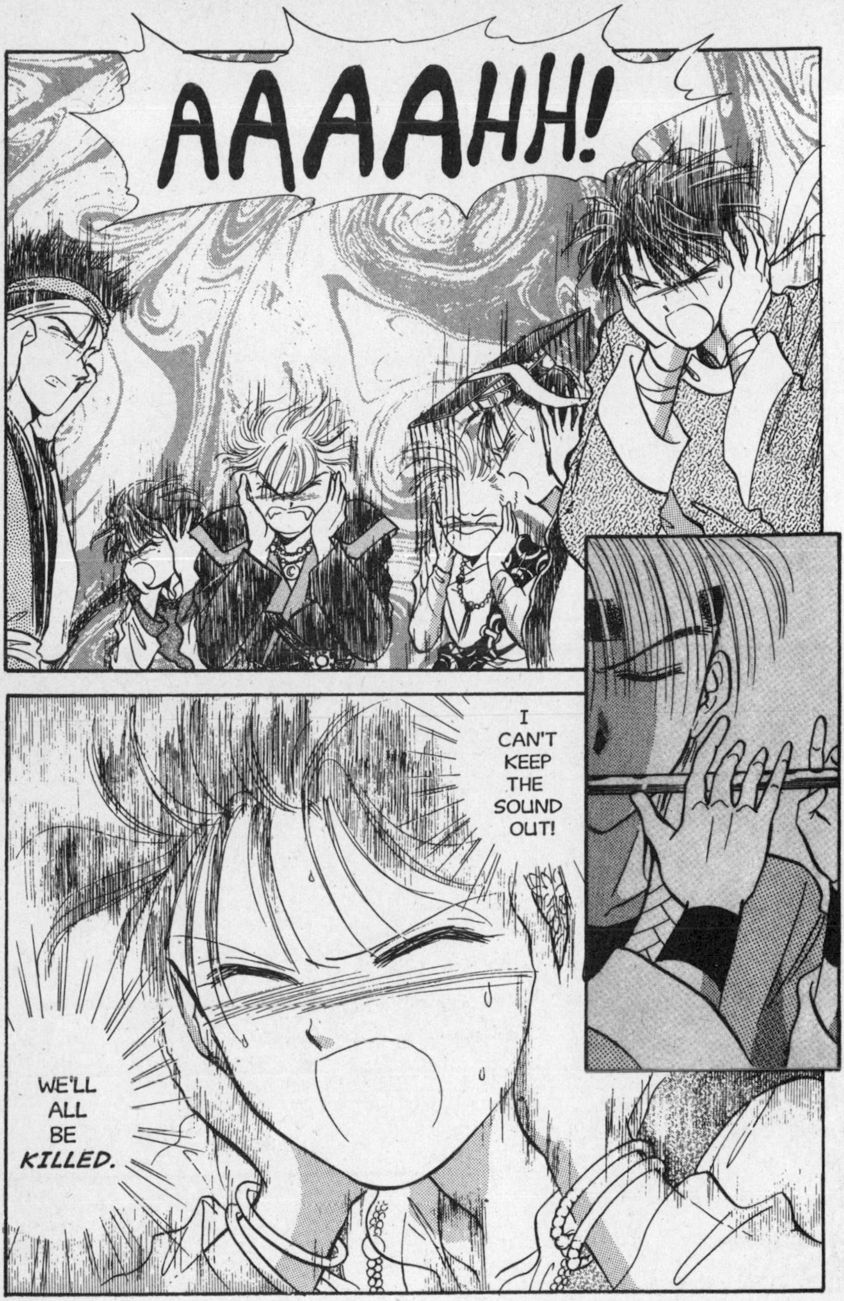
AAAAHH!
I CAN'T KEEP THE SOUND OUT!
WE'LL ALL BE *KILLED.*

The Unexpected Illustration Corner

These were drawn my by assistant M.
(who is in charge of SFX).
They were so cute
I had to
include them.
I once said that
she was an animator,
but it looks like she
still is an animator!

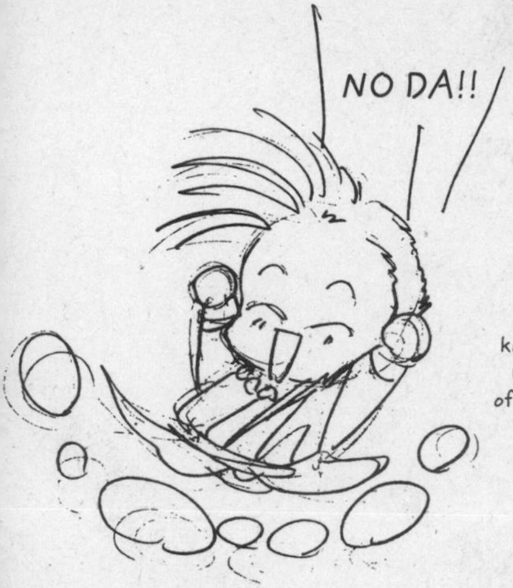
NO DA!!

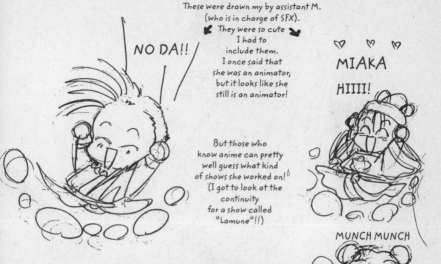

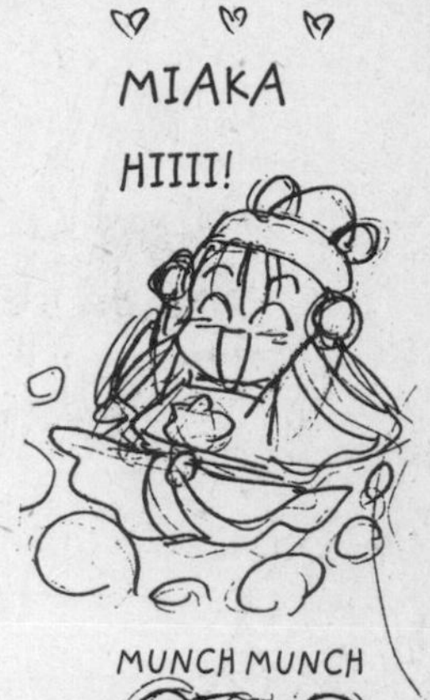
MIAKA
HIIII!

But those who
know anime can pretty
well guess what kind
of shows she worked on!
(I got to look at the
continuity
for a show called
"Lamune"!!)

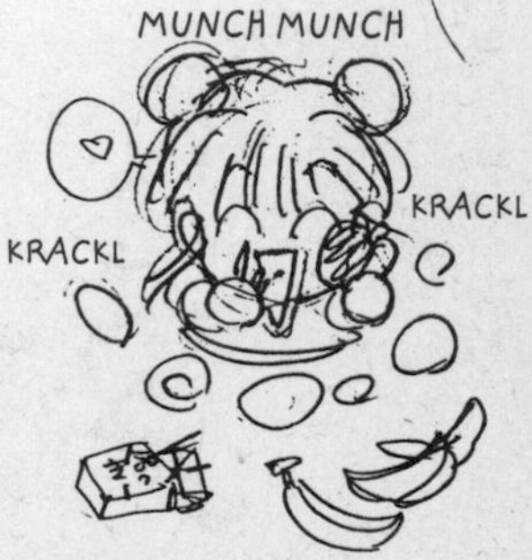
MUNCH MUNCH
KRACKL
KRACKL

This is a picture of Miaka drawn
by my assistant S. Ever since
around chapter six, she has
been doing the highlights in the
character's hair.
(I won't let anybody else do
Tamahome or Nuriko!)
A lot of her drawings make
it into the book.
She has also drawn a Tamahome,
but I'll save that for next time.

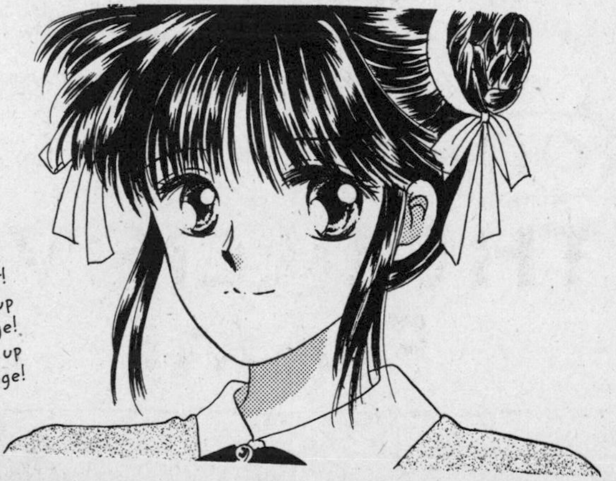

All right!
I filled up
the page!
I filled up
the page!

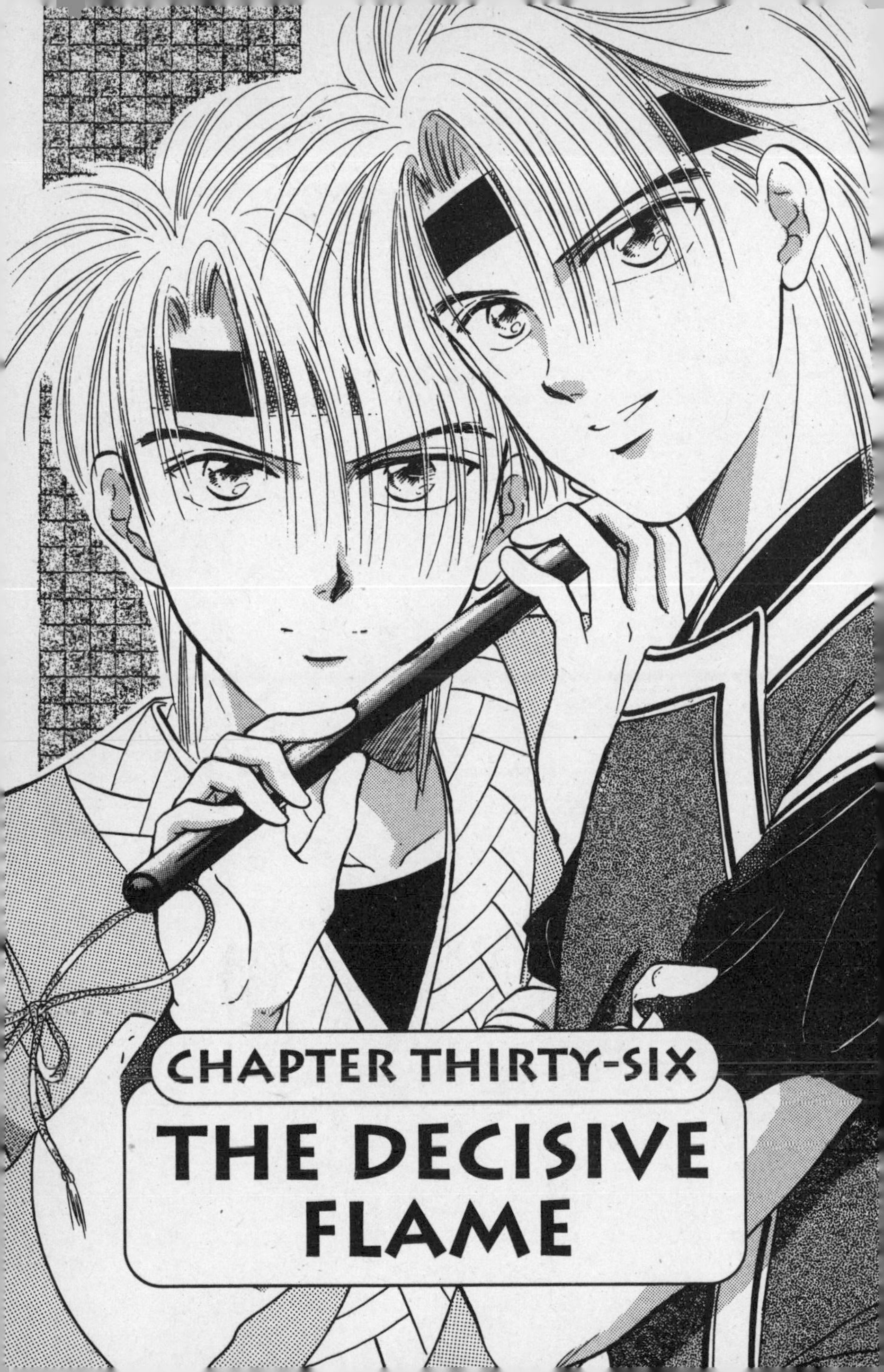
CHAPTER THIRTY-SIX
THE DECISIVE FLAME

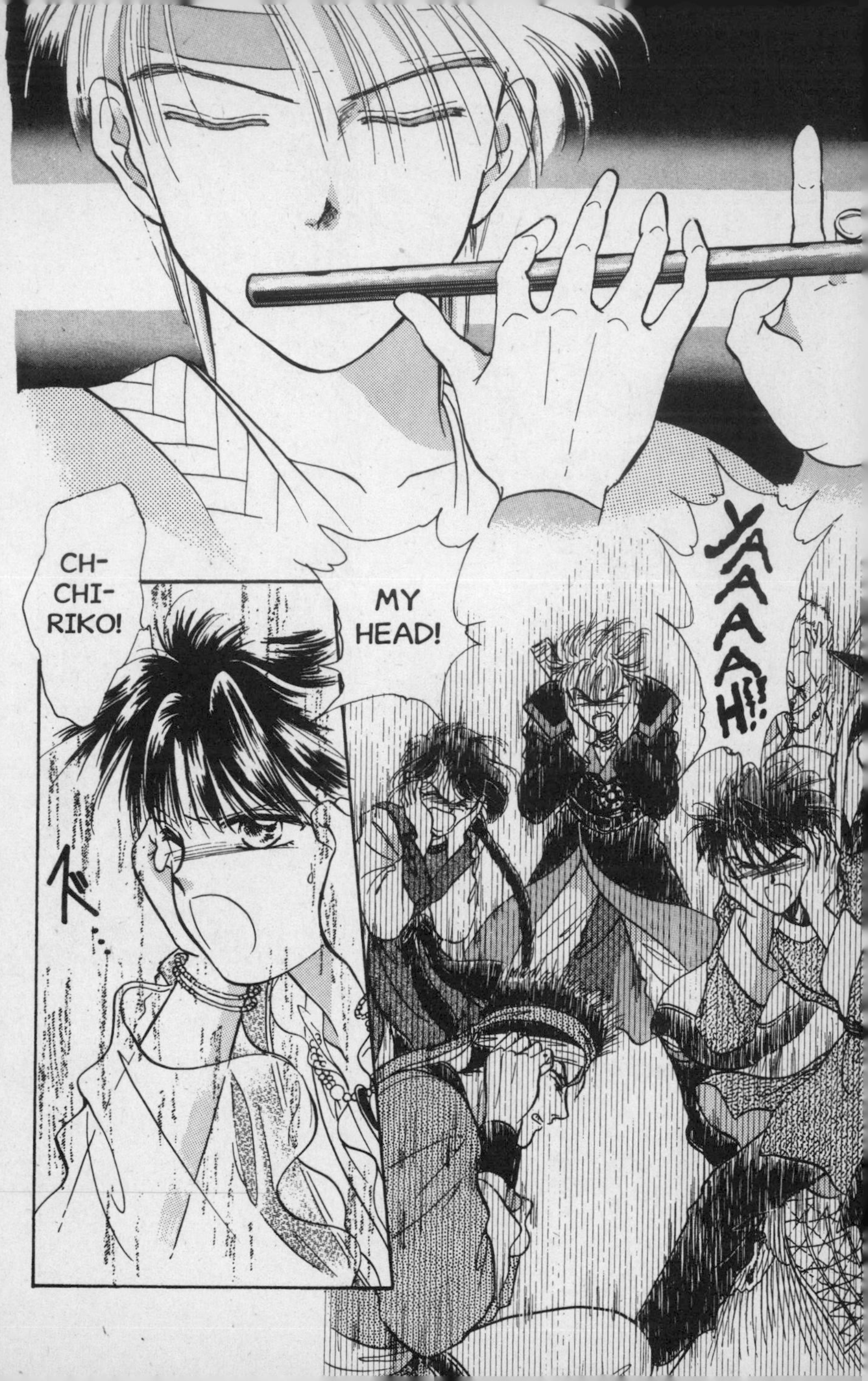

YAAAAH!!
MY HEAD!
CH-CHI-RIKO!
ド...

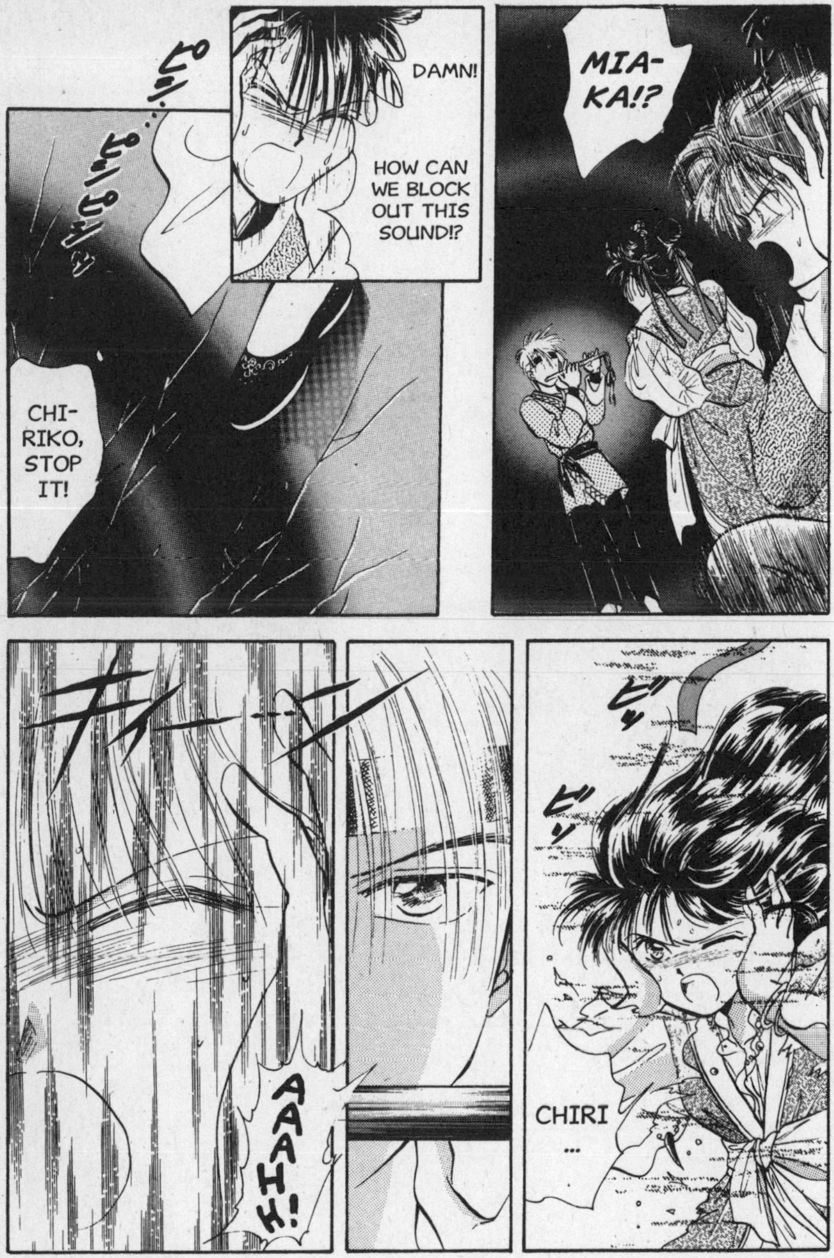
MIA-
KA!?
DAMN!
HOW CAN WE BLOCK OUT THIS SOUND!?
CHI-RIKO, STOP IT!
CHIRI
...
AAAHH!

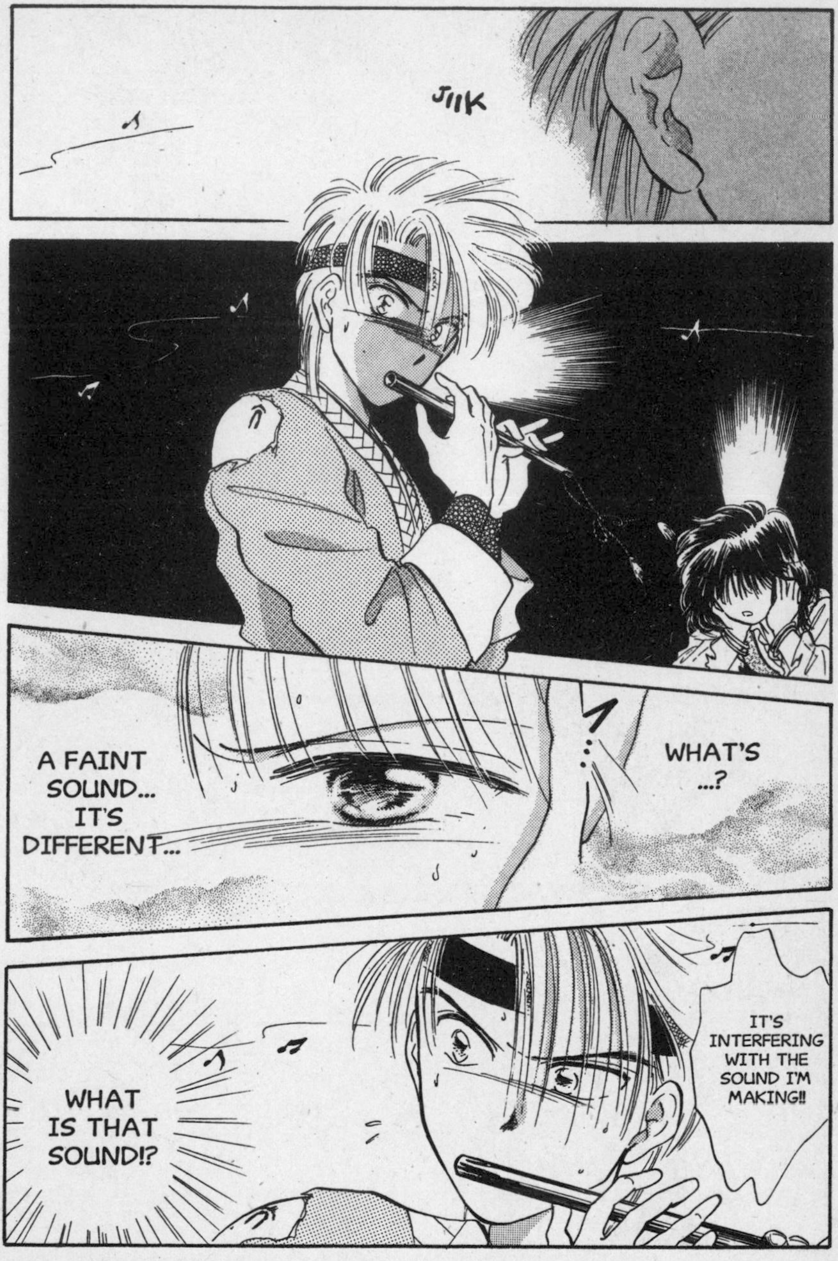
JIIK
WHAT'S ...?
A FAINT SOUND... IT'S DIFFERENT...
IT'S INTERFERING WITH THE SOUND I'M MAKING!!
WHAT IS THAT SOUND!?

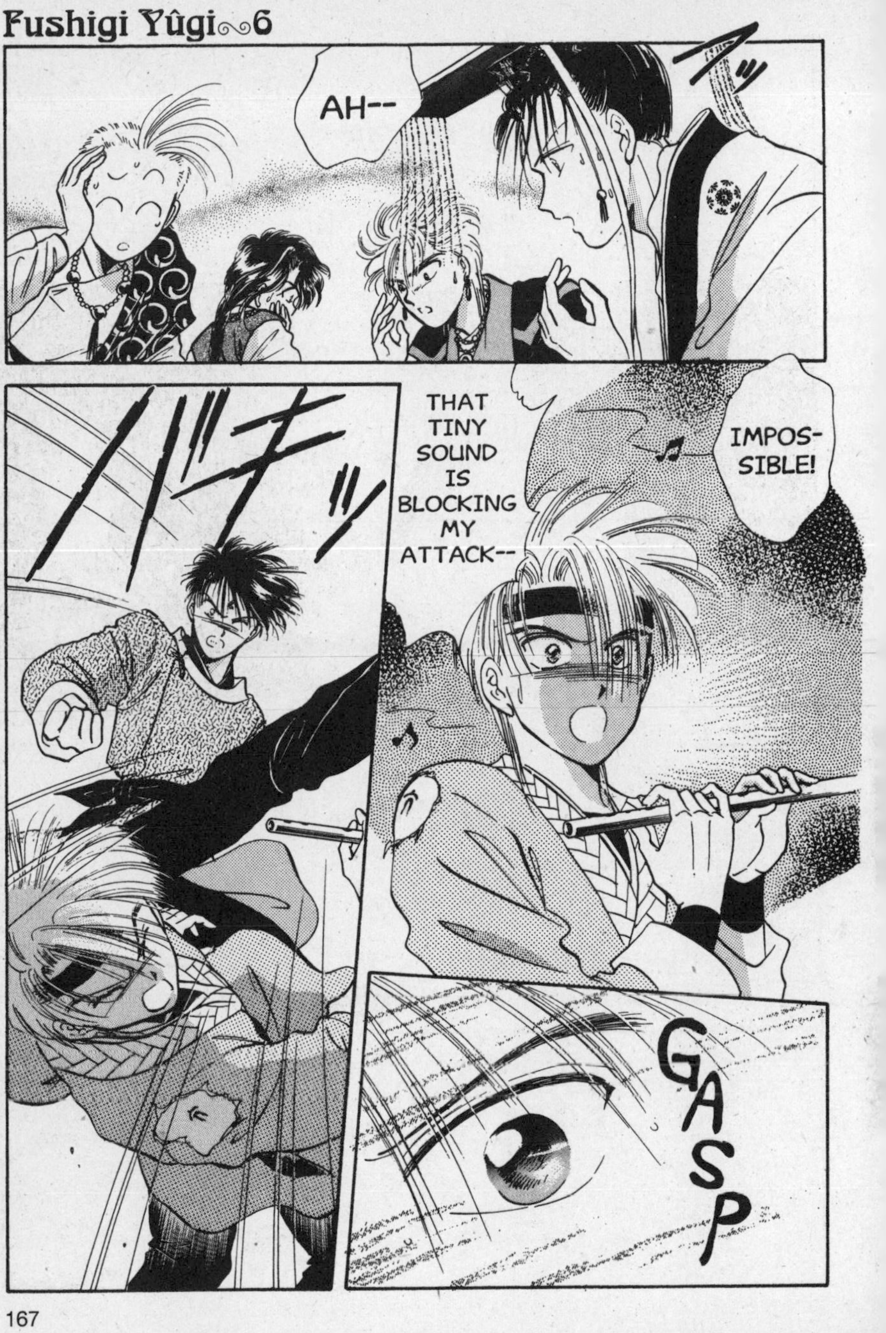
AH--
THAT TINY SOUND IS BLOCKING MY ATTACK--
IMPOSSIBLE!
バキッ
GASP

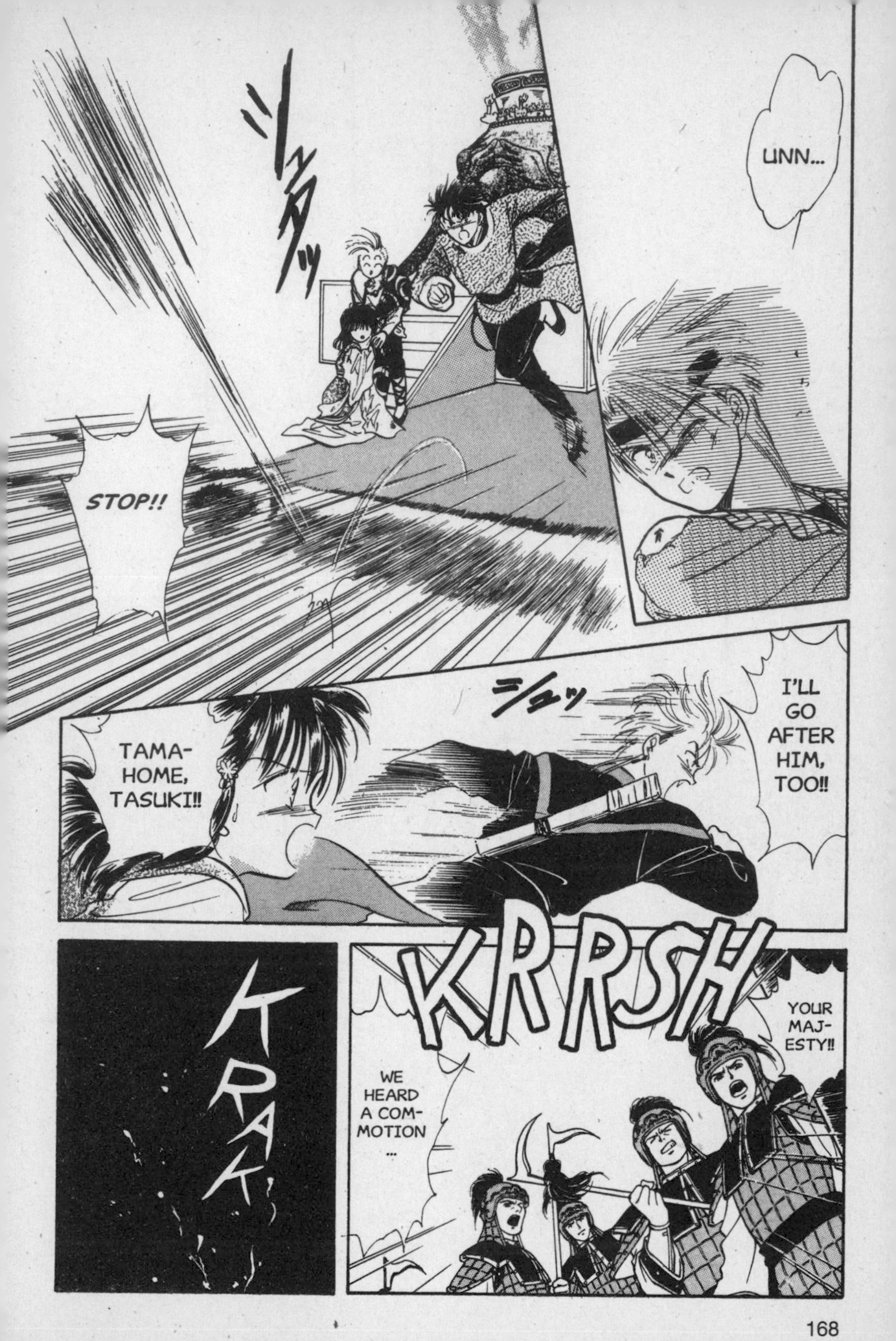
UNN...
シュタッ
STOP!!
I'LL GO AFTER HIM, TOO!!
シュッ
TAMA-HOME, TASUKI!!
KRRSH
YOUR MAJ-ESTY!!
WE HEARD A COM-MOTION ...
KRAK

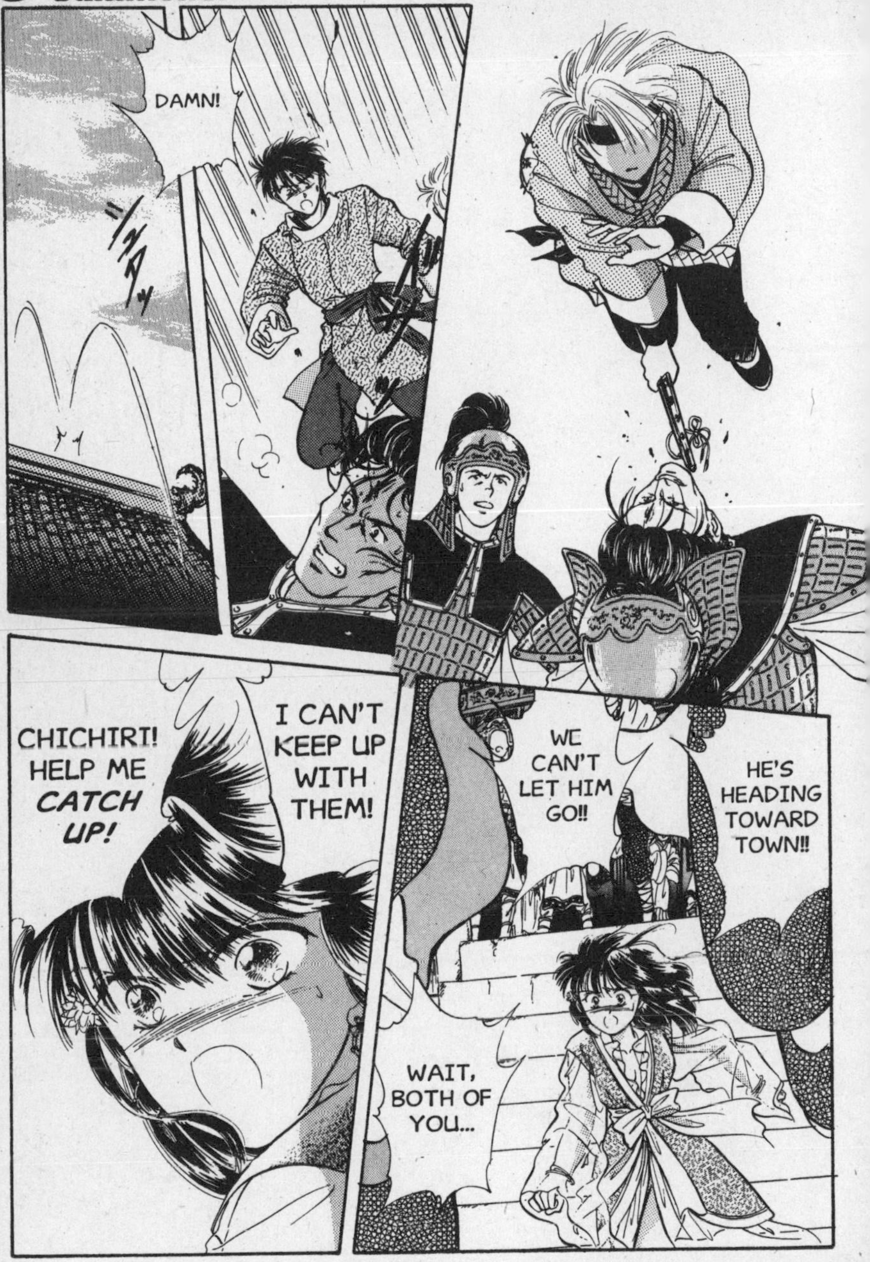
DAMN!
HE'S HEADING TOWARD TOWN!!
WE CAN'T LET HIM GO!!
WAIT, BOTH OF YOU...
I CAN'T KEEP UP WITH THEM!
CHICHIRI! HELP ME *CATCH UP!*

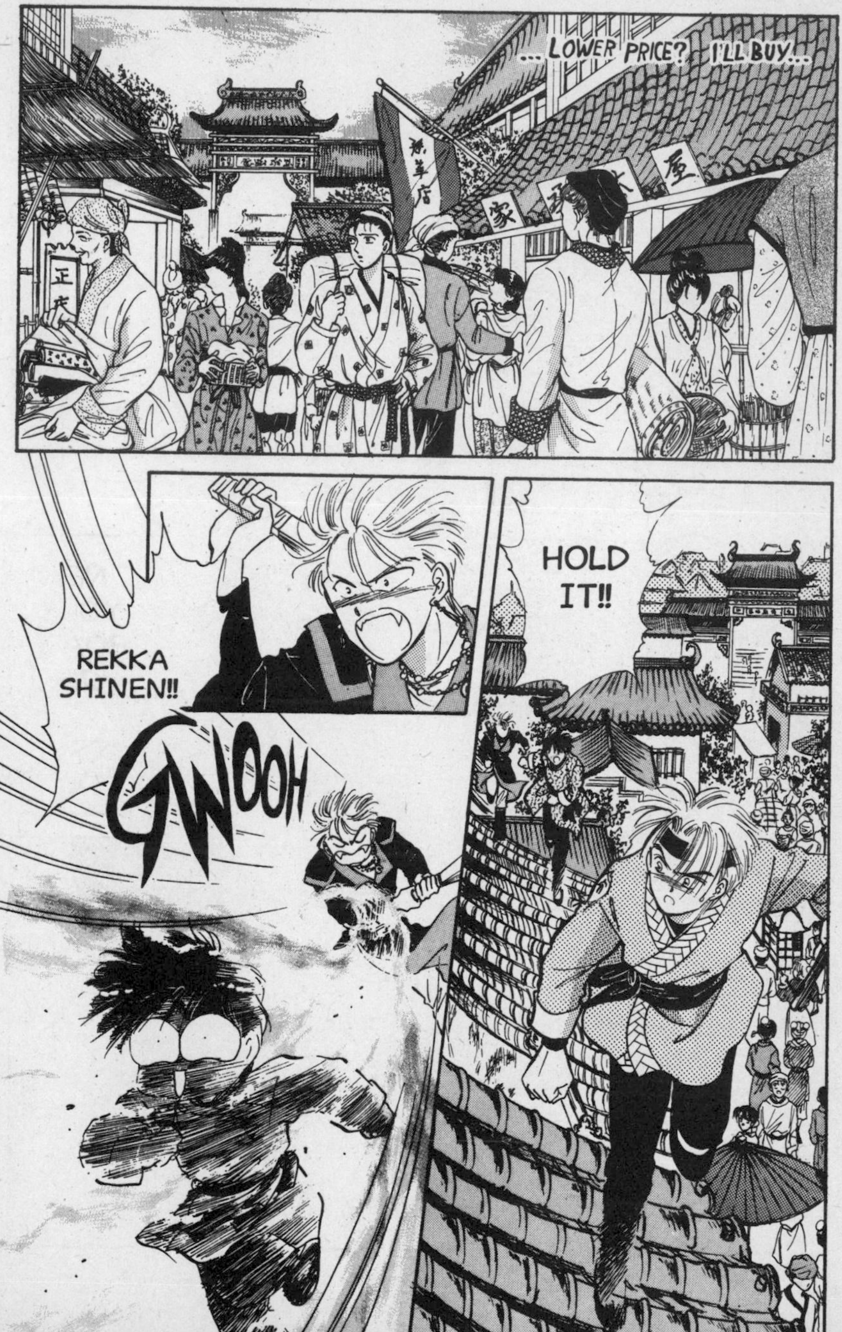
... LOWER PRICE? I'LL BUY...
HOLD IT!!
REKKA SHINEN!!
GWOOH

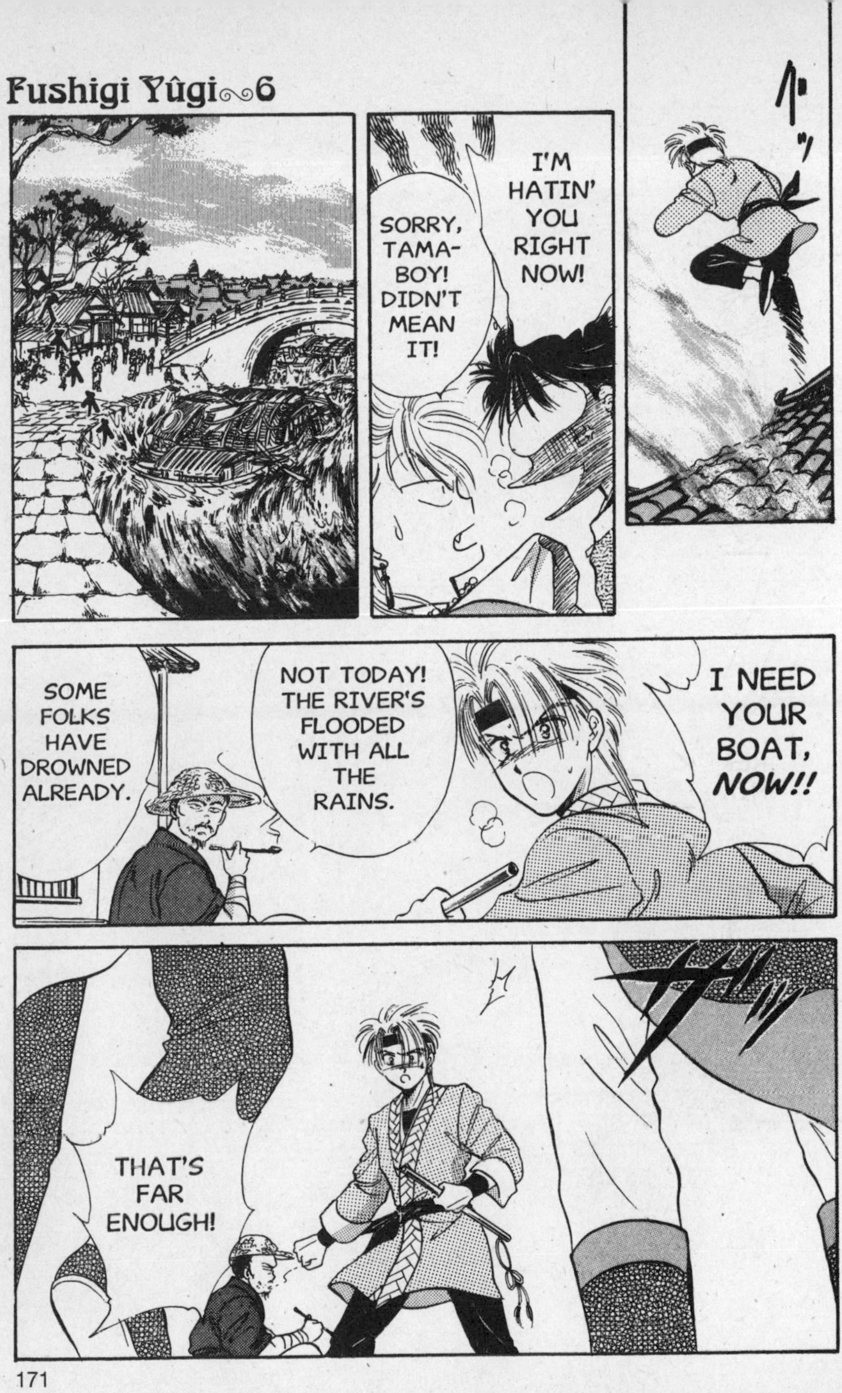
I'M HATIN' YOU RIGHT NOW!
SORRY, TAMA-BOY! DIDN'T MEAN IT!
I NEED YOUR BOAT, *NOW!!*
NOT TODAY! THE RIVER'S FLOODED WITH ALL THE RAINS.
SOME FOLKS HAVE DROWNED ALREADY.
THAT'S FAR ENOUGH!

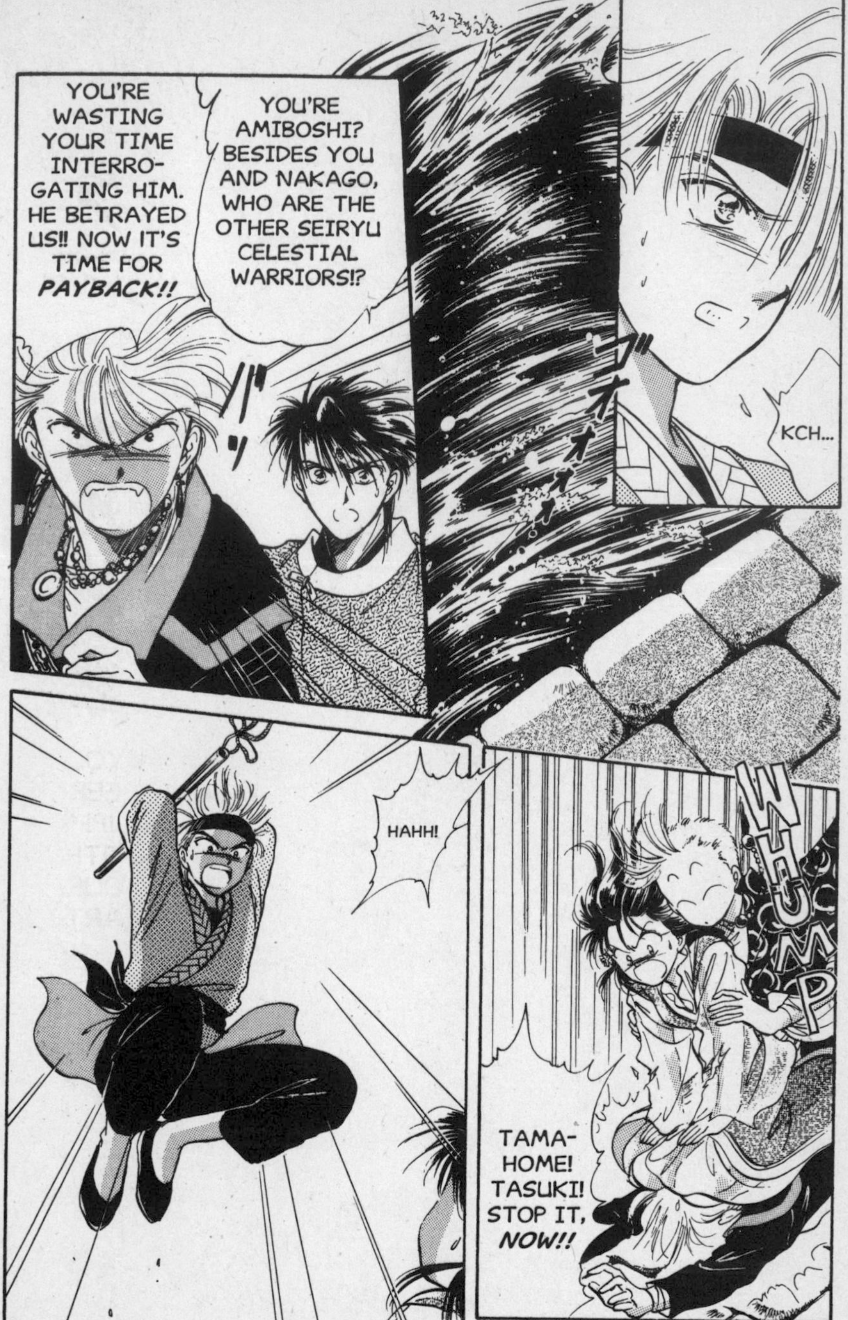
KCH...
YOU'RE AMIBOSHI? BESIDES YOU AND NAKAGO, WHO ARE THE OTHER SEIRYU CELESTIAL WARRIORS!?
YOU'RE WASTING YOUR TIME INTERROGATING HIM. HE BETRAYED US!! NOW IT'S TIME FOR *PAYBACK!!*
WHUMP
TAMAHOME! TASUKI! STOP IT, *NOW!!*
HAHH!

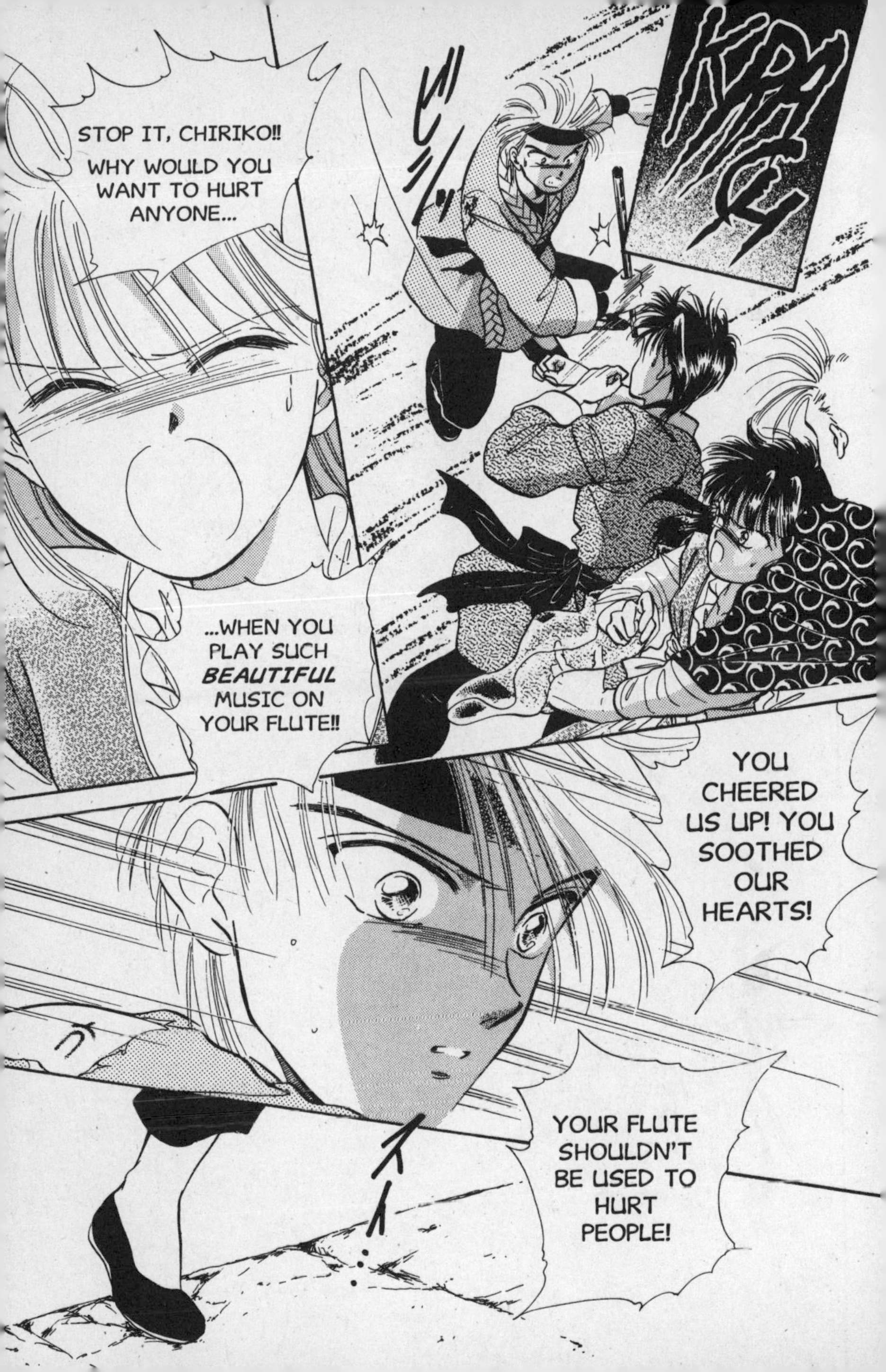

KRAACH
STOP IT, CHIRIKO!! WHY WOULD YOU WANT TO HURT ANYONE...
...WHEN YOU PLAY SUCH *BEAUTIFUL* MUSIC ON YOUR FLUTE!!
YOU CHEERED US UP! YOU SOOTHED OUR HEARTS!
YOUR FLUTE SHOULDN'T BE USED TO HURT PEOPLE!

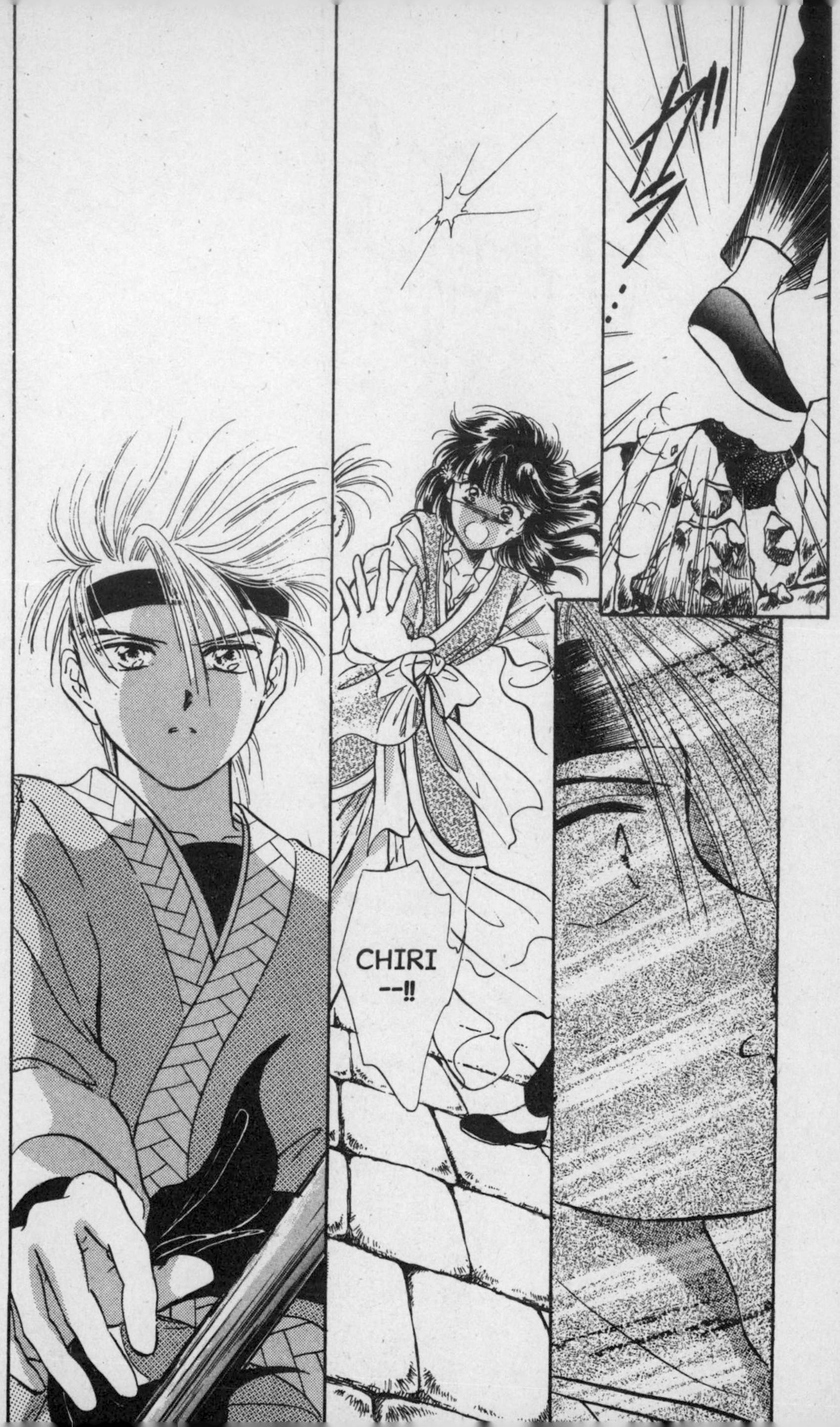
CHIRI
--!!

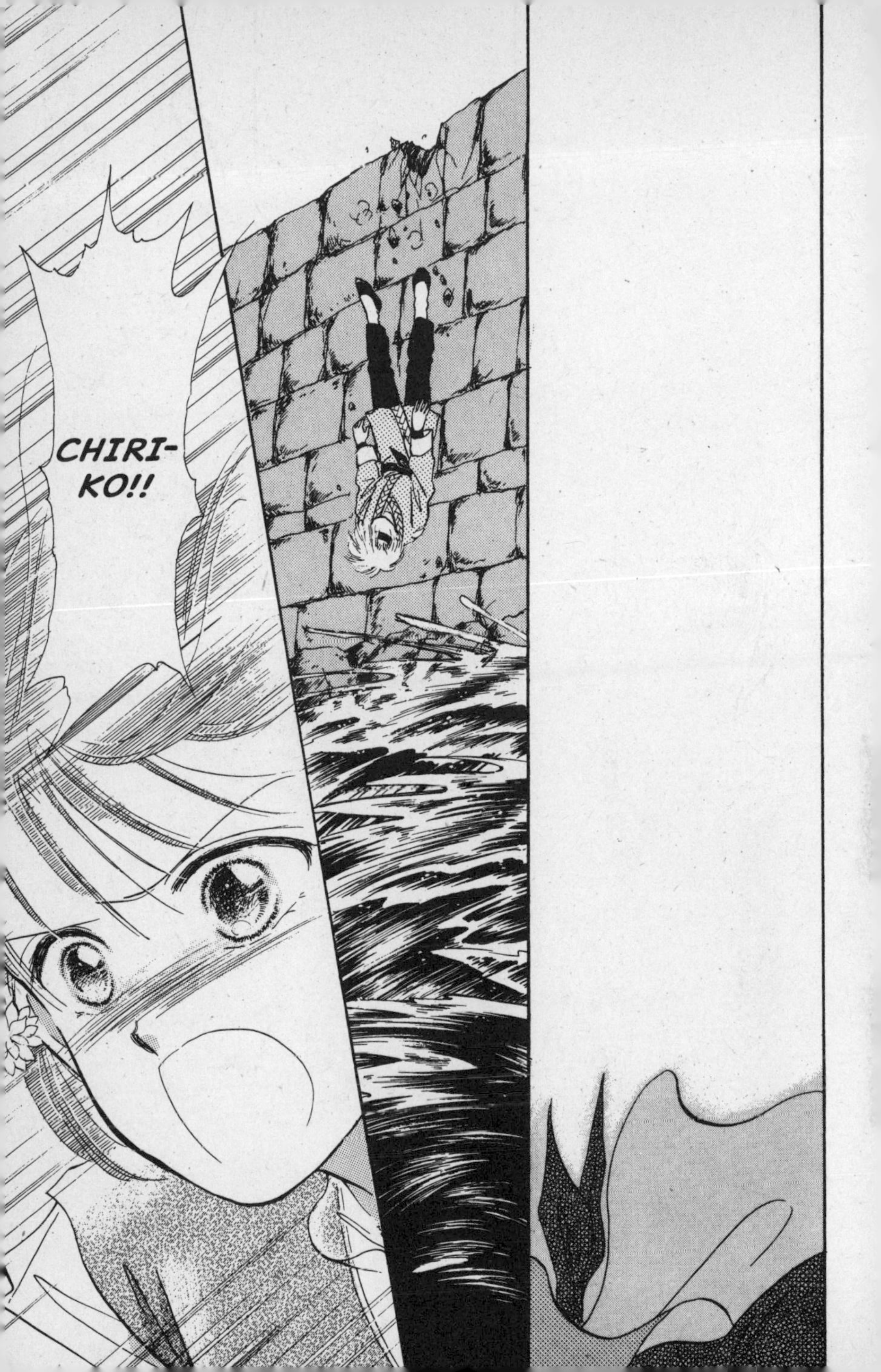
CHIRI-
KO!!

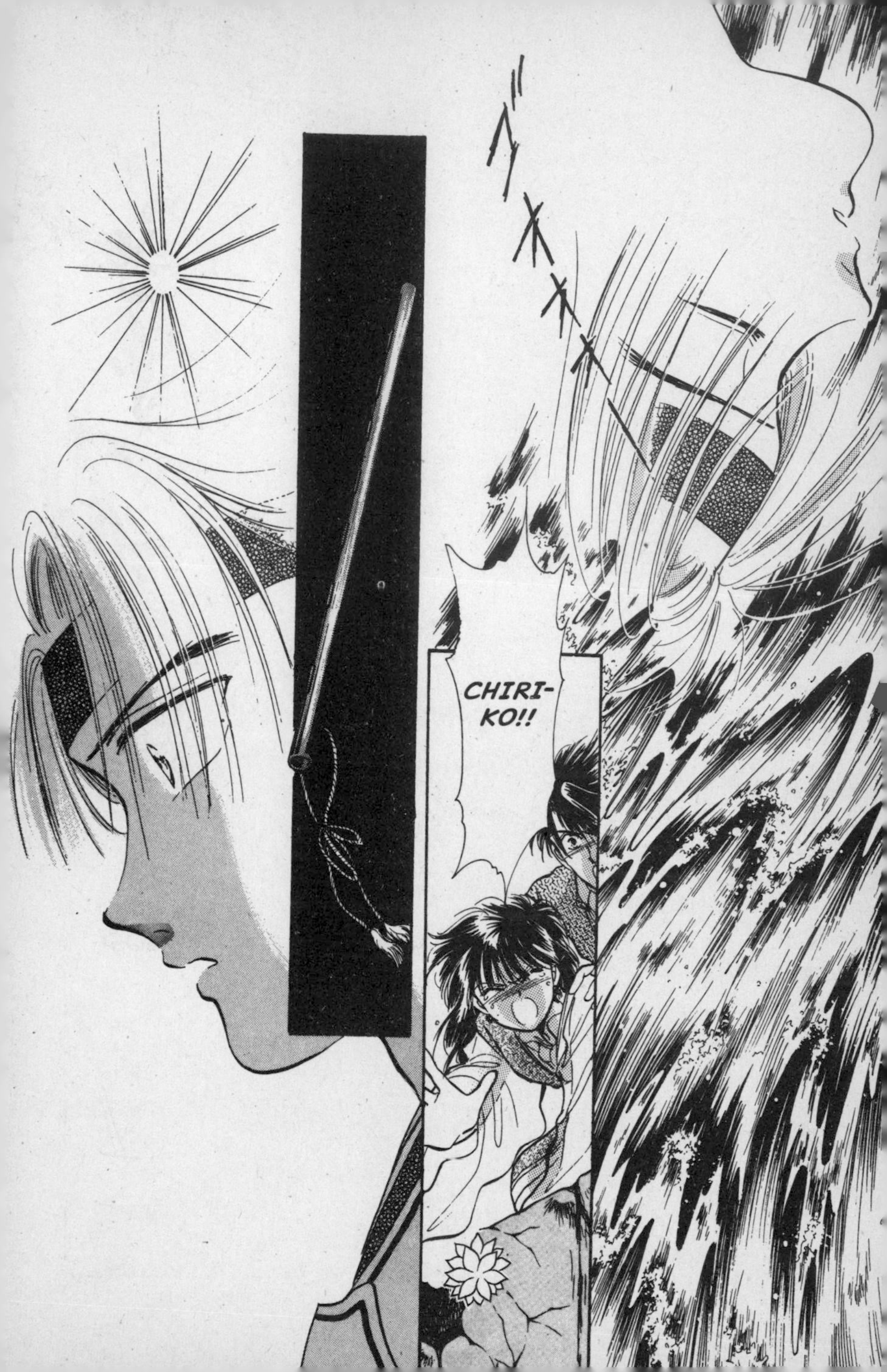
CHIRI-
KO!!

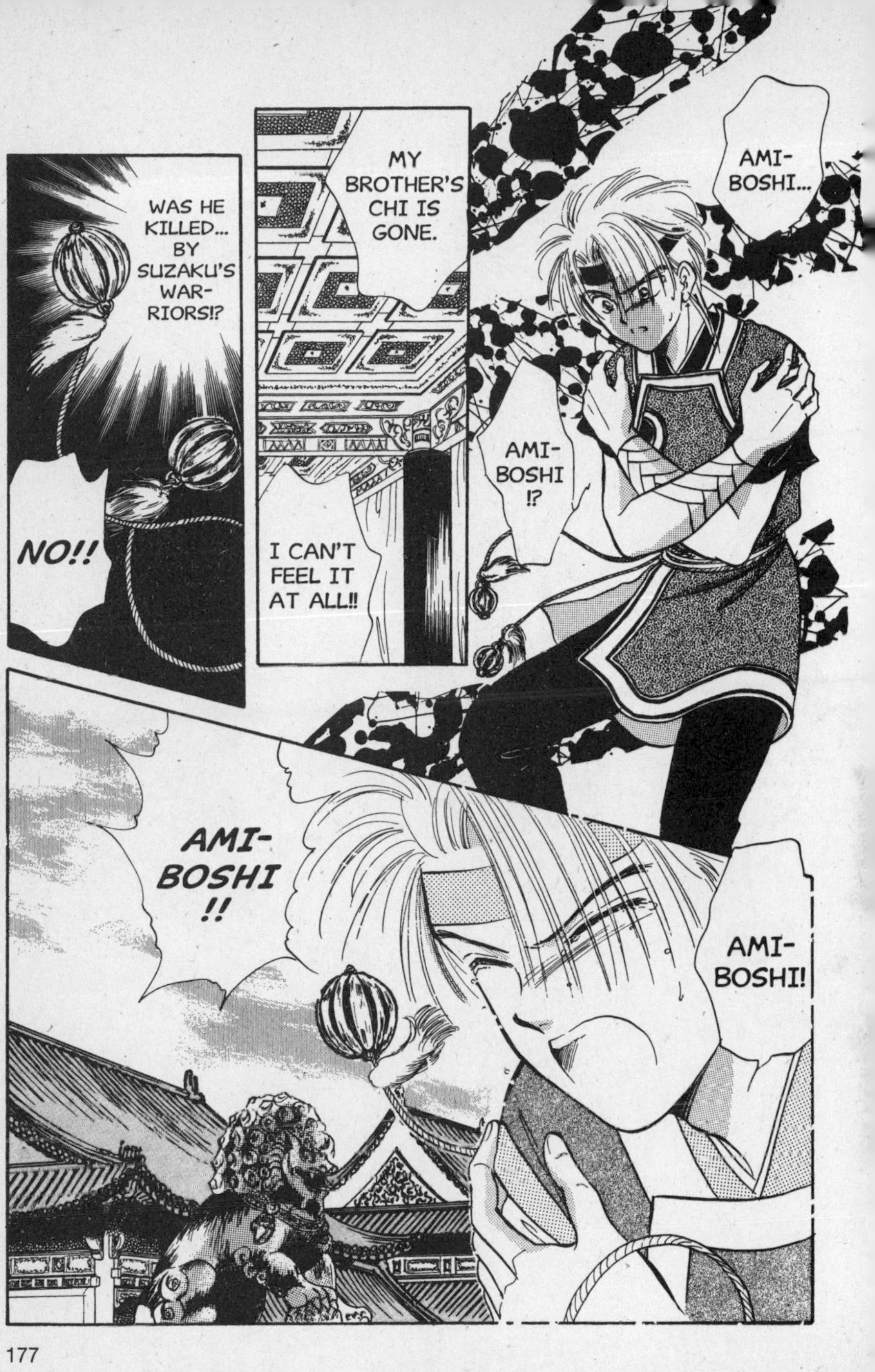
AMI-BOSHI...
AMI-BOSHI !?
MY BROTHER'S CHI IS GONE.
I CAN'T FEEL IT AT ALL!!
WAS HE KILLED... BY SUZAKU'S WAR-RIORS!?
NO!!
AMI-BOSHI!
AMI-BOSHI !!

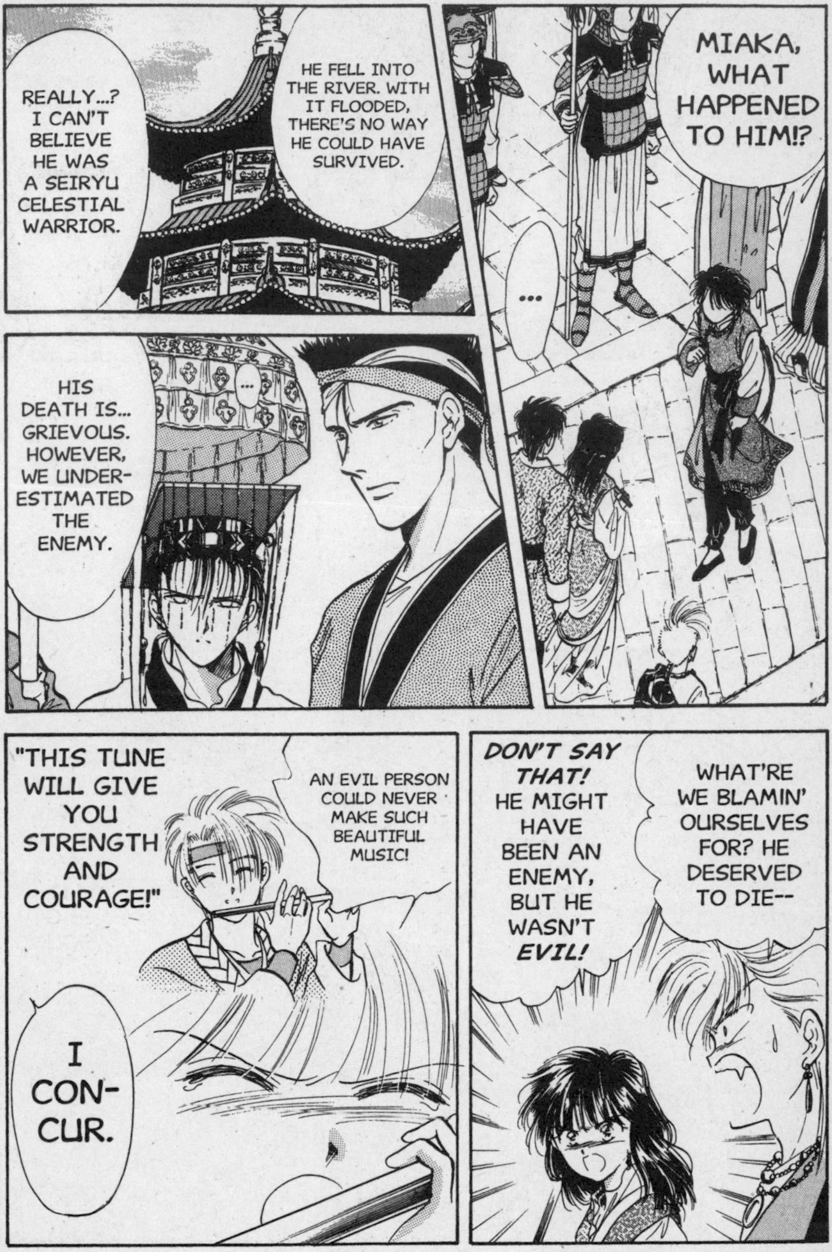
MIAKA, WHAT HAPPENED TO HIM!?
...
HE FELL INTO THE RIVER. WITH IT FLOODED, THERE'S NO WAY HE COULD HAVE SURVIVED.
REALLY...? I CAN'T BELIEVE HE WAS A SEIRYU CELESTIAL WARRIOR.
...
HIS DEATH IS... GRIEVOUS. HOWEVER, WE UNDER-ESTIMATED THE ENEMY.
WHAT'RE WE BLAMIN' OURSELVES FOR? HE DESERVED TO DIE--
DON'T SAY THAT! HE MIGHT HAVE BEEN AN ENEMY, BUT HE WASN'T *EVIL!*
AN EVIL PERSON COULD NEVER MAKE SUCH BEAUTIFUL MUSIC!
"THIS TUNE WILL GIVE YOU STRENGTH AND COURAGE!"
I CON-CUR.

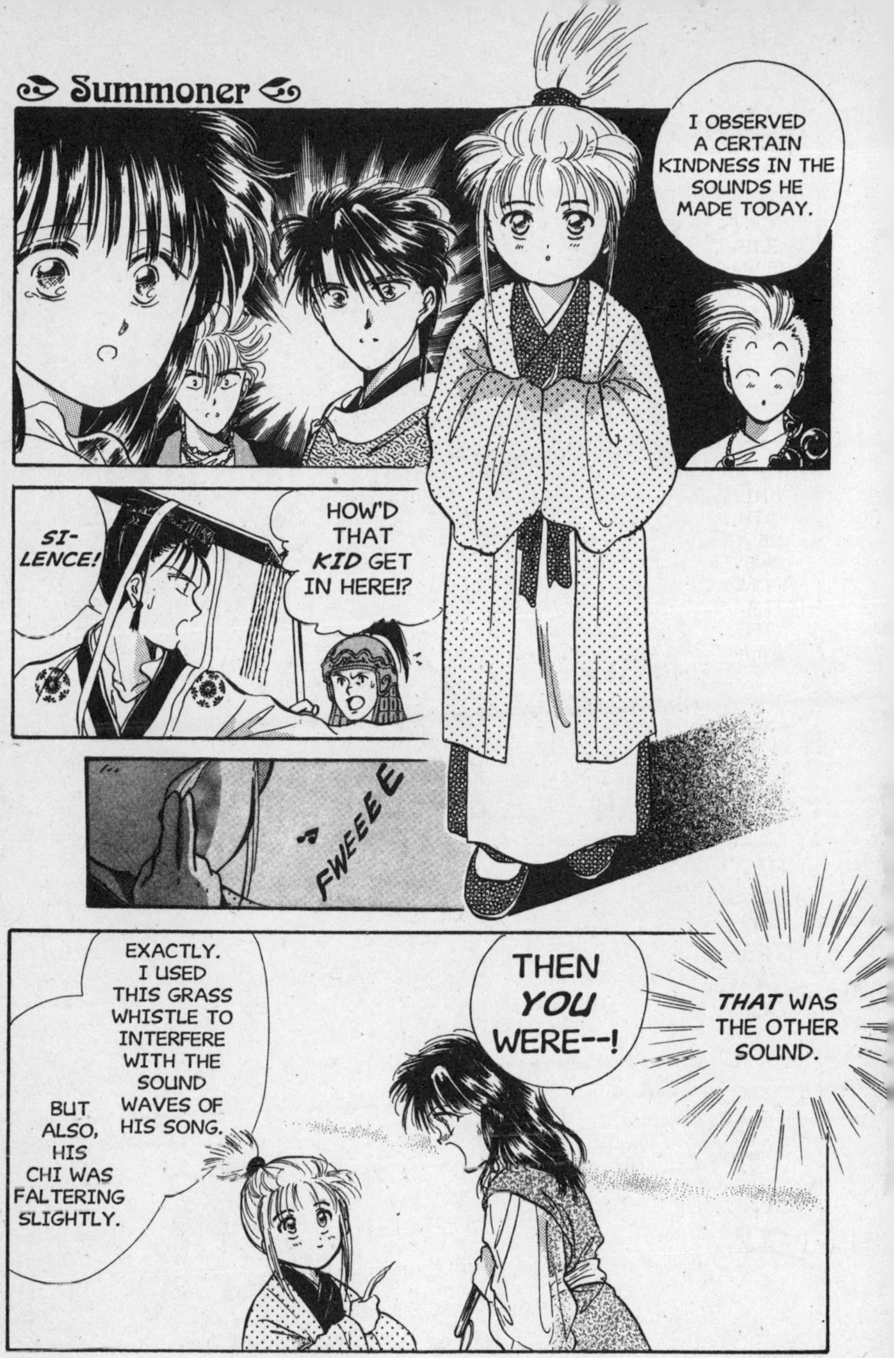
I OBSERVED A CERTAIN KINDNESS IN THE SOUNDS HE MADE TODAY.
HOW'D THAT *KID* GET IN HERE!?
SI-LENCE!
FWEEEE
THAT WAS THE OTHER SOUND.
THEN *YOU* WERE--!
EXACTLY. I USED THIS GRASS WHISTLE TO INTERFERE WITH THE SOUND WAVES OF HIS SONG.
BUT ALSO, HIS CHI WAS FALTERING SLIGHTLY.

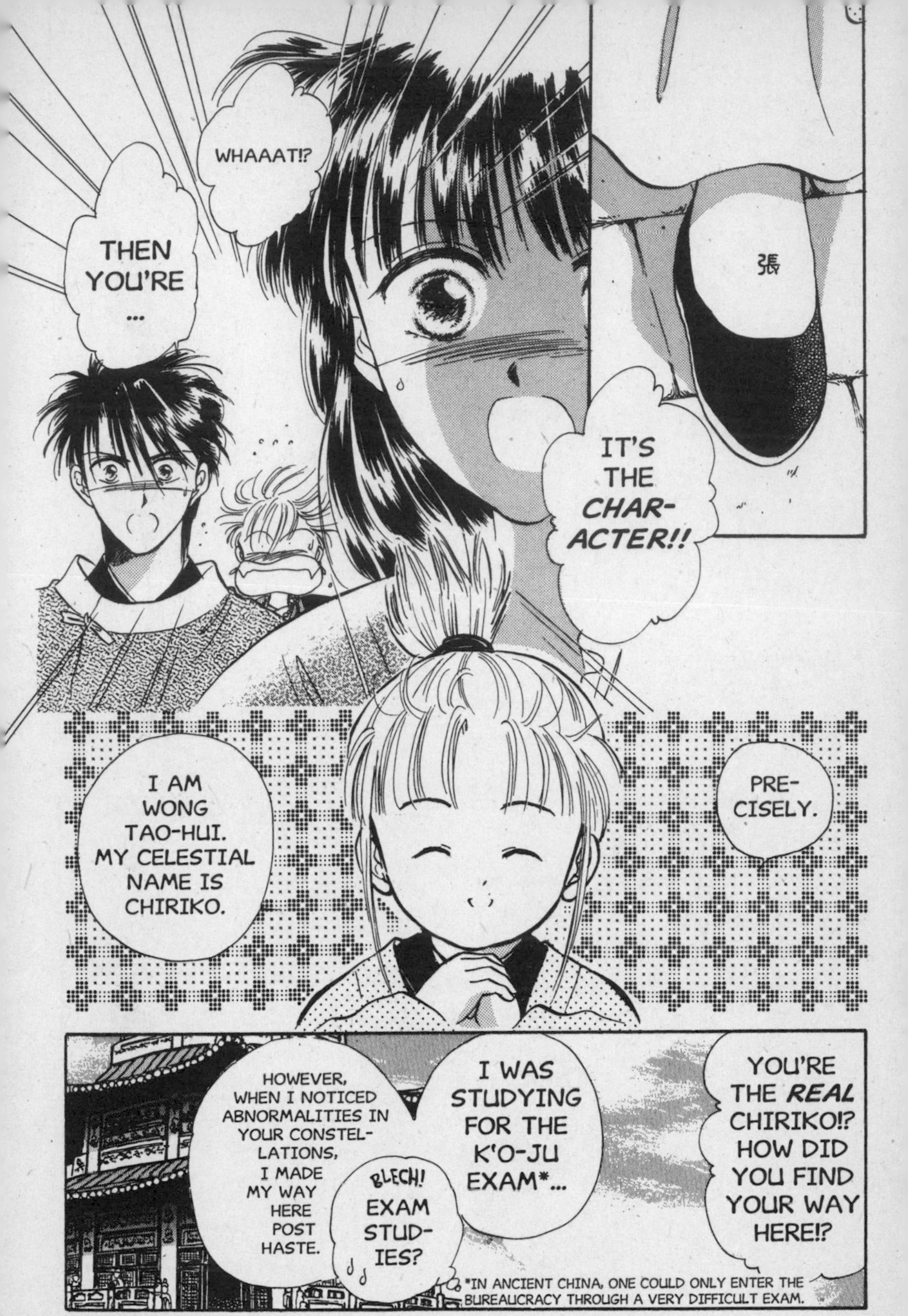
張
IT'S THE *CHARACTER!!*
WHAAAT!?
THEN YOU'RE ...
PRE-CISELY.
I AM WONG TAO-HUI. MY CELESTIAL NAME IS CHIRIKO.
YOU'RE THE *REAL* CHIRIKO!? HOW DID YOU FIND YOUR WAY HERE!?
I WAS STUDYING FOR THE K'O-JU EXAM*...
BLECH! EXAM STUD-IES?
HOWEVER, WHEN I NOTICED ABNORMALITIES IN YOUR CONSTEL-LATIONS, I MADE MY WAY HERE POST HASTE.
*IN ANCIENT CHINA, ONE COULD ONLY ENTER THE BUREAUCRACY THROUGH A VERY DIFFICULT EXAM.

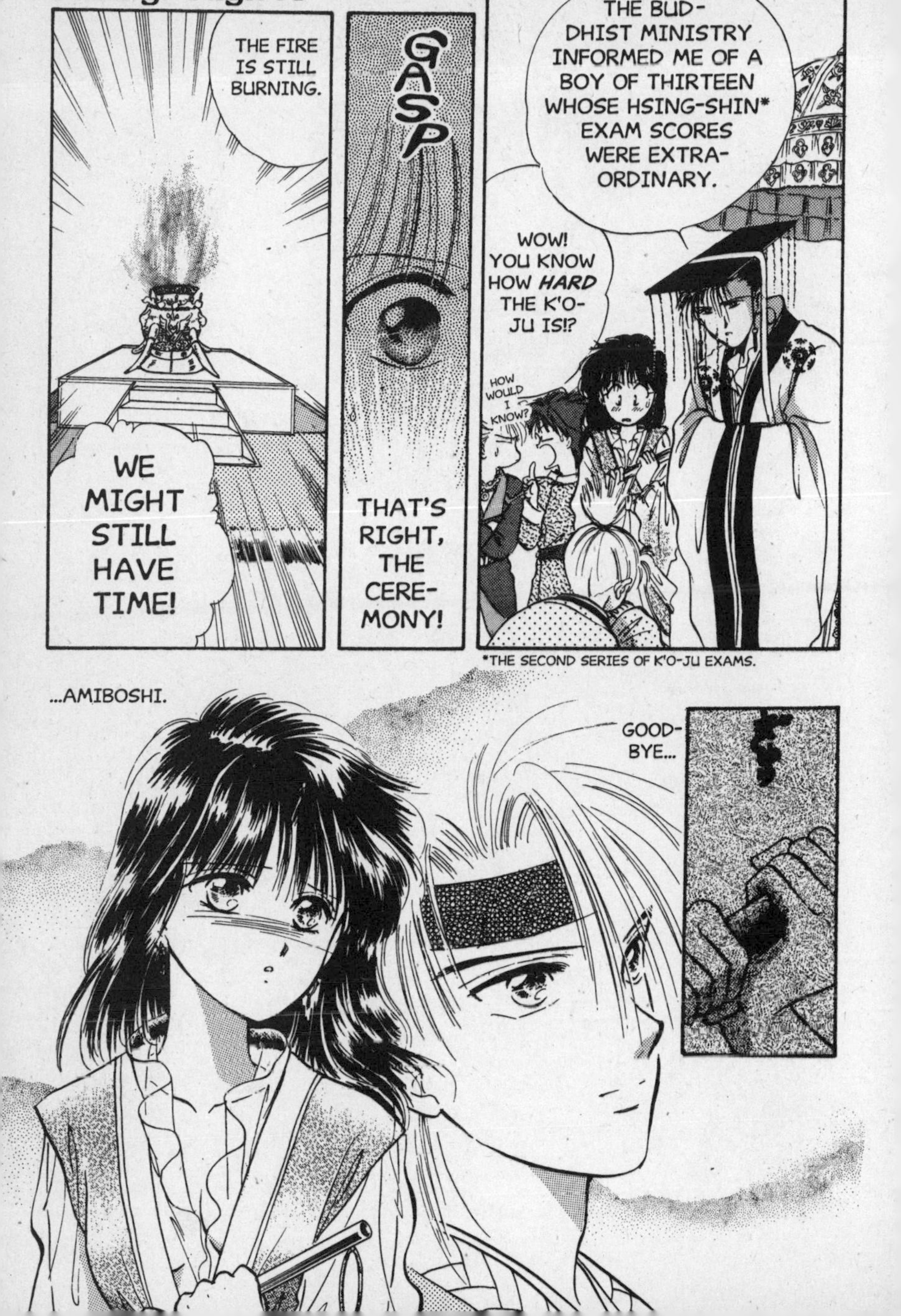
THE BUD-DHIST MINISTRY INFORMED ME OF A BOY OF THIRTEEN WHOSE HSING-SHIN* EXAM SCORES WERE EXTRA-ORDINARY.
WOW! YOU KNOW HOW *HARD* THE K'O-JU IS!?
HOW WOULD I KNOW?
GASP
THAT'S RIGHT, THE CERE-MONY!
THE FIRE IS STILL BURNING.
WE MIGHT STILL HAVE TIME!
*THE SECOND SERIES OF K'O-JU EXAMS.
GOOD-BYE...
...AMIBOSHI.

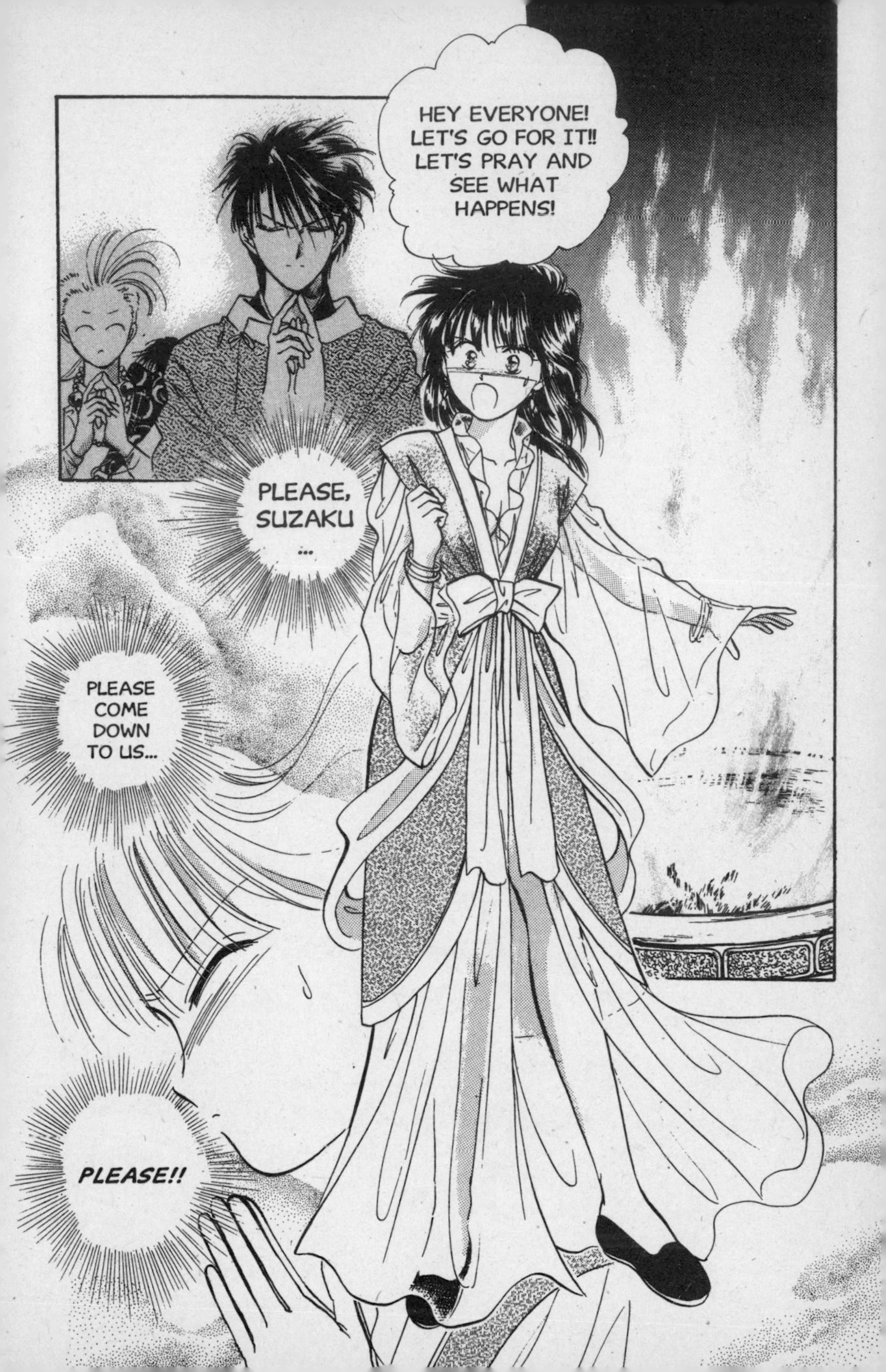
HEY EVERYONE! LET'S GO FOR IT!! LET'S PRAY AND SEE WHAT HAPPENS!
PLEASE, SUZAKU ...
PLEASE COME DOWN TO US...
PLEASE!!

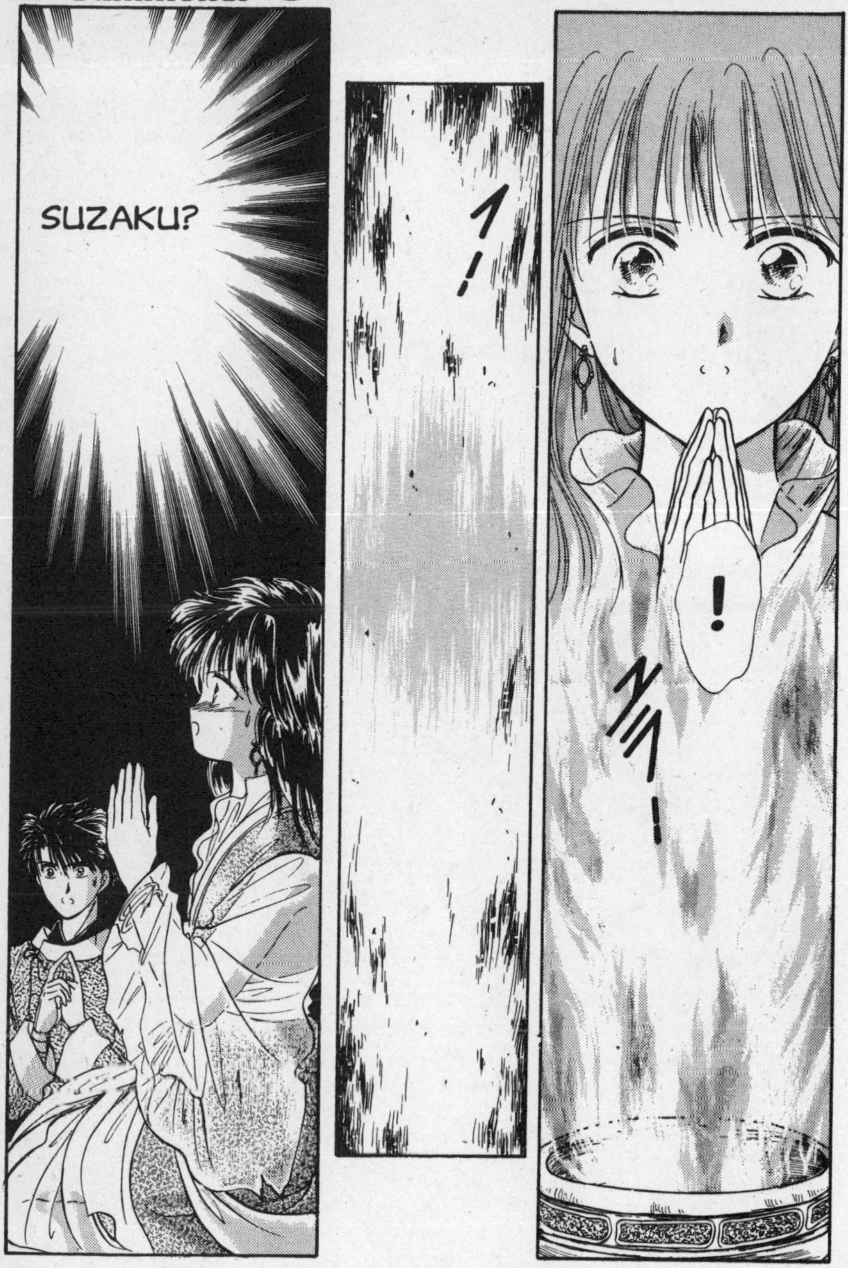
!
SUZAKU?

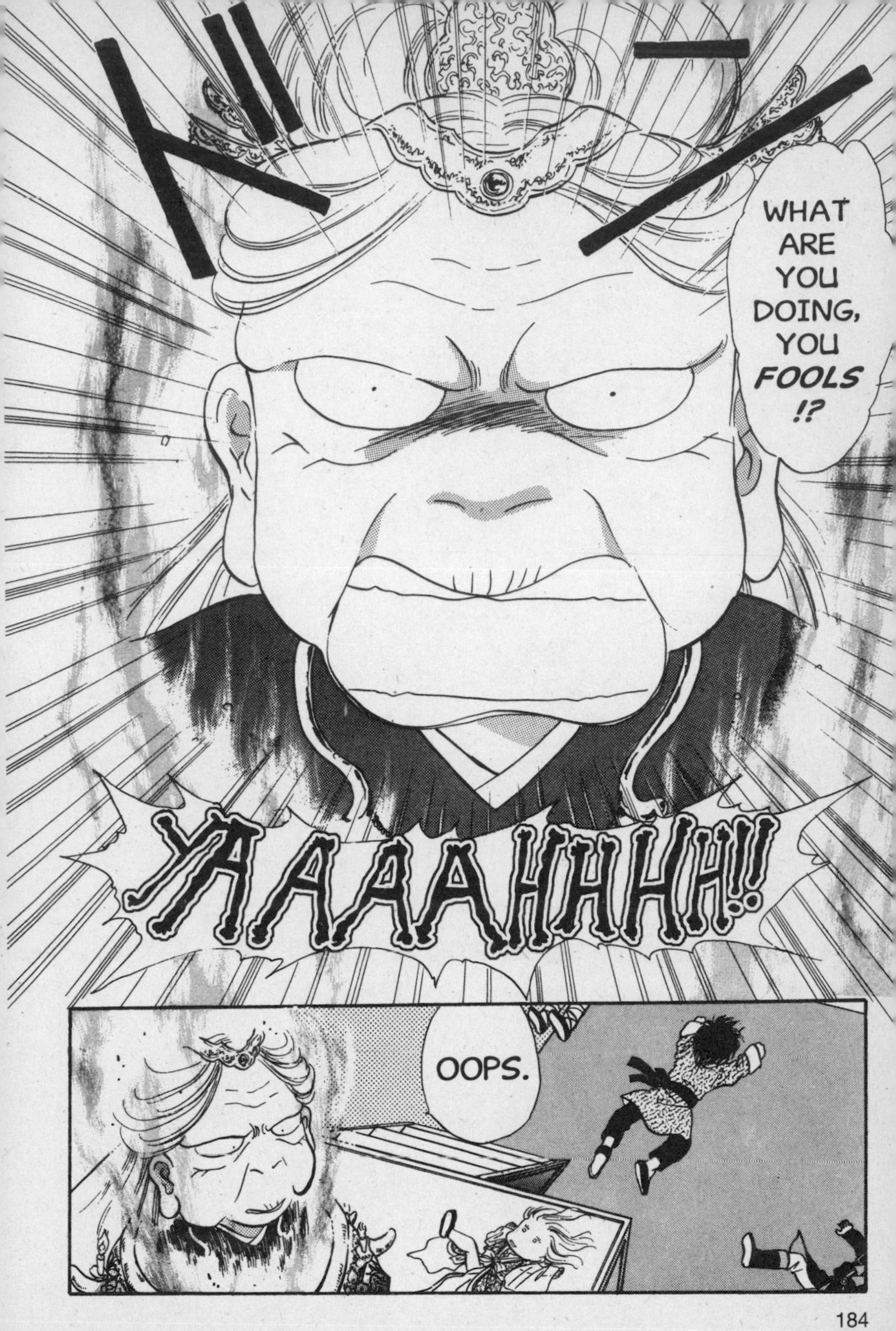
WHAT ARE YOU DOING, YOU *FOOLS* !?
YAAAAHHHH!!
OOPS.

Yui was linked to Miaka by her uniform, so their entire bodies were connected. Keisuke was only linked to Miaka at his wrist (through the ribbon). Their connections are limited to the area in contact. If the ribbon were torn to shreds, it'd reach him, but no matter what bodily injuries are inflicted on Miaka, the most Keisuke would feel is a twitch on his wrist. Do you get it now? Also, let's not forget how much stronger Yui's feelings for Miaka might be compared to Keisuke's. Let's leave it at that for the present.

So now we finally have all seven Celestial Warriors. We're at the end of Part One. It's only Part One!! Titled, "The Seven Celestial Warriors." Now, the story should go in a different direction. But we're talking about Yū Watase, so of course she has no idea where it's going. Waaahh!

Hey! By the way, there's a CD book that's been released along with the Japanese edition of volume 6. It's a novelization that follows the story up to volume 7, so all the Japanese fans should give it a listen. It's all thanks to you. Thank you so much. Also, I have the honor of illustrating Mizuchi Hayase's novel that's to be published by Shogakukan's Canvas Bunko imprint. Please take a look. August: Volume 2 of "New Prepubescence 2"; September: graphic novel of "Tiara of Sand." Hmm, what am I doing providing a list of my upcoming publications!? See ya later!!

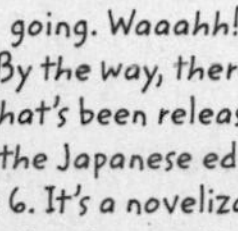
135 is so great. It's Tenmai! Tenmai! I wish all the songs could be used for "Fushigi."
I love Yume Mirai ("Dream Future") on the Tenmai ("Heaven's Dance") soundtrack! It's hard to believe this CD is game music.

Speaking of CDs my friend gave me a character album that goes with the CD of Street Fighter II.

↑

So what!? 135 is Wo Ai Ni.

♪ Wo ai ni. Fly up into the heavens, holy girl (oh yeah). I think a lot of people know the song because it was used for a tea commercial years ago...

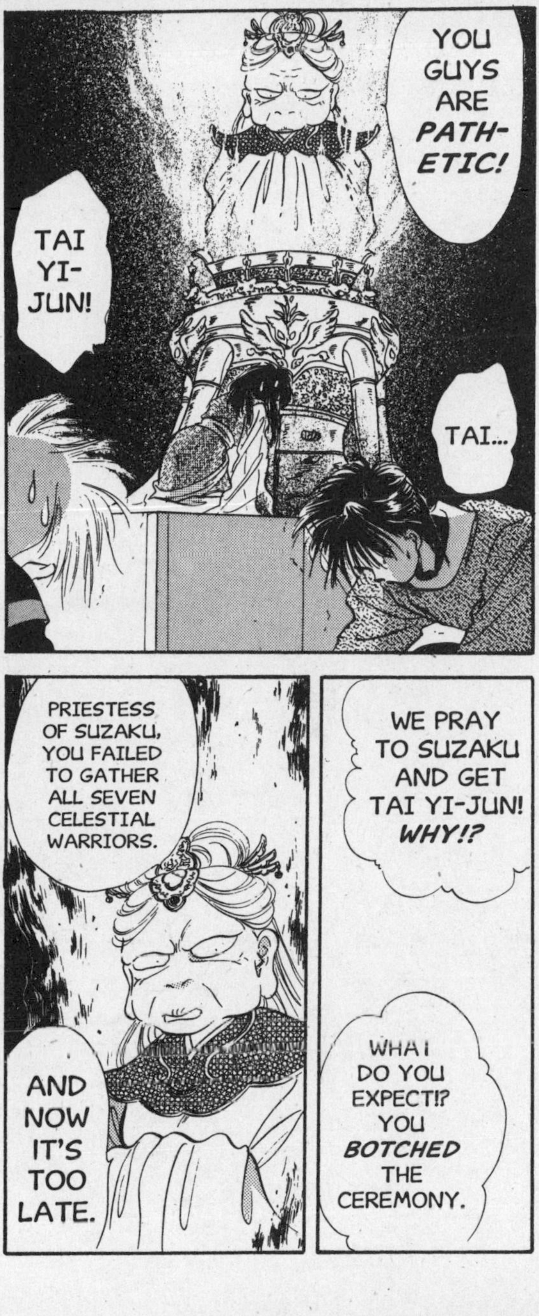
YOU GUYS ARE *PATHETIC!*
TAI YI-JUN!
TAI...
PRIESTESS OF SUZAKU, YOU FAILED TO GATHER ALL SEVEN CELESTIAL WARRIORS.
AND NOW IT'S TOO LATE.
WE PRAY TO SUZAKU AND GET TAI YI-JUN! *WHY!?*
WHAT DO YOU EXPECT!? YOU *BOTCHED* THE CEREMONY.

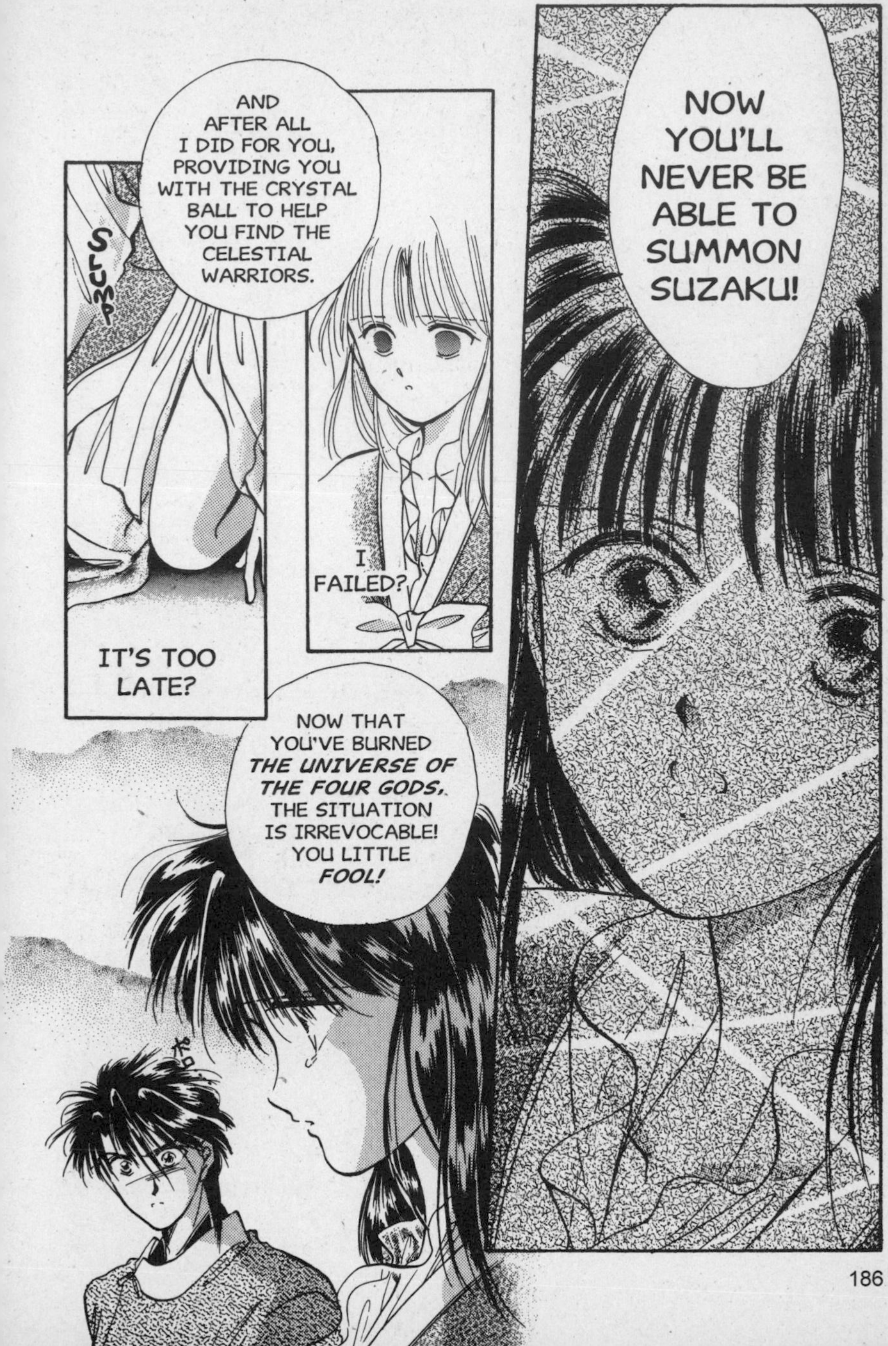
AND AFTER ALL I DID FOR YOU, PROVIDING YOU WITH THE CRYSTAL BALL TO HELP YOU FIND THE CELESTIAL WARRIORS.
I FAILED?
SLUMP
IT'S TOO LATE?
NOW THAT YOU'VE BURNED *THE UNIVERSE OF THE FOUR GODS,* THE SITUATION IS IRREVOCABLE! YOU LITTLE *FOOL!*
NOW YOU'LL NEVER BE ABLE TO SUMMON SUZAKU!

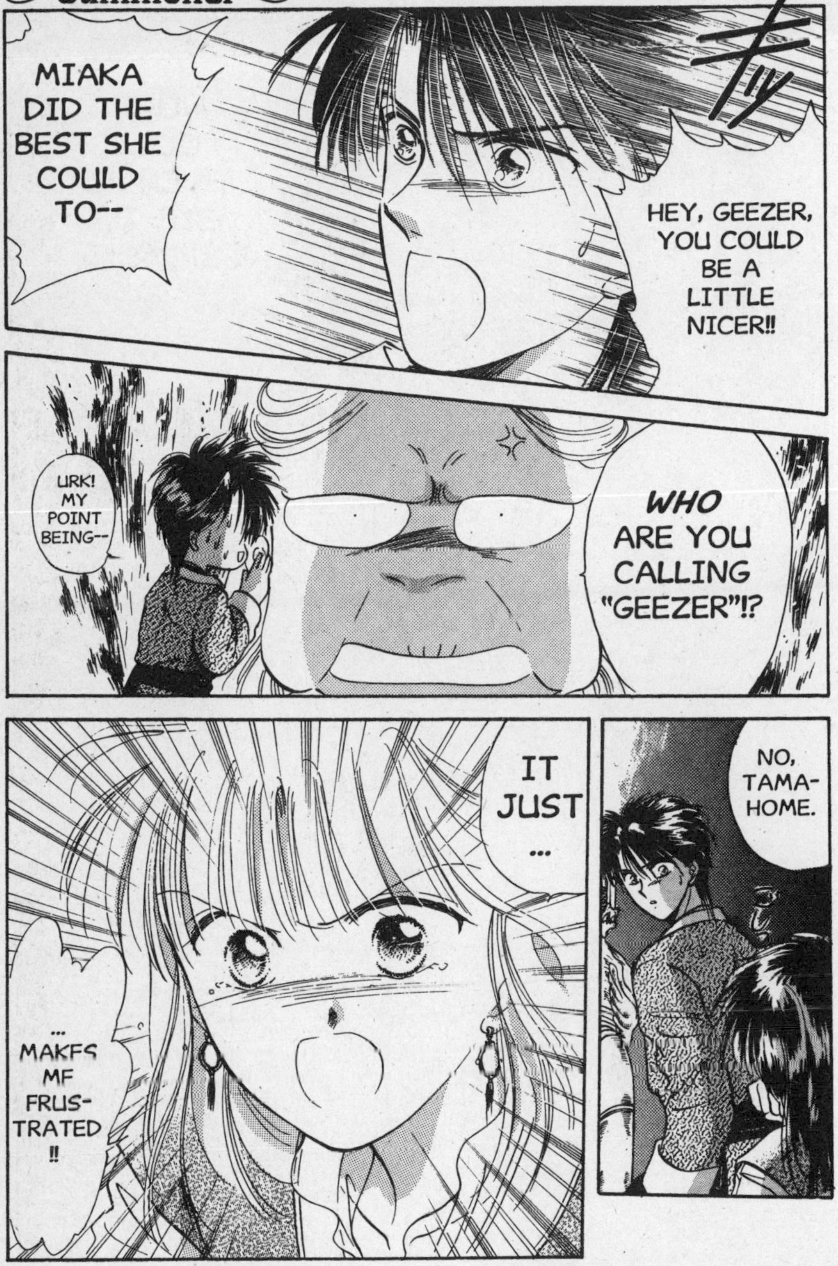
HEY, GEEZER, YOU COULD BE A LITTLE NICER!!
MIAKA DID THE BEST SHE COULD TO--
WHO ARE YOU CALLING "GEEZER"!?
URK! MY POINT BEING--
NO, TAMA-HOME.
IT JUST ...
... MAKES ME FRUS-TRATED !!

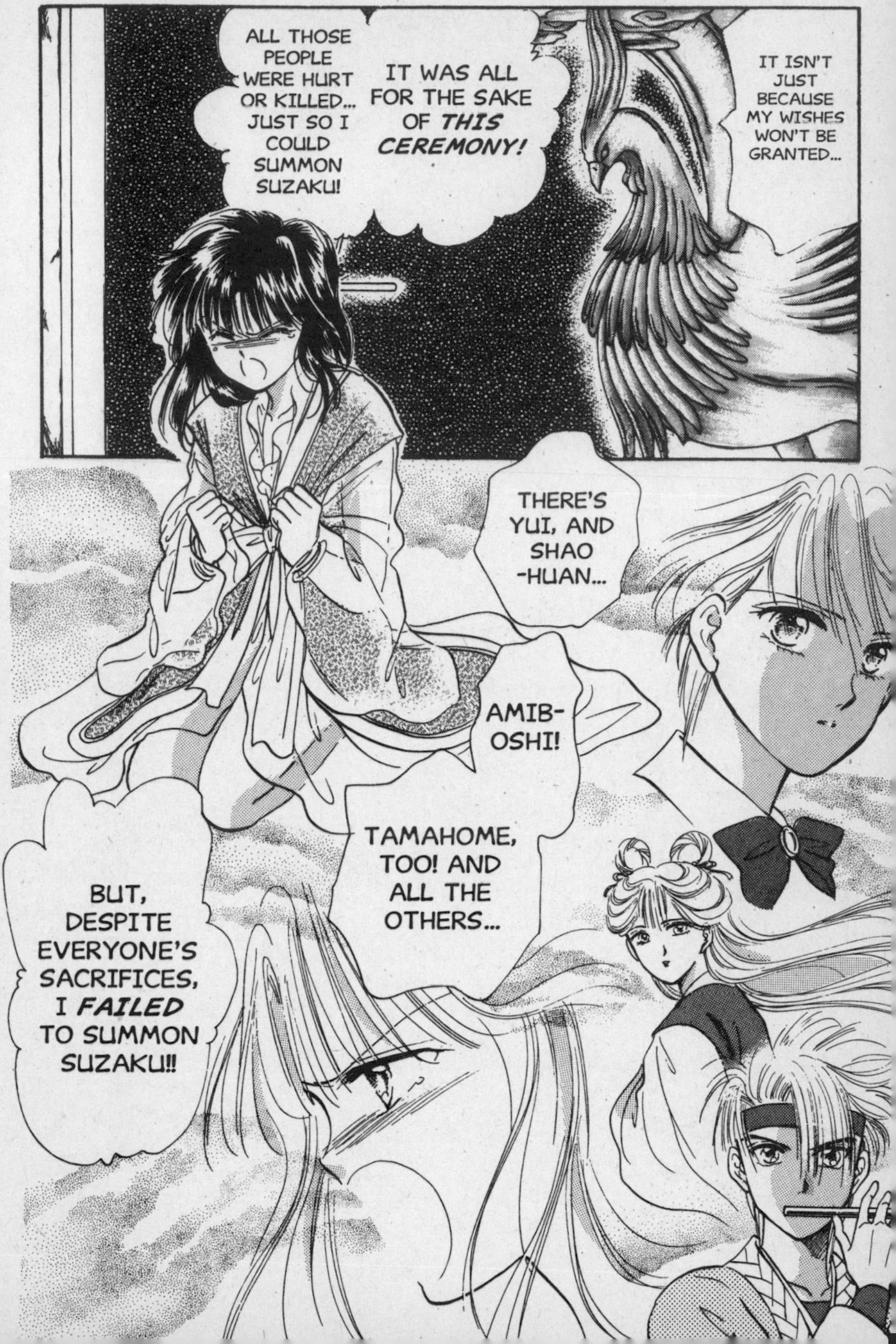
IT ISN'T JUST BECAUSE MY WISHES WON'T BE GRANTED...
IT WAS ALL FOR THE SAKE OF *THIS CEREMONY!*
ALL THOSE PEOPLE WERE HURT OR KILLED... JUST SO I COULD SUMMON SUZAKU!
THERE'S YUI, AND SHAO-HUAN...
AMIB-OSHI!
TAMAHOME, TOO! AND ALL THE OTHERS...
BUT, DESPITE EVERYONE'S SACRIFICES, I *FAILED* TO SUMMON SUZAKU!!

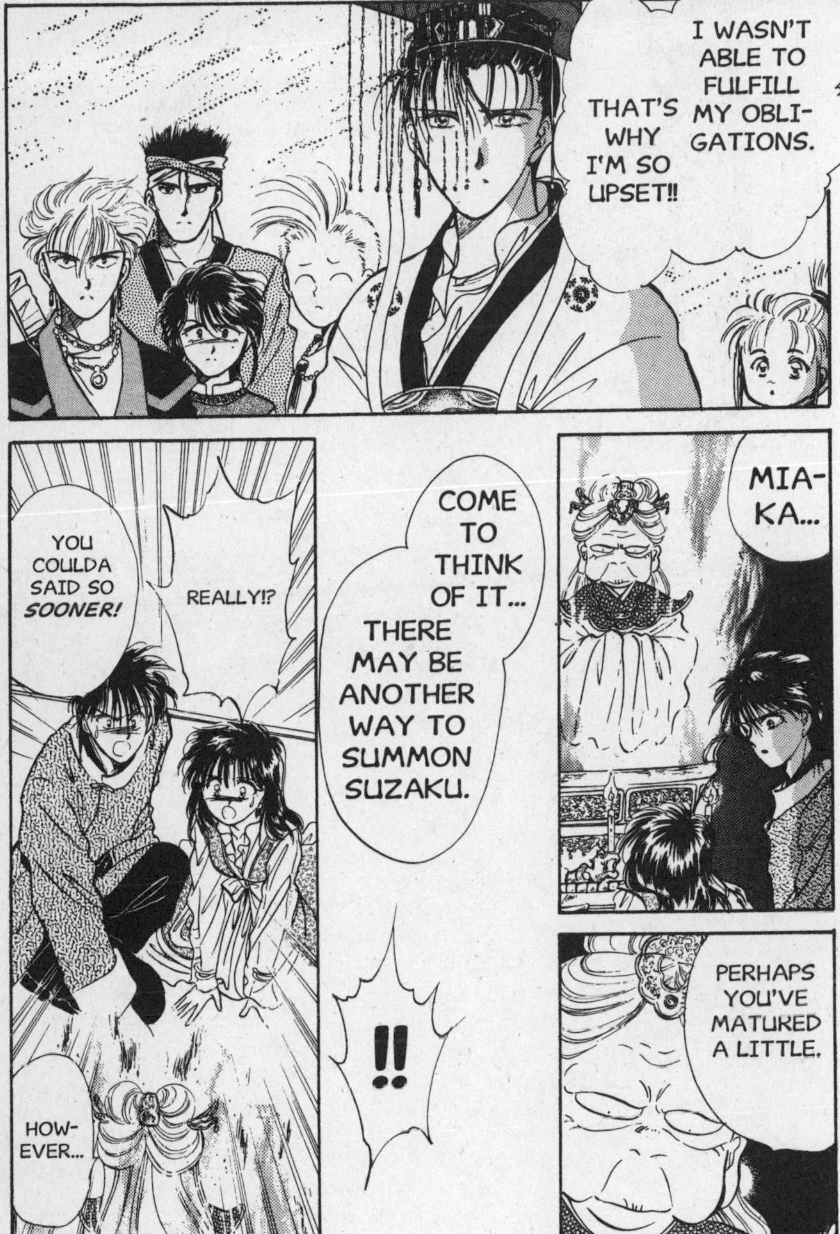
I WASN'T ABLE TO FULFILL MY OBLIGATIONS.
THAT'S WHY I'M SO UPSET!!
MIA-KA...
PERHAPS YOU'VE MATURED A LITTLE.
COME TO THINK OF IT...
THERE MAY BE ANOTHER WAY TO SUMMON SUZAKU.
!!
REALLY!?
YOU COULDA SAID SO *SOONER!*
HOW-EVER...

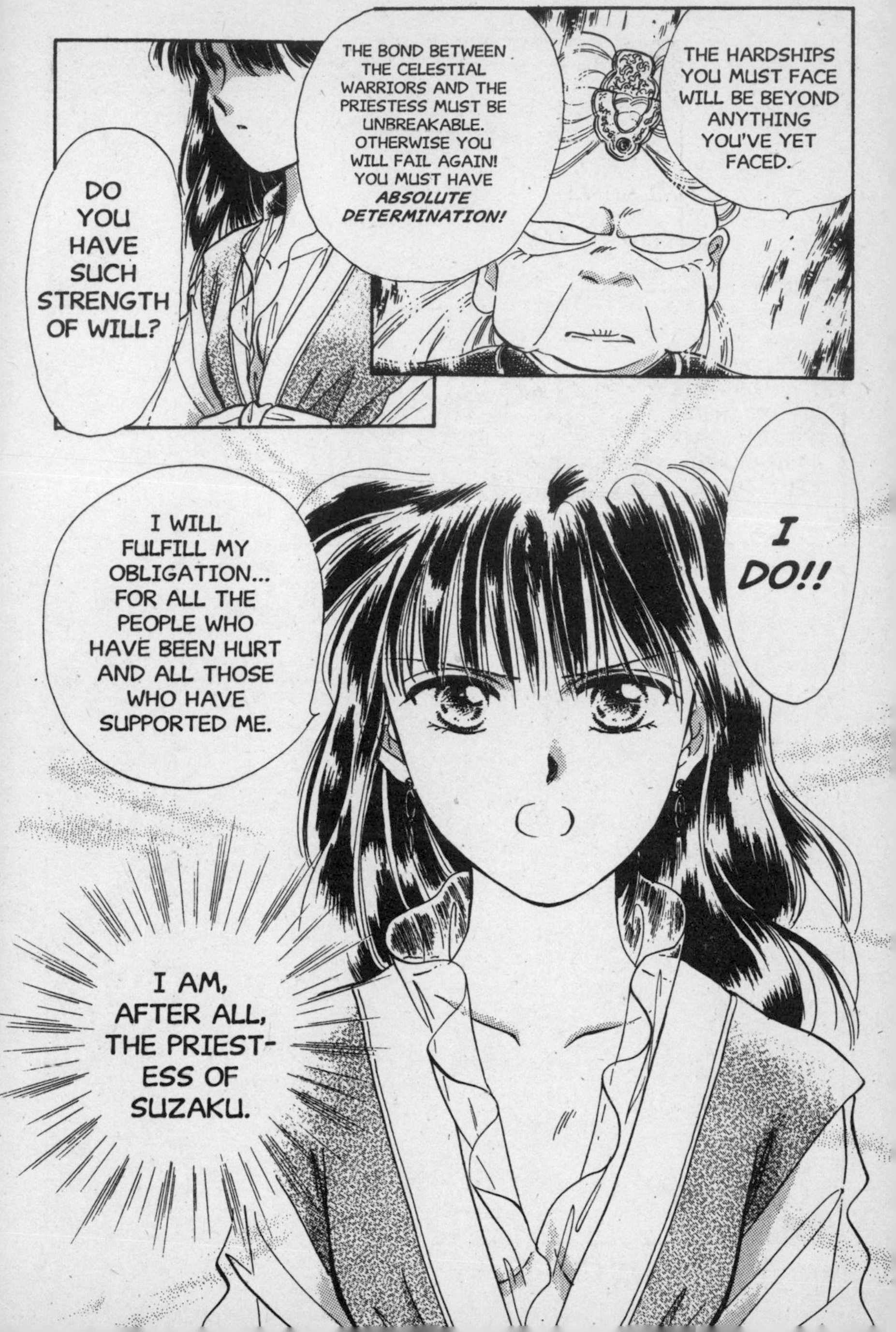
THE HARDSHIPS YOU MUST FACE WILL BE BEYOND ANYTHING YOU'VE YET FACED.
THE BOND BETWEEN THE CELESTIAL WARRIORS AND THE PRIESTESS MUST BE UNBREAKABLE. OTHERWISE YOU WILL FAIL AGAIN! YOU MUST HAVE *ABSOLUTE DETERMINATION!*
DO YOU HAVE SUCH STRENGTH OF WILL?
I DO!!
I WILL FULFILL MY OBLIGATION... FOR ALL THE PEOPLE WHO HAVE BEEN HURT AND ALL THOSE WHO HAVE SUPPORTED ME.
I AM, AFTER ALL, THE PRIEST-ESS OF SUZAKU.

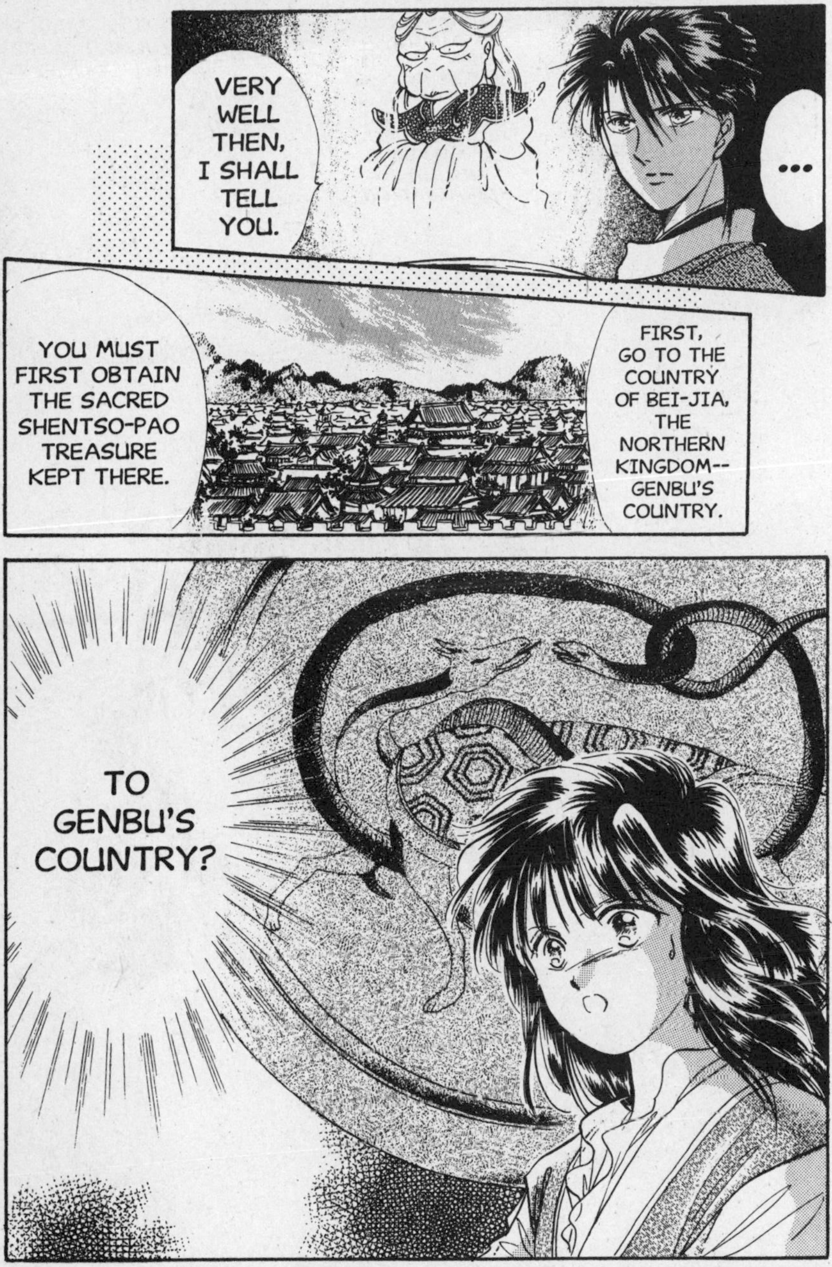
...
VERY WELL THEN, I SHALL TELL YOU.
FIRST, GO TO THE COUNTRY OF BEI-JIA, THE NORTHERN KINGDOM--GENBU'S COUNTRY.
YOU MUST FIRST OBTAIN THE SACRED SHENTSO-PAO TREASURE KEPT THERE.
TO GENBU'S COUNTRY?

TO BE CONTINUED IN VOLUME 7: CASTAWAY

The Fushigi Yûgi Guide to Sound Effects

Most of the sound effects in FUSHIGI YÛGI are the way Yuu Watase created them, in their original Japanese.

We created this glossary for a page-by-page, panel-by-panel explanation of the action and background noises. By using this guide, you may even learn some Japanese.

The glossary lists page and panel number. For example, page 1, panel 3, would be listed as 1.3.

23.1 FX: Zaaa (fssshh)
23.2 FX: Basha (splash)
23.4 FX: Zaba zaba (splosh splosh)

24.1 FX: Bashan (splosh)
24.2 FX: Gabo (glug)
24.3 FX: Gabo gabo (glug glug)
24.4 FX: Zaaa (fssshh)

27.1 FX: Ka (glow)
27.2 FX: Kasa (rustle)

30.4 FX: Zaaa (fssshh)

32.5 FX: Hikku hikku (hic hic)

35.2 FX: Za (walking)

**CHAPTER THIRTY-TWO:
TO PROTECT YOU**

40.2 FX: Sara sara (pitter patter)

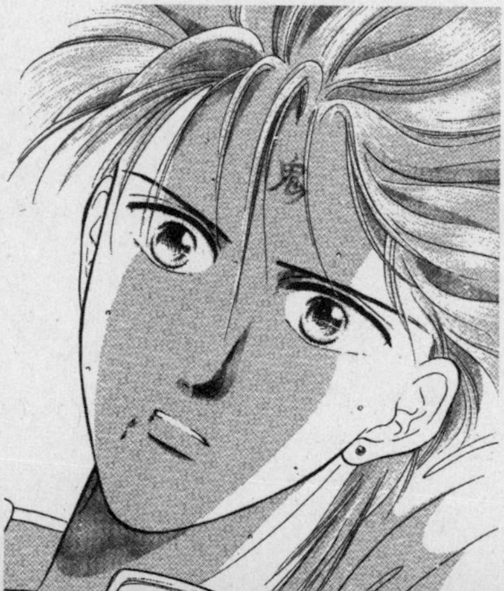

**CHAPTER THIRTY-ONE:
THE WAY TO GOODBYE**

6.3 FX: Basa basa (flap flap)
6.5 FX: Su (swff)

7.4 FX: Pou (glow)

8.2 FX: Su (swff)
8.6 FX: Niko niko (grin)

10.1 FX: Unnn (purr)
10.4 FX: Ba (fwoosh)

12.3 FX: Ha (gasp)
12.4 FX: Sa (twirl)
12.6 FX: Patan (ka-chak)

13.2 FX: Dan (thud)

14.3 FX: Pishi (punch)

16.1-3 FX: Dokun dokun dokun dokun (ba-dump ba-dump ba-dump ba-dump)

17.2 FX: Ba (fwoosh)
17.5 FX: Gyu (squeeze)

20.2 FX: Zaaa (fssshh)
20.3 FX: Kacha kacha (clatter clatter)
20.4 FX: Kii (swing)

21.5 FX: Da (dash)

22.1 FX: Zaaa (fssshh)
22.2 FX: Basha basha basha (splish splash splish)

CHAPTER THIRTY-THREE: NEVER LEAVE YOU

68.1 FX: Do (thud)

70.2 FX: Ha (gasp)

71.2 FX: Ba (grab)
71.3 FX: Gyu (squeeze)

74.2 FX: Byu (whoosh)

75.1 FX: Ba (dash)
75.4 FX: Karan (klang)

79.3 FX: Su (swish)
79.4 FX: Pou (glow)

82.1 FX: Ho (whew)
82.2-3 FX: Ka ka ka ka (walking)

83.1 FX: Ka ka (walking)
83.2 FX: Su (swish)
83.3-4 FX: Ka ka ka ka (walking)

84.1 FX: Byu (whoosh)
84.3 FX: Pan (crack)
84.3 FX: Suto (landing lightly)
84.4 FX: Pashi (thwap)

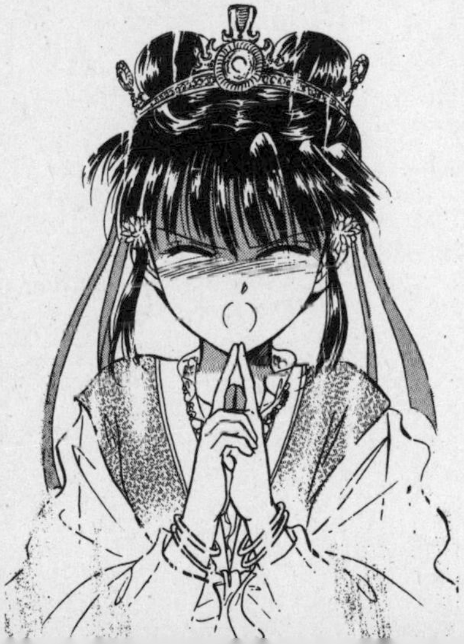

41.1-2 FX: Kasha (click)

42.1 FX: Kusun (sniffle)
42.2 FX: Sara sara (pitter patter)
42.5 FX: Ko ko (walking)
42.6 FX: Su (fwoosh)

43.1 FX: Do (thud)
43.3 FX: Doka (wham)
43.4 FX: Zuru (slump)
43.5 FX: Dosa (thud)

45.3 FX: Ki (glare)
45.4 FX: Pan (slap)

48.2 FX: Niko (grin)
48.4 FX: Bata bata bata (stomp stomp stomp)

49.5 FX: Ga (grab)

50.4 FX: Biku (jolt)

53.1 FX: Ha (gasp)

54.2 FX: Chaki (click)
54.3 FX: Za (standing firm)

55.2 FX: Don don don (bam bam bam)

57.2 FX: Suto (landing lightly)

58.1 FX: Kin (klang)
58.3 FX: Gugu (grrr)

60.2 FX: Bota (thud)

61.1 FX: Zan (whoosh)
61.4 FX: Chaki (clack)

62.1 FX: Ha ha (huff huff)
62.3 FX: Zuru (slip)

63.1 FX: Ba (pounce)

64.1 FX: Do (thwak)

123.2 FX: Ta ta (running)

125.2 FX: Ta ta ta (running)
125.3 FX: Mugyu mugyu mugyu (smoosh smoosh smoosh)

CHAPTER THIRTY-FIVE: THE TREACHEROUS TUNE

136.4 FX: Su (step)

137.3 FX: Tsu (scratch)

138.1 FX: Shulu (fwap)
138.2 FX: Suu (slowly appearing)

139.3 FX: Zaaa (fssshh)
139.4 FX: Zaaa (fssshh)

140.1 FX: Suu (splosh)
140.3 FX: Chapu (splish)

141.3 FX: Gasa gasa (rustle rustle)

144.3 FX: Ba (jolt)
144.4 FX: Doki doki doki (ba-dump ba-dump ba-dump)

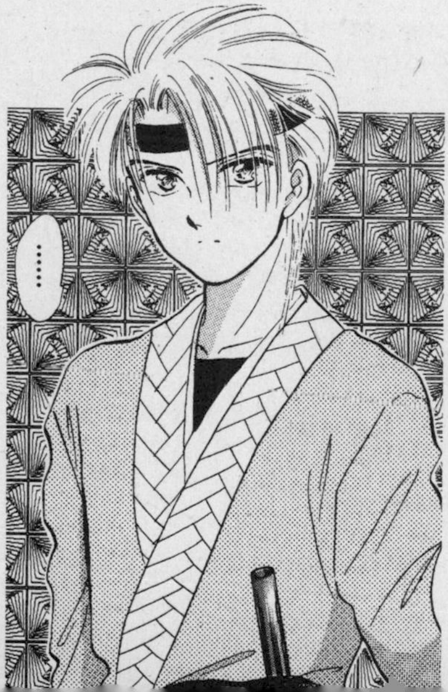

86.2 FX: Shu (fling)
86.3 FX: Pashi (thwap)
86.6 FX: Ka (energy building)

87.4 FX: Ka (walking)

88.4 FX: Ka ka (walking)

93.1 FX: Suku (gulp)

96.4 FX: Kusu (snicker)

97.2 FX: Ba (jolt)

CHAPTER THIRTY-FOUR: THE FINAL EMBRACE

100.5 FX: Chichichi (tweet tweet)

101.1 FX: Chun chun (chirp chirp)
101.4 FX: Gaba (bolt)
101.5 FX: Tatatata (dash)

103.4 FX: Mogu mogu musha musha (chomp chomp munch munch)

104.3 FX: Nihelaa (nye-heh-heh)
104.4 FX: Musuuu (hmph)

105.2 FX: Mu (grr)

106.2 FX: Kya (ooh)

109.4 FX: Ka (walking)

110.3 FX: Ta ta (running)

112.6 FX: Golo golo (purr purr)

113.3 FX: Nyu (nwoink)

114.5 FX: Ta ta ta (running)

116.4 FX: Patan (ka-chak)
116.5 FX: Shiiin (silence)

120.3 FX: Gyu (squeeze)

145.2 FX: Biku (jolt)
145.3 FX: Basha basha basha
(splish splash splish)
145.4 FX: Basha basha (splish splash)

146.2 FX: Basa (fwump)

148.1 FX: Gyu (squeeze)
148.5 FX: Gala gala (rattle rattle)

149.1 FX: Gala gala (rattle rattle)
149.2 FX: Gyu (clench)

152.2 FX: Ba (fling)

153.1 FX: Boo (roar)
153.4 FX: Gooo (roar)

154.1 FX: Gooo (roar)

155.3 FX: Piku (flinch)
155.4 FX: Kiin (fweee)

159.3 FX: Ba (whoosh)
159.4 FX: Su (shoosh)

160.4 FX: Don (thwak)

**CHAPTER THIRTY-SIX:
THE DECISIVE FLAME**

164.3 FX: Zu (slip)

165.1 FX: Zulu (slump)
165.3 FX: Pishi…pishipishi
(crack…crack crack)
165.4 FX: Bi bi (slash vwip)
165.6 FX: Kiiin (fweee)

166.3 FX: Fu (whew)

167.1 FX: Fu (whew)
167.4 FX: Baki (whack)

168.2 FX: Shuta (dash)
168.3 FX: Shu (whoosh)

169.2 FX: Dosa (thud)
169.3 FX: Shuta (dash)

170.4 FX: Boo (roar)

171.1 FX: Ba (jumping aside)
171.5 FX: Za (running)

172.2 FX: Gooo (gshhh)
172.3 FX: Ba (dash)

173.5 FX: Suto (landing lightly)

174.1 FX: Gala (crumble)

176.1 FX: Gooo (roar)

179.3 FX: Piii (fweeee)

181.4 FX: Gyu (squeeze)

183.1 FX: Yula (flicker)
183.2 FX: Fu (slowly appearing)

184.1 FX: Don (boom)

186.3 FX: Heta (slump)
186.4 FX: Polo (plip)

187.1 FX: Ki (glare)
187.3 FX: Goshi (rub)

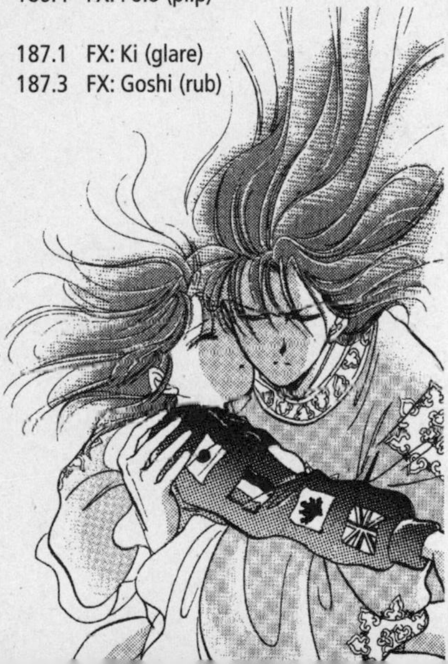

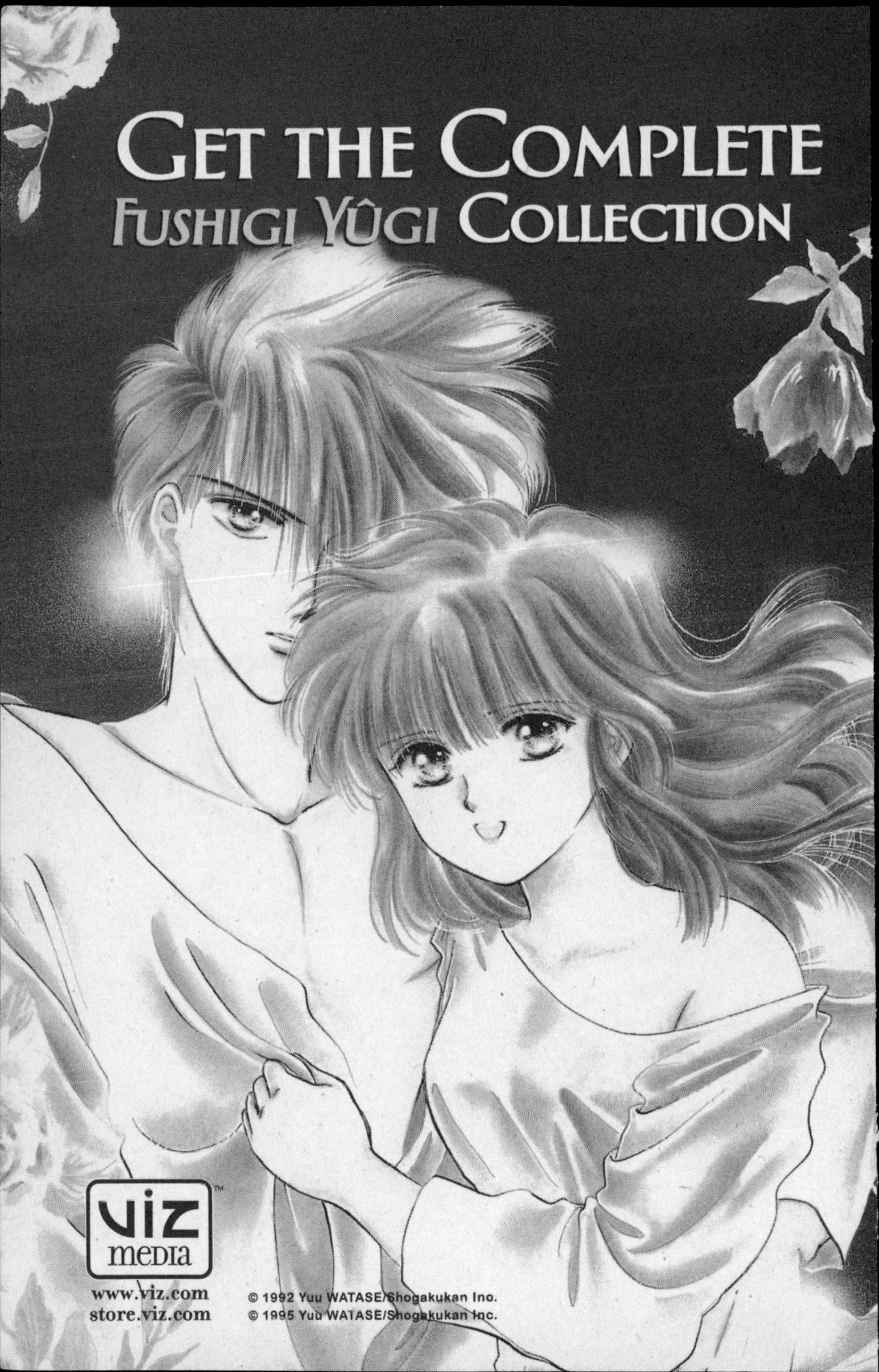
GET THE COMPLETE
FUSHIGI YÛGI COLLECTION
viz media
www.viz.com
store.viz.com
© 1992 Yuu WATASE/Shogakukan Inc.
© 1995 Yuu WATASE/Shogakukan Inc.

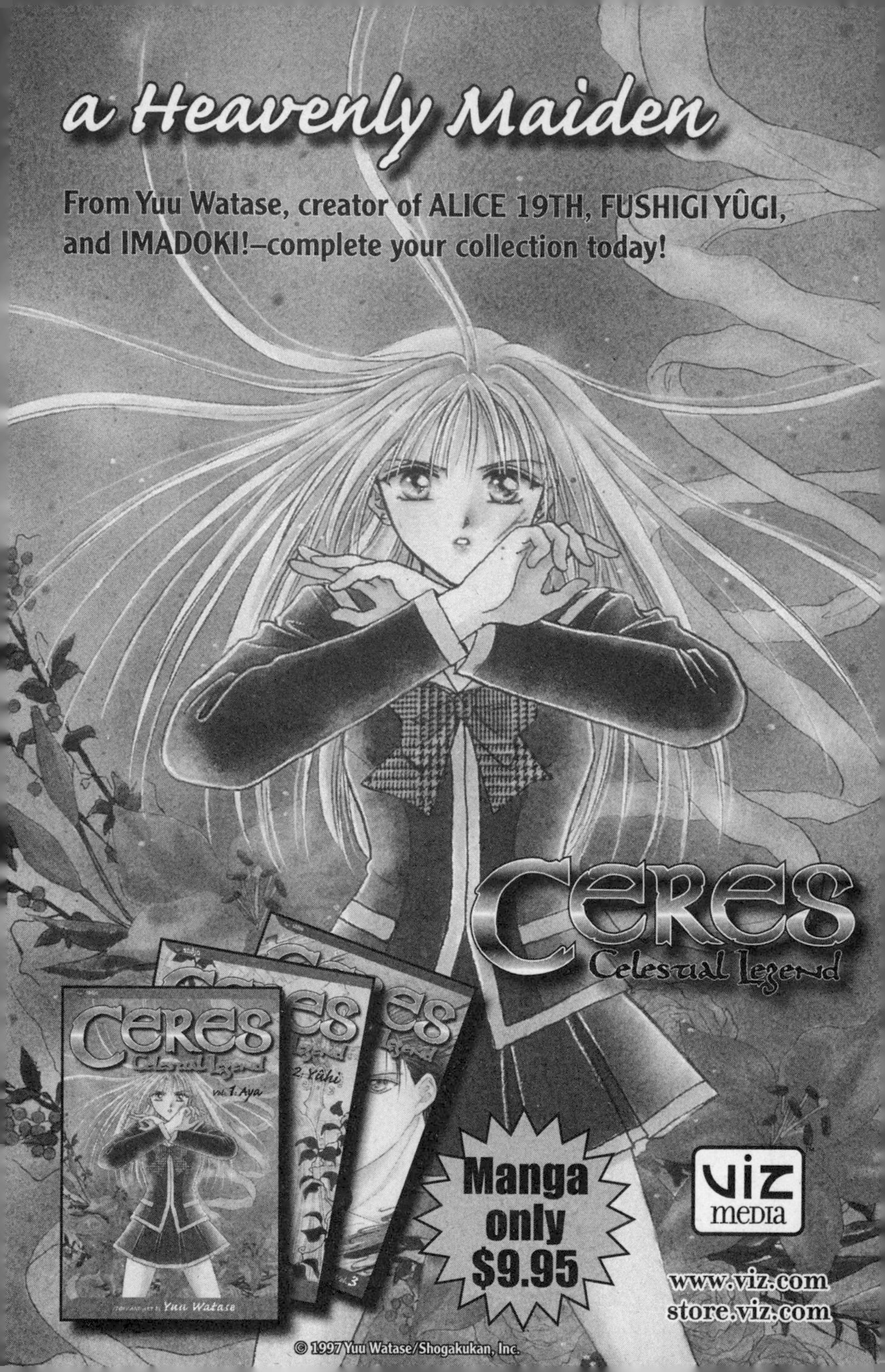

a Heavenly Maiden
From Yuu Watase, creator of ALICE 19TH, FUSHIGI YÛGI, and IMADOKI!–complete your collection today!
Ceres
Celestial Legend
Ceres
Celestial Legend
Vol. 1 Aya
Yuu Watase
Manga only $9.95
viz media
www.viz.com
store.viz.com
© 1997 Yuu Watase/Shogakukan, Inc.

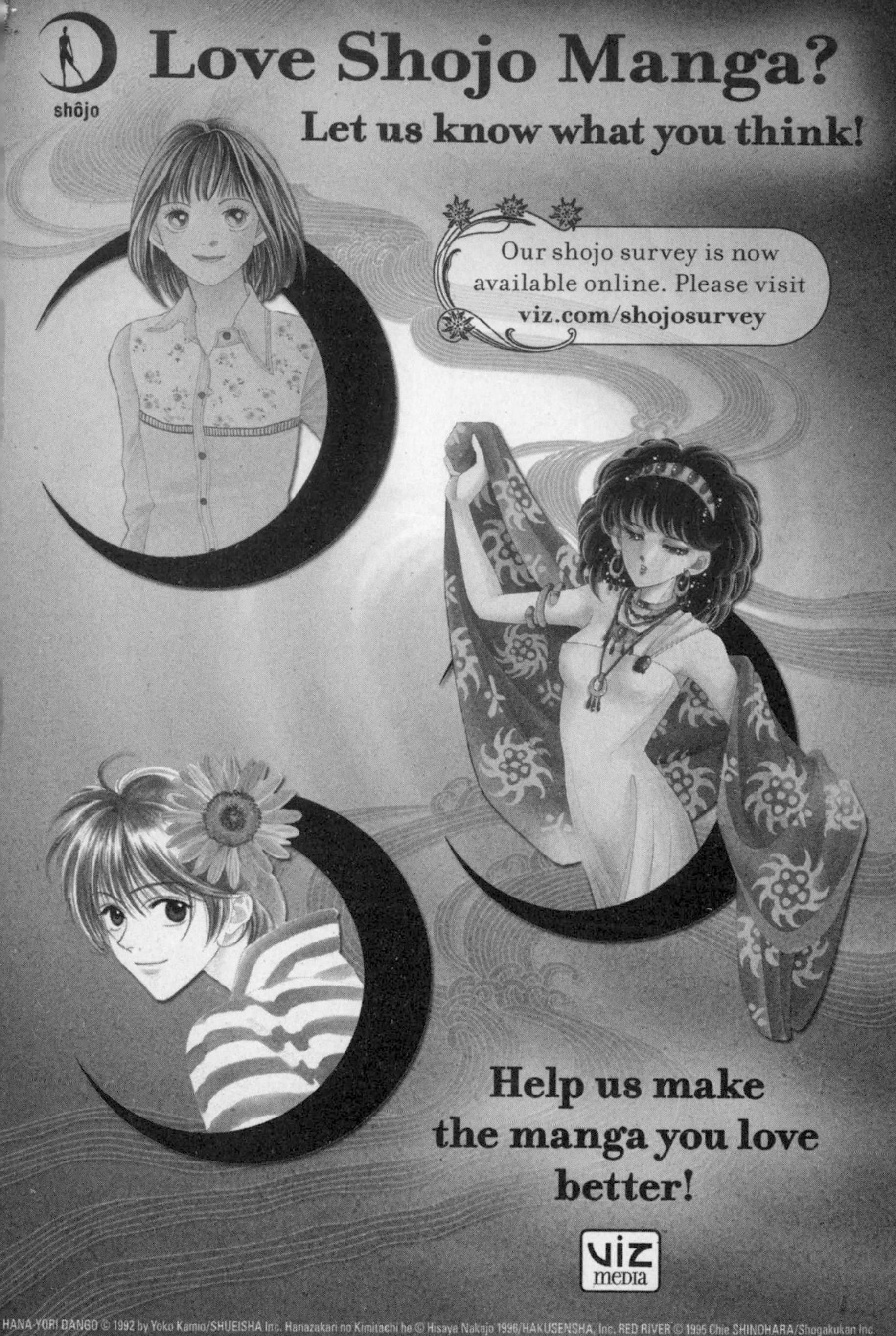
shôjo
Love Shojo Manga?
Let us know what you think!
Our shojo survey is now available online. Please visit viz.com/shojosurvey
Help us make the manga you love better!
viz media
HANA-YORI DANGO © 1992 by Yoko Kamio/SHUEISHA Inc. Hanazakari no Kimitachi he © Hisaya Nakajo 1996/HAKUSENSHA, Inc. RED RIVER © 1995 Chie SHINOHARA/Shogakukan Inc.